NEW YEAR'S BABY
A Memoir of Survival

by

GAIL HEALD-TAYLOR

2025

Copyright © 2025 by Gail Heald-Taylor

All rights reserved. No part of this book may be used or reproduced in any form whatsoever without written permission except in the case of brief quotations in critical articles or reviews.

Printed in Canada.

For more information, or to book an event, contact : ghealdtaylor@outlook.com

Book design by Robyn York

Published by Anchorless Press

ISBN - Paperback: 978-1-927730-17-1

First Edition: September 2025

Introduction

I wrote this memoir for my sons Wesley, Blake and Ron as well as for my three grandchildren, Nathan, Matthew and Amy. Having lived in Ontario for 64 years, my family knows very little of my origins and growing up in Alberta for the first twenty years of my life. My memoir will shed light on my beginnings, the mystery of my birth, family abuse, growing up on the farm, and my teenage years. I will tell you of my travel to Europe to teach, of meeting John Wesley Heald, your father and grandfather, and the birth of my darling sons, Charles Wesley (1961), Colin Blakley (1964) and Ronald Porter (1966). You will discover the effects of traditional roles of men and women in marriage and their consequences, which lead to divorce. I will share my life as a single parent to raise my boys, how I re-established a career, and the struggle to overcome poverty on my road to independence. Much of my memoir revolves around my second husband, John Taylor, with my story of how we met and worked at creating a blended family. I share my dedication to learning—obtaining a BA, Masters, and Doctorate—that led to my successful career as a teacher, consultant, professor, and author of several books. In later years, I celebrated the union of my sons with their partners; and reveal the tragedy of Blake contracting MS. I write about the joy of my three grandchildren, Nathan (1995), Amy (1998) and Matthew (2000) and of the fun we had at the Lodge. The final chapters of my memoir are of growing old and of John's final goodbye.

It is my hope that through this memoir my family will get a glimpse of who I am today as I share the events that shaped my life for over 86 years. It is my wish as well that I might have contributed, in some small way, to the lives of my family.

To Wesley, Blake, Ron, Nathan, Matt and Amy, happy reading.

Introduction

I wrote this memoir for my sons Wesley, Blake and Ron as well as for my three grandchildren, Nathan, Matthew and Amy. Having lived in Ontario for 64 years, my family knows very little of my origins and growing up in Alberta for the first twenty years of my life. My memoir will shed light on my beginnings, the mystery of my birth, family abuse, growing up on the farm, and my teenage years. I will tell you of my travel to Europe to teach, of meeting John Wesley Heald, your father and grandfather, and the birth of my darling sons, Charles Wesley (1961), Colin Blakley (1964) and Ronald Porter (1966). You will discover the effects of traditional roles of men and women in marriage and their consequences, which lead to divorce. I will share my life as a single parent to raise my boys, how I re-established a career, and the struggle to overcome poverty on my road to independence. Much of my memoir revolves around my second husband, John Taylor, with my story of how we met and worked at creating a blended family. I share my dedication to learning—obtaining a BA, Masters, and Doctorate—that led to my successful career as a teacher, consultant, professor, and author of several books. In later years, I celebrated the union of my sons with their partners; and reveal the tragedy of Blake contracting MS. I write about the joy of my three grandchildren, Nathan (1995), Amy (1998) and Matthew (2000) and of the fun we had at the Lodge. The final chapters of my memoir are of growing old and of John's final goodbye.

It is my hope that through this memoir my family will get a glimpse of who I am today as I share the events that shaped my life for over 86 years. It is my wish as well that I might have contributed, in some small way, to the lives of my family.

To Wesley, Blake, Ron, Nathan, Matt and Amy, happy reading.

MEMOIR

In the ink-dark of morning

She sits alone and ponders

An arctic chill pierces like shards of ice

Marking the end of summer

She wraps the shawl tightly round

Like a funeral shroud beckoning winter

Sounds of waves lap the shore

Licking rocks clean like the bones of her life

Geese announcing dawn head south

Blindly disinterested of this old soul

With crepe-like arms, cob webs laced across her face

She recounts the chapters of her life

Flashing before her worn-out eyes

How did she fare?

What will be remembered when she is gone?

Did she bring joy

Along with heart-ache and pain?

Will any good be recalled at all?

Perhaps she does not want to know

Dawn breaks indigo and mauve

She rises to record another memory

TABLE OF CONTENTS

THE FORTIES: EARLY CHILDHOOD 11
    THE DODDS 23
    DAWSON CREEK 29
    FARM STORIES 39

THE FIFTIES: GROWING UP 69

THE SIXTIES: MARRIAGE & MOTHERHOOD 137

THE SEVENTIES: ENDINGS 207
    SEPARATION AGREEMENT 224
    SINGLE PARENTING 231
    JOHN 269

THE EIGHTIES: INVERNESS PLACE 369
    MY CAREER 403
    POINTE-AUX-ROCHES 459

THE NINETIES & AUGHTS 493
    GRANDCHILDREN 494
    RETIREMENT 517
    RECONCILING 565
    THE LODGE 577
    CAREGIVER ROLE 583

THE TWENTY-TWENTIES 669
    WINDING DOWN 669

EPILOGUE: TREASURES TO KEEP 689
ACKNOWLEDGEMENTS 691
APPENDIX 693
FAMILY PHOTOGRAPHS 696
ABOUT THE AUTHOR 710

THE FORTIES

My Beginnings

I was not wanted.

You would think that I would have loads of memories with a school-aged sister and a brother only eighteen months older. But no images of them come to mind at all: nothing of Merla playing hop-scotch, skipping rope, or peek-a-boo with me. I have no memories either of squabbling with Bud over marbles, digging in the sandbox or building towers of wooden building blocks. Nor can I picture a scene of the family sitting around the kitchen table, the smells and taste of food we ate or a program from the radio we likely had in the living room. I cannot recall a stuffed animal or a doll I might have been given under the Christmas tree. I also have no recollection of the bed I slept in, nor do I recall being tucked in at night.

Instead, my earliest memories are with a family *other* than my own—the Dodd's. When I was born, Peg Dodd had been my family's babysitter for my six year old sister, Merla, and my brother Bud, eighteen months older than me. From the moment Peg saw me she fell in love with me—at least that is the story I was told. She whisked me off to their farm as often as she could—I was living with their family full time from my babyhood until I was almost four years old. There is plenty of proof I lived there by the abundance of photographs Peg took of me over those years, as well as the many memories I have that remain vividly clear in my mind. I feel the touch of Peg's warm hands framing my face, and I remember her adoring eyes looking into mine, the gentle murmur of her voice, the swish of her beautiful dark hair when she held me close, and the gorgeous smile on her twenty-year-old lips. In the galvanized tub in the front yard, warm water ripples down my back, as Peg's warm hands sponge me with a face cloth, caressing my body, wrapping me in a soft towel, running her fingers through my hair and winding strands into *'Shirley Temple'* ringlets.

In my memory, giant green spruce trees framed the two-story-white clapboard-farm-house. To this day, I still visualize every room inside—the huge kitchen with the long pine table, the smell of fresh baked bread, the taste of butter on a soft warm slice, and the parlour where Peg knit booties, bonnets and sweaters for me. At night, I slept in a bedroom upstairs and rubbed the soft nubby balls of the chenille bedspread under my nose, my arms wrapped around the cuddly Kewpie-doll that Peg had given me that one Christmas.

It was in the Dodd home that I took my first steps, spoke my first words. I called the fluffy white animals in the field, 'Sheeps.' I couldn't understand why Peg corrected me. "We call them sheep, sweetheart, we call them *sheep*."

My first trip to the outhouse is indelibly imprinted in my toddler mind. The structure, like a big upright coffin, was at the back of the property, camouflaged in a grove of thick-dark- spruce-trees out of sight and smell from family and visitors. It was a long trek down the path for my little legs, and I remember being frightened when something warm and furry scurried across my toes, squeaking as it passed. I reached up and pulled the door open, the inside was dark and smelly. I climbed up onto the wooden bench with the carved toilet hole as big as a dinner plate. My bottom remembers the cold damp wood and the frigid air rushing up like a foul breeze from below as I tried to go, my breath catching with fear of falling in. Finished, I jumped down and ran like the dickens back to the house. Sensing my stress, Peg took pity on me from then on, letting me stay inside and use the shiny white porcelain potty with a handle on the side, whenever I had to go.

I was told that Peg had many boyfriends and when they went out, she insisted that I was included on the date. There is a picture of a dark-haired airman, a boyfriend from the Penhold air-base, perhaps, standing beside the family car with me sitting on top of the hood saluting him.

I have many memories of Ma Dodd and the times I spent with her gathering warm eggs from under the hens and placing them carefully in the egg-basket. I chuckle recalling the time we made a scarecrow by stuffing straw into the arms and legs of an old pair of farm overalls forming the body, the head a white cotton sugar bag we stuffed with straw marking the eyes and mouth with a crayon. Ma laughed as she poked a carrot into the crotch of the overalls saying, "Now he's ready to chase the crows away from the corn field." I couldn't understand how a carrot could possibly frighten crows!

Peg and Ma Dodd were my emotional anchors; they gave me a bank of warm memories and a safe place to grow, creating a firm foundation. Today, on my bedside table, are two brass-framed photos—one of Peg looking adoringly at me, the other of me, a toddler wearing an outfit she had knitted. They remind me that it was with her that I was first cherished and loved unconditionally.

Deep inside of me, I feel that Peg *was* my mother in so many ways, the mother who loved me, the mother I loved back, and the mother I wished for and never had.

Birth Mother: Memories of Pain

When I think of the mother who gave birth to me only two memories stick out in my mind. They are stark, visceral and filled with pain.

In the first memory, I am sitting in a sandbox by myself. There is a cold damp feeling creeping to my bum. Everything around me had a dung-brown hue. The sky was a dull grey mist with washed-out clouds. It was still—no bees buzzed and no birds chirped—when, suddenly, the silence was broken by a blaring sound. Jumping up, I ran to the chain-link fence and peered over to get a better view. Far off and down the field, a puff of black smoke filled the sky from what looked like a toy train. The whistle blasted once again.

"Come on Gail, let's go," Bruce Thorburn, the neighbour boy, called as he sprung the flat metal-on-metal clasp on the gate with a snap-clap. "Let's go! Let's go!" he called again as he reached down and took my hand in his. We raced across the road into the field, my tiny legs churning to keep up and the wet grass slapping my thighs. Tired and out of breath, we reached the black monster, and watched the locomotive glide to a screeching stop, a hiss of steam filling my nostrils with the stench of burning coal. I clung to my friend's hand, both terrified and excited at the same time. A man in the cab engine high above us smiled, waved his gloved hand and doffed his puffed-striped-cap.

"GAIL! GAIL!"—Fear clutched my chest. It was my mother who was screaming and waving her hands. Ripping my hand from Bruce's, I tore through wet grass, as fast as I could, to meet Mom. She grabbed my arm and wrenched it over my head, leaving my feet dangling in mid air. With her other hand, she whacked my bum. Pain shot through me as she slapped my buttocks over and over again. "I told you to stay in the yard," she screeched, as she dragged me across the road through the gate. She thrust me back into the sandbox and I sat, my buttocks stinging, my throat blubbering with sobs, snot dripping from my nose.

The second memory is sharp and clear as if it happened yesterday, not 80 years ago. My mother was scowling, a look of fury in her eyes. "Damn," she said. "I'm out of cigarettes." Her voice was cold and filled with anger. I shuddered. She rummaged in her purse, brought out a scrap of white paper, a pencil and something green (a dollar bill). On her knee, she scratched some scribble marks on the paper, wrapped it around the dollar bill, and thrust it at me. "Go to the drugstore and get a package of cigarettes," she ordered. Gripped with fear and worry, I grasped the paper and wound my little fingers around it tightly. I sensed its importance and did not want to lose it. I headed up the street to the drug store; I knew where I was going because I'd been there before. I skipped along the sidewalk, both excited and proud to be going on an errand all by myself. I squeezed my hand tighter around the note and felt a sense of responsibility. Passing Mr. Roger's Park, I would have liked to play on the swings, but knew that, if I did, I'd get into trouble.

It was a typical prairie day: the sun was high in the bright blue sky and it warmed my back. Arriving at the drug store I reached up and grasped the cold metal door handle. I recall how hard I had to pull to get the door open. I strode confidently to the man behind the counter. He smiled as I threw my arm up over my head and thrust the note toward him; it was sweaty and crumpled by then. Unravelling and flattening it, he swept his eyes across the scribble, nodded his head, and passed me a blue packet with the picture of a sailor in the corner, just like the cigarette packet of Mom's (*Player's Sailor Cut*). With the packet in hand, I headed for home. I rubbed the shiny smooth package along my cheek and under my nose; I liked the scent. It smelled so good that I put the package into my mouth and bit into it to better taste its flavour. I bit once more. The taste intensified with every bite. As I sunk my tiny teeth around every side of the package, my nostrils filled with the sweet aroma of tobacco. Reaching Roger's Park, I looked up and saw Mom waving her arms frantically. I gasped in fear, tore the package from my mouth and ran.

"Where the hell have you been?" she shouted. "I've been waiting for hours!" She snatched the package from my hand, and ripped off the cellophane. Seeing all the bite-holes in the cigarettes, she roared. "Oh my god, you've ruined every cigarette!" Enraged, she tore a branch from a shrub in the yard and stripped off the leaves. All I remember was the sting of the switch as it whipped, again and again and again, across the buttocks, thighs and legs of my three-year-old-body.

As I recall those two episodes eight decades ago, I imagine that my three-year-old self must have been scared to death. I'd never been screamed at before, never felt such pain on my little body, and never cried so many tears. I must have been completely confused, and unable to comprehend what was happening to me. It is hard to believe that the person who inflicted such pain on a helpless little girl, at such a tender age, was my own mother. It was abuse, of course, a term I once bestowed on *other* parents, not mine. While my mother's whip marks healed, deep emotional cuts remained as open wounds; her abusiveness assaulted my *psyche* and left indelible scars, for life. It made me question my worth as a person and fostered the belief that I was not lovable. As Toni Morrison says, "*What you do to children really matters,*" (*Toni Morrison: God Help the Child, 2015)*. What a contrast my mother's behaviour was compared to the affection, kindness, and love Peg and Ma Dodd provided me those four impressionable years.

My Birth Story: Not Wanted

I'd long felt that my mother did not want me, unlike most mothers at least, who embraced their infants in a warm set of arms, where they felt safe and accepted, their physical, emotional and mental needs nourished within the family in which they were born. I longed for a mother like those. Instead, I felt unloved and unwanted.

I was a parent myself on the day Mom told me the story of my birth; I anticipated that I'd get some clues to help me understand the root of her abusive behavior toward me. Perhaps she'd suffered from postpartum depression after my birth; or maybe I was an unwanted pregnancy, especially as I was born so soon after my brother. I hoped I'd get some insights during the visit.

It was a typical October day in Alberta, the poplar trees were shimmering gold after an early frost. It was, I imagined, a similar day to that of my birth—October 1, 1938. She greeted me at her door; she seemed diminished since I'd seen her last; her white mop of curly hair was just beneath my chin. She was in her late 70's and was smartly dressed in an A-line dress that she'd made herself. It was Wedgewood blue and brought out the China blue of her eyes. We sat at her dining room table with cups of coffee and chit-chatted about the nice fall weather, the books we were reading, and her favourite TV shows. Then I broached the subject of my birth. "I'd like to know more about my birth, what it was like and what kind of a baby I was." Her eyes lit up and I was surprised at how eager she seemed to share. This is what she told me.

"The world was on the brink of World War Two in 1938, and it was a heady time in Innisfail, with the Penhold airbase just twenty miles north. War was in the air. I was pregnant with you that fall, and your Dad and I were running the bulk oil business, hauling fuel oil to households, as well as to farmers in the countryside. When he was away, I ran the business and did the books in the evenings. We hired Peg Dodd to mind Merla, who was six, and Bud, who was eighteen months. At the first sign of labour, your dad drove me to the Red Deer hospital, twenty miles north of Innisfail. You were born on October first. When the nurse brought you to me, I examined you from head to toes to be sure you were not deformed in any way. But then, I looked more closely at your face. I was shocked at how ugly you were."

Ugly? I gasped, choking on my coffee.

Her mouth twisted in a grimace. "You reminded me of Mrs. Brett, who was a wizened and wrinkled old lady who lived up the road from our farm when I was growing up. You were so ugly, I covered you with a baby blanket so I couldn't see your face; I couldn't stand the sight of you."

Stunned, I cupped my hand over my mouth; as

a new mother, I was unable to comprehend what she was telling me. Her manner of speaking was strange too: logical, and so matter-of-fact—as if describing my birth to a reporter. It was difficult to hear. Her words stuck in my throat and my stomach twisted into a knot at the lack of emotion in her voice. She had no apparent concern of how this information might be affecting *me*—her grown up daughter looking back at her. She carried on with no crack in her voice, no hesitation, no pause nor any indication that she had changed her opinion of me over thirty years.

Mom continued without skipping a beat. I *had* to cover you up," she said. "I was too ashamed to let anyone see you. I simply *had* to cover you up" she repeated with emphasis. She was so definite, so determined, so resolute, it was as if she was trying to convince *herself* as well as me that she had no other choice. In her mind I would always remain the ugly baby.

Mom took a sip of coffee, swallowed, and let out a deep sigh. Her shoulders lowered and a far-off, wistful look came into her eyes, soft and warm. Her lips stretched into a gentle smile. "Now *Sharon,* she was such a beauty—with her wispy auburn hair, her misty grey-blue eyes, alabaster skin, puffy pink cheeks, just like the baby on the Gerber-baby-food jar!" She paused and added, "not ugly like *you,* Gail."

Beautiful ... pink cheeks ... Gerber baby ... An image wavered deep in the recess of my mind. I was a little girl again, and I was looking down into a brown wicker baby carriage at my baby sister, Sharon. My mother's same words rang in my six-year-old mind, "Not ugly like you, Gail."

I understand why I always feel a sense of foreboding each year as October comes around. I am haunted by my mother's rejection and the resulting feelings they bring on—a sense of vulnerability, dejection, worthlessness and the belief that I am unlovable and unwanted.

THE DODDS

They Wanted to Adopt Me?

On the spur of the moment, I called Mom. Retired now, I pondered ... *What will I do with my time, write another book on literacy, start my memoir?* My mind drifted wistfully to my early memories with the Dodd's sixty years ago, of Peg, Ma Dodd, and the farm. Suddenly, images — of a picnic table, house trailer, my mother — passed through my mind. *How had I been with Peg Dodd one minute and then with my family in Dawson Creek, the next?* Mom would know. Over the years, I had carved out a comfortable, if not close, relationship with her. If I was going to start my memoir, some gaps in memory needed filling in. Mom was the only person who could help me to do that.

She answered on the fourth ring. "Hello?"

"Hi Mom, how's the weather in Alberta?" It was the *weather* game we played. She told me about the freak snow storm they had; I boasted about the daffodils ready to bloom in our front yard in our home in Ontario. She told me about the Alice Munro book I'd sent her, and how she was enjoying it. I took in a deep breath, held it for a moment, and then told her my real purpose for calling. "I'm thinking about writing my memoir and was wondering about that time we moved to Dawson Creek. Can you tell me more about that?"

"Sure," Mom said her voice sounding animated, eager, excited. "It was in 1942 and the Americans had just completed building the Alaska Highway, through the Rocky Mountains to Fairbanks. Your dad got a job with the American government to lead the first civilian convoy over the highway and haul domestic goods from Dawson Creek, British Columbia to the US forces. We sold the oil business in Innisfail and your dad purchased a van for the new job...."

She recalled more from that time and their exciting new venture, which had been an opportunity of a lifetime. She paused for a moment. I heard a honking sound as if she was blowing her nose.

Taking advantage of the break, I interjected. I was tentative and a bit apprehensive because she was always touchy with me, and I didn't want to get her back up. "And the Dodd's and moving me to Dawson Creek?" This was the part of the story I knew nothing about and was anxious to learn.

The line went silent for a moment as if Mom's mind was recalibrating from her story of Dad's job to refocus on the Dodd's, their farmhouse, and sitting around their long kitchen table with Peg and Ma Dodd. Mom cleared her throat, and her tone shifted, no longer full of enthusiasm. "Well," she said, "of course I *had* to tell Peg and Ada (Peg's mother) about our plans to move to Dawson Creek and that we would be taking you with us."

"How did that go?" I asked her, hoping that my anxiety to find out wasn't showing. "They were pretty upset," Mom said. "Peg had a frown on her face when she asked me if they could visit you in Dawson Creek." I heard a snort and a chuckle over the phone line that sounded more like a sneer, as if Peg was an ignorant farm girl who should have known that Dawson Creek was too far away for a visit. "When I told her no, that Dawson Creek was bordering on the Northwest Territories, Peg burst into tears." *'That's thousands of miles away; I may never see Gail again,'* She sobbed. *'Please leave Gail with us while you're gone. She's so special to us, we love her so much.'* "That's when Ada spoke up and said that they wanted to adopt you."

Adopt me? Speechless, my mouth fell open in surprise and a warm flush washed over me remembering their affection and love for me. *The Dodd's wanted to adopt me?* Questions swirled around in my head. *Why would…? Why am I…? How did you…? What if …?* I was astonished, at this new information from the past. *Why was I hearing it now, six decades too late?* To Mom, the request to adopt me seemed like no big deal, an everyday occurrence. She'd have had more passion in her voice had it been a kitten being adopted, rather than her daughter: *me.*

"What do you mean they wanted to adopt me?" I asked, an edge to my voice at hearing this now. "What did you tell them?"

Mom's voice became stern, resolute. "No way! I told them. I can't adopt any of *my* children out." She seemed angry for them to have asked. Yet, her comment, *I can't adopt any of my children out,* sounded unnatural, fake somehow. *Who was she talking about*? She couldn't have meant *me!* I'd been living with the Dodds for the previous four years; she hadn't cast her eyes on me all that time, knew absolutely nothing about me, and didn't seemed to care to find out. Who did she really mean by the term *'my children'*? It would have been my sister Merla, age ten, and my brother Bud, close to six, not *me*! I was certainly not included in the term, *'we'*! Knowing my mother as I did, I surmised that the Dodd's wanting to adopt me would have presented a dilemma for her at thirty-four. I imagined her mind filled with options of what path she should take. *What should she do with this child she'd covered up as a baby, too ashamed to show off, the toddler she beat for inconsequential misdemeanours, the child she didn't know?* I imagined she felt distressed, guarded and unsure of the decision she should make. Was she tempted to take up the Dodd's offer and be rid of this child she'd disliked from birth? Did she weigh the consequences of that decision? Of facing my Dad? Could she withstand the judgment of her friends and neighbours? Who knows what they would whispered about her behind her back. Had any of this gone through her mind? It remains a mystery.

Mom's voice on the phone took on an indignant

tone. "I just told them, in no uncertain terms, that the adoption idea was out of the question, and I'd be coming out the following week to pick you up and take you to Dawson Creek." She was silent—indicating that this was the end of the story. We said our good byes, and the phone line went dead.

The instant I put the phone back on the hook, I was a four-year-old again, metaphorically yanked from the caring loving arms of Peg and Ma and thrust back to a mother who'd never cuddled me in her arms, or tucked me into bed at night. There is no picture in my mind of leaving Peg and Ma on that day in 1942. Nor does my body recall a hug or kiss goodbye.

Now after years of reflection, I puzzle over what prompted Peg and Ma Dodd to consider adopting me. Was it the depth of their love for me? Somehow, I believe there was something more to it than that. As the family babysitter, Peg would have seen the blanket covering my face; it was abnormal for a mother to hide her baby's face. Had she seen the bruises on my body, the welts on my tiny thighs and legs when she bathed me in the galvanized tub? Was their offer to adopt me a way of saving me from my mother's further abuse? Sometimes, in fantasy, I imagine what my life might have been like if they had adopted me. It is a daydream unfulfilled. I know, now, that if it had not been for the love and affection I received from Peg and Ma Dodd, my life would have taken an entirely different course. It was *their* love that has sustained me throughout my life. I feel certain that *'Peg'* was my saving grace, the metaphorical fairy godmother that recognized my worth and saved me.

Instead, the reality was that I lived most of my childhood feeling unwanted, abandoned, continually searching for a place I belonged. I carried open, emotional wounds that never healed. They left indelible marks on my psyche, and this part of my life is laced with sadness, pain, and the effects of unsolved and unresolved questions.

DAWSON CREEK

Landing on Mars

"You're not my mother," I yelled, and pushed my arms out in front of me, splaying my fingers. "Peg does my hair, not *you*." I squeezed past this adult who said she was my mother, ran down the hallway of the trailer, and out the door to the picnic table in the yard, tears streaming down my cheeks. I crawled up onto the bench and banged my fists on the table top till my hands hurt. I didn't know what else to do. Shaking and blubbering and gasping for breath my little body shuddered recalling the sting of the switch. My stomach clenched and shivers ran up my spine. My fingers found my mouth and my sharp baby teeth began to rip and tear the tender skin of my fingernails; I chewed the jagged edges and fibre of each fingernail until I felt pain and saw blood.

What was happening to me? One day I was in the farmhouse with Peg and Ma Dodd who cherished, treasured, and adored me, and the next day I was here, with this strange woman. Nothing was familiar, nothing was the same: this picnic table to eat on, instead of the long farmhouse kitchen table, the trees leafy lime-green, not prickly spruce needles like the farm, a trailer instead of a house, a bunk I had to climb up a ladder to sleep in, instead of a bed with tufts of chenille to tickle my nose to sleep. Nothing felt solid, nothing felt safe, and nothing was. My body cringed with anger and fear, and I kicked out; my feet hit the metal hinges of the picnic table, and I yelled out in pain.

"Where are you, Peg; where are you?" I had so many feelings for which I had no words. I imagine I would have felt cast off to a place I didn't recognize or understand. I would have felt confused, mystified, desolate, and completely and utterly abandoned. In some paradoxical way, it was as if I'd been adopted back to my own flesh and blood, these strangers I had no memory of, and to whom I did not belong.

I lowered my head to the table top, wrapped my tiny arms around my tousled, curly hair and wept in vain.

Feeling Safe, With Dad

My body tingled; I heard his raucous laugh. Daddy was home. There would be chocolate from the American soldiers, and stories, lots of stories. He'd just returned from his trip up the Alaska Highway hauling a load of domestic supplies to the US forces in Fairbanks. He had a few days at home before he'd reload more supplies and head back to Fairbanks again.

"Come to Daddy, my wee girl," he called to me, a

broad smile on his face as he lifted me up, wrapped his long arms around my body, and pressed me close to his chest. He kissed my neck, and whispered, "Ready for a story?" I bobbed my chin, yes. He blew warm air into my ear. I giggled with delight. "I've got a good one today," he said, laughing as he sat down and balanced me on his knee, ready to share his latest adventure. I wiggled with excitement. *What would it be this time?* We all sat waiting and wondering—Merla, Bud, and me.

Dad took a long draw on his cigarette and pulled me closer to his chest. "I was on my way up to Fairbanks, winding up a narrow mountain pass and driving over lumpy wooden corduroy roads made of tree trunks—thick as telephone poles—going up, over and down, up, over and down—with a thump and a bump." Dad bounced me up and down on his knee just like the truck, making me giggle. "All of a sudden, the front wheels jolted with clunk and a thud and the truck stopped dead in its tracks." Frightened, I snuggled close into Dad's tummy. He ruffled my hair and took another drag on his cigarette before continuing. "I zipped up my jacket, put on my toque, and got out of the warm cab to the bone-chilling cold. I crawled under the van to figure out what was wrong. That's when I saw him, the giant grizzly bear." *A grizzly bear?* We gasped in unison. "People have been mauled to death with one swipe of a massive paw." Dad squeezed me with his big hands making me feel safe. He sucked in on his cigarette and blew a perfect round smoke ring. I laughed and tried to catch it.

"What happened then?" We all asked together as if in one voice. "Tell us more!"

Dad's eyes opened wide as he told us how he grabbed his tools and carefully wiggled his body out from under the truck, stood up ever so slowly, and crawled into the cab. The grizzly got to the truck, and peered in at him, he told us. He whapped at the cab window then ambled away, disappearing into the forest on the side of the mountain. We all let out a sigh of relief that dad had narrowly escaped getting mauled by the monster grizzly.

I loved this story and heard it many times over the years. But what I remember most was the joy in Dad's voice when he saw me: the touch of his kiss on my neck, blowing in my ear to make me laugh, ruffling his fingers in my curly hair, and the comforting warmth of his arms pulling me close, when I was scared. He made me feel I was important to him, and that he cared about me. For the first time in this new landscape of Dawson Creek, I felt safe with someone—someone, I could trust.

Almost Getting Kidnapped

Sitting in the plush seat my legs tucked under me so I can see over the person in front of me, scary music rises as black and white images flash across the big screen. A woman is huddled in a corner of what looks like a basement. She is clinging to a small boy not much bigger than me. Her hand is over his mouth for some strange reason and their eyes are open unusually wide like mine are when I'm really scared. I shover with fear. Now there are lots of men wearing funny looking helmets, like upside down bowls. They have on shiny boots up to their knees. Guns are in their hands like the long one Bruce Dodd used for shooting rabbits. They march around the house opening doors, peering into rooms. From the basement cellar the woman hears tramping sounds and words shouted that I don't understand. She clasps the boy closer to her chest. The men in the high boots and funny hats march out of the house shouting loudly as if angry. Happy-sounding-music rises and the mother and child are smiling now with shining, joyful eyes. I believe that they are safe. The music fades and the lights come on. It is the end of the movie.

I left the theatre and started my trek home to the trailer. I knew the way; I'd done it many times before. On the second block a car pulled up beside me and stopped. A woman called to me from the passenger side, "Would you like a ride little girl?" Her voice sounded nice and her smile reminded me of Peg. I climbed into the front seat between the two of them. I recall saying thank you, and told them I'd show them the way to the trailer. Knowing the way by heart, I pointed where the man should make each turn. He followed my directions, ... at first.

But then he suddenly twisted the steering wheel and the car moved onto a street I didn't recognize. An uneasy queasy feeling churned in my stomach and I called out, "No, no this is the wrong way. I want to get out of the car." He stopped the car then and I climbed over the lady and jumped to the ground. My heart was pounding and I felt an electric chill run up my spine. I ran and ran, was out of breath when I got home. Dashing past my mother who was getting dishes out of the cupboard for supper, I climbed up the ladder into my bunk, pulled the covers over my face and began to gnaw. I kept the incident a secret from my mother, unsure of her response. She might not have listened to how frightened I was; instead, she may have punished me for something I didn't understand. As a four-year-old I couldn't take the risk.

I learned something that day. I discovered that I was very brave for a four-year-old; I could trust my feelings and make a decision for my self-protection and well-being, a skill that would serve me well in the future.

The Dawson Creek Explosion

"It was God-damned awful." Dad's words tumbled out, fast and furious. "The flames were so bloody hot you could hardly get near the storage shed...I'd never seen anything like it!...I saw those guys trying like hell to pull that iron cage from the jail to save the guy who was in it...But the fire was too freaking hot and they had to leave the poor bugger to die...I bloody well knew it was gonna blow with that box-car full of dynamite...and Jesus Christ she did...I ran like hell to get away!"

I was huddled with my sister Merla and brother Bud, when it happened. First, a red glow of flames in the distance and then a boom with a deafening roar, like ten thunder-claps reverberating all together; it was a sound louder than I'd ever heard before. Then light shot into the sky, star-like orbs of blue and red and yellow cascading to the earth like a massive firework display, followed by a wall of orange /red flames and billowing waves of black smoke. The smell of soot and burning wood reeked and I could hardly breathe. It seemed to happen all at once. People were running toward us yelling that everything was burning downtown. My heart pounded wildly, and I felt a sinking feeling in my stomach. "Will our trailer burn down?" I shouted at Merla.

"No, no, sweetheart," she replied in a soothing voice. "The fire is too far away. I'll look after you; come close and cuddle in my arms." I ducked my head under Merla's arms and wrapped my arms around her waist. She rubbed her hands up and down my back and pulled the blankets tightly around me, making me feel safe.

Mom's voice woke me up the next morning, her voice, loud and high-pitched. I pulled myself up into a sitting position in my bunk bed, my feet dangled over the edge, and I listened intently. Her voice was charged with excitement; she was eager to share. "It was just after supper when a neighbour rushed over telling me about the huge fire downtown," she said, waving her arms with enthusiasm and a hint of drama. "So, I bundled the three kids in blankets and we sat at the end of the street to watch." She beamed, her eyes sparkling.

"No, no," Merla corrected her, an edge to her voice. "That's not what happened at all." Her voice had a determined tone, emphatic. "You left Bud and Gail with me to look after, so you could go downtown to watch the blaze." There was a bite of anger in her voice. "You do it all the time," she added stressing her point. I nodded my chin up and down in agreement. On that fateful night of the Dawson Creek explosion, February 13th, 1943, my mother was nowhere to be seen. I was there with Merla, not Mom.

The Dawson Creek explosion caused major changes to our family. The blown-up rail lines disrupted the flow of goods from the southern United States, through Dawson Creek, and then up the Alaska Highway to Fairbanks. Dad was out of a job; he was made redundant. We'd left Dawson Creek by the summer of 1943. Fortunately, Dad had earned enough money that we were able to return to central Alberta; they purchased a farm just outside of Innisfail. It was 80 acres, and small by Alberta standards—most Alberta farms were at least a section of land (640 acres) or more. It was too small for wheat farming, and Dad and Mom settled on dairy; they purchased thirty black and white Holstein milk-cows. The farm came with a barn and a two-story clap-board house that had originally been constructed in 1900 from logs hewn from the ubiquitous poplar trees that grew on the original homestead.

There were changes for me as well, during that year in Dawson Creek. On my arrival, I had felt lost, forlorn, abandoned. But when I left, I felt altered in some way. It was my experiences with Dad and Merla that made the difference; it was with them that I grew to believe that I mattered, began to trust, and developed an emerging sense of belonging to this new family that I didn't have before. Would it be enough to sustain me in the long term?

FARM STORIES

Fear of My Mother

As I sat against the poplar tree with my doll in my lap, I curled my finger around strands of its straw-coloured, mop-like hair in an unsuccessful attempt to make ringlets like Peg did with my hair so long ago. A longing for Peg suddenly came over me. I picked up my doll, wrapped my arms around her, pulled her close to my chest and stroked her back softly as Peg used to do; the memory of her touch was comforting. My body bent forward, then backward, against the tree trunk in a rocking motion.

Fear suddenly gripped my heart as I caught a glimpse of Mom through the veranda window. She was coming to the door. Clutching my doll in my fist, I jumped to my feet and took off running, as if being chased by a wild dog. My legs churned in my rush to get away from her. When I reached the backyard, I looked frantically for a place to hide. Nothing! I saw only a field of prairie grass flowing in the warm summer breeze. Taking a deep breath, I waded in, up to my chin, flailing and stumbling through stems and shafts, until I was unable to take another step. When I was tired and out of breath, I crouched down onto my bottom, my heart pounding like a hammer. I held my breath so that I wouldn't make a sound. "Gail, Gail!"

Mom called. Her voice sounded far off; she was at the front of the farm house. "Gail! Gail! Where are you?" she shouted again, her voice sounding harsh and louder. I could see her outline through the wavering stems of grass. "Where are you, damn it!!" she growled "Come when I call you!" Her voice sounded furious and loud. My body shuddered and my shoulders hunched, as I bent my tummy over to make myself as small as I could so she wouldn't see me. "Where the hell are you!?" She shouted so loud that I knew she was very close. I squeezed my eyelids tight and shut out all light believing I was invisible. "I'll tan your hide, when I find you." I put my fingers in my mouth and began tearing off strips of skin from each finger. "Where in the hell are you?" Mom spat out the words, angrily. I started gnawing on my nails. "I wonder if that little bugger is out at the barn." Her voice faded.. I peeked through the shafts of grass and saw her stomping away. My stomach loosened. The air in my chest slowly released my held-in breath. My heart beat slowly.

Fear!

When I looked back at my five-year old self, fear of my mother dictated much of my behaviour, almost every move. To cope with my terror, I intuitively kept away from her as much as I was able. Further, I did as I was told. Those two strategies seemed to keep me safe for the most part, but not always.

It's a Wonder I Ever Learned to Read

"I'm Miss Donovan, your grade one teacher." She pursed her lips. They were painted a bright fire-engine red, and she and scowled as she grasped a long stick with a pointed end and slapped it onto the blackboard. I cringed in fear remembering … "We are going to learn to read," she said as she hitched her tight dress up her thighs in an attempt to hide her bulky behind. *What is she going to do with the stick, hit us if we can't?* "And what does *this* say?" Miss Donovan asked sharply, as if we should know. The sickly smell of her cheap perfume wafted in the air around her and made me gag. The stick pointed at some scribble marks that were under some kind of stick-figure that had curly-cue markings around a circle that sort of looked like a head. A tent-shaped drawing was attached to the waist. I had no idea what any of it meant. "Who can tell me?" Miss Donovan barked again, in a commanding voice. I shuddered and the palms of my hands grew most. Scared, I wanted to get out of there and go home. She waved the pointer in all directions until it found its mark … *me*. Startled, I jerked my head up and followed the stick with my eyes until the stick pointed under the scribbles. Panic rose in my throat; the marks were just a jumbled mess to me. Miss Donnovan tapped her toe on the floor, impatiently, and waited for my response. I whispered under my breath, "Girl? Woman?" I was too afraid to say it out loud, for fear I was wrong and would get a whack of the stick. Instead, I remained mute, shrugging my shoulders in silence. "Well?" she uttered, impatiently. I dipped my chin to my chest, embarrassed; I felt heat rise from my neck to my cheeks, and lowered my head into my arms in shame.

A little blond-haired girl waved her hand madly in the air. "That says *Mother*," she called out boldly, striding up to the front of the room to run her finger under the scribble marks. Fascinated, I wrinkled my forehead. *How did she know?*

When I think back to that day in 1944, 80 years ago, I realize that it was the *Dick and Jane* readers, so popular in the 1940s, that caused the real problem for me when I tried to learn to read. That *Dick and Jane* family made no sense to me. *My* mother didn't stay in the house all day cooking, cleaning and looking after the kids. *My* mother fed the Holstein cows in the barn, milked them and operated the electric milk separator spinning milk into cream. And *my* dad didn't go to work in a tie and fedora. He wore overalls and a straw hat when he rode the tractor in the fields and mowed alfalfa for the cattle. No one I knew called their parents *Mother*, and *Father* instead of Mom and Dad.

I never did learn to read that year, in Grade One,. I struggled and stuttered over every squiggle in the *Dick and Jane* readers. Of course. I *did* eventually learn to read, but not until third grade. By today's standards, I would have been labelled *dyslexic* or a slow learner– as if not being able to read was somehow *my* fault and not that of the system they used for teaching literacy. Who would have predicted, at the time, that I would one day be the author of four published books on literacy–on ways to teach children how to learn to read and write? And the little blond-haired-girl, Beverly? She became one of my best friends in grade school. When I met up with her years later, she had her PhD and I had my Doctorate in Education. Eat your heart out, Miss Donovan!

Babies: The Beautiful and the Ugly

Dad's eyes danced, and his smile filled his entire face when he brought Mom and my new baby sister home that June day of 1945. "Here's your new baby sister, Sharon, born on June 17th," he cried, excitedly. I was full of anticipation of having a new sister to play with. I'd gotten my doll to show her, wiggling with excitement as I waited for Mom to put the baby into the brown wicker baby carriage, so I could see her. Looking down at Baby Sharon I was surprised at how small she was, how perfectly formed, and not much bigger than my doll! I marvelled at her round little face, her long curly lashes on her closed eyelids. Her skin felt so smooth as I stroked her cheek, and her perky toy-like ears were just like the ones on my doll. And her hands…I couldn't help giggling when her wee fingers curled around my thumb. Then, suddenly, Baby Sharon's plump little face scrunched up, and turned angry and red. She let out a roar, scaring me half to death. I was amazed at how such a teeny creature could make such a loud noise. "What did you do to scare the baby?" Mom called out in an accusing voice. I slunk away from the carriage. In an attempt to calm Baby Sharon, Merla wheeled the carriage around the kitchen table a few times, unsuccessfully, and even Bud took a turn. Wanting to care for my baby sister too, I dropped my doll and wrapped my fingers around the buggy handle ready to push.

"No! No!" Mom screamed, waving her hands menacingly at me. "You'll tip the buggy over and she'll fall out!" Discouraged, I hung my head and put my fingers in my mouth.

Mom scooped up Baby Sharon out of the buggy. "Come here my gorgeous darling," she crooned, patting baby Sharon's back until she settled down. "What lovely hair you have," Mom threaded the silky strands between her finger and thumb. "It's so silky and fine, ginger-coloured just like your Grandma Blakley's." She smiled and chuckled softly. "And look how you smile when I tweak your cheeks." She gazed into baby Sharon's face. "And your eyes," Mom's mouth turned up into a smile. "They are so bright I know you are going to be smart as a whip!" Mom's eyes suddenly grew misty as she looked down at Baby Sharon on her lap and drew her fingers lightly across her chubby cheeks.

Mom's voice softened and lowered to just above a whisper, "You are the most gorgeous baby I have ever seen, with your creamy complexion and sparkly grey-blue eyes." Mom blinked her eyelids fast as if to stem the flow of tears that seemed ready to spill over. "You are, without a doubt, the most beautiful of *all* my babies."

With a sudden glance in *my* direction Mom's face twisted into a scowl and her eyes glared into mine. She stated, emphatically, "Not like *you*, were, Gail."

Startled, I felt as if a rock had dropped into the pit of my stomach. Mom's lips spread thin and her eyes glared. "When *you* were born, you were the ugliest baby I'd ever seen." She shook her head in emphasis. "*You* were so ugly, Gail, that I couldn't bear to look at you." Her eyes grew cold—as frigid as icicles. "Get away from the baby; go play with your doll," she scowled, and kicked my doll out of the way with her foot.

Doing as I was told, I picked up my doll, hugged her close to my chest, plodded over to the kitchen table, scrunched under and lowered my head into my cupped hands. I cried.

At six years old, I felt the intensity of my mother's disdain for me. I felt it to the very marrow of my bones.

Learning to Depend on Me

I sat up in my poplar tree and dangled my legs in the air, surveying my domain as if I were the master of the universe. I stared through the wispy clouds scratching the periwinkle blue Alberta sky beyond; in the east, the red headed chickens bobbed and pecked at the ground. I heard the faint thrum of the tractor as Dad cut the hay in the south field. The gully where we tobogganed in the winter was to the west and the Waskasoo Creek threaded through the bushes, north of the farm. It was a place I was forbidden to go. A flock of black cowbirds soared to the heavens and the magpie swooped, his long black tail feathers gliding past like a scarf in the wind; he transferred his power and invincibility to me. A sudden feeling of energy coursed through my body, and for a brief moment, the built-up tension and fear of my mother flowed out of my veins like a river rushing to the sea and set me free.

I climbed my poplar almost every day; it was my favourite thing to do; the one thing I was good at. One day, I wondered *how high I could I climb*? Feeling particularly invincible, I said to myself, *I'm going to find out!* Grabbing the first branch, I put my feet on the trunk and hoisted myself up. Stretching from one branch to another, I tested my weight before moving to the next. When a branch held, I pulled myself up again and again until they became more fragile. When I came to one that was only as thick as my thumb, I paused. *Will it hold?* Tentatively, I tugged. *So far, so good!* Pressing my hands around it, I hefted my chest up and over.

SNAP

A loud crack! My stomach dropped, my breath caught in my throat; my body gave way as I soared through the branches. They tore at my body and ripped my knee open. Twigs snapped and crackled, gouging my face, and limbs clawed flesh as I sped by; the ground raced up to meet me. My heart stopped. *I'm going to die!*

A jolt! Pain shot through my right knee as I hung, dangling, the ground wavering below, my body trembling all over as I gasped for breath. The fat limb held—it saved me. *I was alive!* Sitting on the ground at the base of the poplar, I wiped away blood oozing out of my knee, stroked the welts on my face, and threaded leaves out of my hair. Did I cry? No.

What strikes me now, decades later, is why that seven-year-old me didn't run like the dickens to my mother, to seek a hug or a kiss or a bandage for my scraped knee, as any typical seven year old would? Why did I sit and tend to my own wounds? Did I instinctively understand, at the age of seven, that I couldn't count on my mother for empathy, that I had to look after myself ... alone? That incident is a metaphor for my life. To this day, I rarely ask for help; I rely on myself to solve the problems I encounter.

Bud's Acceptance as Part of the Family

Who is this kid? Where did she come from? Is that what went through Bud's mind when this stranger arrived on the scene in Dawson Creek, a little sister he'd never heard of, had never set eyes on before, who appeared without warning? Over the years, I sometimes wondered this, but not on this spring day.

I was sitting high in my poplar tree when I spied Bud walking out the lane with his friend, Tom. *Where in the world were they going? And how come I wasn't invited?* They crossed the gravel road, climbed into the ditch to the other side, and then under the fence of the Dixon farm across from ours. *They're going to Waskasoo Creek!* Filled with excitement, I scrambled down the tree as fast as I could and followed them. *It wasn't fair that Bud got to go to the creek and I didn't.* Mom told me never to go to the creek; it was dangerous, she said with the spring run off. I didn't care, as I ran across the field into the bush to the muddy bank of the creek. When Bud saw me, he smiled and waved his arm, motioning me to come over. Tom's forehead wrinkled and he glared at me, unhappy that I'd come. "We're playing *Cowboys and Indians*," Bud announced, like a movie director. "And you can be the Indian like in the movie we saw last Saturday." Tom's eyes lightened up when he heard that I'd be the *Indian*. So excited to be a part of the game, I scooped up mud in my fingers and streaked splotches across my forehead and down each cheek, like war-paint I'd seen in the John Wayne movies. Bud and Tom tore branches off the bushes, and stripped them of leaves to make pretend guns.

"You can't shoot me," I teased, prancing around in circles while whooping and hollering, dodging their pretend bullets just like I thought real Indians would. When I think of it now, I am embarrassed at how indoctrinated I was by those old Westerns. But, I never gave it a thought as we chased, shot, screamed and hooted! As the sun lowered in the west, Bud said we should head home. We crossed the field and up our lane. It had been a glorious afternoon playing with my brother Bud and his friend.

When I go back in time, I reflect on my brother Bud and what a good brother he was. Imagine allowing me to butt in with his friend that day, so long ago. I'll always remember how patient he was in showing me how to snare gophers and share in the profits from selling them. Over all those years, we'd become playmates: in winter we tobogganed down the gully. He continued to be at my side during our high school years; he taught me how to curl in the town rink, and drove me to Red Deer to school dances. What a dear brother he was. He accepted me as his sister, a part of the family.

My Chicken Shit Coat

"Here comes farm girl, Gail, in her chicken-shit coat!" David Dunlop sneered, wrinkling up his nose. "Get away, she stinks!" He put his arm up to cover his face as he wiggled past me. I hated that dun-grey, gabardine, three-quarter-length coat; it was a cast-off of Bud's. Chicken shit clung to it like glue. I couldn't wash it off, no matter how hard I tried. I cringe at the memory of it.

Feeding the chickens was my job, morning and night. It was a horrid, messy, smelly, disgusting chore. First, I got a pailful of chop (ground up grain) from the barn, and on my way to the chicken coop, I got a pailful of water from the kitchen. I balanced the two pails until I got to the coop. Setting them down, I unhooked the latch on the door, slid the pails inside, and shut the door fast to prevent the hens from getting out. When I stepped inside, I was greeted with the overwhelmingly acrid smell of urine, shit and sour fermented feed. At the scent of the chop, the chickens swooped down from their nests on the platform in a flurry of movement, feathers batting the air as they landed, as they crowded around me and pecked and clawed at the floor. They squawked with impatience as I scooped out the stinking chop mixed with their shit, splattering some on the sleeves and front of my coat while they were at it. I dumped out the old water and filled it with fresh water. While the hens were feeding, I gathered the eggs encased with a bits of straw laced with shit, put them gently into an empty bucket, and headed to the house to scrub off the chicken shit and store the eggs in the refrigerator. Then I got washed up for school.

I was thankful when spring came. I pitched the filthy old coat into the closet behind the kitchen stove until fall. Then, I begged Mom for a new coat to no avail. That chicken-shit coat caused me grief another year.

Winters in Alberta: How Cold Was It?

It was so God-damned cold, it would freeze the tits off the cows, Dad used to say;

It was so bloody cold, that February temperatures got no warmer than minus 30 Fahrenheit;

It was so freaking cold, we wrapped scarves around faces for the miles walked to school;

It was so blasted cold, that frigid air hit us in the stairwell going up to our bedrooms;

It was so bone-chilling cold, we could scrape hoar frost off the chinked-log-walls;

It was so cold, our breaths made foggy mist like a polar bear ... *inside* our bedroom.

It was so blinking cold, that we needed boiling water in jars to keep us warm at night;

It was so frigid cold, that those jars froze to solid blocks of ice on the morning floor;

It is so cold, it would freeze the balls of a brass monkey! That's something Dad would say.

    A note of explanation about our Alberta farmhouse. The original house was constructed in the early 1900s from poplar logs hewn from the land. A two-story house—two bedrooms down and two bedrooms up—was built with the plaster-chinked logs. There was *no* insulation, *no* wall board and *no* furnace—only a wood stove for cooking and heating rooms. Many years later, a two-story-insulated addition was built, but when I lived there no furnace was ever installed. In the winter, sleeping in the upstairs unheated bedrooms necessitated taking mason jars full of boiling water to bed. We'd climb up the drafty, frigid stairwell to the hoar-frost covered bedroom. In the morning, when the jars had fallen on the floor, they were solid blocks of ice! It *was* that cold! Another fact I must clarify is that we walked the mile-and-a-half to school every day summer *and* winter. No school buses in those days!

My Grandmother's Love

"I bet daffodils are blooming in New Westminster," Dad suggested at supper. "Spring flowers are at least a couple of months ahead of us in B.C." He took another bite of bread. "Your Grandma Pye says everything blooms early there."

I looked outside at the cows in the farmyard huddled together, their rumps backed into the wintry wind to keep warm. Mom's fall dahlias were frozen stiff as sticks. How could I ever do my Grade Four project on fresh spring flowers? *Daffodils in February?*

What a stupid project to assign in the middle of an Alberta winter! It was beyond me! The only Alberta spring flowers I knew didn't bloom till May, three months away—washed-out-mauve crocus and yellow buttercups. I'd only seen flowers like tulips, daffodils and purple muscari, in seed catalogues. They weren't hardy enough for the Alberta climate in the 1940s, according to my mother. Fresh spring flowers in February were a distant dream, the farthest thing from my mind—except for this silly assignment.

Daffodils ... in February ... Grandma Pye ... B.C. ... My mind spun with wild possibility. *I'll write a letter to Grandma Pye.* Right after , I wrote to her to ask if she would <u>please</u> send me some daffodils. I underlined *-please-* because my assignment was due in a couple of weeks.

"You're being ridiculous," Mom chided. "The daffodils will be dead before they arrive!" She shook her head and grimaced. "Grandma Pye won't send daffodils; you're wasting your time."

I sent the letter anyway.

Every day, I checked the metal mailbox at the end of the lane. Every day, I waited. Day after day passed. Days passed into a week. As the deadline for the assignment loomed and I'd heard nothing from Grandma Pye, I began to lose hope. But then, we got a call from the CPR train station in Innisfail to say that a parcel had arrived for *"Gail Pye."* I was over-the-moon excited. My daffodils had arrived just in time for my assignment! As I drove into town with Dad, the minutes seemed like hours; I couldn't wait to get to the station to see my daffodils. In my mind I imagined perky trumpet-shaped-butter-yellow-blooms on long green stalks, just as I'd seen in the seed catalogues. My whole body wiggled with excitement when the stationmaster handed me the long box, covered with brown wrapping paper, with my name on it *"Gail Pye, Innisfail, Alberta.* It was the first piece of mail I had ever received! I ripped off the brown paper and wrestled with the cardboard box, unable to get it open. Dad came to my rescue and undid the folded flaps. I lifted the lid. And there they were: a limp, stringy, straggly, goopy, green and yellow pile of mush! It was a disaster! *My spring flower project was ruined!*

But that's *not* what sticks in my mind today, over seventy-five Februaries later. I learned first-hand how kind my Grandma Pye was. I will always remember the warm feeling that washed over me on that day in the truck, in my anticipation of the gift from a Grandma I had only heard of. It is only now that I recognize what a loving grandmother she was, to send a gift to a granddaughter *she* had never met. My grandparents had moved to B.C. before I was born. With thousands of miles between us, she demonstrated her caring and love for me in the only way that was possible for her to do; to respond to her granddaughter's letter by sending her the daffodils for her project. There were no cell phones or Facetime at that time, and travelling such long distances was out of the question in the 1940s. As a grandmother myself, I am thankful that she modelled the importance of connecting with the next generation in such a loving way. And as for that little ten-year-old girl? She forever held in her heart the feeling of being loved.

I Was a Milkman at Ten Years Old

Sitting on the tailgate with Bud, dangling my legs over the edge, the rattle and banging of the milk bottles against the metal racks rang in my ears as the pick-up-truck bumped along the gravel road to Innisfail. Merla eased the truck to our first stop—my customer. Grabbing two bottles of milk, I jumped down from the tailgate, walked quickly to their doorstep, set down the full bottles, picked up the empty ones—with milk tokens inside—ran back to the truck, hopped up and replaced the empties in the rack. Merla moved slowly down the block, stopping at Bud's customer's house. He repeated the process. We continued working until it was time for school. After Merla dropped us off, she continued delivering milk to the rest of the people on the route. It was a Monday to Saturday job; I felt proud to be working just like a grown-up! I was a milkman at ten years old.

In the evenings, we all donned surgical masks over our mouths and noses, like everyone did over the

Covid years of 2020 and 2021, but we did it to prevent germ-contamination as we prepared the dairy for the next day. My job was to rinse and clean the used bottles with a wire bottle-brush. Once they were cleaned, the bottles were sterilized in a special steam-machine. In fact, everything had to be sterilized, every metal container, every tube, hose and implement used in the process; it filled the room with the steamy, sweet smell of milk. I especially loved watching the milk bottling machine that filled the bottles full before another gadget stamped on the cardboard bottle cap with a snap.

On July 1st *Dominion Day*, as we called it in the 1940s, we decorated the truck and entered the Innisfail parade. Thinking we were very clever, we posted hand-made signs onto the cab of the pickup that read, *"You Can Beat Our Cream; But You Can't Beat Our Milk."* Even now, I get goosebumps remembering how people waved and cheered as we inched our way down Main Street. We didn't win any prizes, but it was a happy memory I'll never forget.

I learned a lot about myself during my childhood on the farm; not only how to be responsible and reliable, but that success comes from hard work. I discovered, too, the feeling of satisfaction and personal pride in a job well done.

Guess Who's Coming to Dinner?

'Guess who's coming to dinner? No, it was not Sydney Poitier in the 1967 movie of the same name. It was Tommy Douglas, the architect of Canada's Universal Medicare program in Saskatchewan, in 1944. As a member of the CCF (Cooperative Commonwealth Federation), the forerunner of the NDP (New Democratic Party), Tommy Douglas was elected as the first social-democratic government in all of North America.

As a ten year old pulling handful after handful of green-stemmed carrots from the garden at back of the barn, I should have guessed the importance of our guest given the tension in the kitchen that morning. Mom was rolling pieces of chicken, puffs of flour stuck on her hands, beads of perspiration building on her wrinkling forehead. *We never have fried chicken for a noon day meal. This must be a big deal.* That had to be why Dad killed the chicken earlier that morning. In my mind, I could still hear the chicken's scream of terror– as if it knew what was coming– as Dad raised his axe. Did it hear the WHACK as the blade hit its neck? The image of its headless body racing around the farmyard in all directions, beating its wings as if it were still alive, blood squirting out of its empty neck, is an image I'll never forget. Did it know it was being sacrificed for the guests coming for dinner, I wondered, as I twisted off the green stems and washed the carrots. I started setting the table with the *Rogers* silverware, normally it was only brought out at Christmas.

Sitting at the dinner table all washed up in clean clothes, I folded in my hands in my lap, as I'd been instructed, as platters of food in the special cut-glass dishes, the first time I'd seen it was used, were passed around.

"Grace?" Dad said as he bowed his head, something we *never* did, ordinarily. I learned later that Tommy Douglas had been a Baptist Minister before he was Premier of Saskatchewan. I didn't understand much of what the adults talked about; I caught words like 'Medicare,' 'social justice,' and 'pensions.' My ears perked up when Mr. Douglas hitched up his wire-rimmed glasses and told the story about a woman in rural Saskatchewan who had cancer and had chosen no treatment, since the cost would have meant selling their farm. "She died a horrible, painful death," he said, lifting his glasses and wiping at his eyes. "Such a sacrifice to save the family's livelihood."

I discovered later that Mr. Douglas was visiting to give encouragement to Dad and his campaign as a CCF candidate. He had an unsuccessful bid for a seat in the Alberta legislature that year. Dad ran again in the 1950 election, and as a teenager I worked along with him; I knocked on doors and handed out pamphlets that pointed to Dad's name, *Auburn C. Pye,* and appealed for their vote for Old Age Security, Universal Medicare, Family Allowances, Employment Insurance, and Social Assistance. These are programs we now take for granted in Canada.

Recalling that afternoon in our farm kitchen seventy-seven years ago, I realize now that Dad was advocating for a better future for all Canadians, despite never winning a seat in the provincial legislature. He was courageous and ahead of his time. I have inherited his vision and always vote for a party that advocates for social justice and equity for all Canadians.

Three New Coats: Would One Be Mine?

"Come see the snowflakes, my darling," Mom called to Sharon and held out a coat I'd never seen before. Sharon toddled over, her arms raised, and fingers pointing, ready to try it on. Mom folded her little arms into the sleeves and zipped up the front. It brought out the indigo blue in Sharon's eyes and the white velvet Peter-Pan collar reminded me of Shirley Temple. The puffed-out fabric, doubling her size, made her look like a puffball, cozy and warm. "Now skedaddle outside and play in the snowflakes." Mom smiled, patting her bum affectionately.

Would I ever get a coat, a decent coat of my own? I filled my buckets with water to take to the chickens. *Oh, how I hated this chicken-shit coat—this boy's coat, a hand-me-down of Buds, the only winter coat I owned. It stank!* Out the kitchen window I watched the mid October snow flakes fall like dandelion whiskers. They glided softly in the air and turned to droplets of rain when they hit the grass. *Jacket weather,* I thought, as I pushed open the back door with my behind to let Sharon out. Without warning, Mom yelled, "Where do you think *you're* going with just a jacket on?" Her eyes glared sharply at me. "It's too cold to go out like that," she barked, waving her index finger in my face. "Take that jacket off right this minute, and get your winter coat out from the closet."

Jaw clenched, I set down the bucket and stomped to the closet, my nostrils flaring with anger at the thought of my chicken-shit coat. Unlatching the closet door, it was stuffed full of discarded garments. I started yanking things out—an old grey shirt of Dad's, a green wool sweater of Merla's, a rubber boot, I thought was probably Bud's. No sign of the stinking chicken-shit coat. My nose scrunched up in disgust at the thought of it as I flung out a pair of woolen leggings, an old housedress of Mom's, and a blue jacket I could not identify. An idea suddenly came to me. *What if I can't locate my chicken-shit coat? Would Mom get me a new winter coat like Sharon's?* That was my plan; it was not a good one.

"Have you found your coat?" Mom's voice rose, crackling with anger.

"Still looking," I answered, smiling smugly.

"Well don't take all day; the chickens need to be fed before you go to school!"

"I know; I know," I said, chucking out a pair of Dad's grey long-johns, an apron, a skirt I'd outgrown. That's when I saw it, the corner of my chicken-shit coat peeking out from under a frayed baby blanket.

"Have you found it yet?" Mom growled her cheeks reddening.

"Not yet," I fibbed, as I wrenched out the chicken-shit coat and tucked it carefully under the mess of clothes, completely hidden. *How clever I am!*

"I can't find it," I lied once more and dragging out the worn-out woolen blanket, leaving the closet completely bare. "It's not here!"

Mom's eyes tightened into slits in a questioning look, her lips pressing into a thin line. Clenching a wooden spoon in her fist she stomped toward me, her shoes clumping across the linoleum floor. She peered into the closet, her head bobbing up and down with a look of surprise. I breathed a sigh of relief—but only for only a moment. Mom turned abruptly to the mound of clothing. My heart sank and I sucked in air and held it tight. In a frenzy she grabbed at the pile flinging items across the floor until she spied my chicken-shit coat. *I was done for.*

Picking it up, she shook it in my face, the veins in her neck throbbing as she raised the wooden spoon above her head. Whack, Whack! I hunched my shoulders waiting for the next blow. Instead, her voice lowered to almost a whisper, her mouth twisting into a trembling ugly sneer. She muttered softly, deliberately, enunciating each word slowly and clearly. "You make me so bloody mad, I could *kill* you!"

Silence hung in the air, tense, taut, terrifying.

The kitchen door burst open and Merla stormed past me loaded with parcels, her eyes dancing. Standing at the kitchen door, I twisted the last button into the hole of my chicken-shit coat, ready to face the November blizzard to make my final trip to the henhouse. Merla flung off her boots and coat, ripped open a huge box and lifted out a cherry-red woollen coat. I'd never seen anything like it; it was magnificent. It fell down over Merla's shoulders, hips and legs and almost touched the floor. Down the front were shiny, ebony-black buttons that were the size of Loonies. She pranced around the kitchen as if she were Ginger Rogers. My mouth dropped open, and I couldn't stop staring at my fifteen-year-old sister; how grown up she looked: her coal-black hair and milky white skin reminded me of Gene Tierney from the movie I'd seen the week before. My shoulders slumped and heaviness hung over me as if my chicken-shit coat was lined with pellets of lead, weighing my spirit down. *Would I be wearing this chicken-shit coat forever?*

Dad whistled, lifting his hand off the barn broom. He wiggled his fingers at me in a wave. "When you're finished with the chickens, get washed up, we're going to town." Once the chickens were fed and my face was sparkling clean, Dad opened the truck door. "It's high time I took you to town to buy you a new winter coat." My eyes widened in disbelief, and my body trembled with excitement. As we drove into town, Dad reached over and patted my knee. "It's about time *you* had a decent winter coat, Gail." A warm flush spread across my cheeks; he made me feel special, important, as if I really counted.

"This little girl is looking for a new winter coat," Dad announced to the clerk in Berscht's fancy clothing store. "Please throw this old one out and show us where the winter coats are that would fit my beautiful daughter." The clerk took us to a rack full of coats. "Now Gail," Dad said, a grin on his face and his eyes sparkling, "You choose any coat you like. Take your time and don't be afraid to try them on and check in the mirror for the one *you* like best." He cocked his head to the side. "And don't be looking at the price tags either." He put his arm around my shoulders. "You choose any one you want. It's *your* choice."

Beaming, I bounced from one foot to the other as I combed through the rack. So many styles, so many colours! I went back and forth, trying on one then another, admiring myself in the mirror. Finally, I found the one I liked best, a heavy, woolen, royal blue coat that came down over my knees with shiny silver buttons. It reminded me of the ones Princess Elizabeth and Margaret Rose wore at Buckingham Palace that I'd seen in last week's *'Star Weekly.'* My eyes sparkled as I ran my hands over the fabric, my fingers tingling at the touch. It was absolutely perfect. As I walked to the truck in my brand-new-coat, I suddenly felt worthy and valued. After seventy years I still recall the smell of newness of that coat... the smell of love.

Over the years I often reflect on that shopping excursion with Dad and why he bought me my very first brand new coat. He'd never done that before; Mom always purchased our clothes. It got me thinking and wondering. Did he recognize mom's unusual treatment of me? Did he want to make it right? I'd like to think so.

Afterthoughts of My Early Years

Who mattered? Who cared? Who made a difference in my early years? These are questions I ask myself, now, in my late eighties. My thoughts turn to my mother first; her abuse had lasting effects on my life. My fear of her, for instance, caused my habit of chewing my fingernails for many decades; I continued the habit until the day she died. Another effect was that—to this day—I seldom look at myself in the mirror. Oh, I study the features of my face when I put on make-up in the morning, and check myself in the full-length-mirror in the hall before I go out, to be sure I am suitably dressed for the event I might be attending. But other than that, I rarely glance at my face. For example, I'll wash my hands in a restaurant bathroom and never glance at the mirror above the sink to check if my lipstick needs replenishing, or if my wind-blown hair requires attention. Am I fearful of what will be reflected—the image my mother saw—a face that, she told me, is revolting, repulsive, unsightly...ugly? Am I subconsciously avoiding that possibility? Why take the risk! Subliminal messages from early childhood run deep. My mother's perception of and behaviour toward me, is related to the sense of foreboding I felt, throughout my life, when my birthday, October 1st, approached. I am haunted by feelings of unworthiness, vulnerability, of being unlovable. Why? What was it about me that drove my mother to such aversion, such repugnance of me? Who did I remind her of? What was going on in her life when I was born that caused her to reject me? In my late eighties, you'd think I'd have figured her out by now, and yet so many questions persist; these are lost pieces of the puzzle that would help me to complete the picture of my life.

Dad comes into focus with more clarity than ever before. I see how he was a counter-balance to Mom's neglect. Throughout my early years, he made me feel as though I mattered; he wrapped me in a shroud of love. I learned the value of hard work, honesty, integrity, and justice from him. He introduced me to a perspective of life that went far beyond the home—of civic responsibility and a global view of the world.

My heart warms when I think of my siblings. Sister Merla was my surrogate mother in my early years; her kindness is embedded in my heart. My brother, Bud, was my first childhood playmate; he accepted and loved me throughout the decades. My sister, Sharon, who grew up adored by my mother? Our mothering experiences are so different. I continually work at bonding with her in a more loving way.

And what became of Peg Dodd? I saw her only *once*, thirty years after I'd left their farm as a little girl. It was in 1972, when I visited my sisters who were living in Vancouver. Peg was still beautiful and her hug was as warm as I remembered. She was thin and wan with cancer. However, Peg's memory came alive once again when, ten years ago, I visited the Dodd farm. Peg and Ma Dodd gone and I was greeted by nephew Terry in a straw hat; he was the image of Bruce Dodd, Peg's brother. Terry opened his arms wide. "Little Gail Pye," he remarked. "I've heard about you, all my life, from my Grandma Ada (Ma Dodd) and from the pictures of you that my aunt Peg showed me so often as I was growing up." He squeezed me close in a tight embrace. "To me, you've always been family,' he whispered in my ear. "Welcome home."

THE FIFTIES

Decade of Change

The 1950s were a decade of change for me; it was a kind of metamorphosis. I'd come through the pupa stage–fed full of love from the Dodds– while the ugly caterpillar phase symbolized my preschool years and my mother's rejection and abuse. The chrysalis period of my teenage years represents fresh possibilities and hope: high school, first boyfriend, Teacher's College, first heartbreak and overseas adventures, teaching.

When Dad suffered a heart attack, brought on by the demands of farm work, he sold the farm and purchased the *'Penhold General Store'*. The business accommodated his weakened physical condition. The move was a welcome change for me. He'd bought our five bedroom, two-story home, and I finally had a bedroom to myself, the coal-stoked-furnace warmed my bedroom. No more hoar-frost on chinked walls for me! Best of all, I had no chickens to feed!

Dad and Mom both worked in the General Store; they ordered produce, stocked shelves and waited on customers –it was a lifestyle shift for my parents. Changes for us kids meant Sharon, at six years old, started Grade One at the local public school; Bud, at fifteen, and I, fourteen, rode the school bus to high school in Red Deer, the largest city in the area, just ten miles north of Penhold. Sister Merla, now nineteen, joined the airforce, and was stationed across the country in Greenwood, Nova Scotia; she was the first of us to leave home. The household was frenzied with excitement, when she came home on leave; we couldn't get enough of her stories about life in the Forces. She gave me her stylish-hand-me-down-dresses that she no longer wore–a bonus, as these were clothes I could never afford from earnings made by baby-sitting or delivering the *Calgary Herald* newspaper around the village.

Seeking Approval: Relying on Myself

In order to seek acknowledgement, approval, and acceptance from my mother, I worked hard at trying to please her. I cleaned our five-bedroom house from top to bottom every Saturday: I changed beds, dusted furniture, scrubbed all the floors, and did the family laundry with a ringer washer. It did not seem to be enough. I was fourteen and what I longed for most was praise from my mother—one single word would do—"Thanks!" Instead, I got the sound of silence.

Now an octogenarian, I recognize this as a pivotal moment in my life. I seemed to be searching to find personal identity and worth—worth that my mother neglected to transfer to me at birth. It appeared that it was *my* job to do the work to accomplish who I wanted to be; I was the only person I could depend on. Instead of being resentful, angry, pissed off at having to do so much work with no acknowledgement, I was proud of the housework I'd done and felt good about myself. In order to become a better person, I wrote letters to former teachers telling them how much I appreciated their teaching, joined the CGIT (Canadian Girls in Training), and the choir of the United Church; we sang at Church on Sundays, and I was the only family member to do so. I was also determined to progress well in school; I did my homework without being reminded, and I studied hard for tests, eventually graduating with honours from high school.

High School Love

"Have you seen him?" Sandy asked. "He's gorgeous!" There was a buzz around the high school (Lindsey Thurber Composite High School in Red Deer, Alberta) that Fall of 1953. "You've just got to see him," Marion whispered to me as we took our seats in Mr. Oak's English class. At the end of the day, I finally caught a glimpse of him—the knock-out good-looking new kid standing beside my brother, Bud! *It had to be him*. What was Bud doing with him? Bud waved me over. The new boy smiled at me. My breath caught in my throat and heat rushed to my cheeks. *Are my white ankle socks sagging? Will he see the scuff marks on my saddle shoes?* "This is Peter Gazeley," Bud said when

I got close. "He wants to get to know you." Peter held out his hand and took mine in his ... holding it just a tad too long.

By Christmas we were going steady and were an item throughout the next three years of high school. We were inseparable those three years; I have an album full of pictures of us ... I still have it...Peter treated me with the utmost respect during that time. Given that Peter was a semi-pro-athlete (baseball & hockey), it was surprising that he was never chauvinistic—a word not used then—since he would have been influenced by the chauvinistic sport culture of the day. When we graduated from high school, Peter went off to the University of North Dakota, and I attended the one-year Teacher Training program at the University of Alberta. We became engaged at Christmas of that year. In my naivete, I imagined marriage, children, a home of our own. However, as so frequently happens with teenage romances, my dream was never fulfilled.

It is only now, in my 86th year, that I realize the impact that Peter's love had on my life. Until I met him, I'd always felt a misfit in my family: I was an outsider always looking in, having to *earn* approval and affection. With Peter, I felt loved unconditionally and was totally accepted as I was, able to reveal my true inner self and loved for it. Peter restored my faith in myself: that I was valued, lovable, and a worthy human being. He was the one person I could count on in every way.

Peter's love gave me the needed strength to survive my destructive first marriage. It was Peter's unconditional love, as well, that helped me recognize it once again when I met John, the man who loved me unconditionally for the next forty years of my life. As tribute, I include Peter in my memoir and acknowledge the role he played in helping me become the person I am today.

Introduction to Chauvinism

Dad seemed nervous. He motioned me to sit down at the kitchen table, facing him. He coughed as if clearing his throat, something he did when he was nervous. It created an eerie, peculiar, uneasy tone in the room, and I felt a sense of foreboding. I took a deep breath and held it tight, listening with my whole being to every word that came from Dad's lips.

"Look Gail," Dad began, his brow wrinkling in a wave. This was not a good sign. My heart clutched tight, and I pressed my teeth firmly on my thumb nail. "Your Mom and I recognize that you want to become a teacher, and we support that." In the back of my mind, I heard a *'but'*! Dad tapped his fingers on the table, nervously, hesitantly. "But we think that you should go the route of taking a one year course." My heart fell. *I qualified for a degree program.* My stomach twisted into a knot; I blinked at the tears bubbling up. "In addition," Dad added, "In all likelihood you will get married, have children and never go back to teaching anyway." *What was he talking about? I was not getting married for-goodness-sake! I just want to get a degree!* I said nothing, but I was hopping mad. "Three years in university would be entirely *wasted*," Dad added as if he thought a woman wouldn't have a career after she married. Suddenly, I felt as if it was *me* that was being wasted. Dad's voice lifted. "I know your mother wants you to have a backup-plan should you ever need to go back to work if something unforeseen happened to your husband." He paused and looked up at Mom. She nodded in confirmation. "You'd have your initial teaching diploma, in that event."

So, the decision had been made. With a sudden twist, I ripped off the nail on my thumb. My voice quivered and lowered in volume, as if it was coming from someone else. "So, what's going to happen to the education fund?" I murmured quietly.

Dad's eyes brightened as if there was a good ending to this story. "Those funds will go to *Bud* for *his* university degree. After all, *he* will be the *'breadwinner'* when he marries and has a family, so he *needs* to have a career," Dad said, slapping his hand on his knee with conviction. *What about me? Aren't I important too? My grades are way better than Bud's. This just isn't fair! I worked so much harder than him. I deserve to get a degree just as much as he does. As a girl, don't I count? Bud gets the funds just because he is a boy!*

As if Dad had read my mind, he shook his head from side to side and mumbled quietly as if he was embarrassed, "We only have enough funds for *one* of you." That was the end of the discussion.

I know, now, in 2025 that this was a classic example of chauvinism, pure and simple, even though the word *'chauvinism'* was not a term generally used in 1956. But this was the 1950s and the way it was done, and girls were expected to accept it without question. Unfortunately, it still happens in some families. Daughters simply get the short end of the stick and are overlooked in favour of sons. It wasn't fair then and it isn't fair now!

I paid the price for that decision to take a one-year-program rather than a degree. Decades later, in the 1970s, I became the *breadwinner* of my family when the boys' father left us.

Long after I had retired from teaching, I met my brother Bud while at my sister Sharon's in Edmonton. We were chatting about our childhood adventures as kids. Bud became quiet suddenly, and set his coffee cup down. "I am very proud of you, you know, with all you've accomplished in your career." I nodded and smiled. "You know, I never wanted to go to university, Gail." I was startled at this revelation! "I wasn't ready to go," Bud said, reaching over and patting my hand. "I went because Dad wanted me to go. It was his dream, not mine." Surprised at this admission, I had no words to respond. "You had the brains and gumption; the education money should have gone to *you*."

Blinking away tears, I squeezed my brother's wrinkled hand. I suddenly felt at peace, as if a band-aid of love had been gently laid over an old childhood wound. Bud died two years later.

Starting My Teaching Career

My heart pounded with excitement as I walked to Bowden Elementary School on that first day of my teaching career: Tuesday, September 4, 1956. There was a hint of frost in the air, and the golden leaves of the poplars stuck to the soles of my shoes. As I stood at my classroom door and waited for the bell to ring, I heard the children outside. Their boisterous, high-pitched voices called out to one another as they laughed and skipped, full of energy. My stomach tightened with anticipation, then shifted to fear, stress, and uncertainty. *Will I like the kids? Will they like me? Will I know what to do? Will I be successful? Should I have become a nurse like my mother wanted for me?* I checked my watch at 8:55 and ran my sweaty hands down the front of my new green dress, my crinoline crinkled like cellophane chocolate bar wrappers and billowed like a balloon over my spanking-new black pumps. I had discarded my white summer sandals, as was dictated by the fashion industry of the day: *No white after Au-*

gust. I straightened my shoulders and sucked in a deep breath in an attempt to settle my jitters. *"I can do this,"* I said to myself. The bell clanged and a flurry of children charged down the hall, chattering and giggling, with smiles plastered on their polished faces and the scent of soap and new clothes hanging in the air. They bustled past me, pushing and shoving in their rush to find just the right desk. Closing the classroom door, I walked to the front of the room. Feigning confidence, I began: "I'm Miss Pye and I am your Grade Two teacher this year." Within a month, I knew I'd chosen the right profession.

Teaching for DND: Saying Goodbye to Canada

The poster stared at me on that fall of 1958: *Department of National Defence* (DND), *Teachers required for the Armed Service in Europe ... Apply ....* So I applied—and was accepted! I packed my trunk, ready to teach in Soest, Germany the following July, 1959; I was just twenty years old.

I visited Mom and Dad to say my good byes in Whitecourt, Alberta. It was an oil boom town, three-hours-drive north of Edmonton. Happy to see me, Dad was still tall dark and handsome at 51. "Wow you're going to Germany, imagine that! I'm so proud of you." He waved his arms excitedly. "Look at all I own, Gail," he said excitedly pointing to the garage and restaurant. "Just hired a new mechanic," he said confidently, giving off an air of importance that he was the owner and the master of the place. "We're going to make a fortune in this town; it's booming with new oil discoveries every week. And speaking of that, there is someone I want you to meet while you are here; he's from Germany, and he's working in the oil-patch. He wants to tell you all about his homeland." Sounds great, I said. "And wait until you see our bungalow; it's fantastic and I plan to purchase two more as an investment," he bragged proudly. He took out a note-pad from his shirt pocket and scribbled directions. "Your mom's waiting for you."

"Come in, come in," Mom called out when I tapped on the door. I stepped into an unfinished floor of rough plywood; in a corner, Mom's coveted three-piece dining set and chesterfield suite were crammed on top of each other. When I went to the bathroom, there was no hook-up for the taps. "You'll have to wash-up in the kitchen sink," Mom called out. This was certainly not the picture *Dad* painted! It was such a come-down from our two-story five-bedroom home in Penhold. "I want to talk, Gail," Mom said anxiously, her cheeks sallow, her eyes dull and listless; she'd suddenly grown old in one year!

My stomach tensed at her unusual request. She'd never discussed anything with me, ever. Her way of communicating was to yell, belittle or criticize. Yet, today, she was behaving as if I was an old friend, a confidante. It was entirely new and made me uneasy, on guard; I braced myself for what I was to hear, what she was up to.

"I'm so worried," Mom stated. "I'm going on fifty and look at what I've got—a partially finished house, a yard full of weeds, and on top of it all, I have to work in the restaurant to make ends meet. My life is a disaster." She went on to describe how Dad wasn't good with money, and purchased equipment he couldn't afford. Without taking a breath, her complaints rolled out of her with the speed of an avalanche—an avalanche of misery. "He makes all the decisions; he never listens to me. Men *always* make the decisions as if it's their right. It's just the way it is, the way it's always been—like it's been forever." She slammed her mug onto the table with a clunk, coffee splashing over the side.

Shocked, I was overcome at hearing this. This was *Dad* she was talking about, my wonderful father who was *perfection* in my eyes. But her words struck a chord of truth, and I recalled the education fund that Bud got, and the male graduates in the teaching profession who got jobs as Principals right off the bat while we women were relegated to classroom jobs at far reduced salaries. Mom paused, a ripple crossing her forehead, her eyes locked on mine with a long and searching look. "Marry a teacher, Gail; a teacher with a secure career. A teacher would be a *very* good bet."

Ernst My German Friend

Ernst, the man from Germany who Dad had wanted me to meet, took me on a picnic on the McLeod River just outside of Whitecourt. Decades later, I wrote a short story about the event. I entered it into the Norfolk County Short Story contest in 2021 and won! I called the story, "The Summer I Was Nineteen"—I was actually 20 at the time, but my writing coach felt it would have more impact if I were 19. She called it 'creative licence.'

~~~

"The Summer I Was Nineteen"

"It seems just yesterday that you were riding your pony on the farm," Dad shakes his head from side to side, pulling me to him in a squeeze. "My little prairie girl's going to Europe."

Dad draws a cigarette from the package he always keeps in his shirt pocket and lights up. "We miss you now that you live five hours away in Red Deer. I'm glad you came up to see your mom and me before you go." He folds my arm in his and twines his fingers into mine. "Let's go have a coffee." Dad tells me all about their move and how well the gas station and coffee shop are doing. "We get piles of business from the oil and gas workers," he tells me excitedly. "Now, what about you?"

"I've never been outside of Alberta, and here I am going to Germany, but because of the war, I have no idea what to expect. "I'm so excited, Dad."

Dad inhales his cigarette and blows a blue mist of smoke. "There's a man from Germany I want you to meet. He works in the oil patch just west of town. I have to tell you that Ernst is different from the other oil patch rig-monkeys," he says. "He comes into the coffee shop regularly, and I've gotten to know him really well." He takes another drag on his cigarette. "He's an intellectual, reads in his spare time, a bit of a misfit compared to the other guys." Dad takes a sip of his black coffee. "I told him that you were going to Germany to teach the kids of the armed services. He's anxious to meet you."

I meet Ernst on a sunny day in July of 1958. We sit on a red plaid car blanket on the rocky shoreline of the McLeod River just west of Whitecourt. The sky is forget-me-not blue, and the roar of rushing, swirling, water tumbling and crashing is all we hear except for the occasional fish jumping and slapping the surface. The river is like a glass of sparkling water; we can see right to the bottom, to the grey-blue boulders and rocks on the riverbed. Beyond the river, the forest is a thick wall of green-black, the trees crowded so tightly that not a shard of sunlight peeks through.

Ernst brushes an unruly strand of hair off his forehead. His thick, ink-black hair, neatly trimmed around his ears, frames his pale, thin face. His eyes are dark and striking. He has a slim build—a bit taller than me—and wears casual tan slacks and a white shirt open at the collar. *Clean cut, not handsome, but nice looking. He's older than me, in his early or mid-thirties but has such a youthful demeanor.*

Sitting with his feet outstretched on the blanket, Ernst kicks off his sandals and smiles. "Tell me about yourself," he says. "What do you like about teaching? What are your interests? What do you enjoy doing in your spare time?" I am taken by surprise at his comment. I expected to learn more about Germany: sights to see, cities to visit, and festivals not to miss. I want to know more about Germany, and he's asking me to talk about *myself*? This is not at all what I expected. Nevertheless, I am pleased. None of the men (boys, really) that I'd known had ever asked me about *my* interests. They always want to talk about themselves or sports, or cars, or how much money they make. Ernst leans forward, placing his elbows on his knees, his fist under his chin listening intently to every sentence, every word I share about my students, and my upcoming teachings at the Canadian base in Germany. He makes me feel comfortable and relaxed. He points his fancy camera in my direction. I finger-comb my shoulder-length chestnut hair away from my face, smooth the wrinkles on my new white slacks, and smile. I hear a 'snap,' and then another. *This is beginning to feel like a date. But he's far too old for me.*

"What is Germany *like*?" I ask him, anxious to get a sense of what to expect when I get there. The images I have of the country are only what I've garnered from old newsreels and war movies, with scenes of streets in rubble, the aftermath of the bombings.

Ernst's voice becomes soft, low, and sentimental as he tells me about growing up in Hamburg. A wistful look comes into his eyes, a kind of longing as he talks about his close friends still there. "We love talking politics, philosophy, going to the theatre, the opera, museums, and reading, we all *love* reading. I also dabble in a bit of writing," he adds, self-consciously.

I'm intrigued. *Theatre, opera, museums, talking philosophy? This is pretty exotic. Never been to an opera or a museum, and the only theatre I've been to is the movie house in Red Deer to watch American motion pictures.* All the knowledge I have of German people comes from war footage in the '40s, like the news we were fed of spit-and-polish Nazi officers yelling, "Heil Hitler!"

When is he going to get around to telling me about the sights?

"What do you like reading?" Ernst asks me. "Who are your favourite authors?"

I don't know what to say. I'd only read novels assigned in high school like *Great Expectations* and Austen's *Pride and Prejudice*, written by British authors whose characters didn't resonate in my teenage mind.

And of course, we had to read *Two Solitudes* by Bruce Hutchison, or had it been Hugh MacLennan? At least that was written by a Canadian.

"I don't do a lot of reading," I say, embarrassed, and shift the conversation. "What made you come to Canada?"

Ernst's eyes darken, a frown creases his forehead, and his voice takes on a different tone, dark, veiled, and somber. He pauses for a moment, contemplating either how much he should tell me or what he imagines a teenager might be interested in hearing. He sweeps his tongue across his top lip, "I came here to get out of Germany, to take time to rethink my life and what my country had become during the war."

Rethink his life? The men I've met think their lives are just fine as they are.

Ernst's voice rises, "I hated Hitler, everything he stood for and what he was doing to the Jews and how he was destroying Europe."

I, too, had been horrified with Hitler's abuses and what he did to the Jews. I watched every movie I could about it. I bob my chin to encourage him to go on. *Finally, he's going to tell me something I can relate to.*

"I was forced to enlist in the German army right out of high school," he says, "like all my friends." His eyes grow wide. His voice fills with emotion. "All men had to, even young boys, at the end."

"I've always wondered whether that was true."

"Oh yes, it's true all right," Ernst replies, taking a deep breath before continuing. "I was so appalled at the gruesome things I was expected to do that I decided to desert."

Oh, my word!

"I fled from an army convoy as soon as I could, jumping off a truck at a railyard," he says. "I hid in an abandoned railcar to escape." His hands are trembling. My heart pounds like a hammer, and my body fills with anxiety, wondering what in the world he did to survive.

Ernst casts his gaze across the river. "I was scared out of my wits, terrified I would be shot." He swallows hard. His breath stutters, in short, fast spurts. "It... was... the... most... horrible... most... awful... experience...of... my... life." The snip snap of his words punctuates the air.

I grapple for words and find none that can adequately express what I feel. I reach out to place my hand alongside Ernst's. His shoulders lower as if releasing years of tension, "I made it … and I have no idea how."

He looks into my eyes then searchingly, filled with feeling, "You are the first person I have told this to." His voice is gravelly. "Thank you for listening."

I feel the heat rise in my face as a wave of emotion washes over me. I'm honoured that I'm the first person he's told his story to, and I also feel empathy, respect, admiration, understanding, and awe at his courage.

A glimmer of a smile crosses his face, "To answer your question as to why I came to Canada—I wanted to come to a peaceful country, where I could reflect on my future." He sips coffee from the thermos Mom sent with us. "And now I meet *you*." Ernst's voice turns serious all of a sudden. "When you get to Germany, I want you to go to Hamburg to see my friends," he says, smiling broadly. "I really want them to meet you."

"Wonderful," I reply.

The next day, Ernst meets me at the coffee shop before I leave Mom and Dad. "I have a book for you," he says and hands me a copy of *The Cremation of Sam McGee* by Robert Service. "It's the first book I purchased when I came here, the only Canadian book I could find," he says smiling shyly, "something for you to read on your trip." On the inside cover is a black and white photograph of Ernst in profile, leaning over his typewriter, hands on the keys, that stray strand of black hair falling over his forehead. Taking my hand in his, ever so gently, he says softly, "Auf Wiedersehen."

Looking back now, I replay those hours over and over like an old scratched vinyl record. What did that afternoon mean to Ernst? What did it mean to me? I sift through what was said, reform the thoughts that went through my still-teenage mind at the time, and revisit the feelings that were developing that afternoon.

I recall how he looked at me, how gently he spoke, the intensity of his feelings, and his reluctance to say goodbye. Why was he so intent on my meeting his friends in Hamburg? And why did Jurgen, Ursula, Rolf, and Gigi treat me so kindly when I stayed with them for an entire week, taking me to all of Ernst's favourite places, the opera, museums, concerts, and the boat ride on the Outer Alster, if they hadn't thought I had some place in Ernst's heart?

Had he fallen in love with me? I'll never know.

And what about me? Did I feel something more than compassion, empathy, and awe? I am left wondering. Perhaps it might have been different had I known him for a more extended period. Maybe if I'd met him in later years when I was more mature and ready for a thoughtful, learned, sensitive man …

Who knows what might have been? At *that* time, my mind was filled with sailing away from Canada to an adventure on another continent, and I'll simply never know.

After much contemplation, I understand now that we were oceans apart as far as our emotional depth was concerned. Ernst was mature, in his thirties, re-examining his life, searching for meaning, while I was a sprite of nineteen whose idea of the future was planning for the next week, packing my trunks and boarding the ship bound for Europe.

Although, even after sixty-three years, I still fondly remember that sunny July day in 1958, when I was nineteen; it was my last summer as a teenager.

****

Recollecting that visit to Whitecourt in July of 1958, over sixty years ago, I realize how much had changed for me. For the first time in my life, Mom and Dad treated me as a grown up. Dad saw me as an equal, an adult, no longer a teenager. And for Mom, I had become more a confidante and friend than her teenage daughter. Most of all, I discovered that I had begun to unravel the ties that bound me to Mom's perception of who I was: that there was something wrong with me–some flaw in my character that needed to be fixed in order for her acceptance. Perhaps, one day, I would crack the chain that bound me to *her* perception of me, freeing me to be independent of *her* and become the person *I* wanted to be. On that visit, I knew, absolutely, that it was possible. I had changed as a person too–I had an education, a job, and a growing career; I could manage money, arrange my own living accommodation and make decisions for my future. On that July day in 1959, I could not know the extent that that visit with my parents would impact my life.

Sailing Away

In my memory, I am standing at the railing of the *The Empress of England*, which is docked at Montreal and ready to sail. The air is filled with noise–stevedores yelling, chains rattling, luggage crashing, and water slapping at the side of the ship. With a clank, the gangplank is locked up, and the ship slips into the water, mute as a whisper; the silence broken only by tearful good byes of passengers on deck. The lady beside me holds a bouquet in one hand and, with the other, waves to a handsome man far below who puts his hands to his lips then extends his hand toward her, blowing kisses. The sweet perfume of her bouquet helps camouflage the acrid smell of fuel and stench of decomposing fish that linger in the dark murky waters of the harbour. The milk-white gulls swoop and glide, squawking and scrabbling over leftover harbour-scraps. They remind me of the gulls that afternoon with Ernst, and I'm filled with anticipation of meeting his friends in Hamburg after I get settled in barracks and prepare my classroom to start school. I smile suddenly, remembering that first day of my teaching career back in Bowden, Alberta. Minute-by-sluggish-minute the ship glides out into the St. Lawrence. It passes homes and their colourful gardens, and I picture our home in Penhold– its yard full of flowers of every hue. I hear Merla's laughter while home on leave as she tells stories of life in the Air Force. Little Sharon is patting the snout of her horse, 'Sparky.' I'm in the picture, too, at the town hall dancing with Bud, and jiving up a storm. A sudden sadness comes over me as I realize that our Penhold home was the last in which our family lived all together. Mom comes into my mind, as I imagine a more hopeful relationship between us, in the future. My nose twitches as I remember the aroma of Dad's tobacco when he wrapped his warm, loving arms around me. The ship rolls from the St Lawrence into the Atlantic, and the Montreal skyline becomes a mystical miniature model–as if constructed by Lego. The wind kicks up whipping my long-chestnut-brown-hair across my face like the flapping laundry on the clothesline, six-years-ago in Penhold, Alberta, four provinces away. The ship is in full throttle, cold wind surges, and I wrap my arms around my body for warmth. Swiftly, the Montreal skyline sinks below the horizon and disappears entirely from view. Releasing my hands from the wet metal railing, I wave my arms wildly in the air like that wet-winged-butterfly of my fifth-stage-metamorphosis and I say goodbye to Canada and open my symbolic wings to embrace the future with hope and new possibility.

Trip to the Army Base

The Empress of England Ocean Liner was luxurious beyond belief. It was 774 feet, and more than twice the length of an NFL football field. It was palatial and majestic; it was pure fantasy for a prairie girl of twenty. We sauntered on deep piled, royal blue carpet, through gilt-panelled hallways, into the music room, or the smoking lounge, or the reading library with books neatly sorted, organized on mahogany bookshelves from floor to ceiling. Peeking into the dining room, I was struck with the size–it was five times as large as our curling rink in Penhold and twice the size of the hockey arena in Red Deer it could seat over five hundred passengers. The moment we sat down to dinner, the wine steward came and offered many kinds of wine—white, red, rose, with a crisp white towel over his arm. "No, no," I exclaimed, shaking my head, "I don't drink wine; could you bring me a glass of milk instead?" The waiter's eyebrows lifted, as if puzzled by such a request; Everyone at the table snickered. A few minutes later, the wine steward came back with a cup and saucer, puffs of steam rising from the surface of the milk. I was bewildered. "The waiter thinks you're sick," a tablemate informed me. I felt a bit like the proverbial wide-eyed country bumpkin. My Alberta-farm-girl-roots dogged me throughout that year in Europe.

As I barrelled across France toward the army

base that summer of 1959, I expected to see bombed buildings in evidence. World War II had ended just fourteen years earlier. Instead, there was no evidence of the war at all. Buildings were pristine, and they were far more modern than the buildings at home.

Soest Army Base: First Trips

At the Soest Army Base, we were assigned the rank of Officer, provided Officer's quarters and privileges, and all living expenses were paid by the Armed Forces. This meant that our teaching salaries, paid by the school boards back home, were ours to spend as we pleased.

Visiting the German elementary school we'd be teaching in, I had imagined they would have been constructed from semi-bombed-out craters hastily built with scraps of lumber found in the rubble. I certainly didn't expect to find a two-story building with large windows and an inviting rotunda and flooring made of crushed-inlaid-stone, instead of the wood or vinyl tiles as was common in schools back home in Canada. A curved cement stairway led to my classroom; it was, by far, more spacious than my classroom in Red Deer; it had floor-to-ceiling-windows that overlooked landscaped soccer pitch. Schools at home were lucky if they had a jungle-gym in their playgrounds. The gymnasium, too, was state-of-the-art, equipped with every piece of equipment imaginable for use by our students. I'd never expected a school of *this* magnitude! Looking back now, I have come to realize that Germans valued education, believing their children deserved the best of facilities and equipment in order to develop capable successful citizens. A lesson to heed in Canada today.

The first trip I took was to Belgium; I carpooled with a teacher friend, and we stopped at various Canadian war memorials from the First World War (1914-1918). The monument at Ypres was particularly impressive, its marble columns stretched two to three stories above us, with row upon row of names of men, from all parts of Canada, who had either been wounded or killed mainly from poison gas used by the Germans, during WWI. 6500 names, etched in marble for posterity. Despite the enormous loss of lives, the Canadians won the battle (1917) and freed Ypres from the Germans . It was a humbling to witness the memorial; it represents such a magnitude of loss and sacrifice. It filled me with pride.

The Breendonk Concentration Camp of World War II was also humbling, but for a different reason. It was an interrogation centre run by the Gestapo. Meat hooks hung on the concrete walls where prisoners—women and men—were tortured. Although there were no extermination ovens at the site, it was gruesome to witness, nevertheless.

Oktoberfest on the Rhein, to the beer gardens in Bavaria, was captivating. Lisa and I wound alongside the Rhein; we saw huge cargo barges inching their way down the river, and steep banks cascading with lush vineyards. Castles from ancient times sat majestically along the top of the riverbanks—it was like a scene from a fairy tale. Every evening, spectacular fireworks burst from each castle and lit up the sky with myriad of colours that fell like coloured snowflakes into the Rhein. They were the first fireworks I'd ever seen!

Exploring Soest: Living with a German Family

Anxious to explore Soest, I made the forty-five-minute-walk from the army base. As I walked through the ancient gates of the city, I gawked, wide-eyed.. Street, after street, was lined with homes three stories high; there was not a shard of sunlight peeking between each. My shoes clip-clacked down narrow cobblestone streets to the market; it held stands of produce as far as my eyes could see, dealers hawking their wares—everything from vegetables to meat, to baked goods to clothing, to chickens, pigeons, and quail, which were hung by their yellow necks, their scaly legs and claws still attached. The customers, mainly women, bartered, and placed their purchases in straw wicker-baskets that hung from their arms. They jostled me as they moved from stall, to stall. All my senses were ignited—the pungent stink of fish and oily eels competed with the sweet waft of fresh baked pastries and the aroma of newly cut flowers. I'd never experienced anything like it.

I thought that living with a German family would be an opportunity to learn to speak German. Fortunately, the Army paid expenses. I met the Wolf family (pronounced Vulf) and their daughter Margaret, a woman in her late twenties. My room, which was up three flights of stairs, was barely large enough for a single bed, table, chair and dresser.

Bathing was an adventure. I was allowed a shower only once a week, and I had to put money into a slot an hour in advance in order to heat the water that was stored in a copper tank above the tub. Sitting with my knees scrunched to my chest in the miniscule tub, I pulled the spigot down. As the water flowed over me, my hands flew over my body with lightning speed; I splashed water on my back and front as quickly as I could, before the hot water ran out!

Learning to speak German was futile, since Margaret was anxious to practice her English. The few words I *did* learn were, "Gutten Tag," (good day), "Sehr gut," (very good), Entschuldigen Sie bitte, (excuse me, please) and "Danke schon" (thank you). Other than those phrases I was pretty hopeless. However, I did get a kick out of Margaret's father's grasp of English–the words that he'd learned in a First World War (1919) prisoner of war camp. He showed off his English skills in broken English that was liberally sprinkled with "Fucking" this, and "Fucking" that. His pronunciation of the "F" word was pronounced flawlessly, as if he were a true Brit! My experiment with living with the Wolfs made me appreciate being Canadian.

My First Date in Germany

I met Otis on a pub crawl with a group of teacher friends from the base. One bar had a particularly good boot-stomping band, and we stayed for a meal and danced to the lively om-pa-pa-music. As I sat down to catch my breath, a young German man asked me to dance. He had a friendly look—with rosy cheeks, a shy smile, short, neatly-trimmed blonde hair, and China-blue eyes that sparkled. He was cute. We danced several sets. In halting English, he told me his name was Otis, and asked me out on a date. Otis seemed respectful and pleasant so I accepted. *It would be an interesting way to learn more of the German language!*

Planning for the date, I tucked my tiny pocket-sized-English-to-German-dictionary into my purse. Otis bowed when he came to the door at number 10 Kessel Strasse; he shook my hand like a perfect gentleman. He took my arm as we walked down the cobble stone street; our feet clapped a staccato echo at every step. "Ich mag dich," he said. I nodded and stopped at a lamp post while I sifted through the tiny pages of the German-English dictionary to discover what he'd said ("I like you."). I smiled and we continued walking down the street. "Du bist schon," he said and we rushed to the next lamp post so that I could look up what he'd said, turning pages for one word at a time to decipher that he had told me, ("You are very beautiful.") My cheeks warmed into a blush; he folded my hand in his and smiled. We carried on down one cobble stoned street stopping at one after another lamppost, looking up words and phrases so I could understand him. It was a long and tedious process. Finally, we came to the main plaza, near where the market was held, several blocks from my room on Kessel Strasse. As we sat down on a bench under the bright lights of the plaza, we conversed some more. "du bist schon," he said again, squeezing my hand tightly and draping his right arm about my shoulders. He leaned over and kissed my cheek and murmured something into my ear. "komm mit mir ins bett, bitte?" I frantically shifted pages, from one page to the other, in a frenzy to find the exact translation of each word. Finally understanding, I yanked my head up angrily, swatted his hand off my shoulder and stood bolt upright. I glared at him. "You want to go to bed with me?"

"No darned way!" Snapping my English-German dictionary shut, I took off from the plaza, my shoes clip-clopping hard against the cobblestones, a fury of indignation ringing in my ears. I tore down the streets and retraced my steps back to 10 Kessel Strasse, and home. That ended my date with a German man.

Meeting My Future Husband

There was a tap-tap at my classroom door. I cocked my head, listening. Hearing nothing more, I finished reading the story to my grade two children. "Tap-tap." There was the sound again. I sent the children to their desks with worksheets and headed toward the door. Through the window insert, I saw a man in gym clothes, a black cotton jacket with a stripe down the sleeve, and matching sweatpants.

"Can I help you?" I asked, opening the door and wondering who he was and what he was doing at my classroom door.

"Help me? Well, yes," he said, smiling shyly. He had a square-rosy-cheeked face. He ran his fingers through his straw-coloured-blond-hair, as if trying to smooth it. "I am Wes Heald; I teach Phys-Ed at the high school for DND, just like you," he said. "I saw you in the Officer's mess the first month you were here, and then you disappeared."

"I'm living in Soest now with a German family."

"I was just wondering," Wes said, rocking from one foot to the other, "if you would go out for coffee with me after school?" He bit his lip, as if worried I'd refuse.

"Okay," I said. He looked so bashful, I thought he might cry if I said no.

A grin spread across his entire face and his blue eyes sparkled, "I'll pick you up after school," his voice sounding self-assured, his confidence now restored. Walking away he had a bounce to his step, and I believe I heard him whistle.

Wes waved to me from the school entrance as he stood beside a squatty, ruby-red, convertible. He wore dark slacks and a blue t-shirt, his blond hair slicked back neatly as if he'd just showered. He was a bit taller than me; he looked to be in his late twenties. He put his hand under my elbow and led me to the passenger side of the car. The door stood open, and he helped me in. *Such a gentleman!* "My car is a Porsche," he stated, enunciating the name, clearly puffing his chest out just a bit. "Got it brand new in Stuttgart at their factory in southern Germany, just a few months ago." He tapped the leather-covered steering wheel. "Always wanted to have one of these babies." He yanked the charcoal seatbelt across his shoulder and clinked it into place. "Got to choose the colour, too, and the upholstery as well, top of the line." He put the key into the ignition, the motor revved up and we roared down the street. As we sped toward Soest, I grabbed at my hair to try to hold it in place so my chignon wouldn't unravel in the wind.

Over coffee, Wes told me about teaching Phys-Ed at the high school, the various sports he taught, the teams he organized, the championships won with other DND schools. "Been doing it for four years—

two years in an air base in the south at Zwi Brucken, and now, two years here in Soest."

"So that's why you are in such good shape," I remarked. "Do you travel beyond Germany with your teams?"

"Oh no, I travel on weekends and holidays; been to most countries in Europe—Denmark, Holland, Belgium, France, Switzerland, and all over Germany, of course." He paused and took a sip of his coffee. "Can't go to East Germany, Poland or Russia; they are out of bounds for anyone associated with the armed services, like us."

I told him about growing up on the farm in Alberta and the places I'd taught.

He smiled politely. "A young farm girl, eh?"

"I'm not so young; I just turned twenty-one!"

When Wes drove me home, he parked the car, climbed out, walked around to my side and opened the door. He took my hand in his and gently pulled me up out of the car to a standing position. Putting my hands between his, he looked into my eyes. "Would you like to go out to dinner on Saturday?" I nodded, yes. He beamed! On my way up to my room, I thought about Wes. He seemed so nice; he was polite, shy really, yet sophisticated, worldly, well travelled, and so knowledgeable. I was impressed.

I was excited to go out to dinner with Wes and I wanted to look especially nice. I bathed in that tiny tub and washed my hair, allowing the chestnut strands to spread and flow across my shoulders and down my back. At six o'clock on the dot, the Porsche came thundering down the cobblestone street, gears grinding as it came to a stop at number 10, Kessel Strasse. I was waiting at the door. Wearing a dark suit, crisp white shirt and striped red and black tie, his black shoes gleamed as if they'd just been polished. *Pretty spiffy for our first date.* He looked sharp, and was handsome in a wholesome kind of way. We drove to the Wildschwein, *(Wild Boar)* the fanciest restaurant in Soest. The table shone of dark ancient wood; the walls and ceiling exposed half timbers. I was filled with awe by the old world charm of the place. The waiter, dressed in a tuxedo, bowed and asked us what we'd like to drink. "Heineken, bitte,' Wes ordered.

"Ginger ale, bitte," I said, one of the few German words I knew.

Over drinks Wes told me that he'd grown up in Ontario, in Fort William: "Situated right on Lake Superior, the largest lake in Canada; it's the largest body of fresh water in the world," he boasted proudly as if it was *his* lake. He told me of his family–two brothers, Lance and Hank and sister, Shirley. "Shirley has MS and it will be good to see her when I get home." I had no idea what MS was. "They are all married with kids of their own." A wistful look suddenly came across his eyes. "I'm the only one that's not married," he said. He gave my hand a light pat.

Wes scooped up the menu, running his fingers down the length of the page reading every item in German. *Wow, he speaks fluid German!* "Are you game for an adventure?," he asked me. I nodded. We had oxtail soup and escargot (snails) as appetizers, "For your main course consider steak, fresh trout, beef bourguignon or hasenpfeffer?" I raised my eyebrow. "Hasenpfeffer is rabbit, and they say it tastes a lot like chicken."

"I'll have that," I said smiling.

Wes finished a bite of steak and put his steak knife down. "Have you been to France yet?" he asked—his eyes questioning.

"Only on the train from Calais to Soest; all I saw was the French countryside."

"I'm going to the Chateaux on the Loire, in the south of France, on the Thanksgiving weekend." He smiled coyly. "Would you like to go with me?"

Startled at his suggestion, I hesitated. *Go away with him on a weekend? What is he thinking, that I'd stay over with him? I hardly know him.* "No, I don't think so," I responded as I took a bite of the hasenpfeffer... *The Chateaux on the Loire ... I'd heard so much about them ...* I swallowed a mouthful of rice. *What if I insisted on paying for my own room?* I took my last bite of hasenpfef-

I was excited to go out to dinner with Wes and I wanted to look especially nice. I bathed in that tiny tub and washed my hair, allowing the chestnut strands to spread and flow across my shoulders and down my back. At six o'clock on the dot, the Porsche came thundering down the cobblestone street, gears grinding as it came to a stop at number 10, Kessel Strasse. I was waiting at the door. Wearing a dark suit, crisp white shirt and striped red and black tie, his black shoes gleamed as if they'd just been polished. *Pretty spiffy for our first date.* He looked sharp, and was handsome in a wholesome kind of way. We drove to the Wildschwein, *(Wild Boar)* the fanciest restaurant in Soest. The table shone of dark ancient wood; the walls and ceiling exposed half timbers. I was filled with awe by the old world charm of the place. The waiter, dressed in a tuxedo, bowed and asked us what we'd like to drink. "Heineken, bitte,' Wes ordered.

"Ginger ale, bitte," I said, one of the few German words I knew.

Over drinks Wes told me that he'd grown up in Ontario, in Fort William: "Situated right on Lake Superior, the largest lake in Canada; it's the largest body of fresh water in the world," he boasted proudly as if it was *his* lake. He told me of his family–two brothers, Lance and Hank and sister, Shirley. "Shirley has MS and it will be good to see her when I get home." I had no idea what MS was. "They are all married with kids of their own." A wistful look suddenly came across his eyes. "I'm the only one that's not married," he said. He gave my hand a light pat.

Wes scooped up the menu, running his fingers down the length of the page reading every item in German. *Wow, he speaks fluid German!* "Are you game for an adventure?," he asked me. I nodded. We had oxtail soup and escargot (snails) as appetizers, "For your main course consider steak, fresh trout, beef bourguignon or hasenpfeffer?" I raised my eyebrow. "Hasenpfeffer is rabbit, and they say it tastes a lot like chicken."

"I'll have that," I said smiling.

Wes finished a bite of steak and put his steak knife down. "Have you been to France yet?" he asked—his eyes questioning.

"Only on the train from Calais to Soest; all I saw was the French countryside."

"I'm going to the Chateaux on the Loire, in the south of France, on the Thanksgiving weekend." He smiled coyly. "Would you like to go with me?"

Startled at his suggestion, I hesitated. *Go away with him on a weekend? What is he thinking, that I'd stay over with him? I hardly know him.* "No, I don't think so," I responded as I took a bite of the hasenpfeffer... *The Chateaux on the Loire ... I'd heard so much about them ...* I swallowed a mouthful of rice. *What if I insisted on paying for my own room?* I took my last bite of hasenpfeffer. It really *did* taste like chicken! I looked up at Wes. "About the Chateaux on the Loire, I will go with you on one condition, that I pay for my own room."

"Fantastic! But I will pay for everything else."

For dessert we had fruit compote laced with kirsch, which was a lovely end to an exquisite meal. I'd never tasted such exotic food before. It must have cost a fortune! *What a generous man Wes was!*

At my door, Wes smiled. "I'm so looking forward to Thanksgiving; I can hardly wait."

Wes was interesting, smart, worldly, and sure of himself. I was struck by his gusto and enthusiasm for life. He was fun to be with. He was sort of cute, reminding me of a cuddly Teddy bear. I felt comfortable with him and he was so generous. I liked him; I liked him a lot. He was taking me to see the Chateaux on the Loire!

The Chateaux on the Loire: Wes' Magnanimous Gift

My hair flapped in the wind, and I felt like Grace Kelly as we flew through the French countryside in the red Porsche, to the Chateaux on the Loire. They were holiday establishments for French noblemen and families, until the people of France revolted in the French Revolution (1789 to 1799) and noblemen and their families were slaughtered. However, the chateaux were saved and kept in pristine condition, as a reminder of times past. Some were enormous–like Chateau de Chambord with over 400 rooms! Others were petite in comparison. The interiors were restored, complete with furniture and paintings of the period. The gardens were elaborately designed in the Baroque style of the 1700s. Many had moats around them, with drawbridges for security. The chateaux remind me of castles in fairy tales that I read to the boys when they were little. I saw the chateaux again, in 1997, when I presented at an education conference in Bordeaux. I brought pictures home of the two largest chateaux and hung them in our bedroom at the Lodge.

What struck me most was the age of the ancient chateaux compared to the Alberta grain elevators only a hundred years old, built at the turn of the twentieth century!

Wes was gallant, a total gentleman. One evening after dinner he walked me to my room, leaned over, and gave me a peck on the cheek. It was sweet. It warmed my heart. True to his word, Wes paid for everything ... except for my room. His generosity was overwhelming.

Soon after that trip, Wes made a most unusual and magnanimous proposal. As we sat outside my favourite baguettery in Soest, and I ate my special raspberry croissant, Wes lit up a cigarette. "That trip to France was fun," he said.

"I loved it," I replied, and took another bite of my croissant.

Wes leaned over, took my hand, and looked deep into my eyes. What he said next was a complete surprise. "I want you to know that I will take you to any country in Europe, on any weekend or holiday."

Stunned, my eyes grew wide. I gasped in astonishment, thoughts churning in my mind. *He'll take me to any place in Europe? On any weekend or holiday?* What is he suggesting? *This is crazy! I can't do this. I won't be beholden to anyone. No way!* Finally, words came to me. "That's so kind and generous of you, Wes," I said nodding my head back and forth, "But I can't accept your offer."

Wes stubbed his cigarette into the ashtray. "But I will pay for *everything*," he said, sounding exasperated.

"No," I said. "I pay my own way."

His brow wrinkled and his eyes had a pleading look. "As a secondary teacher with a degree I make four times your elementary salary, so I can afford this, okay? And besides, I want to see these countries too, if even for a second time."

I was bowled over by his generosity, but I had to at *least* pay for my room. "No," I said, "That won't work."

As if reading my mind, Wes interjected. "I want you to know that I will pay for separate rooms if that's what you're worried about," he offered persuasively.

I bit my lip. "I don't know," I said hesitantly. Wes looked at me with pleading eyes. "That's very generous of you but if I accept, I absolutely *insist* on paying for my room."

Sounding relieved, Wes added, "But I will pay for everything else."

"Well okay," I said, "But it feels as if I'm taking advantage of you."

"No way, I'll enjoy doing it!"

"Okay," I said. "And thank you for your kindness."

Wes smiled and his eyes twinkled.

As my mind flashes back to that day sixty-six-years ago, I realize how extraordinary Wes's offer was. What was his motive, I wonder now? And why did I not question it? At twenty-one, was I simply too naive and inexperienced to do so?

Skiing in Switzerland

"Achtung, Achtung!" (Attention, Attention) screamed a toddler, flying past me down the snow-tipped Alps of Wengen, Switzerland. "Ausweichen!" (Get out of the way!!) Just four months in Europe, and here I was on a skiing vacation during the Christmas break of 1959. I'd never skied before; I'd never been on the top of a mountain peak. Oh, I'd seen the Rockies but I'd looked up at them from the streets of Banff. Being on top of the Alps was a different matter, entirely. Wes bought me a ski outfit and booked skiing lessons on a beginner's slope. "It will be a piece of cake," he assured me. "You'll get the hang of it in no time." He said this, and then sailed past me down the mountain. Gazing down into the valley below, it seemed forever before he reached the bottom. It put me in a full-blown panic mode. Persevering, however, I improved so much that by the end of the week, I'd mastered the beginner slope.

The 'after-ski-party', every afternoon, was fun with gluhwein (hot mulled wine) and fondue (French bread melted in cheese and kirsch). Instead of gluhwein, I washed down the fondue with ginger ale. A great dancer, Wes spun me around the floor all afternoon.

The most vivid memory of that trip was Christmas Eve, when we trudged up the mountain to the tiny church for midnight mass. We were dressed in our ski jackets and sang Christmas carols all the way. Snow fell in giant lacy flakes, gently covering my hair and shoulders, sparkling under the antique street lights as we passed. It was truly a magical, romantic night!

The Proposal

New Years' Eve was a magical night. We met Wes's friends, Gerard and Mary-Lee Kennedy, in Zwi Brucken (Two Bridges), which were the Canadian and American Air Force bases, for a gala evening. I wore a gown of creamy rose tulle lace with wide straps inching off my shoulders. Wes, looked smashing wearing a black tuxedo with a gold cummerbund, surprised to learn that he *owned* it! None of the boys I dated at home ever wore a tuxedo, let alone *owned* one!

The party was held in an enormous airplane hangar about the size of three hockey arenas, back home. Hundreds, maybe thousands, of tables filled the room; they were covered with white linen tablecloths and vases of carnations. Wax candles burned in the centre and created quivering light throughout the hall. Twinkle lights, of various colours, blinked and gave the room a warm and mellow feel. A huge orchestra played soft melodies from the stage at one end. We joined Gerard and Mary-Lee, and the fellows reminisced about old times when Wes taught there two years before. I liked Mary-Lee right off the bat. We compared notes on teaching in Germany. They'd married that summer and were heading back to Canada in August. After a sumptuous meal of prime rib, Mary Lee and I went to the washroom to freshen up. "Gerard sure thinks Wes has hit the jackpot finding you!"

My cheeks warmed. "What do you mean?"

"Well, you are a heck of a lot prettier than that woman he was dating two years ago. Gerard thinks you're stunning!"

For the rest of the evening Wes and I danced to tunes of Glenn Miller and Tommy Dorsey. Light on his feet, Wes could 'jive' almost as well as my brother, Bud.

All of a sudden, the audience broke out shouting, "Tony! Tony!" A tall dark-haired man came out onto the stage. The crowd went wild. It was Tony Bennett. He sauntered up to the microphone. "Tony, Tony," everyone cried, clapping their hands enthusiastically. When the clapping died down, Tony sang all the old songs we loved in that low, easy, mellow way he had. When he started to sing, 'The Way You Look Tonight,' Wes took my hand and led me to the dance floor. He held me close, kissed my neck and whispered into my ear, "You are so beautiful tonight." My body shivered. As we walked back to our table, Mary-Lee and Gerard waved goodbye and promised to meet us the next day. Wes and I continued to dance to all the slow romantic songs. At the stroke of midnight, the orchestra broke into Auld Lang Syne and we sang along, Wes in a deep baritone voice I'd never heard before. He picked up his glass of wine and clinked my wine glass of juice. "Happy New Year, Gail," he said softly. A hush seemed to settle over the room, and the lights went low. Wes took my hand in his, squeezed gently, leaned over and kissed me on the lips, warmly, affectionately. He looked into my eyes. "Will you marry me?" he asked softly, hesitantly, his eyes glistening.

Stunned, I was taken off guard. It was such a surprise. *Get married?* The thought had not occurred to me. *But I like him, he's kind, he's funny, he's a good dancer, he is generous, we have the same profession, he's stable, we get along so well.* These thoughts raced through my mind, in the blink of an eye. The orchestra tuned up for one more dance and Tony Bennett came up to the microphone once again. He leaned into it and crooned, *"Because of you, there's a song in my heart."* Wes lifted my arm. "Let's dance, and you can think about it," he murmured gently, reassuringly.

"Because of you my romance had its start." Wes held me close. I felt so warm, so at peace. I couldn't believe this was happening. *He cares about me ... he*

looks after me ... I'm comfortable with him ... I like being with him ... he respects me. Tony Bennett's voice flowed like velvet, *"Because of you the sun will shine, the moon and stars will say your mine."* Wes sighed. "You make me so happy." He lifted his arm and twirled me around. My heart pounded and warm feelings flowed through me. It was so romantic. I looked up at Wes and smiled. "Yes," I said. "Yes, I'll marry you." Wes fairly skipped to the rest of the song. With his arm around my shoulder, Wes led me gently back to our table. He smiled, reached into his pocket, and brought out a tiny box, covered in royal blue velvet. He raised the lid, lifted out a lovely sparkling blue sapphire ring and slid it gently carefully onto the third finger of my left hand.

The Second-Hand Engagement Ring

I stared at my beautiful engagement ring and twisted it around my finger; the blue sapphire sparkled in the bright winter sunshine. My mind was filled with dreams of the future as we drove back to Soest on that first week of January, 1960. I couldn't wait to write to Mom and Dad, purchase a wedding dress, choose a maid-of-honour, plan the wedding, a honeymoon ....

Wes looked over at me admiring my ring and smiled. "It cost a fortune, you know!"

"I'm not surprised! It's so beautiful. I can't wait to tell Mom and Dad about it."

Wes tapped his fingers lightly on the steering wheel as if thinking of something.

"Oh, I thought I should tell you that it's not new."

My head jerked up, my eyes opening wide in surprise. *What? What was he talking about?*

Wes went on, his voice sounding casual as if he were telling me about a hand-me-down -sweater he once got, or second-hand bicycle. "I gave it to the woman I was engaged to, a couple of years ago."

What! I was stunned, breathless. *A second-hand ring? It was once on the hand of someone else?*

"I was engaged to Bernice, a couple of years ago," he went on. "She was a high school teacher, thirty-five, almost the same age as me."

Speechless, I couldn't believe he was telling me this. *Did she turn him down? Was I second fiddle, the consolation prize? Someone else's crumbs?* I started to twist the ring down my finger, turning and pulling it over the knuckle. *Did he think I was second-best, a discard? Worth a second-hand-ring?* Fuming, I felt like chucking the ring out the window! I fretted and stewed, mulling it over in my mind all the way back to Soest. I didn't know what to think; I didn't know what to do.

Bursting with the news Wes could hardly wait to tell everyone at the base that we were engaged... the romantic night ... pointing out the sapphire ... boasting how expensive it was. With Wes so excited about our engagement, I began to feel guilty wondering if I was putting too much emotional weight on an engagement ring. *Was I being mercenary? Did the ring really mean that much? Didn't the caring count more?* After days of analyzing, I began to wonder if the ring was all that important and continued to wear it.

A resolution to honour our engagement came a few weeks later when a Catholic missionary visited the base. Listening to his work with refugee children, an idea suddenly came into my mind. *We could support a refugee child; it would be a perfect way to honour our engagement!"*

I turned to Wes and told him my idea. He scowled, drew his eyebrows together and rolled up his eyes as if thinking it over. "Yes," he said slowly. "As long as you continue to wear the blue sapphire engagement ring as well."

It was a small concession I thought, if it made Wes happy. While I wore the ring to appease Wes, in my heart, helping a refugee child was how I would always commemorate our engagement from that day forward.

Years later, that sapphire engagement ring became a source of irritation for me. For Wes, it represented great significance in his storytelling—of his romantic proposal with the magnificent sapphire—and of course how expensive it was. But for me, as hard as I tried, I never grew to accept or love that second-hand sapphire engagement ring.

Bull Fighting in Spain and Much More

Two red Porsches, in tandem, racing through Germany, France and into Spain was a sight to see, that spring of 1960. We were travelling to see the bullfights in Spain with Gerard and Mary-Lee Kennedy. We wove in-and-out of secondary highways, two scarlet bombs roaring through the countryside.

Bull fighting was Spain's national sport, and 'a must see,' according to our friends. As we arrived in Barcelona on the day of the bullfight, the city was abuzz with excitement. The energy and enthusiasm reminded me of the Stanley Cup play-offs in Canada. Posters advertising bull fights hung in every restaurant and hotel. The waiter at breakfast noticed I was reading a brochure on bull fighting in halting English commented: "Matadors are revered," he said as he topped up Wes' coffee. "We adore them." It was like how Canadians treated their hockey stars.

Just then Gerard and Mary-Lee joined us and placed their order. Gerard turned to Wes.

"I haven't had a chance to congratulate your engagement, buddy," he remarked, and playfully punched Wes on the arm.

Wes beamed, and his eyes sparkled as he lifted my left hand highlighting the sapphire. "Thank you, Gerard. It was high time I got married. My mother has been pestering me for years to settle down and get married. She'll be thrilled."

My heart lurched and an uneasy feeling swept over me—Why did it feel significant?—I shoved the uneasy feelings aside and focussed instead on reading the bull-fight information.

"Here's something interesting," I said. "It says here that in the grand finale of the bull fight, that a matador, good at his profession, waits for just the right moment with dagger in hand, will leap gracefully in the air above the bull's head and insert the blade into the fatal spot in the bull's neck. When it is done properly, the bull simply slides to the ground in front of the matador's feet ... dead."

We heard the cheering first, as we entered the stadium and squeezed past thousands of people who were screaming and shouting, on our way to our seats. Once settled, we kept our eyes peeled on the enormous grass-filled circle in front of us. We expected to catch a glimpse of the matador, with his fancy cape and colourful clothing, as we'd seen in the brochures. Instead, a giant bull emerged from a gate; the bull was the breadth and height of a pick-up truck. He shook his head, his horns wildly swinging; he pawed at the ground with his hoofs. Two fancy-dressed men (picadors) rushed into the ring; they held poles the length of chair legs that were decorated with coloured dangling ribbons; the poles had sharp blades on the ends. They danced in front of the bull, fluttering the ribbons in his eyes to catch his attention. As the bull charged, the picadors rammed two spears into its haunches. Blood oozed out onto its shoulders and down its legs. "Ole, Ole, Ole," the Spaniards cheered, waving their flags madly. It was incredibly cruel and disgusting to watch. With the bull weakened, two 'toreadors' came out next on horses with quilted covers strapped tightly around their middle in order to protect them from injury, should the bull charge. The toreadors attacked the bull from both sides with long poles the length of hockey sticks. They had razor sharp spears at the end and the toreadors drove them into the shoulders of the bull. The crowd went wild and shouted: "Ole!! Ole!!" I'd never seen anything so brutal in all my life!

The bull, disoriented and bleeding profusely by then, staggered around the bull ring. The crowd roared approval and chanted, "Matador!! Matador!!"

The matador came out, dressed in his slim pants and colourful beaded form-fitting jacket; he wore a large plumed hat and held a dagger in his hand. He waved his red cape to the crowd. The crowd went mad with excitement and anticipation. "Matador! Matador!" they shouted, clapping their hands wildly. In a sweeping motion, the matador waved his red cape in front of the bull, enticing him to charge. The bull confused, bewildered and weakened staggered toward the matador. The matador lunged at the bull thrusting his dagger at the bull's neck. He missed. Nevertheless, the crowd cheered, "Matador! Matador!" The matador bowed to the cheering crowd and waved his red cape in a flourish. "Matador! Matador!", the crowd screamed. The matador doffed his hat and faced the bull once more. He made a series of choreographed moves enticing the bull to attack. The bull lurched forward and the matador leapt at the wobbling bull … He missed again. The crowd yelled and screamed again, "Ole! Ole!" To my disgust, the matador tried a third and fourth time, continually failing to end the bull's suffering. At this point, I felt sorry for the bull, and was disgusted that the matador was simply teasing the tired, weakened, and dazed animal; it had no strength or fight left in him.

In a final thrust, the matador hit the mark. The beast slid to the ground at the matador's feet … a crumpled heap … dead. What happened next was shocking to us, as well as the Spaniards. The matador swung his leg back and, with a swift "Whack!", booted the bull in the head.

Stunned, the crowd went silent.

Over supper we had a good laugh about the matador and how arrogant he was to blame the bull for *his* lack of skill. Shocking!

Later, in my room, I twisted my engagement ring around and around my finger. Wes' earlier comments about his mother niggled at me all night. *My mother has been pestering me for years to get married.... she'll be thrilled.*

It was years later, after our divorce, that I reflected on those comments, made in 1960 on that night in Spain. *Did he marry me to please his mother? Is that why he was so anxious to date me, to take me everywhere, pay for everything, pop the question after knowing me only two months, because his term was up and was obligated to return to Canada that August? Was I the trophy he took home to his mother? Is that why he honed in on a young naïve starry-eyed twenty-year-old prairie girl he could easily impress?* It has been a question I've always wondered about.

The Wedding Dress

A simple, elegant dress was what I wanted; no traditional long gown with a train that would drag along the floor, or fancy veils to cover my face. A good friend, Rhoda, agreed to be my bridesmaid. She was a plucky and vivacious girl from Nova Scotia who I met on the ship coming over. She was my teaching partner in Soest, and we enjoyed doing things together with our classes. She agreed to drive me to The Netherlands (Holland) to shop for a dress.

Fields upon fields of tulips greeted us the moment we entered Holland, of every conceivable colour, shape and size. Their sweet scent filled the air; it was breathtaking. I was reminded that the Dutch send tulips to Ottawa every year—to thank Canada for keeping their royal family safe during the Second World War.

Bicycles were everywhere as we entered the town of Arnhem: bicycles coming at us from every direction, bicycles five abreast, men riding with children in bicycle baskets, mothers with children on the back of the bicycle, children riding bicycles behind parents, bicycles built for two, bicycle baskets filled with produce, bicycles with carts attached, filled with flowers. Bicycles, bicycles, bicycles! We slowed down to a crawl, frantic to get out of their way so the car wouldn't get scratched.

We parked on the main street and started looking for dress shops, hunting for a wedding dress that would suit me. We paraded up street after street and checked out shop after shop. I tried on many dresses, but did not find one that I liked. I'd almost given up, when we spied a dress in the window of a shop, a lovely three-quarter length, off-white satin. It was just what I was looking for.

Excited, the sales clerk took it from the window and we examined it closely; the style was perfect and the size was right and the label read a *'Paris Original!'* I pursed my lips in disappointment. "It will be too expensive for sure," I sighed, dejected.

Rhoda checked the price tag; it was within my

budget! "Try it on," Rhoda cried excitedly. "Try it on!"

In the change room, I slipped the dress over my head. It fit so perfectly you'd think it was made just for me. When I stepped out, Rhoda gasped. "You look fabulous, Gail! It's stunning on you, with your olive complexion, clear skin and dark chestnut hair." I had to agree: the dress *was* lovely. It had a tight-fitting bodice and full satin bouffant skirt with four satin rosettes down the front. It was simple, elegant, and perfect.

Second Thoughts

There was so much to arrange: a date with the United Church Minister, the reception at the Officer's Mess, friends to stand up for us, flowers to order, invitations to get printed and sent … Everything was happening so fast. Six months ago, I didn't even know who Wes Heald was, and in less than a month I would be getting married to him.

Wes suggested we purchase household goods from the American PX, where everything was at wholesale prices for army personnel. "Order anything you want to setup our home when we get back to Ontario," he said. I ordered a toaster, mix-master, pots and pans, Czechoslovakian crystal, Bavarian China, a chest of silver… Herr Wolf on Kessel Strasse built wooden trunks and everything was packed and labelled to Ship To Canada.

There were two incidents that happened and gave me second thoughts. The first was an incident with Wes that put me on edge. Wes contacted a German tailor to have a sports jacket made for the trip back home. He chose the fabric, measurements were made and we went for a fitting. The sport's jacket was perfect and made Wes look trim—he had started putting on a bit of weight around the middle. "You look fantastic," I told him, smiling as I imagined how great he'd look on the ship home.

Wes pointed to the shoulders. "I want shoulder-pads," he shouted. "It's way too narrow." I cringed, embarrassed.

"Oh no," the tailor responded in his German dialect. "Dis suits you, and da curve off da shoulders. Dis make you look slim!" he said smiling encouragingly.

"I think so too, Wes; the jacket makes you look younger."

"No," Wes yelled. "I don't care what you think; I need shoulder-pads to make me look muscular across the chest." His voice rose to a crescendo. The tailor shook his head slowly from side to side. Wes' face turned bright pink, and his eyes blazed. "Put in shoulder-pads, Goddamnit!" he bellowed. "I'm paying good bucks for this damn thing, so put in shoulder-pads you idiot." Then Wes turned on me. "I don't want to look like one of your former Ivy-league boyfriends from Alberta," he hissed. I shuddered. *Is that what I faced if I married him? Is that how he'd yell at our children?* In terror, an icy gust of prairie wind blew over me. Would I be silenced, belittled, made voiceless, powerless—the way my mother had treated me?

The next incident happened days later, when I got a letter from home. Seeing it on my desk, I rushed to open it. It was from Dad. Mom and Dad had split.

I went numb. My hands shook as I read and re-read the letter. How could this be happening? They had their differences, but surely, they could work them out, get back together.

A chill ran up my spine. The only family I knew was crumbling like rubble, thousands of miles away. I felt suddenly alone and abandoned, once again, with no home to go back to.

Making My Decision

Was I doing the right thing? If it didn't work out, where would I go? What would I do? The only home I had now would be with Wes. Would it be enough? Could I deal with his bursts of anger? What choices did I have? The plans were made, the household items purchased, and the trunks built, packed and labelled for Canada. My head spun with these thoughts, ass I lay on my bed and thought about my future.

There were so many things I liked about Wes: he

was smart, knowledgeable, worldly, sophisticated, sure of himself, and full of enthusiasm for life. He looked after me, he was dependable, and I felt comfortable with him ... safe. I was overwhelmed by his generosity, taking me to so many countries and paying for our travel. I was impressed with his values, which included not wanting to have sex until we married. We had the same careers; as a high school teacher my life would be stable, and I'd never be in the position like my mother, worrying if I'd have a roof over my head in my old age. Sure, Wes had moments when he got angry. *Didn't everyone? Didn't his good qualities outweigh the flaws?* I looked over at my wedding dress hanging on the wall and an image of Wes bubbled to the surface: he was holding me in his arms as Tony Bennett sang, '*Because of You.*' It was the most romantic night of my life.

I thought of my friends back home; several were married already and pushing baby carriages. At twenty-one, I'd been a bridesmaid three times! It was my turn now! *It feels right! The cruise tickets are in my purse, my suitcases sit open waiting to be packed...*

My decision was made.

My Wedding Day

A bride! I stand at the entrance of the Protestant church, and the sun is bright in a perfect, cornflower-blue sky. It is a good omen. I feel elegant in my off-white satin dress; it shimmers in the sunlight. I brush a stray wisp of hair from my eyes and tuck it back into my up-swept 'beehive'. This was the style in Europe at the time. I am ready. The organ music filters out the door. I see the heads of friends sitting in the pews. A tear bubbles up as I think of family back home who are not here to wish me luck. I glance down the aisle at the altar, which overflows with ferns and flowers. Wes looks back at me, beaming.

I start down the aisle, full of hope and expectation. The photographer snaps pictures along the way. As I stand beside Wes, I am ready to repeat my vows. Filled with joy, I say, "I do." I am no longer a bride. I am now a wife.

It is all a blur after that–the reception, the appetizers, the toasts, the cutting of Mom's wedding cake, my change from wedding dress to a navy dress and matching jacket, and, finally, placing our suitcases into the back seat of the Porsche. I have an image in my mind of waving to the crowd as they chanted good wishes. Then, we're off to Dusseldorf and my first night as a married woman, filled with optimism and promise.

Honeymoon and Mood Changes

The honeymoon was a whirlwind of travel—through Germany, Italy, Denmark, France, England and Scotland–during that summer of 1960. I was full of anticipation and excitement, but confusion and loneliness as well.

Wes was enthusiastic to go to places he had never been before, like Oberammergau, where the world-famous *'Passion Play'* was held to commemorate the village being saved from the bubonic plague (1618-1648). In response, the residents promised to perform the story of Christ from birth to death every ten years. Since this was 1960, we were very lucky to be able to witness the play. The two thousand citizens spent years preparing for their various roles; the men who were selected to play Christ grew beards and long hair in order to look authentic for the time period, while the girl designated to play Mary had to be a virgin. It was a full day performance and held on the hillside just outside the town. It was, simply, spectacular.

Verona, in northern Italy, was also a city that Wes was anxious to see. The opera *'Aida'*, by Verdi, was performed in the ruins of a Roman amphitheater. We sat on the ancient stone seats, built thousands of years earlier, when Italians watched chariot races and jousting events. When we purchased the tickets, we were given candles; when we lit them, the audience created thousands of tiny pin-pricks of light that illuminated the night. As the overture played, several live horses pranced out onto the stage. When the candles burned down, the overture faded and the opera began. The scene was sensational; I will never forget it.

It was in Venice when I first noticed a mood shift in Wes. We had planned to go together on the hotel tour of the city, but I couldn't get Wes to wake up in time to go. I remember rushing down the stairs of the hotel, just in time to catch the tour bus—along with the other tourists, who were bustling and jostling, their cameras hanging around their necks like dog leashes. Venice was such a gorgeous city, the buildings surrounded by canals. Left on our own for part of the tour, I wandered along the canals and over the various bridges, including *The Bridge of Sighs*. I was enthralled by the Italians, who belted out arias from the local pubs, as I passed by. In Piazza San Marco, along with hundreds of other tourists, I fed the thousands of pigeons. As I stood there alone, I so wished Wes was with me, to share the sights of Venice; it was lonely doing it on my own.

Our next stop in Italy was in Pisa, a concession Wes made to me. I'd wanted to see Rome, but Wes said it was too far south to go, and besides he'd already been there. As we toured the Tower of Pisa, we learned that it took 200 years to complete it (in 1373) and took only five years, after completion, to start leaning. It was hard to believe that, in 1960, it had been leaning for 582 years without collapsing! As we meandered through the streets of the city, I was in awe of the architecture of the churches; they were magnificent.

That afternoon, I wanted to go to the beach, but Wes wanted to have a nap. I went on my own. I put on my turquoise, one-piece, bathing suit (the latest style in Canada at the time), grabbed a hotel towel, and headed for the beach. I was the only woman on the beach to be wearing a one piece bathing suit; I hadn't the courage to purchase a bikini, even though I was told I had the figure for it. The sun was high in the sky as I dodged teenagers holding hands and wove around young couples cuddling on blankets. I almost tripped into a blue umbrella under which a pair of white-haired folks nestled, escaping the sun's rays. When I found an empty spot, I spread my towel on the glistening sand, the only *single* woman on the beach. I slipped off my sandals, walked to the Mediterranean, and dipped my feet into the sparkling ultra-green water, wishing there were four feet splashing instead of two. Forlorn, I wandered back to my towel and stretched out. *Why was Wes stuck back in the hotel room when he could be here with me?* The Italian lifeguard, up on his guardpost, smiled down at me and winked. I blushed and rolled over onto my stomach. How I wished Wes was lying beside me! *Doesn't he find me attractive anymore?* Here I was, a solitary figure on an Italian beach on the Mediterranean *and* on my honeymoon. *What was wrong with this picture?* These thoughts niggled at me as I lay baking in the hot Italian sun. The sun rays lowered in the sky and a breeze came up; I was one of the few people left on the beach. I folded my towel, slid on my sandals and plodded back to the hotel, my body warm and tanned.

Isolated and alone on that Italian beach on my honeymoon, everything had suddenly changed. At the beginning of our relationship, Wes was constantly at my side driving me to and from school, taking me to new countries, and showing me sites he'd seen before. Things were so different now that we were married; Wes seemed withdrawn from me, and distant. He frequently over-slept for morning tours and spent afternoons napping or reading novels, things he'd never done before. Finding myself more and more alone, raw foreboding feelings from long ago suddenly washed over me—I felt deserted, rejected, and unwanted. Abandoned.

I Am Pregnant

I barfed. I couldn't keep any food down. Suddenly, I was bone-tired in the middle of the afternoon and my breasts were tingly and sore. Anyone reading this, in 2025, would wonder why I hadn't taken any birth control pills. But this was 1960 and although 'The Pill' had been invented, it was not widely available to women for another ten years. I'd never heard of it in 1960!

Wes was annoyed at the frequent stops we had to make for me to vomit. "It's slowing down our appointment in Stuttgart," he admonished. "I only have a couple of days to get the Porsche overhauled." While I tried to control the nausea, it came to me in unexpected waves. When I barfed in the Porsche, it was the final straw—Wes insisted that I go to a doctor. After examining me, the pregnancy was confirmed and medication prescribed. The doctor told me that the drug was quite new and was successful with a number of his patients. I had no idea what it was, and in those days, one never questioned a doctor's diagnosis or drugs they prescribed. When we got back to Canada I had a miscarriage. I often wondered if the drug I had taken was 'thalidomide,'; it was discovered, later, to cause birth defects in children. Nevertheless, the drug seemed to help with the nausea, and Wes was very pleased.

Arriving in Stuttgart, we were in time to have the Porsche engine completely overhauled at the factory so that it would last as long as possible when we got back to Ontario. With the drug addressing the nausea, the potential for me to damage the Porsche's spanking new upholstery was no longer a concern; we continued our trip through Europe.

Denmark, England, Scotland and The Three Minute Egg

The visits to these last countries were a bit of a blur, marred by the *'Three Minute Egg Incident'*! In Copenhagen, Denmark, we saw the "Tivoli Gardens" and the "Little Mermaid" statue, before travelling through France to Calais. We then ferried across the English Channel to Britain. England during that summer was unusually warm and sunny; there wasn't a speck of rain. The "Changing of the Guard", in front of Buckingham Palace, was impressive: guardsmen dressed in their red tunics, tall black puffy furry hats on their heads, rode beautiful horses that pranced with precision to the marching band. We didn't see young Queen Elizabeth, who'd been crowned just seven years before. But we *did* see the "Tower of London", where so many wives of Henry-the-Eighth were hung.

Scotland was dark and dismal when we visited. We'd stayed overnight in a hotel in Edinburgh, and in the morning Wes called for room service to order a boiled egg and toast for him and orange juice and toast for me. "The egg has to be boiled for only *three* minutes," he instructed the person taking the order. A few minutes later, the waiter came to our door with our breakfast on a silver tray and placed it on the table near the window. After Wes gave the waiter a tip, we sat down at the table. Wes held onto the egg-cup-holder, raised his knife in his other hand and cracked the top of the egg shell. He scooped out firm egg white and set the empty shell on the plate. Wes then poked his spoon into the yellow-orange-yolk of the remaining egg. He scrunched his eyebrows together in a scowl. "The yolk is hard, goddamn it. This is not a three-minute-egg!" he roared, his face turning red with rage.

Oh no—he's going to start a fuss! I took the last bite of my toast and washed it down with orange juice.

Wes picked up the telephone and dialed. "I ordered a *three-minute-egg*," Wes shouted. "The yolk you sent is *hard-as-a-rock*. The yolk in a *three-minute-egg* is supposed to be *soft*." He emphasized the word '*soft*'. There was a moment of silence. "The egg has to be in boiling water for *exactly* three minutes. Do you understand?" Another pause and then Wes hung up the telephone. *Oh, my word; he's being ridiculous!*

In ten minutes, there was a tap on the hotel room door. I got up to answer. "Sorry for your trouble," I said to the waiter trying to smooth things over.

"About time," Wes called out belligerently. "I'm starving."

"Sorry sir," the waiter said, and took away the first plate before he set down a fresh one. He got no tip this time.

Wes cracked off the top of the egg shell as before. "Oh my God," he roared. "The white's runny and the yolk is spilling down the side of the egg shell." His nostrils flared and his eyes bulged. "I can't eat this," he bellowed, sweeping his arm in the air and knocking over the eggcup, making a gooey mess on the white porcelain dinner plate. "It's damned well *not* a three-minute-egg!" he shouted disgustedly as he lifted up the telephone once again. "This is NOT a three-minute-egg," he bawled into the telephone.

Is this how he will treat me? Mortified, I ran to the bathroom and retched.

Wes repeated this merry-go-round another two times before he was satisfied and would eat his darned three-minute-egg! It was a prelude to what was to come.

Home to Canada
What Have I Done?

Dark clouds hung overhead on that August day of 1960, as I stood at the ship railing of the Homeric, ready to sail back to Canada. It was at this same spot on the The Empress of England that I pulled away from Montreal filled with hope, adventure and new possibilities. Now, twelve months later, I'm clinging to the same ship's railing filled with sadness, regret and dashed dreams. *What have I done? What went wrong?*

Staring down into the slate-coloured water, thoughts come tumbling out as I review it all. I'd been so impressed with Wes, how sophisticated he was, so attentive, so charming, so generous .... taking me to any country I wanted to go. I was in awe by the exotic restaurants and new experiences that he'd introduced me to. Was I dazzled by the Porsche racing across countries like a movie star? I had believed he was solid and dependable; I had believed that I would be looked after and cared about, and would never be let down.

The engines began to chug and groan out and the ship left the South Hampton harbour. Wes seemed so genuine, kind, sensitive and loving. Did I get carried away when he told me how beautiful I was, and that he loved me? Was I overcome by the romance that night he proposed? What was the rush to get married?... His mother?... *She's been pestering me for years to get married!* Was I simply a pawn in his plan? Is that why he chose to court a young woman fifteen years younger ... a twenty-year-old ... and the most naive, vulnerable, inexperienced teacher at the base. *Was I too dumb to see it?*

The wind caught my hair as the ship took on speed, leaving South Hampton in the distance. Everything changed once we were married. Gone was Wes's sensitivity and care of me. Also gone was his generosity and kindness. Gone, gone, gone. Wes withdrew, deserted, and abandoned me.

The Empress of England made its final mournful blast. I took a deep gulp of fresh sea air and thought about my future. I was married, with a baby on the way; I had to make the best of this; I *had* to make it work. *What choice did I have?* I would do as I'd always done ... pick myself up by the boot-straps and pull myself together .... and carry on.

As the ship charged into the Atlantic, South Hampton faded into the horizon like my shattered dreams. I faced rough seas ahead.

Reflections on the Myths of Marriage

It is only now over sixty-four years later that I examine the mystique of marriage. Paul Newman put it so succinctly in his memoir in 2016 when he said of his first marriage, and I paraphrase. "Marriage was as if we were playing by some play-book; it was like following a set of half-earned things we thought were rules...like performing some play that had already been written...you were supposed to graduate from high school or college, find a profession. You're supposed to get married and you're supposed to have children that you are supposed to protect and provide for (if you are a husband); and nurture and love if you are the wife. There was very little beyond that except that the love each felt for the other would naturally follow."

Paul went on further. "We never had any conversations about contraception, no philosophy of how to raise children, never discussed our roles as husband and wife. Everything happened because it happened; I had no awareness that I could shape things myself."

Reading Paul Newman's memoir made me realize that his description of marriage was the playbook for *my* marriage to Wes. It is my hope that I may play a more deliberate role with my grandchildren in posing questions to them *before* they marry, so that they will have more awareness of how they can shape their relationships in marriage.

THE SIXTIES:
Rise And Demise Of A Marriage

Meeting the Heald Family

I made a dramatic entrance into the Heald family home in Fort William (Thunder Bay). "Where is the bathroom?" I called out, holding my abdomen, starting to heave. I saw a hand pointing down the hallway. Racing past a man in a wheelchair, I got to the bathroom just in time. Morning sickness had returned with a vengeance. *What a way to greet my in-laws!* Looking pale and haggard, with dark shadows under my eyes, I returned from the bathroom, wiping my hand across my mouth.

Wes looked angry. His eyes glared, and his lips were as taught as a rubber band as he introduced his mother. She was a chunky lady with greying hair, and she jerked her head in a quick nod of acknowledgement as she held out her arm stiffly. Her handshake had not a hint of warmth; I felt her disapproval instantly. With her round face, puffed-up-cheeks, and light blue eyes, I could see, immediately, that Wes got the bulk of her genetics and temperament. Mr. Heald smiled pleasantly as he sat in his wheelchair, a bright red plaid blanket across his knees. "This is my dad, Charles Wesley Heald," Wes announced proudly. His dad's eyes were friendly, and he responded warmly–

"Welcome to Fort William." His lips spread into a wide smile. He was a handsome man; he had a neatly trimmed greying moustache, and grey-brown eyes that twinkled. He'd have been a real charmer in his day, serving as Captain in the Canadian Army during World War I. It was sad that he was stricken with MS.

We stayed in the Heald home for a week, until we found an apartment and Wes got a position at the Fort William Collegiate as a physical-education instructor. One morning, as I sat on the toilet-seat wiping the puke off my face, I heard Mrs. Heald's voice chatting with her husband, "I know I wanted Wesley to settle down and get married, but why in the world did he choose someone so *young*?" I retched, then, and didn't hear his response.

Life With Multiple Sclerosis

Mrs. Heald had her work cut out for her– both her husband and daughter had MS. She looked after her husband's needs in the morning and then, in the afternoon, took the city bus to the hospital to help with her daughter's evening meal. One day, she invited me to go with her. The moment Shirley saw us, her face broke into a wide toothy grin. She nodded her head-back-and-forth, welcoming me. "Sooo   goood tooo   meeet yooo, Gaal," she said. Her voice sounded hollow as if in an echo-chamber, the effort appeared to sap her energy. I smiled and nodded my head. Shirley had dark, curly hair; she looked a lot like her Dad with her thin face and sparkling brown eyes, and she seemed to have his warm disposition, as well. I caught the scent of urine and noticed a plastic tube flowing into a sack hanging from the side of her bed.

"Hiii...Mooom," Shirley called to her mother.

Mrs. Heald smiled warmly and patted Shirley's hand. "Hello, my dear," she crooned softly. "How are you feeling today?" I could tell that Shirley was Mother Heald's favourite child. At that moment, an orderly came in with a tray of food. At the sight and smell, Shirley's eyes lit up and her body wiggled as she opened her mouth wide like a greedy bird. Her arms lay motionless on either side of her body. It occurred to me then that her arms were paralyzed preventing her from feeding herself. *My word, bed-ridden at age forty! Did this disease have no mercy?* Mrs. Heald took out a large terry-cloth towel from her handbag and placed it over Shirley's chest. She picked up a spoon and scooped up some mashed potatoes with gravy and moved it toward her daughter's mouth. Shirley's mouth opened wide as she slid her lips over the spoon and pulled the food into her mouth. She appeared to have a great deal of difficulty swallowing; the muscles in her throat twitched-up-and-down slowly, moving the food to her stomach. Mrs. Heald waited patiently, scooping up another portion to give to her daughter, when she was ready. I watched in awe at Mrs. Heald's gentleness as she fed her adult daughter spoonful after spoonful, just as she would have done when her daughter was a baby. Dribbles of mush oozed out over the corners of Shirley's mouth. Her mother took a tissue and wiped the spilled food from her daughter's face and chucked it into a waste basket.

Riding home on the bus, I had a whole new appreciation of the load on Mrs. Heald's shoulders. At the time, I couldn't imagine what a drain that was on her, both physically and emotionally.

I know that pain now, however. My darling son, Blake, suffers from the same disabling disease. At 60 years old, his life has been a series of losses. And yet, he is a trooper—he runs his own computer company, lives in his own condo and pays for his own round-the-clock care.

On that day in 1960, however, as I rode the bus with Mother Heald, I couldn't contemplate the possibility. I swept the thought completely from my mind.

Homemaker Par Excellence

As a new wife, I was excited to be a homemaker and was resolved to be the best I could be. I assumed all the household responsibilities: I did the grocery shopping—scanning flyers for bargains in order to keep within the budget that Wes had established for me—as well as meal preparation, cleaning and laundry. With morning sickness still plaguing me, it wasn't easy, but I was committed. I cut out recipes from women's magazines and borrowed recipes from my sister-in-law. I asked for special recipes from Mother Heald so I could prepare her son's favourites. Subconsciously, I hoped my interest in her son might redeem me in her eyes. In a notebook, I recorded each meal I'd prepared over a month to maintain variety, working tirelessly on every meal to make something special, and topped off each meal with a dessert. I also baked cookies, cakes and donuts from scratch—though my first pie was a disaster. "It's sure not like my *mother's*," Wes pointed out.

In a moment of courage, I tried my hand at cooking his three-minute-egg! I got the water boiling, and took an egg from the fridge and lowered it carefully into the boiling water. When the cold egg hit the steaming water, the egg-shell cracked and the white albumin flowed out. It was cooked solid. It was wrecked! For the next try, I warmed the eggshell in hot tap water to prevent it from cracking. Then just as I was lowering it into the pot, my stomach rebelled, and I raced to the bathroom. By the time I got back the egg was over-cooked. I served it anyway. As Wes ate it, I heard him mumble under his breath, "She can't even boil a gall darn egg right!"

Articles in magazines gave helpful instructions for the right way to do laundry: *Tricks to keep socks and underwear sparkling white; Five-easy-steps-to-iron-a-shirt; How to fold sheets and towels.* With so much information, how hard could it be? I ironed all our clothes—including sheets and pillowcases! There were articles, as well, on ways wives could please their husbands: *19 Rules for Keeping a Husband Happy; Be All the Wife He needs; Prepare four-course-meals every night; Have candles or flowers on the table for dinner; Greet your husband at the door in an attractive dress; Put on fresh lipstick.* There was even an article called, *"Ten Ways to Keep Your Husband Happy in the Bedroom!"* —I did it all! I wanted to be the best darned wife possible!

The thing was, I truly *wanted* to make Wes happy. Deep down, I hoped my hard work would make a difference in our relationship, that he'd appreciate me more, respect me, perhaps, and, if I worked hard enough to please him, he might even love me a little.

The Miscarriage

We didn't have an automatic washer or dryer in the apartment, and I was carrying a load of laundry up the stairs when I felt a twinge and tightness in my belly. I didn't want to bother Wes, who was reading a novel in the living room. A wave of pain rolled across my abdomen, and I doubled over in pain. I called out loudly, "*Wes!*"

"What's the matter, now?" he yelled back to me.

"Just come!" I cried.

Shuffling to the top of the stairs in his slippers and pyjamas, he called, "What's wrong?" He sounded annoyed. "Why are you sitting there on the stairs?"

"I'm in pain," I groaned. I vaguely remember scuffling on the stairs … the bathroom … sitting on the toilet … a violent cramp … The next thing I remember was waking up in a hospital room. I'd had a miscarriage.

That fall, the newspapers were filled with the effects of thalidomide: babies born with deformed limbs, eyes, and internal organs. I couldn't help wondering if the drug I took in Germany–the "miracle drug" that had been prescribed as a way to ease my morning sickness–had been thalidomide. I will never know. Yet, in Canada, 400 babies were born with defects. It is interesting to note that, at this time of writing (over 60 years later)—that no pharmaceutical company ever took responsibility for the marketing, or resulting effects, that thalidomide had on families and their babies.

Now, six decades later, I can't believe how hard I worked at being the perfect wife. I am surprised, too, at how happy it made me feel, and the pride I felt at all I'd learned and accomplished. I thought of it as my *job*; it was what I *wanted* to do at that time, and I did it willingly, thinking it was a fair-trade for my husband's role as provider. I realize, now, that I'd bought society's definition of marital roles, hook-line-and-sinker.

It never occurred to me to question our different roles. Like other women of the time, I didn't think I had the right. There was no debate, no discussion on how exhausting the social expectations were: a wife was expected to please her husband. Nor was there consideration about how limiting the role might be—at the expense of her personality, needs, and dreams. Too often, women were expected to curtail their professional and personal aspirations and their intellect was ignored. Little thought was given of the inequality of the roles, and how negatively the role might affect a woman's self identity, and sense-of worth, as well as her confidence. In the 1960s, defined roles were rock-solid in every aspect of society, and most women conformed. That's the way it was.

Starting a Family

I was pregnant once again. When I told Wes the news, that winter of 1961, his response was immediate. "I sure as heck hope you aren't going to be sick like you were the last time," he said, shaking his head. "That was a disaster I don't want repeated." But I was excited and happy at the prospect of becoming a mother. I hoped that having a family would bring Wes and me closer together.

Wes got a job teaching English at St. Catharines Collegiate for that September. We purchased a Vauxhall station wagon—the Porsche had to be shipped with the furniture—to drive from Thunder Bay to southern Ontario, which was a distance of 3,000 miles. "We'll camp," Wes decided excitedly. "I've always wanted to do it." I told Wes that I'd never camped before. "It'll be a piece of cake," he assured me. I was the size of a beluga whale, and I wondered about tenting. I was already having difficulty rolling in and out of my bed! *But what did I know?* I was willing to give it a try. By the time we got to St. Catharines, I ached in parts of my body that I didn't know I had! The experience killed any desire to *ever* camp again.

We found a three-bedroom upstairs apartment in St. Catharines and got settled in. At nine months already, I was anxious to find a doctor, set up the baby's room and purchase furniture and clothes for the baby.

Wes had other priorities. With his new job starting just a week away, he had to get his office ready. He purchased a new desk, office chair and antique oak bookcase with glass drop-leaf-panels in order to keep his novels in pristine condition.

The baby furniture could wait.

Wes spent hours organizing his novels and reading the English curriculum, in readiness for teaching English for the very first time. On that first Tuesday after Labour Day, Wes paced the floor of the apartment; he was nervous and full of anticipation. He checked the mirror several times to be sure his tie was just right and smoothed his fine blond hair once again, before picking up his briefcase and heading out the door. He was as excited as a six-year-old on his first day of school. I was so happy for him.

Now, it was time to plan for the baby. We located a doctor who confirmed that the baby was almost full term. One Saturday morning, while Wes was working in his den, planning lessons, I squeezed into the Vauxhall and went shopping at a local department store. I selected all the equipment we needed—a crib, bassinet, change-table, baby carriage …. The salesman promised it would be delivered in a week. I couldn't wait to tell Wes. After waddling up the two flights of stairs to the apartment, I called out, "Wait till I tell you about the baby equipment I ordered!" I was so excited. "And I got a discount for such a large order," I added proudly. "They'll deliver it next week just in time to get it organized for the baby coming."

Wes looked up from his desk and snapped his novel closed. "How much did it cost?" He scowled at me, looking angry. Surprised by his question, I pulled out the receipt and handed it to him. His eyes scanned the receipt from top to bottom. His eyebrows furrowed. "What?" he exclaimed, his voice rising. "This is an outrageous amount."

"But we need a crib, the change table and...."

Before I could utter another word, Wes bellowed, "Cancel the order right now!" His eyes bulged out, his face turning a flaming Porsche red. "What do you think I am, made of money?"

I was speechless, overwhelmed by his anger. *We are talking about our baby!* I couldn't wrap my mind around what he was saying, what he was thinking. After all, he'd just purchased a new desk, an office chair, a special bookcase for himself and bragged how he'd just gotten a raise in salary. *Why was he being miserly with the baby furniture?* He hadn't batted an eye at buying the Vauxhall and spared no cost for all the camping gear for the trip here. And now, he was quibbling about new furniture for our baby? *What kind of a cheapskate was he?*

I walked away fuming. *What could I do?* Wes had control of all of the money; having none of my own, I had absolutely no power. So, I did as I was told, like a school-girl having spent her allowance on too many comic books. I cancelled the order and trudged to all the second-hand shops in town to scour for used items for our precious baby. It was a hard pill to swallow, and it stuck in my craw for years.

Our Three Babies Are Born

During the last week of September, 1961, Wes began to be interested, acknowledging that he was actually going to be a father. "If it's boy, I'll call him 'Charles Wesley' like my dad," he said enthusiastically. "Dad will be so proud to have a grandson named after him. And if it's a girl," he added in the same breath, "I'll name her Shirley."

"Maybe not," I replied. "I like the name Rachel."

The baby started punching like a boxer, which brought on a cramp that rolled across the underside of my tummy. A searing wave of pain ripped through me. It had started. As I doubled over in pain, Wes helped me down the stairs to the car and whisked me off to the maternity ward of the hospital. I was given medications and doped up. I heard someone say, "Should come by morning." The last thing I remember was feeling something cold and hard thrust inside me …

I woke up on the morning of September 26, 1961. "He's a bruiser," the nurse said, "all 9 pounds 13 ounces of him." She reached over and placed a blue bundle into my arms. His face peeked out from the blanket, the first infant I'd ever seen. I was surprised at his almond-shaped eyes; they were squeezed shut, and reminded me of a statue of a Buddha. I smile at the memory. The tuft of hair on his head was soft and delicate, like the underbelly of a duckling. Peeling away the flannel blanket, I couldn't believe how tiny he was—smaller by far than any doll I'd ever gotten under the Christmas tree when I was a child.. He seemed so delicate, so fragile, that I was afraid to hold him for fear I'd hurt him. And yet, the nurse said he was a bruiser. *You don't look like a bruiser to me!* Running my hands over his body, I remember the silkiness of his skin and his sweetish, delicate scent. It was unlike anything I'd ever smelled before, and uniquely his. My eyes zeroed in on his fingers and toes—perfect, all twenty of them. I remember how his lips pursed together like a fish gulping for air. He made a sniffling, snuffling sound as he latched onto my nipple and sucked. At that moment, a powerful sensation suddenly wrapped around me, the intensity of which I'd never experienced before—ever.

Just then, Wes marched into my hospital room. "We're calling him Charles Wesley after my dad," he announced. "I've already called my folks, and Dad is overjoyed," he said excitedly. "Can't stay; gotta buy cigars and chocolates for my staff to celebrate my son's birth." He rushed out the door.

Our second son, Blake was born on a cold, wintry day, two years and four months later, on January 31, 1964. It was a difficult birth, and my labour dragged on for two days—until I finally blacked out. I woke up in a daze. I called out, "Where's my baby? Is the baby all right?"

"Baby's just fine," a nurse said, as she pulled

the curtain back from my bed. "He's a big guy at 11 pounds, 8 ounces and breech too (Bum first). Don't often see 'em as big as that," she announced. *An eleven-pound-baby? Breech? No wonder I felt as if I'd been drawn and quartered.* After checking his toes and fingers, I couldn't get over how much he looked like Wes—the same round face and fingers shaped just the same.

Wes stomped into my hospital room. "I can't believe it, another son," he said proudly, a smile spreading from ear to ear. "And he looks just like me!" He said it as if he'd done it all by *himself*. "I know exactly what I'll name him," Wes announced confidently ....

"*I* will name our son this time," I interjected. His jaw dropped and his eyes opened wide in disbelief. "His name will be Colin Blakley—Colin after my dad, (Auburn Colin Pye) and Blakley after my mother's maiden name (Margaret Jean Blakley). Colin Blakley," I announced firmly. Wes raised his eyebrows in disbelief.

Colin Blakley Heald born on January 31, 1964 in St. Catharines, Ontario, I wrote in his baby book.

Ron, was the only baby whose birth I saw–I watched as he slipped from my body. I heard his first cry. He was breathing; he was alive; he was healthy; he was mine! Caressing his warm slippery body, I drank in his silky head, his tiny rose-bud lips, and felt the gentle curl of his ears. As I held each tiny foot in my hand, I stroked their soft velvet pads and counted his toy-like toes. His warm body pressed against my chest, and he searched for my breast. I folded him into my arms. There are no words to adequately describe the overwhelming feeling of joy that came over me ... he was so lovely.

Ron's birth was a whole different experience compared to the births of his brothers. Given my history of birthing large babies, the doctor advised medication to bring on premature labour so that this baby would be smaller, and the birth easier. He was right.

Ronald Porter Heald born December 7, 1966 weighed 7 pounds 14 ounces. We called him Ronald Porter (Ronald after my Grandfather Pye and Porter after Wes' grandfather, Porter Grover.) Ronald Porter Heald was a birth to remember!

Surviving Dual Roles: Wife and Mother

Charles Wesley (Wesley) was a dream baby. During the first months, I established a routine of feeding, bathing, changing him and rocking him to sleep. He nursed every four hours and slept soundly between feedings. While he slept, I did my wifely tasks of house-cleaning, laundry and preparing quality meals for Wes at the end of the day.

As the washing machine and dryer were in the basement, two flights below, the extra baby laundry extra laundry was a challenge. After I nursed baby Wesley and put him down for a nap, I would haul the heavy diaper-pail down the stairs to the wringer washer. After washing and rinsing the diapers and chucking the wet loads into the dryer, I would race back up the stairs to our apartment on the top floor– change our bed, clean the bathroom, and vacuum the living-room. After Wesley's next feeding, I dashed back down the stairs to get a load out of the dryer and would lug the laundry basket back up the stairs and set it beside my chair in the living room to fold later. I just had just enough time to peel the potatoes and carrots and get the pork chops ready to bake for supper.

Exhausted by the time I'd prepared supper, cleaned up the dishes and fed Wesley for the night, I joined Wes in the living room to watch "*The Andy Griffith Show.*" Finally able to sit down, I would begin to fold diapers. As the pile of folded diapers mounted, a TV advertisement came on for '*Speedy-Diaper-Service.*' "That would be a great help for me," I commented to Wes. "With the baby, I have to do laundry every second day."

Wes looked over at me, his eyes sparking. "A *diaper service*, are you kidding? That's *way* too expensive." Flinching, I folded another diaper and threw it onto the pile. "All the wives of teachers at *my* school do their own diaper washing," Wes said, a smug look on his face. He paused and put his index finger to his lips. "Of course, the *lazy* ones don't," he snickered. "After all," he added, "you're home all day. What else do you have to do?" My jaw dropped. *How could he say such a thing? Is he blind to all I do, the meals I prepare, the house cleaning, the baking, ironing his clothes? Can't he see how hard it is with a new baby on top of it all?* Paying for diaper service, was the *least* he could do. I pitched a folded diaper onto the pile and stormed off to bed, demoralized and unappreciated.

When Blake was born, everything came to a head. He was a sickly baby and frequently got ear infections that became chronic. The ear infections wouldn't be resolved until he was three when his tonsils and adenoids were taken out. Three long years of hell. Antibiotics worked for a couple of weeks, and then he'd have the infection all over again.

One night was particularly difficult. He started to howl in the middle of the night; I crawled out of bed, picked him up from his bassinet and tip-toed to the living room so that we wouldn't wake up Wes. Wrapping a blanket around the two of us, we cuddled into each other in the rocking chair and rocked ... He howled and we rocked ... He screamed and I continued to rock. I sang lullabies as we rocked and *still* he wailed. The morning light streamed through the window when Blake finally drifted off and I put him back into his bassinet. Dog-tired, I went to the kitchen to prepare Blake's formula for the day. Too drowsy to make scrambled eggs for breakfast, I grabbed the box of '*Red River Cereal*' and got it simmering. My eyes drooping with weariness, I managed to put a lunch together for Wes to take to school. While he showered, I got toddler Wesley up, dressed for the day and at the kitchen table eating his cereal, my eyes blurry with fatigue. Wes marched in and sat down at the head of the kitchen table waiting to be served. I set a bowl of cereal at his place.

"*What*," he barked. "Red River Cereal again?" He scowled. "I was counting on scrambled eggs."

Angry, I turned my back on him. *Can't he see how bushed I am, having been up all night? Does he even care?* Bone-tired, I filled the bottles with Blake's formula hoping I would catch a wink later, while the boys napped.

It was not to be. After feeding and changing Blake, I realized I'd used the last cloth diaper. While the boys napped, I went to the basement again—with the diaper pail full to the brim.

By the time the load was washed and dried, I sat on the bottom step and wept. The echo of Wes' voice reverberated in my head. "*What! Red River Cereal again?*" Tears flowed down my cheeks. "Wes doesn't give a damn about me," I sobbed… "not a speck of appreciation for all I do for him," I wailed at the empty basement. "He doesn't lift a finger to help, doesn't think he has to, simply expects me to do it all as if I am his slave!" A cold rage rose in my throat. I wasn't deserving of a kind word, and not even worth the diaper-service now that I had two babies. I trusted that my hard work would bring me satisfaction, fulfillment, happiness and build a better relationship with Wes. What a fantasy *that* turned out to be!" Furious, something changed inside me that moment. I wiped my cheeks with the back of my hand. The goal I once had to be the perfect wife dissolved like honey in tea. I took a deep breath, stood up, and pulled my shoulders straight. With a sudden spurt of energy, I flew up the two flights of stairs, past the kitchen with the unwashed dishes and the Red River Cereal drying in the pot, and crawled into my unmade bed. I slept.

I'd been hood-winked, tricked somehow, locked into this traditional housewife role and expected to cater to my husband at any cost. I'd become disillusioned and felt de-valued; I felt that I didn't matter to him at all. In some ways, I felt as if I'd been ripped raw, and I didn't know which way to turn. Not only was I no longer treated with respect, but I felt I was destined to a life of dreariness, of disappointment, and of lost hope and dreams. I was stuck, like a metal pole in concrete. I realized that, with no income of my own, and two babies to care for, I had no choice left. *How would I survive on my own?* I had to refocus my energy away from catering to Wes and toward my role as mother of my boys. It was with *them* that I felt worthwhile; it was with *them* I found purpose and happiness. They were the beacon of light and hope for the future.

Finding Happiness in Motherhood

I have so many happy memories of my little boys as they were growing up.

As a toddler, Wesley loved to climb; he climbed up on chairs, crawled in and out of his crib, and scrambled up onto the kitchen table. I couldn't let him out of my sight! When he was three, we purchased a climbing tower for the back yard. The moment it was erected, Wesley clambered hand-over-fist, from the bottom rung to the very top and higher than my up-stretched-arms. I can still hear his voice, as if it were yesterday. "Look at me," he called down to us, waving his hands wildly in the air. His most accomplished climb was up three stories on the outside of the Ontario pavilion at Expo 67 in Montreal. He was five!

Wesley loved the train that ran, several times a week, through the middle of our residential area in St. Catharines. The second he heard the whistle blow, he would call out to me, "The train; the train, train, Mom." We would dash down the stairs to the sidewalk, bolt to the end of the block, and stop dead as the wooden barrier came down over the road. The whistle always blew once again as the engine crawled toward us, its gigantic wheels slowly grinding and making a hissing sound as it puffed out acrid smelling smoke. This would make Wesley hold his hand to his nose while the engine slid slowly past. When the engineer, in his grey-striped-puffed-up-hat, waved at Wesley, he would jump up and down with excitement, and swing his arms wildly. The engineer would pull the cord for the whistle blow, one more time, "whoo, whoo!" Wesley would laugh and call out to him. The train would inch past, the guard-rail raised, and Wesley would keep waving his little arms as the train continued down the track. The train's mournful whistle slowly faded as the engine got smaller and smaller until, rounding a corner, it would disappear from sight. Only then, would Wesley turn and dart back to the apartment. Once he stopped suddenly, bent over in the grass on the curb, and raced back to me with something yellow in his hand. "For you, Mom." My heart melted as I took the golden dandelion, a gift of sunshine.

Blake, at three, had an amazing relationship with Mr. Poloski, the garbage man. As soon as Blake heard the roar of the garbage truck coming down our street on Monday morning, Blake donned his jacket, ran outside, and jumped into his yellow hard-plastic-pedal-car. His wee legs a-churning, Blake blasted down the driveway. I held my breath as he twisted the steering-wheel hard, making a sharp-right-hand-turn onto the sidewalk—never once hitting the curb—just as the garbage truck screeched to a stop beside him. I was relieved when he made it safely. Mr. Poloski hopped out. He was an unusual looking man: his back was humped between his shoulders, his face was contorted, and his mouth twisted to one side as if he'd once been in an accident. His appearance did not bother Blake in the least. He and Mr. Poloski had become friends. One time Mr. Poloski brought Blake a dump truck; Blake was thrilled, even though it had a wheel missing. Blake was mesmerized when Mr. Poloski grabbed our bag of garbage, pitched it into the truck, and pulled a lever to activate a mechanism that shifted instantly with a grinding roar to scrunch our bag and press it into the back, out of sight. After he disposed of our garbage, and headed up the street to the next house, Mr. Poloski would reduce the speed of the truck to a crawl so that Blake could race him past every house on the block—until they got to the next intersection. Then Blake waved and Mr. Poloski waved back and blasted his horn to punctuate his goodbye. Blake would then turn his peddle-car around and charge back home, a smile on his beautiful chubby little face.

Another memory of Blake is an incident at church one Sunday morning. The minister told the children a story with a biblical theme on, *'How good behaviour over time affects spiritual growth.'* Thinking the children would understand the concept, he used the metaphor of spring seeding as his analogy. "So," the minister started, "When your dad starts a new lawn, he puts down lots of good top soil; he rakes it; he plants grass seed over the soil and waters it every day for several weeks." He paused, looking at the children sitting in front of him. "What comes up then?" he asked. Blake's little hand flew up into the air. "What do you think comes up?" the minister asked again.

Blake waved his hand frantically. The minister finally pointed to him for his answer. "Dandelions," Blake shouted. "Dandelions come up." Everyone in the congregation burst out laughing. Blake's face crumpled in a frown, and looked back at me. Trying to hide my smile, I blew him a kiss. Driving home, Blake asked, "Why did everyone laugh at my answer?" He shook his five-year-old-head. "I was right, wasn't I?"

"You certainly were," I said smiling as we pulled into the driveway and I looked over at our lawn covered in a mass of yellow, sunny heads of dandelions.

As a baby, Ron loved to rock in the family rocking chair. I rocked him when I nursed him; I rocked him when he cried, and I rocked him before I put him down to sleep at night. As a toddler he loved to rock when I read stories to him. He often climbed up into the rocking chair by himself; he'd insist that it be situated in front of the picture window so he could look out onto the street as he rocked. (I gave that rocker to Ron when he and his wife purchased their first home; it was the rocking chair in which they rocked their own babies.)

Another event about Ronnie (we called him Ronnie until he went to school), that I remember well, was the day I had to cut his curls. As a toddler, Ronnie had a head of twisty, yellow curls that got curlier and curlier every year. I loved the feeling I got when I wrapped strands of his soft silky hair around my fingers. It was a warm feeling that reminded me of Peg Dodd's gentle fingers in my own hair so many long years before. Such a beautiful boy Ronnie was!

"You have to cut Ronnie's hair!" Wesley yelled, bursting into the house, his nine-year-old-eyes sparkling. "You have to cut Ronnie's hair!" he cried again. The boys had just returned with their dad after having the oil changed in the car.

"Yes," Blake called out running in after Wesley. "The mechanic thought that Ronnie was a beautiful little *girl!*" Blake waved his hands and stomped his five-year-old-feet.

"Why do I have to cut Ronnie's hair?" I asked, surprised at how vehement the boys were. "He's still a toddler, and his hair is so beautiful."

"But Mom," Wesley cried out again. "I told the mechanic that Ronnie was our *brother* but he wouldn't believe me. You *have* to cut his hair, Mom, you just *have* to."

He's only three years old, I thought; *he can have his curls a few years longer. He's still my little baby boy!* I couldn't imagine my little Ronnie without those lovely yellow curls.

"Want my hair cut," Ronnie shouted as he ran into the kitchen, a big smile on his face. "Want my hair cut, Mom," he called again, climbing up onto a kitchen chair as he'd seen his brothers do when I cut their hair.

He started to pound his little hands on the table.

Reluctantly I got out my scissors and draped a towel around Ronnie's wee shoulders. I bent forward and ran my fingers through his hair, building up courage to begin. My shoulders slumped as I twisted a curl around my finger and lifted it up away from his head. My hand trembled as I squeezed the scissors ever so slowly. Snip! A golden curl fell to the floor and my heart dropped with a sense of loss. Wesley clapped his hands. Snip! Another twisty bit of yellow floated to the floor. I winced and bit my lip. Snip, Snip! More curls fell. My baby was disappearing before my eyes. Snip, Snip, Snip. Curl after curl dropped silently one-by-one. An ear suddenly appeared as if announcing that Ronnie's babyhood was coming to an end. Snip! Snap! Snip! Curls mounded in a pile on the kitchen floor. *Why in the world does my baby have to grow up so fast?* With a final snap of the scissors there was no more kinky hair at Ronnie's neck. My eyes teared up and a sadness suddenly swept over me. In a blink of an eye Ronnie became Ron, a little boy. *My baby had disappeared forever.*

Those are the only two memories I have of Ron as a toddler, when I have so many of Wesley and Blake. Why was that? Was I so overloaded with the needs of three preschoolers? Or was something else going on with me at that time? Could I have been distracted living in a house I had no part in choosing, with a man who didn't think I mattered? Was I depressed at that time when I'd lost hope in our marriage—did the effects of my marriage with Wes raise havoc with my memory?

Learning Through Play

Something that I learned from my elementary teacher training was the value of play for my boys in developing them intellectually, physically and emotionally. To this end I purchased building materials of every kind --Lincoln Logs, Lego, Meccano, and Tinker toys. The boys used the materials to build towers, rockets, cars, trucks, diggers. (Wesley crafted so many interesting Lego constructions, he won prizes at the Galt Fair!) I also made sure the boys had lots of materials to express their imagination. They painted, drew pictures, created animals out of play-dough and made everything imaginable from toilet-paper-rolls, boxes and coloured construction paper. I recall the time the boys took cushions from an old chesterfield in the playroom and turned them into a fort in the morning; by the afternoon it became an airplane. The next day they took the airplane apart and created a truck. Their ingenuity amazed me!

The Red Barn Incident: A Parenting Disaster

The *Red Barn* incident was an example of how *not* to parent. Wes was anxious to go to "The Red Barn"; at 15 cents each, they had the cheapest hamburgers in town. The boys thought that the Red Barn hamburgers were even better than McDonald's. Besides, they loved The Red Barn because it was shaped like an old-fashioned barn and painted a fire-engine red.

The boys were sitting on bar-stools waiting for their hamburgers to come; they started to swing on their stools. For a little guy, four-year-old-Blake could swing pretty fast; I was right beside him to catch him if he lost his balance. He spun so fast I thought he might get dizzy.

"Stop spinning, Blake, gal darn it" Wes yelled at him. "You're going to fall!" Blake spun faster and faster. "Stop it right now!!" Wes bellowed so loud that the people around us looked up. "Stop it, I told you!" Wes shouted, shaking his finger in Blake's wee face.

Startled, Blake toppled off the stool; he slipped so fast I couldn't catch him. Down he went onto the floor smacking his head on the step with a loud whack. Screaming in pain, he sobbed, blood pouring out of his tiny head. I rushed over and grabbed him up in my arms. "We have to get him to the hospital," I cried. "He could have a concussion." My hands were shaking with anxiety and fear. Blake wailed in agony.

"It serves you right Blake, gal darn it." Wes roared, his eyes burning with rage. "It serves you darn well right," he scolded, shaking his fist at Blake. "I told you to stop spinning, gal damn it." His lips curled in a fury. "That'll teach you," he screeched. There was a collective gasp of other customers. The room went silent.

"Stop it," I shrieked. "This is *no* time to be blaming Blake; he's only a little boy, my baby for heavensake!" I clutched Blake to my chest, howling in pain, blood all over us. "We've got to get him to the hospital," I pleaded.

"It's only a scratch," Wes said scornfully. "You're worried about nothing," he muttered caustically. Blake wailed and grabbed at his eyes, trying to wipe the blood away.

"He might have brain damage, something permanent," I shouted, in a panic, worried that lasting harm could come to him. "You've got to *do* something."

"All right, gal darn it," Wes grumbled as he got up from his chair begrudgingly, loaded us into the car, and took us to the hospital just blocks away.

Blake had a deep cut requiring several stitches; he had no concussion, thank goodness. "See," Wes snorted derisively at me, "You were worried over nothing."

House Hunting: The Moment of Truth

It was time. We'd been renting for five years, and with two pre-schoolers (five and three) and a baby on the way, we needed to start looking for a home. The promise brightened my spirits. Wes said he had over eight thousand dollars ($8,000) for a down-payment, so we could afford the monthly mortgage payments, especially since he'd been given a new pay-raise at the Galt Collegiate.

I was ready to start looking. I'd fallen in love with two-story brick homes. I had imagined four bedrooms, so Wes would have an office, a formal dining room for entertaining guests, bedrooms for the boys and a nursery for the new baby. I wanted a playroom and a nice big back yard for the boys to play in. We could afford a four-bedroom house, no problem!

I started scanning the newspaper, running my finger down the real-estate section, page after page, seeking something within our price-range. There were so many choices: *Three-bedroom home, living room dining area off the kitchen, basement floor painted ready to finish, $12, 900; large three-bedroom-home, L-shaped living room/ dining room, eat-in kitchen, finished basement, garage, $17,500.* Anyone reading this account in 2025 would be stunned by the 1960 prices. In those days, a single-wage earner could afford a home—factory workers, salesmen, truck drivers, reporters, or teachers. Considering today's market, it's hard to imagine a home could be purchased without a second income. My finger stopped suddenly at a house in Preston: *Four-bedroom-home, with formal living room and dining room; den, kitchen with breakfast nook; finished playroom in the basement; $18,900.* Doing the math in my head, I knew we could afford it.

I couldn't wait to tell Wes as soon as he came home from school. "I've found it," I exclaimed excitedly, picking up the paper. "Come have a look."

Wes scanned the page quickly. "Hrumph," he grumbled with disinterest and handed it back to me.

"But it's in our price-range," I persisted. "And it's only a five-minute-drive to the Galt Collegiate," I argued. "Can we go to see it on the weekend?" I was as excited as a teenager purchasing a new dress.

"We'll see," Wes countered, an odd look sweeping across his face, a hint of a scowl.

Mid-week, I approached Wes again. "Can I set up an appointment to see that house in Preston?"

"I suppose so," he shrugged, not a speck of interest in his voice.

As Saturday neared, I approached Wes again about seeing the Preston house.

"I'm not going," he snapped, "I have marking to do."

Disappointed in his attitude, I still wanted to see it. "Well, I'm going to see it," I retorted, surprised at how confident I sounded.

Wes snorted, "You'd better put the boys down for a nap before you go," he hissed caustically. "I'm not a baby-sitter, you know."

The house was perfect. I fell instantly in love with it with the white shutters against the russet-coloured bricks and wrought-iron planters with green shrubs in each at either side of the door. The owner ushered me into a vestibule with a closet for coats. A room to the right was a perfect office for Wes. To the left was a large living room with tasteful wallpaper and plush carpet. A dining room at the end was to die-for; it would easily seat ten people comfortably. The kitchen, off to the side, had an eating area and up-dated pine cabinets. We climbed the stairs to four huge bedrooms—a master, one for each boy, and a room for the baby. In addition, the basement had a finished playroom with spanking new carpet.

Making arrangements to come back the following day, I drove home full of enthusiasm.

Rushing into the house, my eyes aglow, I could hardly contain my excitement. "I saw the house and it's absolutely perfect," I exclaimed. "It even has an office on the ground floor." I went on quickly describing the rooms floor-by-floor. "Another perk is that it's a five-minute-drive to the Galt Collegiate," I added eagerly. "You've just *got* to come and see it."

Wes lifted his head up from the papers on his desk, a deep crease gouged between his eyes. "Like I told you before," he snarled gruffly, "I'm not interested." He got up and shut the door in my face.

My heart fell.

One day in June, three months later, Wes had a peculiar look on his face when he came home from school. *Something seems amiss!* Making the last preparations for supper, I put Blake in his highchair and Wesley to my right. Wes plunked himself down at the end of the table, his eyes lowered, his fork moving the food around and around on his plate. Usually a hearty eater, he hadn't taken a mouthful of potatoes, meatloaf or vegetables. *What's going on?* An uneasiness came over me. Wes looked up with that lop-sided-grin as if he'd just sneaked a piece of cake saved for company and was caught-out. Sensing something was wrong, I lay my fork across my plate and stared … I waited … Wes coughed to clear his throat. He sucked in a deep breath of air as if building up courage to speak. His voice lowered to almost a whisper. "I put a down payment on a house today." His words came through to me in staccato bursts, like Morse code.

Numb, I sat glued to my chair as his words sank in. *I put a down payment on a house today.* My heart stopped and my lungs turned to concrete; I could hardly breathe. I couldn't believe what I'd just heard. Shaking with anger, I found my voice. "You did *what*?"

"Yes," Wes mumbled. "One of the teachers at school is selling his house. They're moving in July. *This can't be happening! Tell me this is a dream.* Hardly taking a breath, his voice gained confidence, "They're selling it privately so we won't have to pay real-estate fees. It's a real steal, at $16,000" he stated as if trying to convince me he'd made a good deal. His voice rose in volume. "So, I bought it," he announced, as if proud of what he'd done. "I signed the papers today." He smiled triumphantly.

Unspoken words piled up in my head, as I began to comprehend what Wes had done. *You didn't consult me! You never even considered me! You wouldn't even go to see the house in Preston! You were planning to do this all along, you son of a bitch! This is so typical. It's all about you! That's how it's always been!* I pursed my lips and stared daggers at him. *How could you do this to me,* I screamed inside my head. *How could you treat me as if I don't have the right to choose our first house?* I pushed back my chair from the table, raced to the bathroom and threw up. Blake started to wail.

I reflect now, years later on, why I didn't speak up, why I didn't tell Wes how angry I was. I ask myself, *why didn't scream in his face what I was thinking in my mind?* Was it old memories of feeling powerless, growing up with my mother, never feeling I was good enough, never respected or loved, and believing I didn't deserve better? Perhaps it was because I really *had* no power; I'd quit my teaching job so that I could stay at home with the children; I'd spent my pension from teaching to purchase our washer and dryer. I had no income; I had no rights.

In July, we visited that house Wes had purchased without my knowledge or consent. Disappointed. I couldn't help comparing the pint-sized yellow-brick-bungalow to the two-story red brick of the Preston house that I loved. I stepped inside onto a narrow linoleum hallway. The living room to the right was a quarter the size of the one in Preston. The carpet was faded, worn-to-the-bone compared to the velvet plush throughout the one in Preston. Turning left down a short hallway were three small bedrooms, instead of the four I wanted so each boy would have their own. Back up the hallway, we turned left to an eating area, an alcove really, barely enough room for a small kitchen table, not an inch of space for a buffet or China cabinet. My heart sank. *He knew I wanted a dining room, damn it.* From this vantage point, with a turn of the heel, I could view the entire first floor; it was smaller by far than our former apartment in St. Catharines. *What possessed Wes to purchase a house so tiny?*

"Wait till you see the basement," Wes announced excitedly, his voice rising in anticipation. He led us through the galley kitchen and down vinyl steps to the basement. "Look," he exclaimed, "The office!" He waved his hands enthusiastically. "Here's where I can do my lesson-planning, and marking, and reading for my courses, a place to set up my typewriter! And look at the built-in-book-cases for all my novels!"

An office, of course! That's what sold him on this house. There was an office for *him*! *To hell with what I wanted or what would be good for the boys. This is all about him!*

I was devastated, hurt, and disappointed all over again. I felt belittled, as if I were a child with no say, dismissed once more. Something cold and heavy settled in my stomach.

Reliving that scene almost 60 years ago, I realize that our marriage was a sham. It had been all about Wes; what was important to *him*, doing things *he* wanted, acquiring items *he* chose; going on trips *he* planned; purchasing the house *he* decided. *To hell with me!*

During those first years of marriage, I'd been living in a hazy world of dreams foisted on me by tradition of society, thinking I could create happiness. I refused to believe that Wes hadn't loved me when we married even though that truth became evident within a month of saying our vows. Lurking in a dark cloud, I was unable to face that reality head on. I'd been living my life half-asleep on hope, wishes, fantasy and dreams.

That reality suddenly smacked me in the face when Wes purchased our first house without my knowledge. That was the moment I faced the truth.

The Worst Of Times: Making The Best Of It

I felt miserable, alone, completely deserted: I lived in a house I didn't choose, and disliked, in a town foreign to me, had three preschoolers to care for, no family to turn to, and felt unloved by my husband. *How will I ever cope?* I had no choice; I had to make the best of it. It's what I always did to deal with misfortune. *What else could I do?* My boys Wesley, Blake and Ronnie, certainly helped me through. Funny, charming, adventurous, creative and sensitive, they replenished the emotional chasm in my psyche.

I shoved my anger and disappointment about the house aside and threw my energy into making it as attractive as possible. I painted the boys' bedroom banana-yellow and made yellow and orange striped denim roller-blinds, to match. I found a carpet on sale and covered the cement basement floor so the boys had a warm and comfortable place to play. I was particularly proud of carpeting the main bathroom floor; I did such a good job of piecing the stiff fabric around the toilet, that only an expert carpet-layer would have noticed the places I had patched over! By the end of the first year, we had fresh new carpet in the living-room and a classy new French-Provincial chesterfield and matching chair. We eventually gifted it to Blake and Suzie in their new house. My new-found decorating skills gave me a sense of self-worth.

I wanted the outside of our property to look nice:I maintained the rose hedge that grew along the side of the driveway and bloomed all summer long. I had the torn skin to prove it. I weeded the back garden and planted Shasta daisies and mauve phlox. I also regularly mowed the lawn and trimmed the privet hedges at the back yard. Before I knew it, I was taking on *all* the maintenance of our home, inside and out!

At the time, I believed I was doing it because Wes was working hard taking courses to up-grade his qualifications to advance his career. This would lead to a higher salary, and that would ultimately benefit the family. As for me, my hard work gave me a sense of accomplishment and a feeling of pride in our home.

Company and Revelations Come for Dinner

Company was coming for dinner. As the house took on renewed transformation, I wanted to show it off by planning a dinner party for our friends John and Stella. For weeks, I poured over cookbooks, sorted through recipes, and planned a menu. Mid-week, I mowed the lawn and weeded the rose hedge along the driveway. A day before the dinner, I dusted, vacuumed and washed and polished the kitchen floor. On the Saturday morning of the visit, I was in a flurry of activity—getting the boys dressed for the day and preparing breakfast for everyone. Wes finished his second cup of coffee and went downstairs to finish writing an essay for one of his courses. I cleared up the breakfast dishes, tidied the house, made the beds, and ran the vacuum over the carpet one last time. I took the three boys to the Galt market, and purchased fresh chicken, yellow beans, salad greens, and blueberries from the farm vendors.

After lunch, Wes and baby Ronnie napped, Blake and Wesley scampered down to the playroom, and I trimmed the ends off the beans, peeled the potatoes, and marinated the chicken. After making a blueberry cheesecake, I picked some mauve phlox from our garden for a table centrepiece. As I came in the back door, I remembered the last of the diapers in the dryer, I shoved the flowers into a vase, rushed down stairs to fold diapers, and watch the boys build their Lego towers.

Up from his nap, Wes returned to his desk and essay.

At five o'clock, I put the chicken in the oven, the potatoes on to boil and got supper for the children. As I cleared the table, I realized how tiny the eating area really *was*—the table and chairs filled it completely, with hardly an inch to spare. The memory of the dining-room in the Preston house flashed through my mind. I covered the table with the blue damask table cloth from Belgium, which, despite hanging to the floor in waves of extra fabric, dressed it up. The table looked quite elegant with the vase of mauve phlox against the blue damask and the table settings of fabulous Bavarian China and silverware we'd brought from Europe.

Running late, I changed Ronnie's diaper, sponge-bathed him, put him in a sleeper and tucked him into the rolling push-cart so he could paddle around the house.

Needing help at this point, I called to Wes. "Do you think you could supervise the boys' bath?" I asked. "I'm running out of time, and the company will be here in half an hour."

A *harrumph* and a mumble drifted up the stairs. "I'll come as soon as I finish this paragraph." The typewriter clacked away for several long minutes later. I filled the bathtub with water and had Wesley and Blake undressed and in the tub by the time Wes lumbered in and sat down on the toilet seat to supervise them. As I rushed out, I heard him say under his breath, "I shouldn't have to do this, gal damn it. Looking after the kids is *her* job." The comment stung as I raced back to the kitchen to prepare the salad and mash the potatoes.

The doorbell rang. "I'll get it," Wes shouted as he tore out of the bathroom and down the hall to the door to greet our guests, leaving me to dry the boys. "Oh, hello, Stella and John. Come in, come in," he said in a friendly tone. "Let me take your coats. Gail's running late, disorganized as always," I heard him add, as

I came round the corner to wave hello.

Going back to the bathroom I pulled the plug, gathered up the dirty clothes, wet towels, and threw them into the hamper. Wesley and Blake got into their Dr. Denton pyjamas (onesies) and went out to meet our guests. When it was time for bed, I got Ronnie out of his push-cart, carried him to his room, changed him a final time and tucked him into his crib. I kissed Wesley and Blake goodnight. *No time for stories tonight!*

While Wes visited with Stella and John, I returned to the kitchen; got the chicken out of the oven, finished mashing the potatoes and put the beans on to boil.

When dinner was ready, I motioned John to sit at one end of the table and Wes at the other. Stella wedged herself past John and sat facing me as I passed the platters around.

Stella took a bite of chicken. "This chicken is delicious," she said. "I'd like the recipe."

"Thanks," I replied, smiling in appreciation of the compliment.

"These beans taste wonderful," John remarked. "The spice adds a lot of flavour."

I beamed at the acknowledgement.

Wes chewed his chicken. A wrinkled frown crossed his forehead. "The chicken is too spicy," he growled. He lifted a forkful of potatoes to his mouth. He grimaced and chided, "The potatoes are lumpy."

The moment I finished typing the word, *'lumpy,'* a warm flush rose from my neck to my cheeks, and I was suddenly back in that kitchen sixty years ago. Stella winced and her eyes widened with pity. John reached over and patted my arm empathetically.

Tears welled up, and I *willed* them away. "I'll get the dessert ready." Pushing back my chair, I stood up and glared at Wes. Angry, I screamed inside my head. *What the hell is wrong with you? You did nothing to help me! You didn't lift a finger with the meal! You didn't even finish bathing the boys, for heaven's sake! All you are capable of is criticizing, damn it!*

When I reflect on that episode, I see that I still held my anger inside my head, unable to confront Wes and tell him what I really felt. That old fear from childhood held firm; confronting would lead to consequences, the wooden spoon on my backside. *You bet I avoided confrontation*! Perhaps, too, I was resorting to another method, also learned through from my mother's treatment of me: that if I gave enough, worked hard enough .... It was mistaken, but that concept seemed knitted through my body and mind; it was like connective tissue that held me together, as I wished for it to result in a better attitude from my husband. I had not yet internalized that the love I sought was simply not there. It is possible, I realize now, that the marriage may have survived had I received consideration, a helping hand, kind words, to show I was appreciated for all I did.

Criticism was what I got.

The Storm Windows: A Wake-Up Call for Change

The last of the petals had fallen on the rose hedge along the driveway. A hint of frost signaled that it was time to put up the storm windows. These were not thermal-double-plated windows, like we have today. They were a second set of wood-framed-panes of glass that were placed over the permanent windows; they were put up in the fall, taken off in the spring, and stored in the garage. Taking them off and putting them back on was a manual job that I'd done for a couple of years.

I chose to do this job on a mid-September day; the forecast promised sunshine with no indication of rain. As it was an all-day task, I got up first thing in the morning, while Wes was still in bed, and got breakfast for the boys. Now that they were older, they could be on their own until lunch; they could play in the family room, or out on the lawn–where I could keep an eye on them. Before the storm windows went up, I cleaned the permanent windows; I filled a pail with water and got a vinegar spray-bottle, a bunch of dry rags, and a ladder to wash them. I climbed up on the ladder–squeezing in behind the shrubbery at Ronnie's window–hung the pail of water onto the wooden flap, and started washing off the spring and summer grit. Ronnie waved to me from inside as I sprayed the pane with vinegar water and wiped it down with a dry cloth. I continued the process with the next window of the boys' room, and finally the picture window of the living room. I was sweating by the time I got to the back of the house to clean the last four windows. As I finished off our bedroom window, I saw that our bed was unmade–Wes was up. The noon sun was blazing hot by the time I'd wiped our window clean, and rivulets of sweat dripped off my forehead. It was more like a day in July, than September!

After I had made lunch for everyone, I threw the dishes into the sink and decided to put on my old turquoise one-piece bathing suit—the one I took to Europe ten years before when I was twenty–so I'd be cool in the afternoon. I checked the mirror; the suit still fit perfectly in all the right places. *Not bad after three babies!* I thought, as I went outside to start on the last, and biggest, task of putting up the storm window frames.

In the stuffy, humid, garage, I started hauling out the filthy storm windows and lined them up on either side of the garage, careful not to touch the Porsche that was stored inside. By the time all seven were washed, both front and back, I was sweating buckets. To cool off, I dashed through the sprinkler hose that I'd set out for the boys earlier. I manoeuvred the ladder into place under Ronnie's window; it was shiny and clean from the morning. I then hauled the matching storm window in behind the shrubbery, carefully moving it so as not to smudge the clean panes of glass. Grasping it tightly, I inched my way up the ladder rungs, step-by-step, balancing it with both hands. With a heave, I hoisted it over my head, placed it snugly against the permanent pane and twisted the wingnuts tightly in order to secure it. I climbed down, moved the ladder to the second window, and repeated the process. The living-room picture window was next, and it took all the energy I had to drag the giant heavy frame from the garage and rest it against the bricks beneath.

As I clamped my fingers around the frame, getting ready to heave it up, I heard a voice call out behind me, "Looks like you need some help." Startled, I jerked my head around to see John, our neighbour, trotting up our driveway toward me. "Where the heck is that husband of yours?" he cried, his eyes twinkling, a half grin on his face.

My cheeks flushed warm with embarrassment. "He's in the house writing an essay," I stuttered, suddenly feeling uncomfortable that our family life was exposed.

In a flash, John raced around the house to our

back door. With an uneasy feeling in my stomach, I ran after him and got to the back door just in time to hear him call down to Wes in the basement. "Hey man, what are you still doing sitting in your pyjamas in the middle of the day? Your wife is outside putting up the storm windows. You should be out there helping her. What's wrong with you, man?" My body filled with a cocktail of emotions—embarrassment, shame, humiliation, and vulnerability—from there, my mind goes blank. I have no memory of what Wes did, or how the rest of the storm window frames got hooked into place that day.

"What's wrong with you man; you should be out there helping your wife." Those words of reproof rang in my head. They were a wake-up call and forced me to face the reality of my life. Why *was* I putting up the storm windows by myself? Why *wasn't* Wes helping?

It suddenly dawned on me that it was *me* who had done the hard work to make our marriage work. It was *me* who tried so hard to please Wes, by being the perfect wife; it was *me* who cared for our babies with not an ounce of relief from him. It was *me* who did all the housework, with no assistance. And now, I had taken on the outside chores as well so *he* could advance his career. Like hoisting up those storm windows, it was *me* who had done the heavy lifting to keep this marriage together.

Teaching ESL: A Turning Point

I was like a truck in quick-sand, spinning my wheels and going nowhere–purposeless and with nothing to look forward to. I'd been sinking ever deeper into anger, disappointment and loneliness while the wheels of my life spit on my hopes and dreams and future happiness. It was time for me to claw out of this quagmire of despair and search for new ways to find fulfillment in my life.

The answer came, within a week, through the local paper. It had published an advertisement for ESL teachers (English Second Language). *I had teaching qualifications! I could teach in the evenings*. My heart skipped a beat; I felt lightness filling my chest as if the 'ad' was made for *me*.

Imagining the possibility, I could hardly wait to check it out with Wes. The children were tucked in bed for the night, when I approached him the next evening. "I saw an ad in the paper last night," I said cautiously, tentatively. "It's for teaching ESL to new Canadian adults." Wes looked up from his novel, a deadpan look on his face. "It would be in the evenings," I explained quickly while I still had the nerve. Deep furrows knitted his forehead and his lips stretched into a thin, straight, line. "I'd like to apply," I said, like a child begging permission for a sleepover with a friend.

Wes paused in thought and took another sip

of coffee; he swallowed and cleared his throat. "Yes … you … can," he said, enunciating each word slowly and contemplatively. My heart fluttered with anticipation. "However," he added, his voice increasing in volume, "I will expect a four course meal at supper time." *He's putting up road blocks, damn it. What's wrong with him?* But this was really important to me. So, I tilted my head in agreement. "And," he said as if an afterthought. *Oh god what now?* "The children will have to be bathed and ready for bed before you go." *What? Why can't you look after the boys once a week? They're your children too?*

"All right," I said, trying to hide the annoyance in my voice, willing to do whatever it took to do something for *me* for a change, to have the chance to do something *I* wanted to do, instead of being shackled to the house and *his* demands.

As I write this in 2025, I chuckle. Anyone knowing me today would laugh at this exchange. Imagine having to ask permission to teach a night-school class once a week! How absurd to be under a husband's thumb like that! It was unbelievable that I didn't have the gumption to confront him or object to his conditions! But at *that* time, I didn't have the self confidence to challenge his authority, not like I would today.

I applied and got the job.

At five o'clock the boys were bathed, the chicken out of the oven, the vegetables drained, the potatoes mashed and the cobbler steaming on the counter as Wes drove up the driveway. Supper finished, I got the dishes done, kissed the boys and waved goodbye. As I gathered my bag of supplies and headed to my very first ESL class and ignored the scowl on Wes' face.

Things went well—until one evening, a few weeks later, when Wes wasn't home at five o'clock. At five-thirty, he was still not home. I served supper to the children, bathed them and got them into their pyjamas. As it got close to six, my hands started to sweat; my class started at seven, and Wes was still not home. *Where in the world was he?* I was frustrated and angry when the screen door slammed shut, announcing he was home. It was 6:30 and I barely had time to get to my class.

"I got delayed," Wes stated. A smirk creased the side of his cheek, there was not a hint of apology, or explanation. I knew that smirk and the negative memories that went with it; it did not bode well.

"Your plate is in the oven," I said irritation in my voice.

"Aren't you going to stay and do the dishes?"

"Nope," I replied, "I'm late." I kissed the boys and left.

As I drove off to school that evening, I couldn't

help wondering if Wes had *deliberately* been tardy in order to make me late for class, to cause me to cancel it or dissuade me to give up teaching entirely. When I got home that night, his supper dishes were still on the table.

As I reflect on teaching ESL students, reviving the career I loved so much, I gain a renewed sense of success and accomplishment. I'd found a sense of balance—of being home with the boys every day while, for a few hours one evening a week, I did something for *me*. I escaped Wes' demands at home; I felt like a prisoner released from jail.

The Porsche for Supply-Teaching?

"The local Board of Education is always looking for supply teachers, Gail," my neighbour John told me the following spring. I mulled over the idea that summer. It would only be a few times a month. Wesley and Blake would both be in school, so I'd be home at the same time as them. Of course, I'd have to get a baby sitter for Ronnie, who was not yet in kindergarten, on those few days I taught. It wouldn't affect Wes at all, since I'd be home well before him.

When I stopped to think about it, the only problem I could foresee was which car I would use—the station wagon or the Porsche. *It would have to be the station wagon. Wes would never let me drive the Porsche!* He only drove it on special occasions, polished it almost every weekend, and had it tuned-up by a German mechanic every year to keep it in shape so it would run as long as possible. *He'll never let me drive the Porsche!*

When I approached Wes about supply-teaching, I anticipated his response, "It will be all right, as long as you have a four-course meal for supper at five o'clock every evening."

"Okay," I agreed. "The work will be in the daytime, so which car would you like me to drive?"

Wes sat quietly for a very long moment. He drummed his fingers on the table and twisted his mouth to one side—a thing he did when he was trying to make up his mind about something. When he cleared his throat, I knew he'd made his decision. He looked at me calmly and stated in a firm and confident voice, "You can drive the *Porsche*."

Shocked, my eyes grew wide in surprise. I was stunned, completely overwhelmed by his confidence in me, his kindness, and his generosity.

I have to admit that it was a challenge getting used to the stick-shift, and I never revved it like Wes did in Europe to show off its power. But I drove it just fine. On the two or three days I was a supply teacher, the boys were delighted when I dropped them off at school in the gleaming red sports car. For years, I was curious why Wes had allowed me to drive his precious

Porsche, back then. I found out, thirty years later. It was *not* because Wes had confidence in me, nor had it been out of his generosity. In his fifties, son Blake and his friend Gina visited us at our cottage on Lake Erie. Blake was reminiscing about growing up in Cambridge. "Dad had a Porsche," he told Gina. "He *loved* that car." His eyes grew thoughtful and an impish grin tugged at the side of his mouth, just like his father's. Nodding across at me, his smile widened. "When I was a teenager, Mom, Dad told me why he'd offered you the Porsche to drive for supply teaching."

Jolted, I sat up stock still, and tilted my head toward Blake. I didn't want to miss a single word.

"Dad assumed that you wouldn't *want* to drive the Porsche because it was a stick-shift and you'd be so intimidated by its power, you'd *decline* his offer and would consequently give up the whole *idea* of supply-teaching all together."

My jaw dropped open. Fury raged through my body. *What a manipulator! What kind of man does that to his wife? What kind of father brags about it to his teenage son!*

Irony Rules: The Day the Porsche Died

The day I wrecked the Porsche was a miserable, cold, winter morning. I was making porridge for the boys when the phone rang from the School Board. "A teacher called in sick just minutes ago and we wondered if you could come in to supply." Although it was pretty late to be calling, I said yes, since it was for a school about a five-minute drive away. The moment I hung up the phone, I thought of the Porsche. Not made to withstand Canadian winters, it was sometimes difficult to start, and it took a long time for the engine to warm up. I turned the heat down on the porridge, grabbed a jacket, threw it on over my dressing gown, yanked on a pair of rubber boots, snatched the keys, and flew out the front door to the garage. The wind caught my breath, and swirled around my bare legs, and up my nightgown as I pushed up the sliding garage door. Hiking up my nightgown, I crawled onto the leather seat, crackling cold on my behind. A twist and turn of the key, the engine groaned awake. I backed it out onto the driveway and left it idling. *Thank goodness, it started!* I rushed back inside to get washed and dressed, and woke up the boys.

On my way back to the kitchen, I gave the porridge a stir, threw on my coat and boots, and dashed out to check on the Porsche. To my disappointment the motor had stalled. When I turned the key, the engine coughed and grumbled, but finally puffed to life and held with a *rum, rum* sound. I jumped out of the car and I tore up the steps into the house. I got the boys washed and dressed and set their porridge on the table. While they were eating, I went to the front door and listened. *Damn! The Porsche had stalled again!* This time, the engine stuttered and turned over. But, when I lifted my foot off the accelerator, it sputtered to a stop. *If only I could find something to hold the gas pedal down!* I checked around the side of the garage and spotted a brick peeking up out of the snow. Dusting the snow off, I placed it carefully on the gas pedal at just the right angle to keep the motor humming. The car now purred, smooth as a kitten. Ripping back into the house, I cleared the table, and helped the boys into their snowsuits and boots. Stepping outside, I spun the key in the door with a *click*. It was the only sound we heard. A cloud of steam rose in the frosty air. Silence. The Porsche was dead.

The day the tow-truck came to take the Porsche away, I felt embarrassed, and guilty too, at what I'd done. I knew nothing about cars; I had no idea that putting a brick on the accelerator could burn out the engine. I felt terrible.

As the front end of the Porsche raised up, and the tow-truck eased down the driveway, Wes stood in the middle of the street. His face was puffy and red, his shoulders were slumped and his arms hung slack at the side of his thighs. When the tow truck turned up the street, Wes hung his head, his eyes glistening with tears, and his chin trembling, as he watched his beloved Porsche grow smaller and smaller—it rolled out of sight, forever.

Although the Porsche was no longer in sight, Wes remained in the street, looking forlornly in the distance. I wondered what was going through his mind. Did he have visions of past grandeur, his prestige and pride, as he flew around Europe like a celebrity? I imagined that he felt great sadness and despair at his loss.

Wes turned abruptly, then. He stomped back up the empty driveway: fists clenched, his mouth twisted into a glower, his nostrils flared, and every cell of his body stoked with anger. He glared at me for smashing his dream. I don't believe he *ever* forgave me.

Now, fifty years later, I speculate whether Wes ever examined the role that *he* had played in the demise of the Porsche. It was *he* who insisted I drive his Porsche when the station wagon would have suited me far better, given I had the three boys in tow. Did he ever examine his motives for that decision in the first place? He'd hoped the Porsche would be too intimidating for me to drive; he wanted to dissuade me from teaching at all and to spoil my desire to rediscover a profession I loved. Did he consider any of that? It is ironic that his ill-will toward me played such a major role in the whole story. It is true karma.

Not Smart Enough

"It's her first year of teaching, and Sylvia makes way more than me," I overheard a teacher complain, as I hung up my coat in the staff room of the school where I was supplying. "It's only because she has her degree," her friend responded. I perked up my ears and listened. "And it's not fair to those of us who got a one-year teaching certificate from Teachers' College."

This was a revelation to me. If *I* ever went back to teaching, I'd be in the same boat!

On the way home that day, that staff room conversation rolled around in my mind. I enjoyed teaching only a few days a month because I wanted to be home with the boys. But if I ever wanted to teach full time, this would be a great opportunity to start getting a degree, one course at-a-time—like Wes did to get his honours degree in English. *I could start mine!* Eventually, Wes would have free time in the evenings to look after the children, and I could start *my* degree. Afterall, while he was studying those five years, *I* did all the child care and maintained the household to lighten *his* load. *It was my turn, now.*

Opening up the conversation with Wes, I complimented him. "I'm glad that you got your Honours degree; it was a long haul over the past five years and you worked really hard for it." Wes looked up and smiled. *This was my chance.* "Now that you have more free time, I'd like to start *my* degree, maybe take a night course once a week." I paused and took a deep breath. "What do you think, Wes?"

His eyebrows lifted in surprise. "What?" he exclaimed, his lips twisting to the side of his mouth in a smirk. "You're not *smart* enough" he chuckled. "Why, you wouldn't be able to *pass* a university course," he said derisively, his lips turning up into a sarcastic smile. "Why, you're just an *elementary* teacher." He paused then and wagged his head from side to side in disbelief. "Why, you don't even *read!*"

His words punched me in the gut, colour drained from my face, my chest tightened and my throat went dry. Tongue-tied, I got up, grabbed my sweater, and stomped out the door. I was ignited with hot red fury! *How insulting, you bastard, how demeaning! How dare you attack my intelligence! Not smart enough? I graduated with honours from high school, qualified for university ...I'm smart enough. I can pass a goddamn university course, if only I had the chance.* I turned the corner and walked down a side street. *I don't read, you say. When in the world do I have time to read, with babies on my hip for years, meals to prepare, and chores to do so this household works? And what thanks do I get from you? Nothing but criticism!* It was so unfair. All I wanted was to *start* my degree, but without his help to look after the boys once a week, I saw no possible way to get it. Crushed, defeated, and disheartened, I trudged back down the street home.

On *that day,* as I tromped back into the house, I felt as if Wes had plunged a sword deep into the very essence of who I was, leaving me eviscerated. His words festered for years; they caused doubt deep inside me, stomped on my worth and self-confidence, and fed my uncertainty. His words haunted me: *what if he were right? what if I wasn't smart enough to get a degree?* I was terrified when started my BA at McMaster. When I went on to enroll in a Masters at Brock, his words stoked my fear of failure. *Not smart enough?* Twenty years later, at the University of Toronto, I earned my doctorate.

Rubbed Out

I was burdened with unspoken dark thoughts, as the days plodded on. A cloud of despair crept over me. I looked in the mirror; my eyes were dull and hollow with purple smudges beneath. My skin was washed out and sallow. I grimaced. *When was the last time I smiled?* I couldn't recall. My hair was dull and lifeless, and it hung in dank, oily strands. *Who was this stranger? No-one I knew.*

I fell into a listless routine, day after day—nothing gave me hope, or promise that tomorrow would be different. The house closed in on me as I unravelled and became insignificant, diminished, rubbed out.

I stood in the kitchen and looked into the tiny dinette, the electric floor-polisher—the one Wes purchased for my birthday years ago—in my hand. Its whirring motor, which was vibrating through the house moments ago, is silent. Wesley and Blake were at school and Ron was napping down the hall. The beds were made, the dishes were done, the carpet was vacuumed, the linoleum gleamed, bright and shiny, and the smell of wax tingled in my nostrils. I stared into the quiet, stillness ... silence. The house was like a tomb.

"Is this all there is!?" I shouted to the equally soundless table and chairs. Is this what life offers, for the next forty years? How will my time on earth be marked? Who will remember me? And for what?

I stepped up to the reception desk and confirmed my appointment with Dr. Fraser for a bladder infection. I was led into his examining room. Dr. Fraser came in shortly after; he had a kind smile on his lips and my chart in his hand. "So, you've got a bladder infection again," he said, taking out his pen and scribbling down a prescription for antibiotics. I sighed and smiled wanly. "Are you all right?" Dr. Fraser asked kindly, reaching over, putting his hand on my shoulder. His touch was gentle. I couldn't recall the last time I'd felt a warm touch from an adult. "You're looking rather sad. Is something wrong?"

Hearing such sensitive, caring questions, my

eyes thickened with tears, bubbling over, running down my cheeks onto my dress. In an instant, I was engulfed in overwhelming sadness, sobbing uncontrollably, in ragged gulps. I clenched my hands on the arms of the chair in an attempt to stop the flow. I tried to speak over the pounding of my heart. No words would come. Dr. Fraser handed me a tissue and sat patiently, as I daubed my eyes and blew my nose. As my breathing began to slow and my body relaxed, I stuttered my apology.

"No need to be sorry," he said, gently. "You seem depressed—in fact, that's what I've written on your chart for over a year now. Do you want to tell me what's going on?" Once started, I couldn't stop. I poured out my grief, giving him a glimpse of what life was like for me. Dr. Fraser sat and listened patiently. When I finally fell silent, he spoke. "It sounds as though your marriage is in trouble," he said, empathetically. He rubbed his chin for a moment as if something had just occurred to him. He reached for a pamphlet. "Our clinic has a new counselling team that specializes in marriage problems. Would you consider seeing them?" he asked, patting my hand.

"If you think it might help, I'd be willing to try." I paused, and then recalled Wes' attitude toward me. "Though I'm not sure that Wes would go for it."

"I'll have a talk with him."

Will Marriage Counselling Work?

As Wes parked the car at the counsellor's office for the session that day, my heart pounded with anxiety. Fred and Bob had led us through several sessions related to our backgrounds, our perspectives on marriage, how we dealt with emotions, solved problems, shared the work-load of running a house and raising children. It was the spring of 1970. During *this* session, they had summarized our responses from over many sessions and were ready to share their observations and offer strategies for us to work on.

Bob took the lead. "First, we want to compliment you both for engaging in marriage counselling. That takes a lot of courage, and we hope that the sessions have been useful to you both." Wes and I dipped our heads in agreement. "We've reviewed our notes and want to share with you what we observed.

"We noticed that your marriage reflects traditional roles," he said looking over at Wes. "For example, you have taken on the traditional role of *'breadwinner'*, Wes. With your good job, you provide well for your family and manage the household finances." Wes smiled, bobbing his chin up and down, puffing out his chest.

It made me wonder if Wes thought that this is the way things *ought* to be, that he was doing his job as a husband and nothing more was expected of him.

He probably felt justified in not lifting a finger to wash a dish, or change a diaper. I imagined him thinking, *That's Gail's job; I'm not a babysitter!*

"Gail, you have assumed the homemaker role, for the most part, doing all the shopping, cleaning, house work and child-rearing." Wes nodded his head in agreement as if that's how it should be. "In addition, Gail, you have also taken on many of the outdoor tasks traditionally assigned to husbands, like mowing the lawn, gardening and hanging up storm windows."

That was *exactly* how it was for me; I suddenly felt acknowledged, that they had noticed. Maybe Wes will recognise how tired, overworked and exhausted I was, and offer to help.

Bob locked his eyes on Wes. "While these roles may have been the norm for decades, they have become somewhat out-of-date as we move into the 1970's, especially when we consider the effects of the Women's Movement."

A warm flush washed over Wes' face, and his eyebrows pinched together at 'Women's Movement.' He shot a look at me that could cut glass. I found the comment both enlightening and confusing at the same time. Bob seemed to be questioning the validity of the traditional roles, the very roles Wes and I believed in when we got married ten years ago. Much of it had been very rewarding. However, after ten years in the role as full-time housewife, and mother, it had lost its charm. But Wes seemed to want to maintain the traditional role of husband.

Bob turned the page in his notebook. "Now, I'd like to talk about how you both deal with emotions. "Wes, your emotions generally focus on criticism, anger and controlling situations." Wes nodded in agreement. "Gail finds this behaviour unsettling. In fact, she's stated that she is fearful of your anger, and we notice that she does everything she can to avoid any action that might provoke you, or cause an angry outburst." Wes raised his eyebrows in a question. From my perspective, the counsellors had observed our behaviours to a 'T'. I *was* frightened of Wes's anger, when he yelled at me, criticized me in front of others, and demeaned my intelligence. I *did* pussy-foot around him to avoid conflict. "We see this as unhealthy in a marriage," Bob pointed out. Wes cocked his head to one side, and his bottom lip twisted as if trying to make sense of this. Then, his eyes squinted shut, he thrust out his lower lip in a pout, "Well, that's just the way I *am*," he cried out loudly, as if to justify his behaviour. His fingers clenched into a fist. Fred took a sip of coffee and ignored his outburst.

He turned to me. "Gail, we notice that you are positive in your interactions with Wes and the children. But it seems to us that you try to keep the peace at any cost in order to avoid conflict, and we believe that it is at great expense to your own emotional wellbeing. He set his cup down. "We find your passive behaviour emotionally unhealthy in a marriage." I was confused by this. Wasn't being positive and avoiding dissention a *good* thing? *And how in heck is that unhealthy to my well being?*

"Now, Fred will address some specific things we want you to think about that might support your relationship. "Gail, while it's good that you try to appease Wes by taking on additional tasks about the house, we'd like you to consider being more assertive, by stating your feelings. For example, you could tell Wes how tired you are putting up the storm windows by yourself. And you might ask him to take over the lawn mowing sometimes."—*That* pissed me off. Couldn't Wes *see* how over-loaded I was doing all the chores around the house? Couldn't he *see* that I needed help with the cleaning and support with the children? Wasn't it obvious? Shouldn't it be *his* responsibility to help out? Why do *I* have to point it out? Fred's comment made me feel as though it was my own *fault* for being overworked! "We also encourage you to speak up more, Gail, and even confront Wes when you disagree with him, or when his anger frightens you. You could tell him that when he criticizes you, or raises his voice, it scares you, and ask him to stop."

Speak up and confront Wes? Look at how he treats me now when I placate him. I can't imagine his reaction if I dared confront him or argue with him. *He'd blow his stack or worse!*

Overwhelmed, I just shook my head at how unrealistic Fred's suggestions were.

Fred turned to Wes. "And Wes, we'd like you to consider moving out of your comfort zone as 'breadwinner,' and think about taking on more responsibility around the house, like helping with the vacuuming, cooking, doing dishes or laundry, for example." A look of dismay and disbelief came over Wes' face. He sat dazed as if he'd just landed on a different galaxy. A frown furrowed across his forehead, and his lips pursed tight together in a grimace. "And Wes, we also suggest that it would be helpful if you took a more active role with the children, like bathing them and getting them ready for bed, for instance." Wes' jaw dropped as if dumbfounded. His face bloomed red, his eyes blazed, the veins in his neck pulsated. I believe a muscle ticked at his jaw. Shaking his head back and forth, he coughed and sputtered before he lashed out. "What!" he bellowed, his face quivering in anger. "I've given her a house, a car, and three healthy sons. What the hell more does she want?"

Fred looked at him with steady, unblinking eyes and replied calmly, "You are right about how you provide for the family. However, a good marriage requires helping each other, listening to each other, and being respectful of each others' needs. In a good marriage, partners need to be appreciated, and cared about." Fred paused then and took a deep breath before continuing. "We'd just like you to try to be a bit more flexible and think about some of the strategies we've suggested that could strengthen your relationship with Gail. We'd just like you to *think* about it."

Bob interjected at this point. "Now that summer is almost here, we wondered if you might use that time to mull over what we've discussed and try out some of these suggestions. Maybe do something special with the family to reconnect; perhaps go on a trip or take a holiday together."

Their suggestions had some potential. Was it possible for me to be more assertive, speak up more? *Could I?* And, if Wes took any of their recommendations seriously, it would make a huge difference to me and to our relationship. *Would he? Could he?*

Wes closed his eyes and folded his arms firmly across his chest. His lips quivered but no sound came. I could see displeasure written all over his face and imagined the scream inside his head: *This is all a pile of bullshit.*

Who Owns Our Home?
Legality Of Home Ownership

Do I own half of our home on Dudhope Avenue? I think I do....but... two years later, in 1968, I learn that maybe I don't.

I am at the dentist, waiting for my appointment. My friend, Sandy, is looking after four-year-old Blake and Ron, still a toddler. I sort through the magazines on the sidetable: *News Week, Chatelaine, Time* I pick up *Chatelaine. I'll look for recipes*, I think. I thumb through pages. A headline catches my eye: "*Irene Murdoch; Women's Property Rights.*" I'm curious and read on. Irene Murdoch is suing her abusive husband of twenty-five years for a divorce; she seeks half the value of their 480 acre ranch in the Alberta foothills. In the article, she tells the court of the work she did on the ranch. "*I did anything that required doing, like haying, raking, swathing, driving trucks, tractors, and teams of horses, quieting horses, taking cattle back and forth on the ranch, dehorning, vaccinating and branding. I worked outside with him, just as a man would. I just thought when you went into a marriage it was a partnership basis: fifty/fifty.*"

My stomach tightens, I read the phrase again, "*I just thought when you went into a marriage it was a partnership basis: fifty/ fifty.*" That comment strikes a chord. That's what I think too. Fifty/fifty–husbands work outside the home, and wives look after husbands, maintain the household and raise the children. When it comes to property, it's a fifty/fifty deal too. Isn't it?

The dentist is ready. I have a tooth filled and leave the office with a gnawing feeling that has nothing to do with the freezing in my cheek.

As I pull out of the dentist's parking lot, I wonder what relevance the Murdoch story has for me. My mind wanders. *When Wes purchased our home, I didn't question if my name was on the deed. I just assumed it* was, and that the house was half mine. But after reading about Irene Murdoch, I am not so sure. At any rate, there is nothing I can really do about it now. I am committed to the marriage, and as far as the Irene Murdock case is concerned, I'll put my trust in the courts. I can't think about it now; I have shopping to do, children to pick up, and dinner to get ready.

I put the whole thing out of my mind and headed to the supermarket.

****

Five years later, in 1973, after going through to the Supreme Court of Canada, Irene Murdoch lost her case! The Supreme Court ruled that she did not qualify for a share in her husband's property, and Irene was required to pay a portion of her husband's legal costs!

Women across Canada were outraged at the injustice of the verdict. As a result, every province across the country eventually changed their matrimonial laws to protect women's right to communal property; in Ontario, the law was changed in 1979.

After learning of the verdict of the case, I thought back to 1966. I realized, that I had no legal right to shared equity in our Dudhope home. It never crossed my mind that my name would not be on the deed, when Wes purchased it without my knowledge or consent. I had been angry that he had not consulted me. Like Irene Murdoch, I'd put my trust in my husband and the Canadian justice system.

If I had known, in 1966, that I had no legal status to our home on Dudhope, would I have behaved any differently? *What could I have done? What would my options have been? I could have demanded to see the deed, but I had to consider Wes' reaction. He'd have been angry that I'd questioned his authority; he'd yell, be sarcastic. I was afraid of him, afraid of his anger. In those years I did everything to appease in order to avoid his wrath. I wouldn't have had the courage to challenge him.*

I could have taken him to court, I suppose, but I had no money to do that. I'd cashed in my Alberta teacher pension to purchase the washer and dryer. I had no income. I was totally dependent on Wes for everything. Besides, Irene Murdoch lost her case. The law at the time was stacked against me, too. Like Irene, I would have been in society's trap; I couldn't get free.

Thinking back, *I probably wouldn't have acted any differently. I really had no options. When Wes chose and purchased the house, I was too busy to even consider whether I was on the deed. I had two preschoolers in tow, a baby on the way, a husband to care for, and a household to run.* That had become my world. Like wives everywhere, I had put all my faith in my husband, trusting in the myth that we had a fifty/fifty partnership.

THE SEVENTIES:
Endings And New Beginnings

Marriage Counselling: Facing the Truth

The last marriage counselling session with Fred and Bob happened on a gloomy, and blistery, cold February day. We shook the snow off our boots, and hung our coats on the hook at the door. We held hot mugs of coffee as the session started. Bob smiled and nodded his head at both of us. "Have you given some thought about where you'd like to go from here?" He took a sip of coffee and turned to Wes.

Wes tapped his foot on the carpet floor, nervously. "I guess I've been living in the past," he said slowly, thoughtfully. "I have a good job and provide well for my family. It's what I've grown up with, and it worked well for my parents, and my brothers—the men work outside the home, and the wives are homemakers and look after the children—that's what I expect Gail to do. His eyes furrowed, and he hunched his shoulders. "Besides, Gail's a *mother,* she knows how to do all those things, like laundry and looking after the children, and she's good at it."

A chill inched up my spine. Nothing had changed … it probably never would ….

"And," Wes added, "I don't think I *need* to make

any changes. Like I said last time, I've given her a house, a car, and three healthy boys. What more does she want from me?" He made one final tap with his foot, to punctuate his stance.

Bob nodded to me for a response. A feeling of sadness washed over me as I pondered what to say. I knitted my fingers together, and sighed. "I've lived with my marriage like this for ten years now and I'm doing all right," I muttered, folding my hands in my lap. "I *have* to stay in the marriage, for the sake of our boys." Wes smiled contentedly, as if satisfied that I had finally come to my senses.

The counsellors gasped and leaned into each other, chatting softly as if conferring on a response. Bob cleared his throat. "I don't know exactly how to put this," he said slowly, cautiously, yet with deliberation. "Fred and I have observed you for more than a year now, Gail. We believe that you are very unhappy in your marriage and appear to be extremely depressed." His voice lowered to almost a whisper. "Fred and I predict that you are close to a nervous breakdown. We wonder what good you will be for your children if you end up in *Homewood*, the psychiatric facility in Guelph?"

Through a hazy veil, I heard Bob speak to Wes. "When a spouse is not willing to deal with issues in their marriage, or make attempts to meet the needs of their partner, then we believe that the marriage has very little hope of succeeding."

"This is ridiculous," Wes shouted, his voice rising in anger. "Come on Gail, we're out of here.

The Marriage Unravelled

The session was over; Wes stood up, planting his feet solidly on the floor and a look of consternation on his face. Wes lifted his heavy-knit sweater from the hook on the counselors' door. "This counselling nonsense is a pile of crap," he growled as he thrust his arms into the sleeves of his bulky-knit-sweater. "Come on Gail," he barked at me in his commanding voice I knew so well. "We're getting the hell out-of-here." He twisted the last button of his sweater into place. "*I'm* going to see *our* United Church Minister. *He'll* set things straight!"

With sadness, I remembered knitting that sweater last fall, the click-clacking needles the size of broom handles, weaving the wool thick as rope, as if I were *knitting* our marriage together, strengthening it with every stitch, holding it firm. At times, I unravelled sections and started anew, like the pattern of our marriage that kept coming undone. I was hopeful that this last marriage counselling session would bring our lives closer together with renewed direction and change for the better.

I sat immobilized. The words of the counsellors rolled over me like a paving machine. They had warned me; *You are close to a nervous breakdown if you stay in this marriage...end up in a psych ward ...* At that moment I felt something strange come over me, a shift, as if I were suddenly a different person with a renewed spirit. "What good will I be to my children, then?" I said to myself with sudden resolve. *My children need me!*

Wes frowned, rocking side-to side on his feet with impatience. "Get a move on, Gail," he roared.

Reluctant to react to his order, I rose slowly from my chair. With a determination new to me I grabbed my winter coat, and yanked up my fleece-lined-boots.

As we opened the door, a blast of driving snow greeted us. The car was a mound of white, like meringue on a lemon pie. I trudged through the drift to the passenger side, the snow whipping at my legs as I climbed in.

Wes slid into the driver's side, started the engine, and reached for the snow brushes in the side pocket of his door. He flipped one over to me.

I sat glued to my seat and, with knees bent and my hands clasped on my lap, stared straight ahead, *I'll be damned if I am going to clear the snow; I've had enough of this man!*

"Aren't you going to help brush the snow off the

car?" Wes asked, sounding surprised that I wasn't already out of the car and helping, like I'd always done in the past.

"Nope!" I said with confidence I didn't know I had. *How does it feel to do a job all by yourself with no one helping you?* I muttered under my breath. *You didn't lift a finger to change a diaper or wash a dish, or sweep a floor ... not ever!*

Wes scowled, his eyes squinting as if he couldn't understand what had just happened. "Gall damnit," he mumbled as he slammed the door and stomped to the front of the car. He swiped the brush across the hood of the station wagon in a fit of rage.

It was unnatural for me to be so saucy—flippant even—not to lend a hand. But I took a certain amount of satisfaction in the reversal of roles. *Where were you when I was mowing the lawn, putting up the storm windows, and shovelling the driveway by myself so you could write essays for your Honours English degree!* The snow pelted the windshield so hard I could barely see a thing. *After all I'd done for you, the gall of you telling me that I wasn't smart enough to pass a university course.* "You're only an *elementary* teacher," you'd scorned. *The arrogance of you, demeaning me like that!*

As Wes swatted the car with the brush, snow flew in all directions; he glared at me through the side window. I pursed my lips and glowered back. *I wanted to save our marriage, but you refused to do a thing that the counselors suggested. You didn't think you had to.* "After all," you insisted, "I'm the *breadwinner* of the family. It's the wife's job to look after the kids, make good meals and manage the household."

Thwack! went the brush, releasing the last of the excess snow from the car. Wes opened the car door and slid into the driver's seat, his face flushed beet-red, . "At least you could have helped sweep, gall damnit," he sneered curtly, as he slammed the door shut, like a clap of thunder.

The shoulders of his heavy-knit sweater glistened and sparkled with the melting snowflakes. I could hardly see the rust-coloured triangles peeking through.

How I'd loved knitting every one of those triangles … back then.

Now … I had the greatest urge to *snip* a strand of wool with my razor-sharp, sewing scissors, and *yank* … unwind every strand like he'd unravelled our marriage and my life … unstitch every dream, every promise, every wish, obliterating all hope. With the mountain of multicoloured skeins of wool heaped on the car floor in front of me … I'd stomp on it like he had on my heart.

But . . . I didn't have my razor-sharp, silver, pair of scissors.

We Saw Our Minister

"I'm going to see our minister" ... "He'll set things right!!" Wes was determined that our Minister would see things differently. Within days we were sitting in his office, at the church we'd attended for the past ten years. We spent several sessions with him; we went over the same issues and questions we'd done previously with the marriage counsellors. Over those sessions my mind floated in and out of reality as if I was in a dream ...

"It was all a pile of crap," Wes argued, "they wanted me to do chores" ...

... Bob's voice echoed in my ears. *You are depressed, Gail* ... My lips quivered, tears misted ... . . . Wes ranted on ... "they said I should vacuum, do dishes" ...

... I blinked my tears away. *You could end up in a psychiatric ward.* ...

... "I provide for my family, had a good job." ...

... *I'll be damned if I'll end up in Homewood* ...

... "gave her a house, a car, and three healthy boys" ...

... I clenched my teeth ... *my boys need me!* ...

Wes cried out, seething, "What the hell more does she want, gal damn it?"

Jarred by his outburst, I was dragged back to the present.

The room fell silent; the atmosphere grew heavy with emotion. I braced myself for what was to come.

The Reverend sat still, as if he was deliberating on how to proceed. His lips turned up at the corners, but concern lurked behind his smile. I swallowed against the lump that was forming in my throat, and waited for a verdict. His voice calm, the Reverend focussed his eyes directly on Wes. "You don't seem to grasp that you're not providing Gail the emotional support she needs in order to make your marriage work," he said ruefully. "You're stuck in the traditional role of 'breadwinner' as if that's enough," he stated, his voice rising. "You need to *listen* more, try to respond to what Gail needs, help with the housework, and the boys, be more affectionate and appreciative of what she does for you."

My heart lifted; maybe Wes would see the light and make some changes. The Reverend—the one person he seemed to trust—would be by his side to give him the support he needed.

Wes scowled; the colour drained from his face.

The Reverend went on. "But you can't seem to do that, and you're not even willing to *try*," he added, sounding exasperated.

Wes sat quietly for several long minutes; his

brow wrinkled as if in thought.

I held my breath—hoping ....

A far off look in his eyes, Wes finally spoke, his voice slow, deliberate, contemplative. "I guess I *can't* change," he muttered. "I'm too set in my ways." His voice was flat, detached. "I guess the marriage is *over.*"

My body went numb, a boulder settled in the pit of my stomach. I couldn't believe what I was hearing. *Was he throwing our marriage away after all the counselling, after all our hard work?* Here was a chance for him to make a difference, with someone he admired, someone he trusted. How could he sit there, so stoic, so unmoved, so resigned, and so detached? He'd shown more feeling when I wrecked his Porsche than he had for his children or for me. My throat tightened in anger. *Where were his tears? Where was his pain?*

"So, what do I do now?" Wes asked, his voice calm and steady.

"What?!" Rage coursed through me. "You're going to give up? You aren't even going to try to make our marriage work? What's wrong with you?"

Wes shrugged his shoulders, "It's over," he repeated, sounding resigned.

Fear and panic slammed into my chest.

"Are you sure?" the Reverend queried. "Have you completely given up?" There was a glimmer of optimism in his voice.

"I'm done," Wes said, his voice rising. "So, what do I do now?"

The Reverend shifted in his chair, hunched his shoulders and took a deep breath before answering. A sombre look came across his face. "I guess," he said soberly, "You *could* move out of the house." He sounded uncomfortable making the suggestion.

"When?" Wes asked, his voice unemotional as if he were inquiring about the date of vacation plans.

"I suppose," the Reverend responded, shaking his head, "as soon as possible." He sounded ill-at-ease with how Wes was expecting him to make decisions for him.

"I can't move out *now*," Wes stammered. "There's three months left of school!"

"Move out in the summer when school is over, Wes," the Reverend retorted, sounding annoyed. "Get yourself an apartment in Guelph to be near your work."

"All right," Wes mumbled calmly, his voice relaxed, relieved. "I guess I can do that." He paused, drumming his fingers on the desk. "Yes, yes, I'll move out this summer." He sounded unruffled, unperturbed as if everything was falling into place.

"Move out? Leave us?" I yelled. "What the heck are you talking about?" Fear and anger gripped my throat. "Are you going to leave the boys and me, simply walk out?" I took a deep breath. "You'd rather leave your family than wash a bloody dish?" I slammed my hand down on the desk. "What kind of a fool are you?"

My emotions were in a turmoil—dread, fear, pain ... *What will the boys and I do if he leaves us? Where will we go? What will become of us?* Wes was behaving erratically, crazily; surely, he'd come to his senses.

But Wes was dead serious.

When he started looking for a place in Guelph, I had to face the reality. He was leaving his sons, Wesley age 10, Blake at 7, little Ronnie only 4... and me.

"You'll have to tell my parents we are separating," Wes announced one day in the middle of June. "No-one has ever divorced in *my* family and *I'm* not going to tell them; *you'll* have to."

"Why the hell do *I* have to tell them," I argued. "You are the one leaving us."

"Just do it, gal damn it," he snarled.

I complied.

Whisking the Boys and Me to Friends

Wes was leaving in the first week of July, 1971; he'd purchased a townhouse in Guelph. I realized that the boys and I couldn't be there when he packed up his things and left; that would have been way too much for the boys to deal with. In anticipation of Wes leaving, I signed up Wesley for summer camp for a week and made arrangements to go to my friends, the Goertzen's for a few days. As I drove up their driveway, my vision began to blur . . . I managed to get Blake and Ronnie inside before my legs melted to rubber, and I collapsed.

"Mom, Mom!" Ronnie's voice woke me up the next day; he was crying, calling out for me. When I called back, the door opened and my little Ronnie ran in. He scrambled onto the bed and snuggled into me, his warm body so comforting. "She wouldn't let me see you," he cried. I held him close and beckoned Blake to come up on the bed too. Wesley, when he arrived the next day, looked forlorn and confused. During those days at the Goertzen's, I was totally out of commission, when my little boys needed me the most. How could I ever make it up to them? How would they ever forgive me?

Leaving the Goertzen's, I pulled into the driveway of our home in Galt. Fear gripped my heart, and a gulf of emptiness opened up inside me. All I had in the world were my three little boys; they were my only family now, my responsibility. *How would I manage all alone?* I took a deep breath, squared my shoulders, and walked up the steps to the door, one wooden clunky step after the other. A click and the door unlocked. Wesley, Blake and Ronnie bolted past me to race across the kitchen and down the stairs to the playroom.

Standing there, in the entrance-way, everything looked the same—yet, in the space of three months my world, and that of my sons, had irrevocably changed. I felt we'd been deserted, discarded, and abandoned in no-man's land.

Understanding Patriarchy in My Life

As I revisit that scene, on that February day in 1971, I ask myself why I swallowed my husband's chauvinistic behaviour for so long. The woman I am *now* certainly would not have tolerated such disrespect. What was preventing me back then?

In order to respond to that question, I remind myself of the times; it was the 1960s. I'd been whitewashed by the after-war years, when the men came home and those self-sufficient women working in the munition factories were sent back to the kitchen. Housewifery was glamorized by the propaganda found in magazines, in movies and TV shows like 'Father Knows Best.'

I didn't have the language to even *describe* what

was happening to me. Heck, the word *patriarchy* wasn't in common use then—certainly not in *my* neighbourhood in southern Ontario—I was *living* patriarchy without knowing what it was called!

The rights of women? Who read about *that* in the 1960's—certainly not in *Chatelaine* or *MacLean's* magazines. *Feminism* was a word I'd never read or heard about. Gloria Steinem's "Women's Movement" was in its infancy then. Men dismissed her work, or ignored or disregarded her. They laughed at the notion of women having equal rights.

Of course, I *believed* I had equality. As a housewife, I had allowance money for groceries, clothes for the children and myself, and I *thought* that I had a share in the ownership of our home. That's what women like me *understood* by the "Social Contract." But it never crossed my mind if I had the *right* to the finances or ownership of our home. That was the *myth* of the *social contract* ... there was nothing *legal* about it. In fact, it worked *against* Canadian women at the time, as the Irene Murdoch case in 1968 * demonstrated. After working on their ranch in Alberta for over twenty years, ranching alongside her husband, doing everything he did—driving cattle, dehorning and branding them—Irene was thrown out five years later when the Supreme Court of Canada threw out her case. She had nothing but the clothes on her back. Despite the fact her husband was abusive to her and her son, she even lost custody of him. On top of that, she was required to pay a portion of her husband's legal expenses. Women across Canada were so outraged, that matrimonial laws were changed in provinces across Canada so that women had equal property-rights. Unfortunately, Ontario matrimonial laws did not come into effect until 1979, too late to advantage me.

Why was I so meek and mild, so self-sacrificing with regard to my husband? That behavior is explained by generations of women who were unable to serve in public office, but glorified in their role in chauvinistic marriages—like me—or looking after children (*governesses*) as servants, or caregivers of aging parents. Read the work of the Bronte sisters; they had to take pseudonyms of male names in order to get their work published.

The Courts worked against women as well—Canadian women did not receive the right to vote until January 27, 1916—after my grandmother's time. My mother, born in 1909, was not declared a *persons*, in the legal sense, until October 18, 1929, at the age of 20. My sister Merla and I were the first women in my family to be legally born persons. Generation after generation of women have been locked into subservient roles, and undervalued and underpaid, compared to men of the same qualifications.

Of course, my childhood experiences played a role as well; my memoir is riddled with how powerless I felt growing up. It contributed to my docile, passive behaviour in my chauvinistic marriage. Back then, I had no knowledge of the history of women and their plight over the generations. I'd been kept in ignorance, in the true sense of the word, blanketed in generations of conditioning which I both experienced and was uninformed about–giving me little choice.

I'd remained powerless until February, 1969 when, fed up with his emotional abuse, I finally found the courage to rebel against my chauvinistic husband, and refused to clear the snow from the car.

My children and I paid very dearly for that outburst of power on that wintry day.

Questions, Understanding and Forgiveness

I hurt . . . all the time . . . all over my body. I never dreamed that I could feel so much pain, when there was nothing physically wrong with me. *How could this be happening to us.* A profound sense of failure crept into my heart. *Had I done enough to save the marriage? Was there anything else I could have done?* "No," I told myself. I *had* done everything I knew how to save our marriage. I'd worked so hard at the counselling. I was willing to stay in the marriage in order to shelter my sons from the heartache of a broken family. But if I'd stayed, I would have collapsed, ending up in a psychiatric facility. *What good would I have been to my boys then?* For decades, I couldn't figure out why I did my husband's bidding. Was I still doing what I was told out of habit? And what of Wes? Why couldn't *he* tell his parents that he was leaving us? Was he afraid of his family's reaction? Was he fearful of being *judged*? Was he side-stepping the role *he* played in our failed marriage? Was he making *me* accountable for the failed marriage so *he* would not be blamed? Perhaps it was a combination of *all* those things.

As I reflect now, in 2025, those questions still haunt me. *Why did my husband walk away from the marriage and leave me and our children?* I still can't understand it. I accepted that he was not able to change and was willing to stay in the marriage for the sake of the boys. Everything would have remained as it had for the previous ten years. Why was he so anxious to get out—away from us—to purchase a home in Guelph? What would he gain? Why was he so emotionless, dispassionate, and so cold-hearted as he made his exit plans? Did it have to do with his childhood—raised by a military father and an emotionally distant mother? And yet, his relationship with his mother was special—they corresponded weekly during his war years and throughout our marriage.

After almost 55 years, I speculate as to why he married me in the first place. His mother *wanted* him to get married—he'd told me that in Spain. Had he married me to please *her*? Was he following in the traditional paths of his married sister and brothers? *What other reason was there?*

At 86, I still wrestle with the concept of forgiveness for how Wes treated me in our marriage. The best I can do is try to understand him—his family background and the chauvinistic times. But did he have to be so nasty and so cold-hearted? What I find difficult to reconcile is why he deliberately told untruths to my children—when they were vulnerable little boys—untruths for the marriage break-up: "*Your mother didn't want to be a stay-at-home mom anymore; she wanted a career instead; your mother wrecked the marriage when she wrecked the Porsche.*" Those were some of the stories my sons told me as adults, years later—too late for me to set the record straight. Those tall tales—told to my little boys at such an impressionable age, would have an effect on them as they grew up. How did they react to those untruths throughout their childhood and beyond? What wounds remain? So many questions unanswered and unresolved.

The Separation Agreement

Standing at the picture window in the middle of July, 1971, I smiled at my three wonderful sons, Wesley, ten, Blake, seven, and Ronnie, almost five; they were cracking their hockey sticks on the hardtop of the dead-end street, with the neighbour kids. The tennis ball suddenly smacked the glass and a wild cheer went up as the boys hooted and yelled," We scored!" As Wesley scrambled to retrieve the ball, Mr. Harris, the mailman, strolled up the driveway, the Canada Post canvas bag slung across his chest. He climbed up the three steps and with a click-clack of the metal flap he stuffed in the mail. He waved and smiled. Opening the door, I was greeted with the high blue Alberta sky, a good omen, I thought as I waved to the boys and took out the bunch of mail—the telephone bill, flyers, a white-business-sized-envelope, and an electric bill. After chucking the junkmail into the garbage, and putting the bills in a basket on the kitchen counter to deal with later, I studied the long white six-by-eleven inch envelope more closely. Glancing at the return address, a law firm from Guelph, my stomach twisted. A thread of fear wormed its way up my back. *What in the world does Wes want now?* Getting a kitchen knife, I opened the envelope carefully so as not to damage the contents inside. I took out the letter unfolding it slowly, cautiously. *What in the world can it be?* My fingers trembled as I folded over one flap and then the other until it was flat, staring back at me.

BRUCE PAYNE

SOLICITOR

Terror coursed through my veins. My eyes blurred as the words crawled across the page like black ants. I focussed. I gasped.

ON BEHALF OF MY CLIENT JOHN WESLEY HEALD, HE DEMANDS SOLE OWNERSHIP OF THE HOUSE, _____ AVENUE, GALT.

Dizzy, I stumbled over to the chesterfield and crumpled in a heap. *What the hell is this? He's the one who left us, walked out on us for goodness' sake!* Anger kindled in my stomach as I ran my finger under the sentence again. **'Demands sole ownership of the house.'** *What is he talking about? The house is half mine, for Godsake. I thought that our marriage was fifty-fifty; that all we accumulated was half mine. Isn't that how it's supposed to work? It's the boys' home too. Are you throwing them out on the curb, chucking your children onto the street, making them homeless?*

At that moment Ronnie came rushing in, "Gotta-pee, gotta-pee," he shouted, his little round face flushed pink and sweaty. He waved at me when he came out of the bathroom and raced back outside, Blake's boisterous laughter floating in off the street through the open door.

I refocused and read on.

...THE TRAILER AND ALL VEHICLES.

What? You're taking my car, the VW bug? You already took the six-passenger-van and you promised me the Bug—that's what we agreed to. The boys and I need a vehicle; how the heck can I take them to cubs, to church, or shopping? Did you think of that?

And the trailer too? *Oh, now I get it; you want the station wagon to tow the trailer. So, you drive around in a huge six-passenger-station-wagon for ten months of the year while me and our three children are crammed nose-to-nose in the VW bug!*

MY CLIENT OFFERS NO ALIMONY, AND NO CHILD SUPPORT.

No support for the boys? Do you have no conscience? How can you do this to your three sons? You make pots of money as a high school teacher with your fancy Honours degree. You walked out on them and now you refuse to support them, feed them, put clothes on their backs?

And no alimony?

I'll need something *to tide me over. After all,* you *have control of all the finances!*

How can this be happening? Don't I deserve half of the house, half of our property and half of the finances? Aren't I worth something?

RESPOND AT YOUR EARLIEST CONVENIENCE,

BRUCE PAYNE

SOLICITOR

I recognize that name! Bruce Payne is a friend of Wes! He's one of the best-known lawyer's in Guelph! I was hopping mad. They knew what they were doing, the bastards. Without access to any funds, I wouldn't be able to hire a lawyer. *How could Wes do this, knowing I don't have a cent to my name. What kind of father does this to his children? What kind of shyster lawyer executed it?*

I'll respond all right; you can bet on that! You can't bloody well do this to Wesley, Blake, and Ronnie; No bloody way!

The separation Agreement below:

BRUCE PAYNE
SOLICITOR

SEPARATION AGREEMENT

ON BEHALF OF MY CLIENT JOHN WESLEY HEALD, HE DEMANDS SOLE OWNERSHIP OF THE HOUSE,

_____ AVENUE, GALT, AND ALL VEHICLES AND TRAILER.

MY CLIENT OFFERS NO ALIMONY, NO CHILD SUPPORT.

RESPOND AT YOUR EARLIEST CONVENIENCE.

I REMAIN,

BRUCE PAYNE
SOLICITOR

According to the laws in Ontario in 1971, *everything* in the separation agreement was completely legal. I had no claim to the house, nor the trailer, nor the station wagon, nor the VW Bug. I had no worth, not a silver quarter, dime or nickel or a copper-coloured-penny!

It was a low blow. I felt pummelled, beaten up, thrown under the bus, once again.

THE SEVENTIES:
How I Made It As A Single Parent

New Beginnings

My whole world was shifting, and it turned sideways on that day in August, 1971. Overnight, I was on my own with my three sweet, little boys. I was paralysed with fear—how would I manage to maintain the house, car, and get ready for my first teaching position in ten years? The magnitude of this new responsibility weighed heavily on my shoulders, like chunks of concrete. Completely overwhelmed, my mind flashed with questions: How can I work and look after the boys, too? How do I get a baby-sitter for them when I'm working? What about servicing the car? How will we survive on my meager income? Will I be a success at teaching, after ten years out of my profession? *Who will pick me up if I fail?*

Why was everything such a gigantic task for me to accomplish? I asked myself. I was already looking after the house by myself. *Hell. I'd been doing it all for years.* In addition, I'd gotten my feet wet doing supply teaching—when I started my new job in September, that would hold me in good stead. *Why was I fretting?*

As we continued trekking up Concession Street, Wesley skipped up the road ahead of us. The trees, limbs hanging on either side, were tinged with August gold. The fingers of my right hand were laced with Blake's; I held Ronnie's hand firm in my left. Ronnie, suddenly, squeezed my hand. "Look Mom, a squirrel; it's got an acorn in its mouth!"

A surge of love wrapped around me like a blanket. I had my boys, my beautiful little boys, Wesley, Blake and Ronnie! They would see me through. We crunched through the golden leaves, as we made our way home.

Fighting Back for the Boys and Me

"Can my husband throw us out on the street? I asked Gary, the lawyer I'd found that July of 1971. "Can he really do that?"

I passed him the letter from Wes' lawyer. When he'd finished reading the Separation Agreement, Gary pursed his lips and shook his head. "According to the present matrimonial laws in Ontario, it would appear that he *can* if *your* name is not on the deeds of your home or the cars or trailer."

Blood drained from my face and my voice rose in panic. "I can't believe what I'm hearing. This is outrageous, Gary. He's never done a damned thing to that house. I've done all the painting, and decorating and even laid the carpet in the bathroom, for God's sake. He never lifted a finger while I did the gardening, lawn mowing, and even put up the storm windows for winter. I deserve half of that house too, by God. I've earned the right to it!" My head was spinning. What about the social contract? I was led to believe that I would have the right to half of what we'd accumulated as a couple. It's what every wife in Canada believed in the 1960s. It was a fifty-fifty arrangement, the accepted norm of society, or so I believed.

"Will the boys and I be left with nothing?" I asked, my voice fading to a quiet murmur.

"Not if *I* can help it," Gary said, reassuringly as he picked up his pen and started making notes on his yellow legal notepad. Ripping off the page, he handed it to me and sent me home with research to do.

A week later I had the information Gary had requested—Wes' yearly salary ($25,000), with 23 pensionable years; my projected yearly salary ($6,200), with zero pensionable years. I'd just been hired by the School Board in Wentworth County.

Gary's eyebrows raised in surprise. "His worth is more than *four times* what you will earn, and each year he'll get regular increases as well," Gary announced, eyes flashing, his mouth twisting with determination. "And the boys' expenses?" I'd estimated an amount of $10, 000 a year. It included expenses such as food, clothing, child-care, and a percentage of the heat, hydro and water they'd use in the house. Gary nodded, making a notation. "This is very pertinent information to start negotiating with Wes' lawyer," he remarked, glancing up at me with a look of hope.

"Before we go any further, Gary, I want you to

fight for custody of my boys. Come hell or high water, he's not going to take my boys from me."

"Absolutely," he assured me, as he scribbled that down on his pad.

On the way home I caught a news report that the Irene Murdoch case was going to the Supreme Court. I'd been following the case since 1968. Irene Murdoch had worked equally alongside her husband, on their ranch, for over twenty years She'd done all the ranch chores—herding, branding, farming pastures—as well as maintained the household and looked after their son. She took him to court when he broke her jaw; she'd had enough. During the court case, she was required to remove the neckbrace she wore because the judge thought it was prejudicial to her husband. The ruling of the Supreme Court favoured her husband. Irene was left with absolutely nothing; she even lost the custody of her son! There was such an outrage across Canada, that the laws changed one-by-one in every province. Unfortunately, Irene never benefitted from the new laws and was left destitute. Since the Matrimonial law did not change in Ontario until 1979, I was in the same boat unless Gary could negotiate a fair deal.

In mid August Gary had news. "There is good news and bad," he stated, tapping his pen on his desk. Dread settled like a stone in my stomach. "The good news is that you will have custody of the children.

Thank goodness! I breathed out a giant sigh … Gary went on. "Wes will get visiting rights every second weekend and alternative holidays. That was okay. "In addition," Gary went on. "Wes will continue to pay the education funds for the boys." *Well, good for him …* "You will also retain the VW bug, though I fought for the six passenger station wagon– it is far more suitable for you and the three boys than the tiny VW Bug, but Wes wouldn't budge." I dipped my chin, knowing that Wes wanted the station wagon to tow the trailer in the summer.

Gary looked up and smiled. "Another good piece of news is that I've also worked out a deal so that you can live in your home rent-free." *Oh, my goodness; this was an unexpected surprise.* I was so thankful that the boys wouldn't be disrupted with a move… "And regarding equity in your home." I listened intently. *Would I get anything*, I wondered? "You will maintain *half* the value of your house at time of separation which amounts to $10,000. I was happy with that, though I could see a 'but' coming. "However, in the event that the house is sold, any equity accrued *after* the date of separation will go to Wes."

> Flashforward *Two years later I sold the house for $35, 000. Wes got $15, 000 in increased equity, plus $10,000, the original half at time of separation. The total Wes received from the sale and our agreement was $25,000. I received $10,000.*

Gary frowned. "Now for the *bad* news. I also fought for alimony for you, because you needed some money to survive until you started your job, but that was completely rejected.

"I don't want alimony, Gary. But what about child support?" I asked. "I will certainly need that!"

Gary looked down, a glum expression on his face. "Wes is willing to provide $120 per child, each month, for food and clothing," Gary said, shaking his head. "It's an insult, given three growing boys; our teenagers eat us out of house and home!"

"That is totally unacceptable, Gary. That won't even cover the cost for clothes to start school, and they all need new coats and boots for winter!" Blinking back tears, I added, "When they're older, there will be costs for fees and equipment for hockey, and according to my friends, the cost is astronomical."

"I know," Gary affirmed sympathetically. "I tried to get that amount increased, but your husband dug in his heels and wouldn't give an inch!" He scowled. "I can't understand why he is so cheap when it comes to his children!"

"How will we ever survive on that skimpy amount?" I cried.

Gary flipped through his papers once more and his eyes lit up. "We *could* take him to court for more," he suggested. "After all, the child support is a pittance and you should get substantial alimony since *he* left *you*. The courts don't look kindly at a man who deserts his wife and children, especially a man earning *his* salary—four times what you'll earn."

I bit my lower lip. "Thank you, Gary, but frankly I am utterly drained; I don't have the energy, or the money, to go to court. I haven't got a penny to my name, and I won't get a paycheck for another month." I twisted my hands together, my eyes bleary with exhaustion. "I only have a week before I start my new job, for goodness' sake. And I haven't got new school clothes for the boys yet." *How could I possibly pay for a lawyer to go to court? ...* I pondered over the agreement. It reeked of being so unjust, so unfair, so inequitable. But I had no more fight left in me. I accepted the offer.

A twist of panic wrenched in my stomach on my way home. As a single mother raising three little boys, a new job, and with no family to turn to, I was wracked with doubt, uncertainty and fear; I was barely holding myself together by a thread. *How could I ever make it on my own?* I was a strong woman, but how much more could I withstand? I took a deep breath, rolled my shoulders back and lifted my chin. "You're damned right, you can," I railed to myself, smacking the steering wheel to bolster my courage. "You'll *make* it work, because you've got Wesley, Blake and Ronnie to think of."

Now, I still find it hard to believe the power that men had in society and how little women knew about the forces against them. It was a shock to come to grips with the fact that, with the stroke of my husband's pen, my boys and I were put in such a perilous situation.

My Credit Card Is Rejected?

"Come on boys, we have to go shopping for new clothes for school." It was the last week of August and the boys were playing in the basement family room.

"Awe, do we have to?" Blake whined. "I want to finish my Lego rocket. I hate shopping!"

"Me too," I countered. "But if you want something decent to wear to school next week we have to.

While I waited for them to put away their toys, I checked my wallet for money: I had my Zeller's credit card as back-up. We scrambled into the VW Beatle and headed to Zellers; it was the main department store in Galt in the 1970s. The parking lot seemed full, but Wesley, my little right-hand-man, spotted a parking space at the far end of the lot. Women and children were streaming out of the store arms laden with bags, other chattering children following behind. We entered. It was pandemonium. Parents were lined up, several deep, at each check-out, there was a cacophony of sound from the ka-chinging cash registers, there were children crying, mothers yelling, and the clank of shopping carts and squealing wheels making a clamour in the aisles.

"Find a shopping cart," I called to Wesley, as he ran to where they were stacked.

"I got the second last one," he claimed proudly. I lifted up Ronnie and placed him into the rack-seat at the front of the cart; Wesley volunteered to push. "Where to, Mom?" he asked.

"Let's find the children's clothing section," I replied, and Wesley led the way with Blake and I following behind. Wesley zig-zagged up and down the aisles, past crying babies, toddlers clinging to buggies, whiney children, and exasperated mothers. Wesley and Ronnie were way ahead of me. I called out. "Come back to the Boy's section!" Pawing through a mound of T-shirts, I told Wesley and Blake to pick out three they liked, while I helped Ronnie. The two boys dug into the pile, examining every T-shirt until they found ones they liked. If they fit, they threw them into the cart. Miraculously, we managed to find T-shirts, hoodies, jeans and shoes that satisfied the boys. The cart was filled to the brim when we headed to the checkout. There were lineups at every one—Wesley chose the one that seemed to move the fastest. "I want to go home," Ronnie cried, yawning. "I'm tired. I hate shopping."

"I know," I said, patting his wee hands. "We'll be only a few minutes longer," I promised. We inched our way, step-by-step, to the cashier.

The clerk transferred each item from the cart

onto the counter, checked the prices of each, and punched the cost into the cash register. When she was finished, she handed me the receipt. Glancing at the total, I knew that I didn't have enough cash, so I handed her my Zellers credit card. She took it and inserted it into the cash register. It didn't work, so she tried again. "It should work," I said. "I paid last month's bill."

She tried one more time, then looked at the card and turned to me and handed it back. "I'm sorry ma'am," she said, "but this credit card is no longer valid; it is valid only for John Wesley Heald." A warm flush crept up my neck to my cheeks. Angry and humiliated, I loaded the items back into the cart, and stepped back. Customers gave me a disgusted look as they shuffled aside to make way for me and the boys.

"What's wrong?" Wesley asked anxiously.

"What's going on?" Blake wondered out loud.

"I want to go home," five-year-old-Ronnie cried.

Embarrassed and mortified, I said, "We'll have to come back another time when I have cash!" Fuming, I knew what had happened. Wes had cancelled the Zellers credit card.

When I reflect on that day, I congratulate myself that I hadn't told my boys the *real* reason for having to unload our purchases and go home. What was running through their minds at that moment? Did they think I was incompetent and unable to manage money? I'll never know.

What I should have done was taken my lawyer's advice …. *I should have sued the bastard!*

The Minister Hits on Me

"We have some unfinished business to discuss," the Minister said to me on the telephone one Saturday in September, 1971.

"Why do you want to see me?" I asked, curious about what this could be about.

"It's something I have to talk to you about in person," he replied. "Come by the church at about three." He was my minister, so I felt obliged to go. The boys were with their Dad in Guelph, so I didn't have a good reason to refuse. I went up the side door leading to the church office. Before I put my hand on the doorknob, he pushed the door open and stepped out. "We'll go in *my* car," he suggested. It felt less like a suggestion, but not quite a command, and I felt a bit uncomfortable as he put his hand at my elbow leading me to the parking lot behind the church. He opened the passenger door, and I crawled in. My stomach twitched with uncertainty as he drove south down Main Street and out of town. Although nervous, I rationalized. *I'm with the Minister, for crying out loud. He counselled Wes and me. What's wrong with you?* He turned into Pinehurst Lake Provincial Park, wound toward the water and parked the car in a copse of evergreens and shut off the motor. "What's this all about?" I asked anxiously, somewhat apprehensive.

"I just felt that we should talk," he said warmly, turning towards me with a smile on his face. "I know how unhappy you were with Wes." *Of course, he knew from the sessions we had with him.* "I just want you to know that I think you are a wonderful person and deserve someone better than him." *What the heck is he getting at?* The Minister inched across the bench-seat of his car toward me, and raised his arm as if he was about to put it around my shoulder. My body tensed. *Oh my God, he's going to make a pass at me!* I put my hands up in front of me. "No, no," I cried. "Don't come any closer."

"Oh, I'm sorry," he said ruefully and slid back to his side of the seat and put his hands on the steering wheel. "It's just that I know how you feel, being in an unhappy marriage; I feel the same in *my* marriage, and I'd just like to talk." No longer feeling in danger, I let him talk for a few minutes before insisting on leaving. Without hesitation, he started the car and drove me back to the church. It was a relief to get home.

He started calling me in the evenings, and although I told him to stop, he wouldn't. When he became a nuisance, I talked to my neighbour, John. "Tell him if he calls again, you'll call the police." John said smiling. "He sounds like a nutcase." The phone calls stopped. I left the church!

Years later, I told this story to my friend Mary. "Was his name David?" she asked. "Did he have a New Zealand accent?" I nodded my head affirmatively. "He was the minister of our United Church in Markham years ago, and we booted him out for the very same thing, for coming on to female members of the congregation; he had quite the reputation!"

Now in 2025, I see this episode for what it was. I had believed I was safe with him: I had respect for his position as my minister, and as the person who had counselled us on our marriage, I had accepted the meeting. He'd used my respect against me. He'd used his power and authority as if it was his *right* to prey on me, knowing that my husband had just left me, and I was most vulnerable. In my naiveté at the time, I hadn't yet learned to question the possibility that a man of the faith might have negative intentions. And what about the role that the United Church played in this fiasco? Despite the minister's past indiscretions, they moved him into our United Church in Galt. Their actions put *me* at risk. And as he was moved, from church after church across Ontario, how many others were victims of him over fifty years? The United Church should have had the courage—at the very least—to remove him from the church. It is only luck that saved me from something which could have been much worse.

Peaches For?

The doorbell rang. Sweaty and sticky from mowing the lawn, I was not in any state for company. The bell rang again. Walking to the door I peered out through the small rectangular window in the door to see who it was. It was Fortunato, a neighbour from up the street; he and his wife came to a neighbourhood party a couple of years ago. As I opened the door, I saw that he was carrying a basket in his hand. "Hello Fortunato," I said smiling. He was dressed formally in a dark blue suit and a sparkling white shirt. They complimented his cinnamon complexion. His raven hair slicked back, and his amber eyes shining. He smiled, and his jet moustache twitched nervously.

"Hullo Meesus. I bring you dis basket of peaches. I hope you like," he said in halting English as he handed me the basket brim full of peaches the size of grapefruit. My arm dropped with its weight as I set it down on the floor beside me.

"Why thank you," I said. "How much are you selling them for?"

"Oh no Meesus, dey for you," he stammered. "Dey for you." He paused and looked up at me, his eyes gleaming with sincerity.

"Why thank you very much," I said gratefully.

"How very thoughtful of you. The boys will be so pleased to have some fresh fruit."

Ready to shut the door, he waved his hands. "Momento, Meesus, momento," he cried anxiously.

Puzzled, I wondered if I'd misunderstood Fortunato. *Maybe, he wants to be paid for the peaches after all.* The door ajar, I waved to my boys playing ball on the street.

Fortunato cleared his throat and swallowed. "I hear your man leaving you. I so sorry."

"Thank you for your concern," I said, beginning to feel uneasy. I sensed that something was awry.

"Want you know I understand." He shuffled his feet nervously. "You be lonely." He paused. "I help when you want."

Oh my God, he's propositioning me!

"I be very discrete," he continued with a bit of a smirk, a half grin.

Taking a deep breath, collecting my thoughts and stifling a giggle. I calmly lifted the basket of peaches from the floor and pushed them out toward him. His eyes blinked open wide in surprise as he took them back.

"Oh Fortunato," I said. "You do not understand me." *I do not accept peaches... for sex!* That's what I *wanted* to say. Instead, I slowly, gently, shut the door firmly until the latch clicked shut.

When I think back to that episode, fifty odd years ago, and remember how amused I felt, I now see the situation differently. It makes me question attitudes of that time. Did Fortunato think he had the right to approach me, knowing my husband had left me? Did he believe that a woman couldn't survive without a man? Did he think that, because I was on my own, that I had loose morals and was fair game to be taken advantage of?

Of course he *did* know exactly what he was doing! *Why wouldn't he?* With the patriarchal attitudes of the 1960s and '70s, men like my minister and Fortunata were conditioned to believe they had the *right* to treat women as fair game. *What was available to tell them any differently?* Certainly not other men, or TV shows like Father Knows Best or Leave It to Beaver or articles in current newspapers. Furthermore, most of the feminist literature and the women's movement, which aimed to educate both women and men, had barely begun to scratch the surface. There was little research at that time regarding male power, and, men behaved as if they had the right!

Hectic Days: Making Ends Meet

"Hectic" and "chaotic" are the only words that properly describe life as a single mother and full-time teacher. On a typical day, I was up at 6:30 a.m., and had showered, pulled on a skirt and top, rushed to the kitchen to start breakfast, and make my lunch for work. I set the Shreddies box on the table, along with the pitcher of milk—No more porridge like we once had. I grabbed the apple juice from the fridge. *Damn, it was almost empty.* I rationed it out into three glasses. I woke up the boys at 7, and helped Ronnie get dressed. One particular morning, he cried, "Where's my blue T-shirt? I want my blue shirt." I rummaged in his drawer for another one, while Blake called out that he couldn't find matching socks. I told him that any pair would do.

"What? Shreddies again?" Wesley complained as he poured the last brown square into his bowl. His eyes lit up. "Oh good," he smiled, as he raced to the cupboard for a box of Cheerios. Eating our cereal too quickly, we threw our dishes in the sink, grabbed our jackets and raced to the door. "Don't forget our hot-dog money," Wesley called out and I rummaged in my purse for a five-dollar-bill. Scrambling into the Volkswagen Beetle, I drove the boys to the sitter before traveling down Highway 8 to Rockton and Beverly Central School, getting there just as the last bell clanged.

After teaching all day I left school as soon as I could in order to pick up the boys at the sitter and drive home. While the boys played, I made supper– I always prepared meals that included meat, vegetables and dessert. By 8 o'clock, and the dishes done, I bathed the boys and got them ready for bed. I had good intentions to read a story to them every night before I tucked them into bed at night, but unfortunately that didn't always happen. After planning lessons for the next day, I collapsed into bed myself. On weekends I shopped for groceries, cleaned the house, did laundry, and mowed the lawn. It was a gruelling regimen.

I soon found out that it was one thing to be a substitute teacher a few days a month, but teaching full time, running a household, and raising three small children, was quite another. It was all very daunting, especially when all the responsibility rested on my shoulders ... alone.

When my first monthly pay-cheque came in I discovered that my yearly salary of $6,200, below the Canadian average in 1971, didn't go very far after deductions came off for income tax and pension contributions. The babysitting expenses ate up most of the child support money I got from their father, leaving the rest of the entire cost of raising our boys, up to me. In addition, if I wanted to increase my income above the poverty line, I had to consider taking costly courses. It was hard not to feel resentful of Wes, who was making more than four times I was.

To make ends meet, I budgeted and cut back. I bought powdered milk and mixed it up myself, split pork chops in half and made a lot of ground meat casseroles. Spaghetti became a staple, as did meat-loaf, mashed potatoes, and root vegetables. We picked strawberries in season and froze them; in the fall, I purchased bushels of sweet corn, blanched it, cut the kernels off the cobs with an electric knife, filled plastic bags, and stored them in the freezer for winter.

I made do; I managed.

When I relive that time, I have a lot of guilt that I didn't spend enough time with my darling little boys. It seemed that I was forever running: shopping for groceries, cooking supper, cleaning the house, and planning lessons. I wish, now, that I'd done more things with them—like playing board games or cards. I hardly took any moments to even watch TV with them. I regret that. Sure, I taught Ron how to ride his bike one weekend at the grounds of his public school, and took Wesley and Blake to Cubs and Wesley to play softball. But I regret that I didn't do more.

The Wiener Roast Explosion

A camper I was not! Nevertheless, I was excited to take the boys on a picnic one day in early October, after school. I packed wieners, hot dog buns, a large can of pork and beans, and marshmallows, and we headed out to Valen's Lake Conservation area. It was a pleasant evening, around dusk. There was still enough light before the sun went down, yet it was warm enough that we didn't need jackets. I parked by a picnic site with a fire-pit surrounded with stones--at least that's how *I* remember it. According to Wesley, however, it was an open Bar-B-Q pit! While I got all the food out of the car, Wesley and Blake gathered kindling for a fire. Wesley started it; he'd learned how from his Dad, or at Cubs. The fire caught quickly, and I placed the can of beans in the centre of the ignited sticks. As Wesley added the larger blocks of wood that he'd found on the site, flames shot up—until it was a blazing inferno! We made thin branches from shrubs we'd found, and we stripped their leaves. We hadn't brought a jack-knife,, so I used a kitchen knife to carve the end of each stick into enough of a point for the boys to spear their hot dogs. By this time, the fire had died down to a mound of red and orange glowing embers, and the paper around the can of beans had burned off. The boys put their sticks just above the hot coals. As bits of meat fell off of Ronnie's stick, he cried out: "I've lost my hot dog!" He sobbed. "It's fallen into the fire." As he started to lean over the embers, in order to fish the wiener out, I grabbed him and held him back so that he didn't fall in.

"Let me skewer another one for you," I said, as I took a kitchen knife and tried to whittle the end of his stick into a better point. His stick was now a jagged mess of frayed, stringy, green pulp. Getting another branch, I tried again, but this time I poked the stick into the centre of the wiener to make the shape of the letter 'T'. Just then, Wesley took his wiener out of the fire, and I got a bun out for him to put it in. By this time, too, Blake's wiener was black on one side. "Do you want another one? "I asked him.

No," he said. "It's okay, I'll eat it the way it is."

Ronnie's wiener had finally browned nicely. With a fork, I lifted it gently off the stick and put it into the bun. Then, we all sat back on the blanket and munched on our hot dogs; I was going to wait until the beans were ready and have *them* for *my* supper. As I walked over to the car to get out plates and forks for the beans, there was an explosive *BOOM,* which scared the life out of me. "Get back," I called to the boys as the metal bean can soared into the air. Brown beans flew everywhere! They stuck to the car and also left a gooey mess that covered the blanket. It was raining pork and beans! As the hot beans landed on our heads and arms, I yelled, in a panic, to the boys: "Pick the beans out of your hair, and brush them off your arms so you won't get burned!" I grabbed little Ronnie and madly whisked beans off of him. I spotted the bean can on the ground, two picnic sites over.

No one was hurt, thank goodness. We were safe, and that was all that mattered. The boys ate their marshmallows on our way back home. And that was the last outdoor wiener-roast we ever had!

Re-establishing My Career in Teaching

As I drove down the highway to my first teaching job after ten years, on the Tuesday after Labour Day, 1971, my chest tightened with trepidation and fear. It is a memory I will never forget. I'd gone to the school days before meeting my Principal, Cec Hamilton, and got my first-grade classroom ready to greet the children.

Within months, I had organized the class into learning groups, to be team-taught with my partner, Jan Dunn. She became a lifelong friend; we are still in contact. In the fall, we took our classes, to the local apple farm, and in the spring, to the sugar bush down the road. I remember when all the primary teachers developed a theme on Canada; every class focused on a different province. My class explored Alberta, of course, making murals of the grain elevators with the Rocky Mountains in the background. The children made paper cowboy hats when they shared what they had learned with other classes.

I remember fondly the special friendship between students Stephanie and Hermona. Stephanie was a tiny wisp of a little six-year-old, with fair skin, sparkly blue eyes and blond-white hair that hung straight past her shoulder blades. Hermona had a mop of curly kinky hair, like a halo around her dark, and cocoa-black eyes in a sandalwood face. They were inseparable–the best of friends. In the classroom, Hermona showed Stephanie how to solve number problems, and Stephanie helped Hermona use scissors to cut out circles and squares. At free activity time, the girls cuddled in the reading corner; Hermona read stories to Stephanie.

During an art lesson one day, I asked the children to paint pictures of themselves. Hermona and Stephanie each sat at a different easel, facing each other, and went to work with enthusiasm. Every once in a while, I saw them cock their heads and look critically at each other as they painted. At the end of the lesson, the children shared what they'd painted, one-by-one. Stephanie waved her hand wildly, anxious to show the class her self-portrait. She bounced out of her chair, blond hair bobbing, blue eyes sparkling as she danced up to the front of the room; she held her picture close to her chest. Carefully she turned her portrait around so it faced me and the class. There was an instant gasp, a collective 'ahaa,'—a look of surprise. The children pointed their fingers, taunting. "You've made a mistake, Stephanie," a classmate cried. "That's Hermona's picture." I wondered, myself, if she'd made a blunder.

Stephanie's face fell, a tear rolled down her cheek. "It's *me*," is all she said.

"Tell us about your picture," I asked gently, hoping she had an explanation.

"This *is* me," Stephanie responded again, emphatically.

Finally figuring it out, I smiled. "It's a great picture, Stephanie," I said looking closely to admire every detail of a beautiful little girl with skin as tan as a Jersey cow ... eyes deep pools of chocolate ... her hair a mass of kinky, twisty curls as black as night, just like Hermona's! Then Hermona shared *her* painting of herself. It was the image of Stephanie, complete with golden locks, and indigo-blue eyes, that glistened in her milk-white face! As best friends, their love for each other ran very deep indeed!

Fifty years later, I looked up their names on the internet. I couldn't find Stephanie under her maiden name, but I *did* locate Hermona. She was a flight attendant for West-Jet. We had a good chuckle about the story, even though she sadly did not recall the incident.

Another memory sticks in my mind, of which I am very proud. I went to court on behalf of the mother of one of my students. At a parent-teacher-interview, she broke down and told me how she had left her abusive husband earlier in the year. "And now he's suing me for custody of my precious little Bonnie," she cried, tears streaming down her face. Over a few months, I kept notes on Bonnie's behaviour and on the few interactions I'd had with her father. When the court case came up, I had documented enough information about the family to testify on the mother's behalf. The judge must have valued my testimony, because Bonnie remained with her mother. I was pleased that I'd played a part in the verdict.

When I reflect on that year, I see how I'd gained a renewed confidence, both in the profession I loved, and my skill with teaching children. That year, I gained renewed faith in myself—joy, value and fulfillment.

Starting University

My friend, Arleen, had been nagging me for a couple of years about getting my BA. "Your salary is frozen unless you do and you've got three children to support." In March, 1974, I registered at McMaster University—although my body tried to resist, with stomach cramps all morning.

I'd taken so many Ministry of Education courses—on Early Childhood Education, Environmental Studies, Special Education—and had proven that I was capable. Still, I was paralysed with fear at starting my BA. That little voice in the back of my head hammered away. *You are not smart enough to go to university; you're only an elementary teacher!* My husband's scorn had heaped a mountain of doubt on me and made me question my intelligence. *What if I fail? What if he's right?*

When I stopped to think about it, I'd always

liked school even as a kid; it was something I was good at and a way to be acknowledged by my mother. I'd graduated from Grade 12 with Honours. Success in school made me feel that I counted for something and gave me a sense of self-worth. I reminded myself that I'd achieved my elementary teaching certificate with flying colours from the University of Alberta's Faculty of Education. I'd also taught successfully in Alberta, Germany and Thunder Bay. I was competent, and successful.

Still, I fretted. *I'm thirty-two, an over-the-hill old lady. Everyone will be looking at me!*

Arleen gave me the final push by promising to take me to the Registrar's office to sign up for the first course. She even promised to type all my essays. *How could I refuse?*

I was nervous and anxious on my drive to Hamilton; Wesley's comments still haunted me: *You're not smart enough, you're not smart enough, you're not smart enough.* "Shut up!" I yelled, as I drove through the McMaster arch and pulled into the parking lot. Arleen waved. My stomach unknotted. I knew I'd be all right.

Life was hectic for me those years. I remember living my life in half hours—a half hour to drive to work; a half hour at lunch to do my course reading; a half hour drive home; a half hour to make supper, and a half hour to get the boys bathed and into bed before spending a half hour planning lessons for the next day. Somehow, I still managed to get the boys to music lessons and hockey.

Three years later, in 1977, I graduated with my Bachelor of Arts (BA) at McMaster University, my first university degree. At the time I did not know that my Masters and Doctorate would follow.

FRANK

Meeting Frank

"Let's go out on the town," Merla said, all of a sudden on the last weekend of her visit. Months after Wes left us, Merla, my older sister, had come from Alberta to see me. She was someone with whom I could confide and share my grief with for the loss of a failed marriage. She'd experienced divorce and knew the heartache and feelings of desolation, of starting life anew, all alone.

Merla was five years older than me and had always been a special person in my life—a kind of surrogate mother for me, as I grew up on the farm in Alberta. As a frightened five-year-old going to school for the first time, it was Merla who took my hand and settled me into a desk in the first grade classroom. It was Merla, not my mother, who told me at seven years old, to be wary of men who got too familiar, not discovering until I was a teen what her warning really meant. And when I was in high-school, it was Merla who gave me her fancy dresses she no longer wore, so I would have something fashionable to wear to high-school dances. Oh, how I wished she could have been with me in Germany in 1960, to give me counsel before I got married.

But she was here *now* to listen, to lend her shoulder to cry on. She gave me the time to grieve, and made me feel safe, cared for, and loved.

"Let's go out," Merla suggested once again. "You need to meet people, feel like a woman again." A shiver of excitement rippled through my body like a teenager. "Are there any cultural clubs in Galt?" she asked. "We have some in Calgary, and they are usually fun, with live music and dancing."

Within the hour, we were sitting at a table at the Schwaben Club in Kitchener eating sausage and sauerkraut on a bun, people polka dancing to a live band. "Come on, let's polka, like we did as kids in the Penhold town hall." Before I could object, we were kicking up our heels to the oomp-pa-pa beat.

As a slow waltz started, a tall, slim man in a silk-like shirt and dark slacks came toward me from across the room. Smiling, he extended his hand and led me to the dance floor. I caught a whiff of Bryl Cream. Glancing over at Merla, she smiled and nodded her head in approval. Folding my right hand in his, he put his other arm about my shoulders. I shuddered at the warmth of his hand and the gentleness of his arm about me. It had been years since I'd felt my body touched.

"My name is Frank," he said with a hint of a European accent, that I couldn't quite put my finger on--German? Italian? He was a smooth dancer, and Frank asked me to dance again. And by the third dance, the tension in my shoulders eased. As he drew me closer to his chest, I felt warmth course through me, for the first time in a decade. In that moment, I realized how empty of emotion my twelve years of marriage had actually been.

On our way home that night Merla--ever the big sister--counseled me. "Now remember, Gail, you are pretty vulnerable, and men could take advantage of that, so just be cautious about falling off the deep end too soon."

Of course she was right. It had been just months since my marriage fell apart and I knew I was emotionally wrung out, bereft of any self-worth, feeling lonely and needy, and desperate for a kind word or any hint of positive attention, after twelve years.

It was a sad day when Merla left for Alberta. At the Toronto International Airport, she wrapped her arms about me and held me close. "Remember," she whispered softly into my ear, "I'm only a phone-call away."

I felt comfortable with Frank and, later in the month, accepted his invitation to go out. However, I heeded Merla's advice; I remembered I was vulnerable and took things slowly. Frank was a proud Italian from northern Italy, near Verona, and he bragged of his sophistication. "I'm not like those gangster southern Italians in Calabria," he said proudly, his chest puffing out just a bit. As we dated off and on that fall, I learned that he worked in construction, brick-laying, tiling bathrooms and kitchens in new houses in Kitchener. "I can do anything with these hands," he said, spreading his fingers wide apart as if ready to snatch a pile of tile. "My ex-wife told me they were golden."

One weekend, Frank came over to the house when the boys were with their Dad. He repaired the boys' metal swing-set, fixed the hinges on the screen door and repaired a leak in the toilet bathroom downstairs. I was surprised at how handy he was and grateful for his help.

When our relationship grew, I eventually introduced Frank to my boys. Soon he was helping with chores around the house, like mowing the lawn, cleaning out the garage and even putting up the storm windows before winter. It was a marvelous new feeling to be supported: to be relieved of chores, and to be dating a man who was not afraid to wash a dish or the car if it was needed. It was such a welcome change from the past. On Sundays, Frank often took the boys and me to *Leisure Lodge* for family day, something I could never afford to do on my own. The boys had a great time dancing to the music and having their fill of food and German pastries for supper.

With Frank I felt appreciated and cared for, something I'd longed for but hadn't experienced in a decade. I began to feel doted on. Frank wanted to move in, but I was not ready; it would be too overwhelming for the boys. But it was something I thought about.

Partners With Frank

I craved independence: a house of my own, one for the boys and me, that was completely mine with no strings attached, and to be free of the shackles of my previous marriage. I started thinking about my future and where the boys and I would be in the next ten years. After examining my finances, it didn't look promising– my salary was near poverty level, and a quarter of what my former husband earned. In addition, the equity in the house was locked in at $10,000. I knew that the longer the boys and I stayed at this home, the faster I slipped backwards financially. As house prices steadily increased in value, the increases automatically went to my former husband.

Investigating all avenues, I discovered that I could borrow on some insurance policies to raise enough money for a down payment on an older house that could be renovated and rented out. Frank loved the idea. "I certainly have all the skills necessary to do the renovations," he said enthusiastically, rubbing his magic hands together. Within a year, we had a house on Norfolk Avenue in north Galt. There were renters in apartments upstairs and down, as well as a basement apartment for Frank to live in. I smile when I remember Ron, at age eight, and I planting gold chrysanthemums along the front of that house. Our success with the first rental property led us to purchase, renovate and rent another two-story house, on Spears Avenue in north Galt.

I no longer felt adrift and alone; I felt appreciated and valued, and I grew very fond of Frank. I'd found a partner, someone with whom I could share my life. We made a plan to move in together. We reorganized our finances and purchased our first home together, on Lowry Avenue in Galt. Frank ripped out carpets, built closets, and designed and constructed the dining room buffet and hutch. He repainted an antique pine dining room table that I'd found in an old barn. On my sewing machine, Frank even sewed green velvet cushion covers over foam for the seats of the matching chairs. Ron still has that dining set in his kitchen in their home in Kitchener. We brought the 1930 ice-box from the old house, and Frank restored it, laying black ceramic tile on the inside walls and cutting mirror-glass shelving. That old ice box moved from home to home from Lowrey, to Highway 8, Inverness place, Pointe-Aux-Roche, Port Dover and finally to *The Lodge* in 2020. Frank created the dining room I'd always dreamed of. He painted walls, hung wallpaper, laid carpet in all the rooms– upstairs and down. He even retiled the front of the natural fireplace. He truly performed his magic on everything he touched. We created a home we were proud of.

The boys transferred from Chalmers Street School to Lincoln Avenue; Wesley had a paper route, reminiscent of the one I had at about the same age in Penhold. During our first winter at Lowrey, Blake and Ronnie took figure skating lessons, in preparation for playing hockey. I have the cutest picture of them in alligator costumes at the spring Ice Follies. We had become a family.

Life on Highway 8

Always interested in up-grading, Frank and I started looking for another home and found a country property, an acreage on Highway 8 south of Galt, just a blink of a drive to my school at Rockton. We sold our home on Lowrey Avenue, and used the increase in value for the down payment on the Highway 8 property. The house was a 'side-split-level', with a carport at one side. With three bedrooms, Wesley had a room of his own and Blake and Ron shared another. Life in the country, meant the boys were bussed to schools in Galt. On the long driveway, the boys played road hockey, had car washes, played in the old cars on Oliver's property next door, and skated on Mr. Thornwell's pond on the property to the other side of us.

Over the years, Frank cultivated a garden, and grew all kinds of vegetables. I can still smell the aroma of his authentic Italian spaghetti sauce, simmering on the stove from the tomatoes we grew. We also raised chickens one spring; in the fall we plucked and froze them for winter. Ronnie's heart was broken when we had to kill the lame one that he loved. Ronnie was the most sensitive of the boys.

One summer, Frank built a swimming pool in our front yard from scratch; he even constructed the side forms in which to pour the concrete and mixed the cement in an electric cement-mixer. The boys pitched in and shoveled gravel into the mixer, while Frank poured the cement into the wheelbarrow and hauled it to the wooden forms. When the pool was finished, Frank built a fence around it, and I planted flowers around the deck. We had many summers of fun in that pool.

We also designed the entrance to the property, with clumps of pine trees to welcome guests. We never did get around to making the sign, *Villa Paradisio*, the name Frank wanted to call our home. *We were going to make it after all.* At least that's what I thought at the time.

Stormy Days Ahead

Stormy days came in our relationship when Frank began to take on the parenting role, reprimanding the boys for misbehaviour, sending them to their rooms, and withholding TV privileges. It soon became a cat-and-mouse-exercise between Frank and the boys, each trying to outwit the other. The more Frank got frustrated, the more the boys became disrespectful. Feeling caught in the middle, we sought help with family counselling, but the counsellor lacked the skill in dealing with step-parenting, so the attitude between the boys and Frank deteriorated.

During this time, I was taking courses at McMaster. Fascinated by course readings, I was anxious to share what I'd learned with Frank. He wasn't much interested in how society was dominated by patriarchal ideology; how to build a shack for the swimming pool was more up his alley.

Our relationship gradually deteriorated, until it finally collapsed. When we parted, I transferred one of the rental properties to Frank's name; I couldn't leave Frank in the position *I'd* once experienced. It was the only fair thing to do after all Frank had invested in our lives.

When the boys were adults, and in their fifties, they shared some memories of growing up on Highway 8.

"Remember Minnie, that ornery Shetland pony we adopted?" Wesley recalled. "When I rode her, she'd head right to an apple tree in the front yard, on purpose, just so she could knock me off on my butt! In the winter, Frank made a harness so she could pull us around the yard. It was great fun."

Ron started to laugh. "And remember the Bantam rooster that used to wake us up at dawn every day; he was so annoying!"

Blake interjected. "It's the car washes in the driveway on weekends, that I remember; we made pots of money."

The boys went on and on recalling story after story of the fun they'd had on that home on Highway 8. They expressed no ill will toward Frank; in fact, Ron expressed some appreciation. "After you'd split up with Frank, he contacted us kids and told us how much he'd enjoyed his time with us during those years." Ron dipped his chin, thoughtfully. "That took a lot of courage, and I gained a lot of respect for him."

That chapter of my life closed in the summer of 1973. Now, in 2025, I can see more clearly the role that Frank played in my life. I met him when I was at my most vulnerable, at my lowest ebb, emotionally. During our time together, Frank restored my faith in myself as a person; he helped rebuild my confidence and trust in myself, which restored my self-worth.

JOHN

Who Is That Handsome Dude?

"There he is." I nudged my friend Sylvia, pointing to the back door of the amphitheatre of the Sociology class at McMaster University, on a rainy September day in 1975. "Late again," I mused, as I waited for the class to start. "I wonder who he is?" He was a tall man; he wore a navy trench-coat, with the collar turned up and the shoulders glistening from rain. Removing his coat, he shook off the droplets and folded it over the arm of his three-piece, navy pinstriped suit. *Man, he was a handsome dude!* I couldn't take my eyes off of him. He had dark, salt and pepper hair, almost to his shoulders; it framed his long narrow face. He had bushy, dark eyebrows that matched a neatly trimmed moustache. He was in his forties—early forties—and trim, with a slim build. He exuded confidence and style. I wondered if he'd just come from work; if he was an executive of some sort, a bank manager maybe, or the CEO of a steel company. He certainly wasn't a teacher—who typically had a corduroy-pant-frumpy-look. *He had to be a professional.* I twisted my head around, my eyes following him to the back of the auditorium. He turned into a row and squeezed across several students, until he found a seat among a bevy of young women who looked to be their late twenties.

One woman stood up to let him pass, her long, blond hair flowing down her back to the place where her behind bulged out—Heck, I used to have hair like that when I was a teenager! I bobbed it in my 30s, when I started to colour it to hide the silver strands that were emerging—she was skinny as a rail, and her chest flat as plywood. In an instant, my hand went to my chest, my thirty-seven-year-old breasts bulging the buttons of my blouse. Her legs went on forever, to her armpits! I shook my head. *She was a spring chicken compared to me.*

He threw his coat over the back of the seat and turned to sit down. He was out of place in his three-piece-suit among a couple of hundred casually-attired teachers. *He was over-done, and dressed for a CEO, meeting not a classroom.*

Every week he was late, every week he sat with those skinny twenty-year-olds, and every week, I drooled. One night, when I arrived late, the mystery man was already on the stage, with a group of teenagers. I sucked in my breath at the sight of him. Instead of a suit, he wore a T-shirt, jeans and, black western boots. *Oh my goodness, he was just as handsome in casual dress! No one deserves to look that good.* "I'm John Taylor," he said, his voice deep and low. "This is my ball team, all high school students," he said pointing to the group of teenage girls dressed in T-shirts and jeans sitting in a semicircle on the stage facing us. They doffed their ball caps. "Tonight, they will talk about *their* perspectives of high school life." The girls were silent at first, as if intimidated by the sea of adults—mainly teachers—staring back at them. Instantly realizing their anxiety, John gently prompted and encouraged the girls to talk. It was obvious they trusted and respected him. As their stress subsided, they started to talk, one-by-one. As their confidence increased, they gradually took control of the presentation, even fielding questions from the audience at the end. It was unbelievable how comfortable and self-assured John was—a natural teacher. There was something warm, sincere, and considerate in his manner that I liked. My internal radar went up a few notches.

A few weeks later, Sylvia and I gave our team presentation; we showed a film about self-esteem. As I was gathering up my materials, I glanced up and saw a tall head above the tide of students rushing down the aisle to the exit. He turned toward me. *Oh my goodness, it was him!* John smiled, his eyes sparkling as he exclaimed, "That was a powerful presentation you two made tonight; I liked the overall message." He held up the long index finger of his left hand and added, "But I especially appreciated *your* contribution," he said pointing directly at *me. No wedding ring!*

"Thanks," I said, my stomach fluttering at the compliment. He walked away and disappeared into the crowd. *Oh my word he noticed me, not Sylvia! Where the heck did he go?* Every class I mooned over John, hoping he'd notice me once again ... He never did ...I lost hope.

Meeting John

Shivers of excitement crawled up my spine when, two years later, I saw John at the reunion for Jack Hawes. He was a favoured sociology professor; we were acknowledging our appreciation of his classes. Looking smart in casual tan slacks and shirt—Nehru style—John was in the centre of the room. He introduced a mixer-type game that got people up on the floor and interacting with each other. I was fascinated by his skill with people, how comfortable he seemed, as if he did it all the time—a born leader. *Who was he? Was he a Human Resources director for a company?* Once everyone was engaged, John sauntered over in my direction. My hands trembled, clammy with anticipation as he got near, a whiff of shaving cream tingling my nose. "I remember you from your presentation in class a couple of years ago," he said. His lips turned up at the corners of his mouth in a half grin.

My heart raced. "How is your ball team doing?" I stammered nervously attempting to start a conversation ... We chatted ...His brown eyes were warm and friendly. I felt an instant connection. To my surprise he drew out a pen and tiny notepad from the pocket of his shirt and looked at me. *Oh my goodness, he's going to get my phone number!*

The boys bustled in the back door, cheeks

flushed pink with cold from playing road-hockey in the laneway after supper. *My word, they were growing up so fast!* "Bath time," I called to them as they raced up the stairs two at a time to their bedrooms. "After snacks?"

"Toast and peanut butter coming up!" Just as I was lifting the giant peanut butter jar down, the phone rang-- *Rrrrrring.*

"I'll get it," Wesley called, lifting the receiver up off the cradle. "Heald residence," he said, attempting to be formal. "It's for you, Mom."

"Hello?"

"Hello Gail."

The voice? *It was John!* My hand trembled and it took a moment to find my voice, "Hello, John."

"How did you know it was *me*?" he responded in that soft velvety voice; I imagined a wink and a half grin at the other end of the line.

"Oh, I-I could tell; I remembered the sound of your voice," I stammered nervously, sounding like a ridiculous school girl, not a thirty-nine-year-old woman. "I was wondering if you'd like to join me for dinner next Saturday, for a wedding reception I've been invited to."

"Oh yes, I'd like that," I said, sounding more enthusiastic than I'd intended." We arranged a time.

"5:45 would be perfect."

"Got it," John said confidently. "I'm looking forward to seeing you next week."

"Me too."

First Date

The boys were bathed and ready. I put on Hamburger Helper for their supper, while I packed their clothes for the weekend with their dad and lined up their suitcases at the door. "Can we play hockey while we wait for Dad to come?" Blake pleaded, his hockey stick already in his hand.

"Sure," I said, as I washed up their dishes.

"I scored," Ron whooped, as the puck slapped passed Wesley in net. "Dad's here," Ron called as they threw their hockey sticks and net into the carport, just as their dad's station wagon rolled to a stop.

"Good bye, Mom," the boys called as they scrambled into the station wagon with their weekend bags.

"Bye," I waved from the front step as they took off down the driveway.

Rushing back inside, I slipped into my outfit and glanced in the full-length mirror. *Looking darned good!* Making one last check on my hair and makeup, I splashed *Shalimar* onto my wrists and behind my ears, when I heard the light tap on the door. Pulling it open I was taken-aback by how handsome John was– he was clean-shaven, his skin almost glistening except for his neatly trimmed moustache. His wavy salt and pepper hair was immaculately styled with a touch of curl at the ends. Did I notice a faint smell of soap or lotion, something sweet? He was wearing a grey, herringbone three-piece suit and exuded class and self-confidence. *How in the world could anyone be so absolutely gorgeous?* He looked at me and smiled that half crooked grin, and my cheeks flushed.

"It's so nice to see you again." His hazel eyes gleamed. "What a nice home you have." He reached and took my coat from my hands, helped me put it on, and guided me out the door to his car. "You have boys?" he asked glancing at the hockey net and hockey sticks.

"Yes, three boys, Wesley, Blake and Ron, and as you can see, they all love hockey." John opened the car door, wrapped his giant hand over mine and gently lowered me in. The touch of his fingers sent shivers through me like an electric shock. Forty years later, the memory of his touch still resonates, deep in the recesses of my heart.

John smiled at me as he twisted the key. The car purred out to Highway 8 and toward Hamilton on our first date.

John led me to the table with the black and white lettered *'Reserved'* plaque on it and pulled the chair out for me. *Such great manners!*

A shout from the next room, *"Another drink to the bride!"* Hands clapped, glasses clinked. *"Here, Here.!"*

John grinned, "That's for Joan, the bride. She's a friend from Jack's class," he said as he took out a silver cigarette case from the inside pocket of his suit jacket, the letters *JT* engraved on the front. *First class, this guy!* He took out a cigarette and snapped the lid shut with a clap. "So, tell me about yourself," he said, as he lit up.

I told him about my boys, our life in our country home with all our animals, and how engaged they were in hockey.

"And do you have children, John?"

John blew a puff of smoke into the air. "I have a son, Adam, who lives with his mother in Ancaster … and … I … A look of sadness crossed his eyes … At that moment the wine steward approached, a white napkin over his arm.

"What can I get you folks to drink?"

John's eyes lifted. "What would you like, Gail?"

"I'm not much of a drinker, John; so, I'm fine with water and lemon, thanks."

"What kind of red wine do you have?" John asked. "a Cabernet?" John made his choice and the wine steward left. In our 44 years together, John drank only dry red wine.

John took a drag on his cigarette. "And what do you do, Gail?" Are you a teacher like many of the friends I sit with in Jack's class?"

"Yes, I've been a teacher for several years, but now I'm a consultant for the Waterloo Board of Education."

"And what does that entail?" John asked, as he blew out a puff of smoke.

He really seems interested in what I do. I'm impressed! "I work with more than a hundred teachers giving classroom demonstrations, writing curriculum and conducting workshops," I explained, as the wine steward arrived with John's red wine and my water. John put his nose to the rim of the glass and nodded affirmatively. I am reminded of the time I was in Bordeaux, France giving a presentation, when I went to their winery and purchased a bottle of the driest red wine I could get for a hundred dollars—expensive for us at the time—though they had bottles that cost well into the thousands! John said it was the best red wine he'd ever tasted!

Smiling up at John I took a sip of water. "And you, John? What line of work are you in?"

John tipped his wine glass up and took a sip. "I've always loved reading and I'm getting my degree in English literature. I have a dream of teaching high school English one day," he mused wistfully. "It would be a welcome change from my work as a credit manager."

My shoulders stiffened. *Surely, he doesn't work at "Household Finance" that squeezes money from poor clients who can't get credit at a bank!*

Sensing my shift in mood, John countered. "I'm a credit manager for a major steel company in Hamilton," he explained. "I approve terms of payment for large firms across Canada and out of country conglomerates that purchase steel from our company."

My shoulders lowered in relief. "You live in Hamilton?"

"Yes," he said, a glimmer of a smirk on his lips. I live in a condo, since my wife ran away with my best friend."

"Oh, my word," I gasped, "How terrible for you."

"Yes," John said, a deadpan look on his face, "I didn't know what a good friend he *was*." ... He paused then ... "until he ran away with my wife."

I burst out laughing. "That's too funny!"

The server came over then and asked us if we'd like to order. We nodded and poked our noses into the menu. After making our selections, John looked up. "Where did you grow up, Gail?" he asked.

"On a farm in Alberta." ... I told him about the cold winters ... riding my pony ... delivering milk as a kid ....

"Alberta?" John enquired. "That's right next door to Saskatchewan, the home of the NDP (New Democratic Party)," John noted as he took another sip of wine.

"You know the birth place of the NDP!" I gasped in surprise. "My dad ran for the CCF (Cooperative Commonwealth Federation), the forerunner of the NDP, and I used to go with him door-knocking at election time when I was a teenager."

The server came with our meals. John took a slice of salmon, smiling. "In the last election, I voted for the Marxist/Leninist Party in Hamilton and my vote was one of the four in all of Hamilton," he bragged. *My goodness, John was humanistic, interested in social-justice issues, like me.* "It's so refreshing to be able to talk about politics with you without feeling judged, like I was as a kid."

"How so?"

"It was during the McCarthy years, and we were called Communists, dissidents or subversives, just for *advocating* for universal health care."

I swallowed a bite of my fillet-mignon. "For years I kept my mouth shut about my socialist beliefs." All of a sudden, I felt a real connection with John. "But with you, I can be honest and open to my true self." John smiled.

Feeling relaxed and comfortable in his company, I went on sharing stories about growing up. It felt good to share a part of myself with John and to hear his stories in return.

Finishing my meal, I suddenly felt the urge to go to the bathroom. John put down his fork and walked around to pull the chair out from behind me. *My word he's so polite. I could easily get used to this!*

Heading to the washroom, I followed a group of women dressed in party outfits, probably from the wedding-party next door. I recognized the striking blond from Jack's class, one of the groupies that John used to sit with in the back row. As I was washing my hands at the sink, she stood beside me and ran a comb through her long blond hair. It hung down to her hips. She peered into the mirror at me; her deep blue eyes snapped, and her mouth twisted into a grimace. "You're with John Taylor, aren't you?" she stated, her voice sharp, acerbic.

"Well yes, yes, I am," I stammered, stunned by her accusatory, reproachful tone.

"Don't you *ever* hurt that dear man," she blurted

out caustically, puckering her mouth in disapproval.

I stared back at her, rubbing soap over my hands, feeling accused of something I knew nothing about. *What the heck was she talking about? I'd only just met John, for heaven's sake. Was she a former girlfriend?* I wondered, feeling suddenly insecure. I felt uneasy. I finished washing my hands, and left the bathroom.

John stood when he saw me coming and pulled my chair out for me to be seated. As I sat down, I tried to cool down, collect my thoughts, and steady my trembling hands.

"What's wrong?" John asked, empathy washing over his warm eyes.

I told him what I'd experienced in the powder room.

John sucked in a long draught of air and sighed. A look of pain crawled across his face. His voice fell to a throaty whisper. "That was probably Josey. She's just a friend, but she's very protective of me." *Protective? What the heck for? Nothing was making any sense.* "It's about my daughter, my daughter Kimmy." Colour leached from his cheeks, and his lips quivered.

My anger suddenly turned to empathy. *His daughter? What in the world happened to his daughter?*

"My daughter, Kimmy, was killed in a car accident two years ago." His voice cracked. "She was fourteen." His eyes moistened with pain. "I miss her so much; she was my sweet little girl."

John's sadness wrenched my heart. He sounded as if Kimmy were killed yesterday and was mourning her loss all over again. Feeling the sting in my eyes, I reached over the table and rested my hand on top of his. John wrapped his hands around mine and held on. There was an oppressive silence, heavy with questions unasked, and unanswered.

As we stood in the vestibule at my home, John looked deeply into my eyes. "May I kiss you?" he asked. His request was so gentle, so old fashioned. I lifted my chin. His arms rose up and his long fingers cupped both cheeks. His head lowered, and his lips met mine, lightly, like the brush of a butterfly's wing. "You are a breath of fresh air," he murmured into my ear as he slowly untwined his hands. He smiled that lop-sided-grin. "Until next time."

Waiting For a Phone Call

As I closed my door, my mind flashed with memories of the evening with John. We had so much in common. He was so sensitive and warm. He was so genuine, engaging and funny. It seemed like I'd known him forever, not hours. *It was absolutely impossible not to like this man.*

Constantly in my thoughts the next day, and I

hoped he would call. *He'll tell me what a great time he had.* He didn't. Nor did he call the next day ... or the next ... I sat in the quiet of each evening, after the boys had gone to bed, staring at the black box on the wall and willing it to ring. It didn't. A week went by, and the telephone remained silent. A second week passed without a word. After a month, I was resigned that I might *not* ever hear from him. I thought we had something going on between us. I really liked this guy, *more* than I wanted to admit. Disappointed, I gave up waiting.

The boys kept me busy from late October through to December. With both Ron and Blake on hockey teams, the Rockton arena became our second home. Supper was frequently hot-dogs at the arena confectionery booth before the practices and games. I sat in the stands on frigid benches, cheering on the boys. After the games, the VW was filled with smelly, sweaty hockey shirts until we got home and put the hockey gear into the basement storage room.

Wesley had his music lessons and skiing as an outlet. I couldn't afford the hockey equipment to have him in hockey too, something I regret now, because Wesley had a great spirit for the game. Wesley was especially keen on skiing, so I took up skiing at the Chicopee Ski Club, in Kitchener. He attached the ski rack onto the back of the VW—not following instructions—and somehow made it work anyway, so we could attach our skies onto it. We had many enjoyable weekends skiing together.

As for John, I'd finally given up on him. *I'd probably just imagined all those feelings.* Was I wishing for some kind of dreamy romance, believing that I needed a man to make my life complete, a partner, a companion–someone to help raise the boys? No. I found that I was enjoying *not* having a man in my life. I had a good job, the boys were healthy, and I could finally afford the mortgage on our home by myself. Life was good ... Perhaps I no longer *needed* a man in my life. I was beginning to feel quite liberated and was enjoying independence.

It was a cold, blowy, blustery day on Christmas break. As usual, the boys were over at Mr. Thornwell's place playing hockey on his pond. I was making another batch of shortbread cookies for them to have when they came home. My hands were sticky with butter and icing sugar when the telephone rang. I scraped off as much goo as I could and reached for the phone, a blob of dough falling with a 'plop' onto the kitchen floor.

"Hello?"

"Hi," says the voice at the other end of the line. I instantly recognized that voice from the past, almost a forgotten memory. *Oh, my word, it was John.* A shiver ran up my spine.

"Why haven't you *called* me?" he asked calmly, as if *I* had somehow been negligent.

"What are you talking about?" I replied, feeling annoyed recalling all those days and weeks I'd pined for the phone to ring. *Does he think he is funny?*

Recognizing the reserve in my voice, John started to explain. "I just discovered that women always called *me* for dates," he chuckled, sounding a bit embarrassed. I imagined him smirking, shaking his head. "And *you* are the first woman who hadn't done that." *Is he serious?*

"So," he said, a hint of an apology in his voice, "I'd *really* like to see you." He sounded *sincere* all of a sudden. *Was he being honest? Did he truly want to see me after leaving me dangling for so long?*

There was that flutter in my stomach, I couldn't control.

"Could I come up sometime soon?" There was a sense of urgency in his voice.; "I have something important to talk to you about."

I didn't know what to make of this. *He hadn't called for over a month and now he wants to see me? Why the heck would I want to see him, after the way he'd treated me? What was the urgency?*

He had my attention …I was feeling just a bit curious. I bit my bottom lip. Part of me was dying to see him again, but still, I didn't want to sound too eager. "I'm busy the next couple of days," I lied, "but what about Wednesday afternoon around two."

"I'd like that," John replied with a long, whooshing kind of sigh, slowly releasing air out of his lungs.

See you then," I chirped more brightly than I'd intended. My body quivered at the thought of seeing him again.

John Came with Gifts

I was on pins and needles as I tried to figure out what John wanted to tell me. I didn't get a wink of sleep for the next two nights. On Wednesday morning, the boys shoveled the driveway, grabbed their skates, and rushed over to Thornwell's pond to play hockey once again. *Mr. Thornwell was so generous to let them play so frequently. I must take them over a box of shortbread.* I did the dishes and took hamburger out of the freezer to thaw for supper. The boys came in for grilled cheese sandwiches for lunch. I did the dishes, then sat in the living room to wait for John. Large, lacy, snowflakes came sliding from the grey sky, to settle onto the driveway. *Before long, the boys will have to shovel once more.* I checked my watch—it was one thirty; *John will be here in half an hour.* I looked out the front room window and watched cars passing on their way to Galt. Nervous and twitchy, I went down to the laundry-room, took out the dried clothes, and started folding the boys' jeans, T-shirts, underwear, plaid shirts, and socks. I'd started on the towels when

I heard a knock on the front door. Racing up the steps two-at-a-time to the family room, then five more to the vestibule, I stopped and composed myself before I turned the door handle. Snow glistened on his felt cap, and melted on the shoulders of his three-quarter length black leather coat. His arms were laden with parcels.

"Come in, come in," I invited him.

He banged his black western boots, with a *'whap, whap'*, on the door ledge to knock snow onto the cement entrance before stepping over the door frame onto the rug in the vestibule.

"Here, let me take those things." I reached to take some of the parcels he was carrying. "What in the world are these for?" I asked, as I stacked them onto the end table beside the chesterfield.

"Thanks," John said, setting a final parcel on the floor. It was wrapped in green tissue and had red ribbon tied around it. He took off his jacket, and I hung it in the closet while he removed his boots and set them at the side of the door. He was wearing jeans and had a black leather buckle with JT stamped on it; it was almost hidden by a long blue denim shirt over a white T-shirt. He was dressed so casually, so differently from the three-piece suit he'd worn on our date in October. *My goodness, he looked so good, regardless of what he wore.* I guided him into the living room, where he sat opposite on the wing-back chair. "It's wickedly cold out there," he commented and, rubbing his hands together, pointed to the parcels. "I brought some presents for you and the boys."

I was completely perplexed. *We'd only been out only once.* It seemed unusual, so unexpected to be bringing presents.

John passed me the rectangular-shaped one in green paper and red ribbon. "This is for *you*," he said smiling a crooked nervous grin.

"This is so nice of you, but is totally unnecessary." *Why in the world was he doing this?* I was totally confused. "Can I open it?" I asked, curious as to what he'd brought.

"Of course," he said, his brown eyes sparkling.

I tore off the wrapping paper ... *Lady Oracle* by Margaret Atwood. *I didn't read Atwood, but it was so sweet that he'd been so thoughtful.* I opened the cover. It was her most recent book. "Thank you," I said, with less enthusiasm than I would have liked. "This is so kind of you." Over the years I've read every novel that Atwood wrote!

"And what's this?" I asked, pointing to a wrapped parcel with a handle sticking out the side.

"Oh, that's a present for the household," John explained with excitement. "It's to roll newspapers into logs for your fireplace."

"Thank you, John. Thank you so very much."

John pointed to a square box-like package. "And this is a game for the boys." I was overwhelmed by his generosity; I couldn't figure him out.

"You can give it to them when they come in from the pond," I said. "Would you like a cup of coffee?" I asked, finding my manners.

"Love it," John answered. "It will help me warm up."

"What do you take?"

"Cream and sugar, thank you."

At that moment, the boys burst into the back door, hockey sticks clanking, door slamming, boots clunking off. "Blake, that goal went in, and you know it!" Wesley yelled. They came rushing up the stairs, their faces ruddy with cold.

I introduced them to John; John stood up and up and shook their hands, and then gave them their present. "I thought you guys might enjoy this game."

"Gee, thanks," they said and dashed down to the family room, the sound of rustling paper floating back up. "Who wants to go first?"

John and I spent time sharing anecdotes from our Sociology classes, talking about the weather, and the holiday crowds in the stores, until we finally ran out of things to say.

What is the important thing he wanted to tell me? When in the world am I going to hear the serious topic that he'd come to talk about?

The Big Revelation: New Year's Eve

"I have something I want to tell you," John said, clearing his throat, his voice sounding tentative, hesitant. *Finally, I'll learn the mystery of his visit.* He took in a breath of air and began. "I have plans for Christmas with my family." *Of course, he'd want to spend Christmas Day with his family in Hamilton. That's no big deal. I'll be with my boys.*

"I'd like to spend New Year's Eve with *you*." John's voice lightened.

My heart soared. This was almost too good to be true, since we'd only been out on one date. A warm glow washed over me and goosebumps prickled over my arms. In an instant, I knew what I'd wear—that off-white gown with the hood—like the one Margaret Trudeau wore on her wedding day. "Why, that's lovely, John, thank you." I flashed a smile, my eyes all aglow.

John bit down on his bottom lip and his fingers opened and closed in a clench. His body language was all wrong. *Why was he so nervous? Had he changed his mind about asking me out?*

Wavy lines creased John's forehead; he paused, as if rehearsing in his mind what he wanted to say next. Splaying his fingers firmly on his thighs, he spoke. "But I *can't* take you out on New Year's Eve." His voice was dry, gravelly, a hint of disappointment crossing his eyes.

My mouth dropped open; my eyes grew wide in surprise. *What! First, he asks me out on New Year's and then reneges? What the heck is going on here?* "What?" I managed to mumble, disillusioned with this whole conversation.

"You see," John responded slowly, almost painfully. "I already *have* a date."

This was too much! He asked me out, took back the invitation and then had the gall to tell me he already had a date! This was the important thing he wanted to tell me? Nuts to that! I picked up the crumpled green tissue and crunched it into a ball. *Have I read this man all wrong? Why was he so anxious to see me? Why did he come with gifts? And then this? It makes no sense, no sense at all!*

Fuming, words sat on my tongue like fly-paper; I couldn't think of a single word to say.

Seeing my disconcerted look, words suddenly poured out of John's mouth. "You see, I promised my friend, Ruthie, months ago that I would take *her* out on New Year's Eve." *Yeah, right! Go ahead, pour salt on the wound. Why not pour vinegar on it for good measure!*

John's eyes lit up. "But now that I've met *you*," he said, his lips lifting up into that lopsided smirk, "I can't go out with Ruthie, because I'd rather go out with you." His tone was almost joyous.

I was dumb-struck! *What in the world is happening here? This is the most confounding man I've ever met.* "Let me get this straight." I frowned, searching to find my voice. "You'd rather spend New Year's Eve with *me*?" I said, sounding flustered and confused. "Is that what I just heard?

John threw his hands up off his thighs, "Yes, yes!" he said excitedly, "I want to go out with *you* on New Year's Eve."

This was all too bewildering and it took me a few moments to get things clear in my mind. I didn't know what to make of all of this. I was delighted of course, that he'd chosen *me* and yet ....

John's voice lowered then and he seemed to struggle with his words once again. "But you see *that* wouldn't be *right, either*," he said quietly, almost in a whisper. "It wouldn't be *ethical* to take *you* out."

Air rushed out of my lungs, leaving me gasping and unable to breathe. I shook my head in disbelief. *What is he saying? It wouldn't be right to go out with me? Is he nuts? Am I crazy for putting up with this nonsense?*

Before I could utter a word, John added quickly. "You *see* it wouldn't be *ethical* to break a previous date with a friend and then take out someone else instead." His eyes pleaded for me to understand.

Ethical? What the heck is he talking about?

"Therefore," John continued quickly, his voice gaining momentum and strength. "I am *cancelling* my date with Ruthie and will be spending New Year's Eve *alone*."

Now he'd really gone off his rocker. He wanted to go out with me; he was cancelling his date with Ruthie, and he was going to spend New Year's alone?

It was a very long moment before I could speak. *Ethical? Morally right?* These were concepts that had not occurred to me. "Are you saying that you can't take me out on New Year's Eve because it wouldn't be right to break a promise to your friend, Ruthie?"

"Yes, that's right," John said, light coming into his eyes again as if pleased that I was beginning to understand.

"So rather than take out *either* of us, you are going to spend New Year's Eve on your own?"

"You've got it," John said as he breathed a soft sigh, relieved that he had finally made himself understood.

"Are you *really* planning to stay at home by yourself on New Year's Eve?"

"Yes, I certainly am!" He said it with determination and conviction in his voice. "That's the only *honest* and *ethical* thing I can do!" His shoulders lowered, the creases lining his forehead faded, and his whole body relaxed. His eyes glistened brightly again, and his lips curled up into that silly half-grin.

I got up out of the chesterfield, walked over to John, placed my fingers lightly on his slender cheeks and kissed each gently, first one cheek, and then the other.

I'd never before met a man so full of honesty, integrity, and morality. At that moment, I knew that John was the man for me.

~~~

John is now gone. Wherever he is, I want him to know—*You were such an extraordinary, remarkable human being! How blessed I was to have had you in my life for those forty-five years. My beloved John, you will be in my soul as long as my memory lasts ... until we meet again.*

Dinner For John

The table would look romantic when I lit the blue candles, held in cream-coloured onyx candlesticks designed with a vein of pale rose that ran through them. My off-white, Bavarian China plates that I saved for special occasions stood out boldly against a cobalt blue Belgian table cloth that flowed over the dining room table and kissed the floor. Grandma Blakely's crystal goblets looked perfect at the tip of the knives just so, exactly as she'd have placed them. *Perfect, simply perfect!* A warm glow ran through my body and stirred up emotions from those times I spent with 'Gran' when I was a little girl. I lined up Roger's silverware beside each plate; they gleamed from last week's polish. I smiled. I must really like this guy to be doing all this fussing over a meal.

My nostrils suddenly tingled with a whiff of something tangy—the sweet smelling aroma of the chicken I was cooking. It was simmering in white wine. The recipe in the French cookbook seemed to have done its trick. I put wild rice and carrots on the stove to boil, and sat down for a moment to take a break—letting the classical music on my FM station wash over me. I recalled the concert by Harry Chapin that John had taken me to a few weeks earlier, at Hamilton Place, and it suddenly occurred to me that classics may not be the kind of music John liked. Then again, he loved

Joan Baez—we listened to her music that day we went to his condo—the classics would have to do.

I looked out at out at the raging, end-of-January storm: the wind whipped and swirled down, filling the driveway with snow. The limbs of the apple trees out front looked like crooked, witches' arms, covered with layers of frothy white. Lacy patterns clung to the plate-glass window, blocking my view. *What if the storm was this bad in Hamilton?* Thank goodness I'd had the boys shovel the driveway before they left with their Dad for the weekend. *Why the heck had the storm come up today; it was so nice yesterday. What if John canceled? What in the world would I do with all this blasted food?*

Adding another log to the fire, it crackled and hissed an orange glow. "He'd better come, that's all there is to it."

My hand-mixer whirred to life, as I whipped the egg whites into soft curly peaks of meringue, for the baked Alaska dessert. *Why in the world had I tried this crazy recipe anyway?* What if the ice cream melted in the 500-degree-oven, and the whole thing came out a red and white gooey mess?

Wham!--the slam of a car door. It was John. I fastened up the button on my ivory blouse and ran my hands down the sides of my hips, wiping off imagined particles of food and smoothing out invisible wrinkles on my long black skirt. I raced to the door. Frigid air rushed in, and turned John's breath into vapoury plumes. He stomped snow off his boots onto the stoop before stepping in, and shook off the white flakes that covered his felt navy driving-cap, before he took it off and placed it on the closet shelf.

"Nasty day, roads are getting snow-covered and slippery, the visibility's almost impossible; the wiper-blades could hardly keep up." He shoved his gloves into his coat pockets and hung up his coat. He rubbed his hands together before reaching over and pecking me lightly on the cheek. He looked fantastic in his navy sports jacket, the deep blue so pleasing against his fair skin. Windblown, he spread his fingers like a comb through his fine, silky hair. Looking beyond John, the picture window was now solid glistening white.

"Red wine?"

"Please," John said, his soft eyes lighting up, his lips turning up at the corners as if attempting to conceal a grin.

"Thank you," his smile replied, his gentle eyes making me feel relaxed and comfortable. "Something smells awfully good," he said, nodding his head in the direction of the kitchen.

"I hope it will be; I've tried some new recipes—making baked Alaska for the first time."

"Sounds interesting."

"It's a layer of cake, strawberries and ice cream

covered with meringue." I said proudly.

"Sounds fascinating, never heard of it; I can hardly wait to try it."

It better turn out now that I'd blown the surprise dessert. "I just have a few more things to do in the kitchen," I turned down the heat on the chicken, buttered the carrots and stirred the rice.

"Would you like to come to the table, John?" I transferred the meal into serving platters, and lit the candles, motioning to the chair on my right facing the dining-room window. I topped-up his wine.

"This looks fantastic," John said, as he cut into a chicken breast. "What makes this delicious aroma?"

My body stiffened upright with pride at the unexpected complement. "Simmered it in white wine," I said, nonchalantly, as if I cooked with wine all the time, pretending I knew what was doing.

"And this rice is absolutely scrumptious," he said, as I offered the parsley carrots.

When we were finished eating, I cleared the plates and stacked them in the sink. "Pour yourself another glass of wine, John, while I prepare the baked Alaska."

"It sounds so exotic."

Setting the oven on to broil, I got the block of

vanilla ice-cream from the freezer, sliced a hunk, and placed it between the strawberries and cake, then covered the entire conglomeration with meringue, carefully sealing the bottom edges to the plate for insulation before placing it into the scorching hot oven. *Oh, my word! This better work!*

John watched from the dining room. "Boy, you are going to a lot of trouble."

I looked up and smiled. *Great, he's impressed! Things are going better than I thought.*

Folding a white hand-towel and placing it on the table to act as a pot-holder for the baked Alaska, I went back into the kitchen and stared into the glass opening of the oven. When the meringue was a light toasty brown, I put on my oven mitts, lifted it out carefully and placed it on the towel. It looked spectacular and the sweet smell of the meringue, strawberries and ice cream was heavenly. John's mouth dropped open. "This is amazing! I've never seen anything like it."

I basked in his appreciation.

"You know, Gail, this is the first time I have ever accepted an invitation for a home-cooked-dinner, from a woman I'm dating."

My heart flickered, thinking that was meant to be a compliment.

John took another mouthful of cake.

"Why is that?"

John licked a dab of meringue from his lip. "When women asked me over for dinner, I assumed they wanted a commitment." John took another bite of cake. "This is really delicious, Gail." His Adam's apple wriggled as he swallowed.

Is that what I am doing? Does he think I'm looking for a permanent relationship and prepared this meal to soften him up for the kill? Is that what I'm doing?

"I usually steer clear of those invitations." John continued, licking the last bit of meringue off his fork. Taking out a cigarette from his silver case, he lit up and took a long drag. "I dodged those invitations," he repeated, "because I was not ready to settle down with anyone. But ...." He left the sentence hanging in a blue smoke ring.

Not ready to settle down? But? What's coming next? Do I really want to know?

Suddenly, John's dark eyebrows rose into an inverted "V" as if that thought had just occurred to him. *What's going on in that handsome head of his?* "Come to think about it," he muttered slowly, as if he'd realized–at that very moment–something for the first time. "*This time* I feel different; it feels quite *natural* to be having dinner prepared for me by a woman, like *this* dinner tonight, made by *you*," he said, sucking in another drag. "I've suddenly become aware that

I *like* this," he paused a mini-second, "I really *do*." He sounded as if he was surprised at what he was saying. He took the cigarette out of his mouth, set it carefully onto the ashtray, and looked at me, his eyes sparkling, astonished at the revelation that had just occurred to him. "*This* feels so normal…so right!" A full smile spread across his face from ear to ear.

A thrill raced through my entire body, while my mind was a jumble of alarm and worry. *Is he thinking about commitment? Am I ready for this?*

We took our coffee into the living-room, and John joined me on the chesterfield. "This has been a lovely evening with you, Gail, and I've enjoyed it so much." He lifted my right hand and cushioned it between both of his, as warmth surged through me. I felt a deep longing and the sensation of being safe, protected, and adored. It left me weak.

John's right hand rose, hovering over mine like a humming bird as he stroked each finger. His lips caressed one finger-tip at a time and left me breathless with emotion.

"I really must go," he said, releasing my hand gently, hesitantly, and unwillingly. "Before the roads get any worse." His hands on his knees, he leaned forward, slowly rising from the couch He stretched his legs up and stood, his six-foot-three body towered over me. He buttoned his jacket and prepared to leave.

Reluctantly, I stood too. My mind screamed: *Don't go! Don't leave me like this.* My body cried out for more. John turned to face me and smiled. He placed his hands on either side of my face and moved closer, his warm breath on my ear, sending shivers of delight up my spine. He murmured something that I couldn't decipher and looked down at me, his eyes warm and deep with feeling as he pulled me into a long embrace. Our foreheads met, his lips parted and met mine with a kiss, gentle at first, and then deep and intimate, almost primal in its power.

My heart quickened. "Stay," I whispered. I nuzzled my head against the soft wool fabric of his sports jacket, ran my fingers to the buttons of his jacket and twisted one free out of its hole. I took his hand in mine.

"Come."

To this day, I can still smell the sweetness of his skin, the small indentation in his neck was like vanilla against the tip of my tongue. His touch, so soft, so gentle, was full of tenderness and kindness; he had a touch that didn't need words, as a near growl was pulled out of my throat.

The morning sky was cloudless and coloured a bold sapphire blue. The pale winter sun shone down, its warm breath like an Alberta Chinook that melted the drifts along the driveway. Tufts of white plopped from the branches of the apple trees onto the yard, and water drip-dripped from the eves. The storm was over. The baked Alaska was a red, white, runny, gooey, and sticky mess on the dining room table.

John Proposes: I Refused

"I want to marry you," John blurted out, just a little over a month later, when the boys were with their dad. Sitting at the kitchen table eating breakfast, John swallowed a mouthful of scrambled eggs, and repeated. "I want to marry you."

I almost choked on my toast. "What? What are you talking about, Hon? I've known you less than four months, for goodness' sake; you can't be serious!"

"I *am* serious and I'm telling you, I *really* want to marry you." His voice was filled with conviction, making it perfectly clear about what he wanted. He lifted his cup of coffee, took a sip and set his cup back down on the table as if it were settled.

This is ridiculous! I was not ready for a permanent relationship, and I wasn't sure I *wanted* one, either. *Talking marriage so soon—he must be mad!* My stomach clenched in fear as I remembered my failed marriage, how I'd given it my all for twelve years and got royally screwed at the end. I had been abandoned, with three little boys to raise alone, with no job or means of support, nor the right to a single solitary piece of property. I never wanted to go through that again. My relationship with Frank hadn't worked out either. *I had to head him off at the pass.*

On the other hand, I had survived being the lone parent. The boys were settled in their respective schools. I had my BA—having overcome my fear of intellectual failure. On top of that, I had security in my position as a consultant with the Board of Education, and was finally able to earn enough money to pay the mortgage on my own. For the first time in my life, I felt independent, settled, and in control of my life. "Do I want to give any of that up?" I asked myself, "*Heck no!*" I answered silently. But I really liked this guy. We had so much in common … but marriage, after knowing him only four months? I was not so sure.

I calmed my nerves and turned to John, ready with a rebuttal. "You are coming at me way too fast. I'm not at all sure if I *want* to get married. There are a few things you need to know about me up front." I bit my lower lip. "And when you hear me out, you might change your mind."

"Okay, what's on your mind?" John asked with that adorable smirk. *He's so darned charming!* I almost lost my train of thought.

"Well," I started, "I'm not moving to Hamilton."

"That's all right; I wouldn't expect you to. This is *your* home, where you and your boys are established and comfortable. The boys need to stay in their own schools and keep their friends. I would never disrupt your life or theirs." He stopped and took a sip of coffee. "I love you and want to be with you, that's all."

"Well, I'm not giving up my position of consultant; I love my job, and I've worked too hard to establish myself with this school board to make a change."

John smiled as if he'd already considered that. "Of course! I'd never think of disrupting your career; I'm impressed by your accomplishments and proud of the position you have as consultant. You have a great career ahead of you, and I am certainly not going to interfere with that." *He was impressed with my accomplishments, proud of my career?*

"I'm not giving up my university courses; I may want to continue on and get my Masters." *What will he think of that, having a wife with more education than him? That'll turn him off for sure.*

John shook his head and pulled out a cigarette and lighter. "Listen Gail, I recognize your ability and your desire to further your education; I applaud your ambition and drive. Of course you will want to get your Masters." He lit up and blew smoke rings, showing off. "One day you may even want to get your PhD."

I could hardly believe my ears. *He admires my intellect!* This was too good to be true. "And, I have one more thing."

John smiled and winked. "I'm ready."

Such a flirt! Why the heck is he so darned cute? "If I were to get married, I would want a pre-nuptial agreement." I was not about to give up the assets I had accumulated thus far.

"And that's all right too," John agreed. "You've worked too hard to give up anything you own." He took one last drag and stubbed out his cigarette into the ashtray. "I am not after your house, Gail." He reached over and took my hand, his eyes deep pools of warmth. "I just want to spend my life with *you*, that's all."

I'd never met a man who respected and admired me like this; and loved me to boot! But still ... Struggling to process all this, I remained unsure ...

"Well ... I'm not ready," I argued.

"That's all right. I'll wait until you are."

All of a sudden, the obvious occurred to me. "And I can't marry you—because I don't have a divorce!"

John's jaw dropped, his bushy eyebrows raised and his eyes widened. "Well, we'll have to do something about *that*." Despite my protestations, John hung around.

John introduced me to his son Adam and on every second weekend when my boys were with us, John brought Adam to join the crew. Adam fit right in between Blake and Ron. On those weekends, it began to feel like a real family.

Eventually, John asked if he could move in, and that was that. I got my divorce, and we married the following year, April 21st, 1979.

~~~

As I revisited John's proposal, forty years later, on a blistering hot day in August in 2018, a year before John died, I read this chapter to him. He was sitting in the blue wingback in the corner of the 'Lodge,' his silver head was buried in Leonard Cohen's latest book, and his round, silver-rimmed John Lennon glasses were perched on his nose. He was gaunt, and his extra-large flannel track-suit hung limply on his frail bones. He was so emaciated that he needed to wear a fleece-lined vest over top to insulate him from odd drafts.

Listening to every word I read, John was particularly attentive, as if checking for accuracy, to be sure I'd gotten everything right. When I came to the part, "*I want to marry you*," *he blurted out*" John stopped me, mid-sentence. He inclined his head to one side and frowned. "Very forward wasn't I—pretty cock-sure. Not very romantic, that's for sure."

I smiled remembering that moment over forty years before as if it were yesterday. "I *loved* how you proposed; you were so spontaneous, honest and authentic, so sure of what you wanted. I was too insecure to say yes immediately; I was such a dummy."

After finishing the rest of the chapter, I asked, "So, what do you think?"

John was quick to respond. "When you came to the part about my respecting your *intellect*, I wouldn't want readers to think that I was just in love with your mind; I thought you had a great body too!" His lips curled up into that half smile. "And when you wrote, "*I asked if I could move in*?"

"Yes?" I said, "What's wrong with that?"

John winked. "I would *never* have asked you if I could move in."

"I *thought* you had, but of course I could be wrong."

"Asking to move in would have been far too forward," he said grinning. "I moved in by osmosis, one suit at a time, until I had more clothes in *your* closet than in my apartment in Hamilton." He paused, flashing that smirk again. "Besides, the reader might think that I was only after your baked Alaska!"

I laughed out loud. *My gracious, that man still had his sense of humour even at the end of his rope.* "I guess I have some revising to do." I said with a smile, a tear bubbling at the side of my eyes, wondering how many months together we had left.

Our Unconventional Wedding

"I'd like our wedding to be casual, a family affair with all the boys involved. It's important to me that the boys are comfortable and a part of everything."

"If that's what you want," John replied, a grin spreading across his face. John and I were sitting at the kitchen table in our home on Highway 8, in February, 1979 making wedding plans.

"And I don't want to leave the boys after the wedding reception and take off on a honeymoon, leaving the boys behind. I just couldn't do that to them, Hon."

"I have an idea," John said, his eyes lighting up. "Why don't we go on our honeymoon over March break, when the boys are away with their other parents?"

"Good idea, and we could get married right after that, in April, maybe. That way, the boys will come home with us after the wedding so it will be a very natural transition for them to our new life."

"And," John suggested excitedly, "Why not have our reception on the May 24th weekend, allowing more people to attend?"

"That's a great plan," I agreed.

When we told the boys of our plans, Wesley said he'd like to take the pictures and would check with the art teacher to borrow a camera. Blake was quiet, deep furrows gathering across his forehead that I failed to enquire about. Ron had a questioning look in his eyes. He approached me later, when I was preparing supper. "Will you be changing your name to *'Taylor?'* " he asked. "I don't want *my* name to change."

"I hadn't really thought about it, sweetheart," I replied. "But now that you've drawn my attention to it, I think I'll call myself, Gail Heald-Taylor?" The glint returned to Ron's eyes.

John and I went to Niagara Falls, our wedding plans in place for April 21st, on that March break. It was the only conventional thing about our wedding—the very *last* place any self-respecting Ontarian would ever choose to spend their honeymoon!

I found the perfect dress—an off white, two-piece, silk dress with a flowing skirt that came to my calves. When I sent pictures of the wedding to my mother, she wrote back that I looked fat. Soon afterward, we took the boys shopping for new clothes at a men's shop in Cambridge. At seventeen, Wesley had shot up; he was almost up to John's eyebrows. As Wesley came out of the dressing room with his new clothes, the clerk commented, "Not hard to tell whose son *he* is!" There was dead silence for a very long moment. Then, we all broke out laughing at the clerk's mistake. *Yes, Wesley would soon become one of John's sons—very soon, very soon indeed!* We left the men's shop, carrying the wedding clothes for the boys. We were ready for the big event in just a few days.

Our wedding day was a blur. Only a few things from the day remain in my memory: Wesley taking pictures of the family in the driveway; tripping down the aisle of the church to a jazzed-up version of *A Closer Walk with Thee* by Joan Baez (that John had picked out and Wesley had taped for the ceremony); reading our marriage vows–"You are now husband and wife."; Adam, as John's best man, signing the wedding certificate; piling into cars; the wedding supper; and the sound of laughter. When we got home, the boys got changed and went out to play road-hockey in the driveway.

Our wedding reception was on the long weekend in May. It involved all the boys—from ordering the liquor, to tape-recording the music, to bartending. The hall was filled with both John's friends and mine. Even John's all-girl ball-team was there. The highlight, of course, was being in John's arms dancing the first dance to Elvis's *Can't Help Falling In Love*. The rest of the evening was a jumble of dancing, laughter and chatter of voices.

One story *does* stick in my mind. My friend, Sheldon, cornered me in the middle of the evening. "I ordered a rye and ginger from your son Ron," he said smiling. "And I almost gagged when I took a sip," he exclaimed. "Ron had mixed a glass with *half rye* and *half gin*! My twelve-year-old, Ron, was bartending and mixing wicked drinks!

The next day, Ron summed up the event. "That was the best party ever!" he exclaimed. "I loved the music and the dancing and everything." He paused and smiled: "And, of course, John's all girl ball-team. We should have a party like that every week!"

I smile when I think back to our unconventional wedding. It was over 45 years ago, and it was a family affair. Every step of the way was a natural transition that introduced the boys to a new chapter of our lives.

~~~

"Happy Anniversary," Blake called out—twenty-six years later—as he and his partner, Suzie, pulled into our driveway at the Lodge, our cottage on Lake Erie. It was April 21st, 2005. Suzie got the wheels of Blake's wheelchair out of the back seat, and the rest of it from the trunk, and pieced it together. My eyes glistened. I remembered the day Blake was diagnosed with MS. It was when he was twenty-seven, fifteen years earlier. Blake eased into the wheelchair, and Suzie wheeled him to the deck. It was a wonderful surprise, and we settled into a long visit.

Later, as they roared away in their cardinal-red Mazda convertible, turned the corner of Maple Bay and disappeared, out of sight, John turned to me. "I have a story to tell you about Blake, on that morning of our wedding day, back in 1979."

"Really?" I said, dipping my head to one side, a questioning look in my eyes.

John squeezed my hand and began. "I didn't want to tell you at the time, because I knew it would upset you on your special day."

My breath caught in my throat. *What on earth was it?*

"I was in our bedroom," John said, "when I heard a tap, tap on the door. When I opened it there was Blake, still in his pyjamas. "What's up?" I asked him.

Blake looked up at me, his forehead furrowed. "I don't want to come to the wedding," he stammered. He twisted his hands nervously in front of him, and tears glistened in his teenage eyes.

"Oh," I said, taken aback, thinking what I should say to him. After collecting my thoughts, I said, "Do you feel that you are being disloyal to your father if you came?"

"*Yes*," he said, "so I don't want to go to the wedding."

"I understand how you must be feeling," I told him. "I want you to know that this is *your* decision and only *your* decision to make." Blake looked at me kind of surprised, suspecting perhaps that we'd *make* him come to our wedding whether he wanted to or not. "But," I added, "while you are making your decision, I want you to think about how your *Mom* will feel if you decide *not* to come to our wedding." Blake's eyes grew wide, as if he hadn't considered that.

I patted him on the shoulder. "I also want you to know that your Mom and I will respect whatever you decide." Blake's eyes brightened then, and I told him to go back to his room to think about it. "And remember the decision is yours," I reminded him.

Tears welled up in my eyes. I squeezed John's hand. "Thank you for keeping this story from me for so many years. "You knew it would have broken my heart if I'd heard it back then."

Of course, Blake *did* come to our wedding; he is in all the wedding pictures I have hanging on our walls.

It is 2025, and my wonderful husband has been gone for seven years. I look at the pictures that were taken of our new family, that spring of 1979, as I sit in the bedroom of my condo, on the teal-blue, antique pine blanket box. Memories of that day, forty-five years ago, come flooding back to me—clearly and as warmly as my love for John ever deepens in my soul. I relive our wedding all over again.

When did I know I loved John?

I recall a sweet memory from 2018:

Shutting down my computer for the day, I went out onto the west deck where John usually preferred to sit. He wasn't there. A cool wind—too cold for August—caught in my throat, and whipped at my hair. Lake Erie was roiling and wild today, there were great waves crashing onto the rocky shore. Shivering, I rushed to the east deck, out of the wind. There was John, sitting on the hard wooden seat of one of the white Muskoka chairs, without the padded seat cushions. He was wearing his hoodie and puffy down-filled winter vest—he needed those in order to keep his frail body warm, even on these hot, humid days of summer. *Oh, my word, he doesn't have the energy or strength to bring the blue cushions out of the shed to soften the hard wooden seat!* Getting the cushions, I brought them to John. He placed his hands on the flat arms of the chair and levered up his weakened body so that I could place a cushion under him, and quickly slide another behind his back. Then, he lowered himself back down gradually, gingerly to the seat, air seeping out of his mouth in a soft sigh at the effort. "Thank you, Gail. That feels so much better."

Sitting down beside him in the matching chair, I stroked his hand and looked deeply at my beloved John, his thin sunken cheeks furrowed with deep ridges, like beach sand after a storm. I didn't know that this was the last August that he would spend with me. I leaned over and kissed his cheek, now riddled with wrinkles, like crumpled-up Christmas wrapping paper.

"I love you so much," I murmured. He smiled wanly and took my hand in his, like he did on that first date at that Hamilton night club, forty-five years ago– my tall, six-foot, handsome dude, his black hair sprinkled with silver, his dark mustache, perfectly trimmed, and so sophisticated as he led me to the dance floor, wrapped his arms about me, and waltzed with me to the "Four Lads". I squeezed his hand and wondered how many more months I would have him by my side.

"How are you feeling now, after your nap?" I asked.

He looked at me and tried to focus. "I slept some." His voice was low with a gravelly sound—unusual, I thought. *This is a decline compared to last month.* "How did your conference call go with Patti?" he asked.

"She liked some pieces, but not all of them. She always pushes me for more depth. She wants my pieces to have more detail, to answer questions readers might ask, things they might like to know. I find her frustrating sometimes. But she makes my writing better. I can see that."

"What did she want you to think about today?"

"She wanted to know when I knew I loved you; when was the moment I knew for sure. I think that's a stupid question to ask. I've loved you forever."

"What did you tell her?"

"I told her that I didn't know, I didn't know the *exact* time that you were the man for me. I felt stupid, but I really couldn't remember." I took the last sip of water from my turquoise plastic water bottle. "What does it matter when I first knew I loved you? I've loved you for over forty years, that's all that counts," I added defensively. "Do *you* recall the moment that *you* knew that you loved *me?*

John's soft cow-brown-eyes suddenly lit up, and his lips turned up in that adorable half-grin. "I loved you right from the *get go*," he said with more conviction than I'd heard in months.

"What do you mean, you loved me from the *get go*. When was that?"

"I was impressed with your presentation in Jack's Sociology class, that's for sure. And I was thrilled that you came to Jack's reunion party. Then, there was our first date, and the dinner you made for me, and of course the baked Alaska!" A wistful look crossed John's eyes. "Maybe my body knew that I loved you before my head did." He took a sip of water from his blue glass. He was grinning now. "Yes, I loved you from the *get go*."

"That's so very sweet, Hon. I'm feeling guilty now that I can't recall the moment that I first knew that I loved *you*. I wish that I could remember more clearly."

John sat quietly for a moment. "I think you told me that you loved me right after you went out with that bozo that your friend Sylvia introduced you to."

Bozo! My mind suddenly rewound, like a tape from an old news-reel, and spun back forty years. "It's all coming back; it was when we were first dating. I went on a blind-date with a man Sylvia and Doug introduced me to—I can't even remember his name. We went out for dinner and then back to Sylvia's for the evening. I spent the night fighting him off me. It was so dumb, so ridiculous! I couldn't wait to get back home." I shook my head, laughing, I remember driving down 401 yelling, '*I love John, I love John.*' As I flew past Guelph, I screamed '*I love John; he's the one I love.*' I spun off 401, onto Highway 24 to Cambridge, almost home, and excited to get back so that I could call and tell you.

I took John's cold hand in mine and looked at him. "That's when I knew I loved you!"

John smiled, a self-satisfied look crossing his gaunt face, his amber eyes twinkling, sparking with emotion.

"I could have saved you all that trouble," he

smirked. "You should have checked with *me* first!"

****

Our relationship has deepened so much from when we said our vows on April 21st 1979. I am still discovering things about John and about myself, all the time. I am discovering that life just continues on. We keep on living and learning until we can't.

RENEWAL

Reaching back in memory,
I review my life more clearly now
I see how your unconditional love
Is pivotal in my rebirth
With you I am
Adored not abandoned
Accepted not rejected
Worthy not worthless
Valued not criticized
Affirmed not spurned
Encouraged not belittled
Hopeful not hopeless
Empowered not powerless
Truly loved unconditionally

Life As a Blended Family

John and I had so much love for each other, that we felt sure our love would spill over onto all our children automatically. *How can it not? We have enough love to make it happen.* During the first few months, life seemed idyllic. Not much changed for the boys and me. We all headed out in different directions every morning—John to Hamilton, me to Kitchener, and the boys to their respective schools via school bus into Galt—Ron to Branchton, Blake to Stewart Avenue, and Wesley to Glenview High School. Blake and Ron continued playing hockey at Beverly Central Arena, while Wesley was involved in the drama club at Glenview as part of the lighting crew for a big spring production. Adam still came every second weekend. We now had four boys between the ages of 12 and 17. We imagined being a blended family like the *"Brady Bunch,"* the early 1970s TV sitcom.

I cautioned John that it might be difficult for my boys to have him in our home permanently.

"I agree that it will an adjustment for the boys to accept a new adult male in their lives, but I want to be clear, Gail, that I don't want to take on a *"father"* role, that's for sure; they have a father, and I respect that, and am not going to interfere with their relationship with him."

John took small steps to interact with them. He played touch-football with them in the back yard even though football was certainly *not* his forte. On his way home from work, he stopped at the Rockton arena to join me and watch Ron and Blake's hockey games.

"What do think of my reading to the boys?" John asked me, one evening. I thought it was a great idea.

John introduced the boys to *"Night"* by Elie Wiesel and read the first chapter to them. The boys sat, politely listening, but as soon as John finished reading, the boys jumped up and raced downstairs to get on their coats and boots. They took off to the neighbour's pond to play hockey before it got too dark, slamming the door behind them. The thought was a good one, but the selection was a bit over their heads. I gave John an *'A'* for trying.

Noticing how much Wesley enjoyed playing the guitar, he invited him to attend the *Harry Chapin* concert with us at Hamilton Place. It felt so good to be on a date with two important men in my life. Although Wesley didn't say much about whether he enjoyed himself, I overheard him telling his brothers all about it the next day.

My boys and Adam seemed to be getting along just fine. Adam and Blake enjoyed going to the local dump to scavenge old electronic junk with which to reinvent new gadgets. That summer, they worked weekends at the 'Lion Safari' in Rockton—Blake manned the corn-roast-booth, and Adam cleaned washrooms. Sometimes, we drove the boys to work, and other times they rode their bikes the five miles down the road.

John was impressed that my boys could cook. "I'm so impressed that they can cook for themselves, and Ron certainly *loves* garlic," he chuckled. "You can smell it on his sweater a mile away!"

"Yes," I agreed, laughing. "They *had* to on those days when I was away and taking evening courses for my BA."

John took the load off me in terms of meals. The first time he brought home cold-cuts and rolls for supper, the boys were ecstatic. "Wow," Blake exclaimed, his face lighting up, "Will you do this *every* Friday?" Some Fridays, John took us out to a restaurant, which was an extravagance that I could never afford. I remember the time that John took us to 'George's,' the local Chinese restaurant in Galt. Not accustomed to Chinese fare, the boys ordered hamburgers and fries! Eating at restaurants became a regular event. The night we went to 'Frank Vetere's', they couldn't contain their excitement that they could make all-you-can-eat ice cream sundaes for dessert. Their boys' smiles told me that they loved *this* change that John brought to our family!

I was also overjoyed when John took on family responsibilities too, like helping with the dishes, weeding the garden, and taking turns mowing the lawn. He even volunteered for a job on the Thursday night cleaning regimen that I'd established when I was on my own. Within a month, John decided to pay for a cleaning person to come once a week! The boys cheered.

Complimenting John, I told him, "You can't fully understand how much I appreciate your being such a helpmate, a true partner, after what I experienced in my former marriage." I reached up and gave him a big juicy kiss.

One Friday morning, John noticed me gathering up all the laundry, putting it into green garbage bags and dragged them to the front door. "What are you doing?" he asked, his forehead furrowing into a frown.

"Well, our washer broke down last year, and I couldn't afford to replace it," I explained. "So, on my way home after work, I stop at the *Dominion Plaza* in Galt, at the Laundromat there. I put the dirty laundry into several washers, before I go grocery shopping at the *Dominion* store. After I put the groceries into the car, I go to the Laundromat, take out the loads of laundry, pack it all into the green garbage bags, and bring it home to dry in the automatic dryer downstairs."

John shook his head in disbelief. "It's been a Friday ritual for me for over a year."

One Monday morning, I gathered up the garbage into green bags and had them at the door. "Where are you taking them?" John remarked, his mouth twisting in surprise.

"I drop off the garbage at the landfill on my way to work."

"Why?" John asked, perplexed, his eyes widening, "Why in the world are you hauling the garbage to the dump?"

"I can't afford the price of rural garbage pick-up." My initial salary in 1972 was at a poverty level, until I got my BA.

"Well, you can *now*," John said emphatically. "Taking the garbage to the recycling station is way too much work for you. Please make arrangements for next week's garbage pick-up, okay?"

The following Saturday, John took Wesley shopping for a new washing machine. Wesley couldn't wait to tell me all about their excursion. Then, John took his turn doing the laundry.

In John, I'd found a *real* partner to share my life and make our family stronger. *What a wonderful man I have found! Or did he find me? Hell, we finally found each other!*

I basked in how our blended family was working; it was a fantasy come true. Taking stock of how our children were adjusting, I believed that things would be fine. Life seemed better for all of the boys. Adam seemed to be enjoying being with boys his age; my sons were overjoyed at our Friday routine of going out for dinner; there wasn't any evidence of negative attitudes, and there was no disruptive behaviour. They seemed to be accepting of this new man in our family. Although I didn't observe any outward demonstrations of affection toward John, as I had hoped, I believed my sons were gradually learning to trust him. I couldn't believe my good luck! *A husband who actually helped and appreciated what needs to be done in running a home! I'd hit the jackpot!* What a good role model he was for my guys!

I was satisfied with that.

Natural Consequences

The need to discipline the boys, at times, soon raised its ugly head. Wesley disappeared for a week during March break. We had no clue where he was—he'd left no note and his brothers didn't know. We were worried sick and contacted the police.

Then, we got a phone call. Wesley was in Atlanta, Georgia. He asked if we could send him fare to get home. We wired money to him. I was so relieved that he was safe and alive.

Wesley's school had planned a trip to Disney,

and he decided he would hitchhike with his buddy. To this day I don't remember what the reason was for his going–was he angry at us? I really had no clue.

"So, what are we going to do?" I asked John, after we'd wired Wesley the money.

"I think that using *natural consequences* will work with Wesley," John suggested, sipping his cup of coffee as we sat on the couch in the living room and contemplated what to do when Wesley got home.

"Well, I disagree!" I argued, "I think he should be *punished* for leaving without telling us and making us worry like that," I said angrily. "On the phone, Wesley didn't seem to give a whit that he had caused us so much worry." Dissatisfied with John's solution, I thought that Wesley should at *least* apologize, at the bare minimum, "If *I* did anything like this when I was a kid, I'd have gotten a licking for sure; my mother would have beaten the crap out of me." I flinched remembering the sting of the switch, the smack of the wooden spoon. *Oh my God, am I behaving like my mother, believing that punishment is the solution? I certainly don't want to be like her!* I tried so hard to do just the *opposite* of how my mother had parented me.

Sadness crossed John's eyes. "I was beaten as a kid, too," he remarked, his voice almost a whisper. "And I believe beating is a brutal way to discipline." He took my hand in his. "I abhor *any* kind of abuse, both physical and verbal." In a flash I thought of Wes Sr.

Does he verbally abuse the boys, like he did me?

John set his coffee cup down on coffee table. "I certainly don't have all the answers" he said calmly, his forehead wrinkling in waves as if sifting through his thoughts. "But instead of punishment, I believe in the idea of *natural consequences,* and I'd really like to try the concept with Wesley."

"So, how would that work in *Wesley's* case?"

"I think that we should just ignore Wesley's actions." John's voice seemed sure, confident. "Look Gail, think of it this way. It couldn't have been an easy holiday tenting every night on some lonely Florida beach, and then camping on the inter-state in the rain would have been abysmal."

I nodded, trying to understand John's point of view. "And I guess it was pretty terrifying to be in downtown Atlanta," I admitted.

"A white boy in a predominantly black area," John added. "I can't imagine it."

"I never thought about it like that."

"So, I suggest that we chalk up this episode as a *natural consequence.*"

"Okay," I said hesitantly, still somewhat skeptical, "I understand what you're saying, and I am willing to go along with it."

John became quiet, suddenly, as if deep in thought. "I have a certain amount of empathy for Wesley," John said wistfully. "My high school years were pure hell!" His eyes grew wide; his lips pinched together in a thin straight line. "Teenage years are really tough on boys, and I can understand how difficult adolescence might be for Wesley."

Oh, my word, John really cares about my son; he seems to understand him.

John went on. "I believe that we should continue to be positive and look for ways to support Wesley."

My spirit lifted and my concerns evaporated; I suddenly felt optimistic. "You are wonderful," I said, gently taking his big hand in mine. "I trust you and really think this might work."

It was such a relief to have Wesley home safely, that I ignored how he shrugged the whole thing off and didn't apologize for the incident. I was hoping, like John, that Wesley's harrowing experience was enough of a *natural consequence* for his unruly behaviour.

In August, 2018, when Blake was visiting, I asked Blake about Wesley's misadventure in Florida. I asked him point blank: "Did you know that Wesley had hitchhiked to Florida that March break?"

"Sure, I did," Blake replied with a grin. "Lots of teenagers did it in those days."

"So, you knew where he'd gone when I'd asked you?"

"Yeah," he smiled. "I wasn't going to squeal on him; he was my brother!"

At that moment, I learned the strength of brotherly love.

Teenage Rebellion

"I'm out of here," Wesley yelled, slamming the door with a loud *BAM!*.

Oh, my word, it's happening again! I can't go through this again. My God, this is becoming a pattern. It was always the same thing; Wesley wouldn't do his chores, and I was getting sick and tired of it. I was too angry to be worried when Wesley didn't come home for supper that November evening in 1978, but when it started to get dark, I began to fret. *He's probably in the trailer out front, sleeping off his anger. It isn't the first time he's done it.* I threw on a jacket, slid into my sneakers, and went outside to check but there was no sign of him. At my insistence, we got into the car and headed out onto Highway 8 toward Galt; I scoured the ditches and looked up side roads. It was futile.

"He'll come home when he gets cold," John assured me. "I'm sure he will; I know how *I* was at his age."

But Wesley didn't come home, and I spent another frantic, sleepless night of worry, thinking he'd been in a car accident or abducted.

The next morning, standing at the stove making scrambled eggs, I promised myself that I'd call the police right after breakfast. As I reached for the garlic spice bottle to sprinkle onto the light-yellow mush of eggs, I heard the squeak of the front door opening, a soft whosh-click. Startled, I dropped the spatula and turned just as Wesley walked into the kitchen, nonchalantly, looking well rested, and seemingly unconcerned about anything at all.

Pissed off, yet relieved at the same time, I yelled louder than I intended, "Where in the world have *you* been? I asked, unable to keep my impatience in check.

Wesley's lips lifted into a crooked grin. "I was in the trailer when you looked in, and I saw you and John drive out the driveway, probably looking for me," he said as if unconcerned about how worried I'd been. "I'm starving, can I have some eggs?"

I was suddenly furious. *What a cocky son-of-a-gun! Who does he think he is scaring me half to death?* I lost my patience. "If you saw us leave," I said, my voice raising, "then why the heck didn't you come inside?"

Wesley looked at me and twisted his mouth to one side in a half grimace, and grin, shrugged and was silent. *Is he doing this on purpose? Is he trying to make me angry? What the hell is going on with him? Natural consequences don't seem to be working on him!*

John and I talked. "I think Wesley is having difficulty adjusting to the changes in the family now that *I* am a part of it," John offered. "I've worked overtime *not* to be a *"father figure"* for him; I recognize that he's *got* a father. And I respect that. I'd just like to understand what is going on in his head that's causing this negative behaviour."

"I agree, but I can't take much more of this."

"Maybe it's time to have a talk with him?" John suggested. After supper the next evening we invited Wesley to sit with us on our bed. John started. "We're worried about you, Wesley," John said calmly. "You seem troubled; is there anything you want to tell us?" John asked empathetically.

Wesley stared straight ahead, pursing his lips in silence, hunching his shoulders as though anticipating a fight.

I looked into his eyes. "Is there something we can do differently that would make you feel better?" I asked.

Wesley was deaf to my question.

I continued, "Why don't you do your chores? Why do you run away from home instead?"

Wesley looked away, silent.

"This is the *second* time you've done this," I said, frustration rising in my voice. "Don't you understand how worried we are about you?" I was struggling to maintain control, yet at the same time could feel my body begin to stiffen in anger. *I am not dealing with this very well, but I am so damned frustrated with him.*

John reached and placed his hand over mine. I felt my heart-rate slow down. "Help us understand why you choose to take off rather than talk to us," John asked gently. Wesley remained mute.

Pausing, I looked deeply into Wesley's eyes and hesitated just a moment before asking slowly, cautiously, "Are... you.... unhappy.... living.... with.... us?" I asked, struggling with each word, unsure if I wanted to hear his answer.

Wesley shrugged his shoulders, looking puzzled, raising his eyebrows as if this was something he hadn't thought about. But he remained stoic.

John turned to Wesley and asked again, "Are you unhappy living with your mother and me?" he asked kindly.

I closed my eyes. *What if he wants to live with his father instead of us?* I wanted to know, but I was terrified at the same time, afraid that he might *want* to live with his father instead of us.

The air was thick with unspoken words. I looked up to see the skin between Wesley's eyebrows crease as if he was pondering the question. But no sound came from his mouth.

I've got to find out. I've got to know if he wants to live with his Dad regardless of the anguish it may cause me. I've got to be able to support him if he does. I've just got to. I closed my eyes and pursed my lips. Mustering all my courage, I said, "Would you rather... live...with... your...father?"

"HECK, NO!" Wesley shouted emphatically.

I jerked up in shock. I was totally stunned by his answer; it took a moment for relief to settle in and my heart to stop pounding. He doesn't want to live with his dad. *Then what the heck does he want?* He certainly acts as though he doesn't want to live with us. *What's going on in his head?*

John's body relaxed, seeming to also be relieved by Wesley's answer. Changing the subject, John asked, "Is there something wrong at school?" John knew that life at school could be difficult for teenage boys.

Wesley sat mute.

John added, "Would you like to go to another school, a private school like Ridley College in St. Catharines?" John offered quietly. "It's a *great* school."

Wesley's eyebrows scrunched up instantly and worry lines wove suddenly across his forehead. His eyes grew wide with panic. "NO," he called out in alarm.

His pupils wide with fear, he stammered. "I don't want to be sent away to a private school," he shouted, his lips quivering.

"Then what is it you want?" I asked.

Wesley just looked at me and I saw disdain on his face. Did I notice a smirk? As if signalling this meeting was over, he stood up and left us.

John and I sat quietly for a long moment, each of us deep in private thoughts.

"What are we going to do?" I asked, my voice shaking. I wondered if we'd done the right thing, by using natural consequences instead of some kind of punishment, when Wesley had gone to Florida without our permission.

John broke the silence. "I wonder if some of Wesley's problem is that he can't participate in extra-curricular activities at school because he is bussed every day?" John asked, concerned. "Maybe that will be an issue for Blake too when he enters high school next year."

Surprised at John's comment, I asked, "Do you think the boys would be happier living in town so they'd have access to more school clubs, and sports?"

"I think it is something to consider."

In February of 1979, John and I started looking for a home in Cambridge, even though it meant

John had a longer commute to Hamilton. We found our next home on Inverness Place, in Galt.

When I reflect on that conversation with Wesley, 46 years ago (in 1978), many things come to mind. First, we discovered very clearly what Wesley *didn't* want: he did not want to live with his Dad, and he didn't want to leave home and attend a private school.

Through hindsight, I also now understand that Wesley *was* going through puberty; he was flexing his wings and fighting for independence and power. He needed to cut his ties to *me*, something a boy needed to do to become his own person. John knew this, but I was too locked into a pattern of *rules, chores,* and *punishment*. I was part of the problem. I was trying so hard to maintain my own power and control that I couldn't see John's point of view. I regret that, for both Wesley and I. It would have saved a lot of grief for both of us. As I re-examine John's approach, so thoughtful, empathetic, full of understanding and possibilities to make Wesley's life better, I wish in some way that I could have followed *his* example.

My son Ron, now fifty-eight, visited me recently. I asked him what it was like, as a little brother, with Wesley's antics. "Hell, Mom, Wesley did crazy dangerous things all his life! Ron listed them, one anecdote after another: there were at least ten outrageous things his brother had done when they were growing up, either with his Dad or with us. "I think Wesley was

ADHD before it was invented!" he chuckled. Ron's eyebrows came together and his mouth twisted into a grimace. "But then, you always took *his* side, Mom."

"What do you mean?" I asked, perplexed.

"Wesley was *not* the kindest brother to me. He was often quite mean, and he got away with everything, because *you* always took his side."

"Really?"

Ron began to name incident after incident. "But the worst time was when you cut Blake's hair and mine—when the style was long like the Beatles. But Wesley raised a raucous and you let *him* have his way." Ron's voice rose, twenty-six-years of suppressed anger evident.

"I'm sorry I did that," I said, wondering *why* I had always taken Wesley's side… In a faint and distant memory of fifty years earlier, I could hear his dad yelling at his ten-year-old son, Wesley, for some innocent misdeed. Somehow, in that moment, I felt particularly protective of my little Wesley. Had I unconsciously shielded him from his own wrong doings from then on? Did I do that at the expense of my darling Ron's childhood? *Oh, my God! What a terrible Mother I was!* How hurtful that must have been for my little Ronnie, not to have been believed by his mother, his truth dismissed as if he didn't count, or wasn't loved. How awful for him to have harboured that hurt these past twenty-six years. Could my apology diminish his pain?

Teenage Boys: First Jobs

It was a houseful of teenage boys, that ten years we lived at Inverness place. It was a time when the boys, Wesley, Blake, Adam and Ron, experimented with finding jobs and purchased vehicles of their own.

They found their first jobs when we lived on Highway 8. Wesley was the first to get a paying job—gluing eyes on pet rocks for a friend's company. "I get five cents a rock, Mom, five dollars a hundred," he told me. "And I make hundreds of them. I'll be rolling in dough before you know it." But Wesley soon found that it was tedious work. He decided, instead, to work for Mr. Decker on his nearby farm. Wesley would drive the tractor and do other odd jobs around the farm.

A year or two later, Wesley got a job working at *Canadian General Tower*. "The company makes vinyl products like baby-pants," Wesley explained. "One job was to fill baskets of plastic pellets and dump them into a tower. On the first day, I filled the whole tower in five hours! And I was really proud of myself," he said proudly. "But the supervisor was really upset."

"Slow down," he told me angrily. "The union has this job time–measured and assessed at a three-day-job."

"That's unions for you," Wesley commented.

When we lived at Highway 8, Adam and Blake found work at the *Lion Safari* in Rockton.. It was easy for them to get there; they would ride their bikes there from our home. On weekends, when Adam was with his mom, he worked at the *Ancaster Golf and Country Club*.

When we moved into Inverness Place, Blake and Adam became teenage entrepreneurs. The two of them loved going to the local dump to gather discarded electronic gadgets or wire that they could use to experiment and build things. One time, they built an electric hotdog cooker with a nail hooked up to a battery and wires. It cooked the first hotdog to perfection!

One of Blake's most lucrative teenage ventures was selling discarded black-and-white TVs, when he was sixteen "It was our biggest money making-scheme...ever. Adam and I brought one home to try it out and it was perfectly operable."

Blake explained how their scheme worked. "We put up a hand-made sign in *Buck's Variety Store* and advertised them at bargain prices."

"But where did you store them?" I asked him. "I don't recall old TV's in the house."

"We didn't have to store them anywhere," Blake answered. "When we got an order, we just went to the dump, picked it up, and delivered it to the buyer."

I shook my head. "What little entrepreneurs you were!" I remarked, laughing.

Blake just smiled. "At the time, Adam and I couldn't understand why people were throwing out perfectly good TVs. We didn't realize until years later that it was because coloured TVs had just come out. Most people wanted coloured TVs and threw out their black-and-white ones." He paused. "I see now, that not everyone could afford a coloured TV, so people purchased the black-and-white ones rather than have no TV at all. We had a ready market to fill. They sold like hot-cakes," he laughed.

Over the years Blake got jobs in a variety of places—*Brick Oven Pizza, Babcock/Wilcox, Granada TV, Cambridge Cycle* and *Sunny's Gas Bar.*

Ron's first job was at *Brick Oven Pizza.* That late night job has affected Ron's sleeping habits ever since.

Ron's Scariest Hallowe'en Costume

In October 1975, Ron was in Grade 5 at Branchton Public School, which was a country school just south of Galt, Ontario. His goal that year was to have the scariest Hallowe'en costume, ever. Up until then, Ken Schmidt had always won first prize. But *this* year, Ron was determined to win. He enlisted Wesley to help make his costume. It was to be the absolute scariest costume, bar none. Here is his story, written in his own words.

RON'S SCARIEST HALLOWE'EN COSTUME

BY RON HEALD

I used to love Hallowe'en as a kid. It was a great holiday. You dressed up and walked the neighbourhood, and people gave you candy. Whoever thought of this idea was a genius. A true genius. My brothers and I liked making our own costumes. We used to get right into it. My oldest brother, Wes, would help me with my costume, and also try and out do himself each year. My brother was very creative. Each year he came up with good ideas for costumes.

I went to a small two room school for grade 4 and 5. It was the best school I ever attended. I had a lot of great memories there. Hallowe'en at that school was one of them. Each year, our principal would dress up as a vampire and hide in a coffin in the library in the basement. The coffin was an old wooden box used to store sports equipment. But on Hallowe'en, it became a coffin. Our teachers would lead us to the library in the basement of the school, get us settled, and read scary stories to us. The wooden box was placed in the centre of the room, and we students would sit in a circle around it. The Grade 5's knew what was going on. The Grade 4's had no idea. The Grade 5's were all smiling, as they knew what we Grade 4's were about to experience. The Grade 4's had no idea that our principal was lying silently in the coffin, waiting for the lull in the story so he could slowly emerge and frighten us. The first time I experienced that, I was frightened. It was an exhilarating feeling. It is a great memory. Fifty students, all dressed up in our costumes, sitting in our basement library listening to scary stories. Hallowe'en was a big celebration at Branchton School when I was a kid. Not only were there scary stories and vampires in coffins, there was the costumes contest..... Ah... the costumes contest.

In the fall of Grade 4, we were told that we were going to have a Hallowe'en party in our school. Both the Grade 4 class and the Grade 5 class would participate, together. It would be a whole school celebration. There were going to be prizes for the best costumes. One of the prizes was for Scariest Costume. I really wanted to win it. With Wes' help, I was sure I would. We came up with the idea to make a medieval executioner. We used an old hockey stick and some cardboard to make the long-handled-axe. I had a black hood, black gloves... black everything. It was scary. It was a great costume.

When it came time to the judging at the end of the day, I was sure I was going to win. Nobody's costume even came close to mine. When my teacher announced the prizes, I won Most Original. "Most Original?" I don't want to be original..... I want to be scary. It's Hallowe'en after all. Ken Schmidt won Scariest. I was shocked.... Ken Schmidt?.... Seriously? All he had was a rubber werewolf-mask. He even wore his normal clothes. How is that even scary? I was a guy who chopped off people's heads. But Ken Schmidt was the Golden Boy. He was taller than me, better looking than me, and a slightly better hockey player. We were friends, but I was a little jealous. He had it all. I thought for sure my costume was scarier than his. I went home on the bus, disappointed. I vowed that I would win the Scariest Costume when I was in Grade 5. I would think of something that no one could beat. Not even the Golden Boy.

Sure enough, in Grade 5, it was announced that we would be having another Hallowe'en party, with prizes for the best costumes. I was determined that I was going to win. I had to have a really scary idea. I had to have something so scary that it wouldn't even be close.

Wes and I came up with an idea for the scariest costume ever. We thought about a Zombie costume, with blood all over his face. We thought that was pretty cool. Then Wes said, "What about a zombie that had a real knife stuck in his neck?" I loved the idea, but how was that possible? We needed a fake head, of course. We thought about it for a bit, and we remembered that my Mom had a few wigs. The wig stands were made of styrofoam heads. They were all white, but perfectly head-shaped. So, we decided to use one of my Mom's styrofoam wig-heads. My Mom was pretty cool, so she said, "You can have it." She thought our costume idea was pretty cool, as well. We painted the white styrofoam to look like a real head and face. We looked through our kitchen drawers to find the largest and scariest knife we could. We found a large butcher knife with a serrated edge and stuck it in the neck of the wig head. We then painted blood coming out of it. It looked great. It was scary as hell.

Next, we borrowed one of my Mom's boyfriend's dress-shirts. We asked my mom for one. Frank would have never given it to us. He was kind of an asshole, but that's another story. She gave us one that he never wore any more. We used a board for fake shoulders that would rest on top of my head–my real head. The fake head we attached to the board. We draped the shirt over the board. We cut out eye-holes in the shirt, so I could see. We made fake hands to come out of the cuffs at the end of the sleeves and tied them with string to each end of the board. I tried it on, and it looked great. I was gonna win Scariest Costume for sure.

It was the night before Hallowe'en, when Wes said he had an idea to make it even scarier. He asked me, "What if fake blood oozed out of the neck?"

"You mean like real blood? … Can we do that? Do we have time?" I asked.

"I think so," Wes said.

So, Wes got some tubing from his aquarium and

a squeeze-ball. We hollowed out the head, (the fake one) and ran the tubing up through the shirt so that it came out at the hole where the knife was sticking out. We filled the tube and large squeeze-ball with red food colouring and water. Wes put the costume on and tried it out. It looked fantastic! The fake blood was a deep red that trickled down the side of the neck and soaked into the shoulder and chest of the white shirt. It was so cool! I knew right then I was going to win. There was no way that anybody, not even Ken Schmidt, could come up with something that good.

It was getting close to bedtime, so we had to put the costume away. I didn't get a chance to try it out. Wes told me to remember to squeeze the ball gently when I was wearing it the next day at our class party. I didn't ask him why, I just agreed.

I was so excited, I couldn't sleep. It felt like Christmas Eve. I couldn't wait for the next day.

When I got up the next morning, I packed up the costume in two large garbage bags and headed for the bus stop. Everyone was asking me what I was gonna be this year. I said, "You'll see." They asked if they could see the costume. I told them they'd have to wait for the party in the afternoon. So, when the bus arrived, we got on and went to school. I was keeping my costume a secret.

The morning seemed to last forever. We were told that, after lunch, we could change into our costumes for the party. Finally, lunch was over and we all headed to the washrooms to change. I looked over to see what Ken Schmidt had in his bag. I couldn't believe it, as I watched him pull out the same rubber werewolf mask. *That was it? That was his costume?* I knew right then I had the prize in the bag!—Pardon the pun. He had the same costume as last year. There was no way he'd win Scariest Costume now. All the other boys watched as I removed my costume from my two bags. There were lots of gasps and comments of, "COOOL!" heard throughout the change room. They all thought the real knife coming out of the neck was pretty sweet. I didn't tell anyone that blood came out of the neck. I wanted it to be a surprise. So, after everyone left the washroom, I filled the tube and ball with water and added the red food colouring. I left the bathroom and headed to class for the party.

The party was good. Everyone loved my costume. No one complained about a real knife sticking out of the neck, not even the teachers. I can't imagine that happening today. The day was nearing an end, and it was time for the two teachers and our principal to do the judging. All of us that wanted to win a prize for our costumes were to go to the front of the class. This was my chance. When everyone was looking, I would start the blood flowing out of my fake head. About ten of us went to the front. There was a prize for the prettiest, funniest, most original, and… scariest, in my mind, the only *real* prize. It was Hallowe'en, and I wanted the prize for scariest costume ever. When we got to the front, I faced the class and the ten of us vying for a prize were all lined up in a row. Ken was on my left. I thought to myself, *"The rubber mask aint gonna cut it this year."* I think I even felt a little sorry for him. Hilda Brun with her white angel costume was on my right. Lisa Brethauer was next to her dressed as a princess. Those two were going for prettiest, I was sure.

Once we were all lined up, our principal told us to pose and show off our costumes. Now was the time to show off what my costume could do. As I posed, the blood would come out of the neck and I would scare the hell out of everyone.

But just then, I remembered Wes telling me the night before to squeeze the ball gently. I never asked him why, I just figured it was to save the fake blood or something. I really didn't think it was an important instruction. I didn't think it was really important how hard I squeezed the rubber ball. I only had about fifteen seconds to make my mark. I wanted there to be lots of blood. So..... I squeezed... I squeezed hard... I squeezed fast. I heard screams from the rest of the kids at their desks.... It was working. My costume was scaring them. I heard Hilda and Lisa screaming beside me. Everyone was scared. This might be a good time to tell you that the knife was sticking out of the right side of my fake head. The fake blood was coming out to the right. I must also tell you that I had no peripheral vision. I could only see straight ahead through the tiny eye-holes in the shirt. I could only see the reaction of my classmates at their desks and the teachers and principal at the back of the class. I could not see my fellow contestants. I could only see the students at their desks. The look of horror and fear and terror and disgust on their faces was thrilling! I had this context wrapped up! There was no denying that I had the scariest costume!

Miss Bates came running to the front waving her arms. She's stopping me?... *It's so scary, that the kids can't take it*, I thought. She calmly asked me to stop the blood and she turned me to the right to face Hilda and Lisa. Now *I* was scared. The white angel and pretty princess costumes were splattered with droplets of fake blood. Hilda looked like one of our fall chickens freshly beheaded! Her white angel feathers were spotted with blood. Lisa had fake blood freckles all over the top of her princess costume.

I didn't realize why Wes had told me to squeeze the ball gently. I just figured it was to save juice. I didn't realize that it was to prevent the red food colouring from spraying all over the place. I don't quite remember what happened next. I felt so bad that I'd ruined two costumes. I was also a little worried. What if the butchered angel and the bloody princess were now the scariest costumes?

After we were all settled in our seats.... And the

blood was cleaned from the floor, the teachers and principal left for a few minutes to determine the winners. I needn't have worried about Hilda or Lisa taking my rightful award for Scariest Costume. Scariest costume went to Ken Schmidt. And me... you guessed it. I got Most Original. I really wanted to be Scariest! I really couldn't argue with their decision. Mine was a very *original* costume. But Ken Schmidt? .... Really? Two years in a row? Hilda Brun's bloody angel was way scarier than a rubber werewolf mask!

Just say'n.

~~~

Camping With the Boys

Our first experience of camping was at the Ontario Teacher's Federation (OTF) campground east of Parry Sound near the village of Dunchurch. Wesley was in his glory, as he setup the trailer

"I can do it," Wesley told John. "I can back the trailer into the campsite," he said enthusiastically. "I've done it a million times before."

"Sure thing, Wesley," John encouraged, throwing him the keys. To my surprise, Wesley jumped into the van and backed up the trailer like a pro, perfectly between two trees.

"Fantastic," I told him. "My goodness, you are a good driver."

Wesley beamed.

That was the summer of 1978. John and I took the family on two excursions, believing that a holiday together would help us connect in more relaxing settings, even though John and I were *not* campers by choice. The boys were excited about going up to the OTF camp-grounds in Parry Sound, something they did with their Dad every summer.

I made the meals every day at camp so the boys were free to participate in all the activities with the other campers: they played down at the beach, went on hikes with young friends, and fished off the wooden wharf down at the lake. In the evenings, John, the boys and I played softball before sitting around campfires, singing.

One afternoon, as John I walked down to the beach, he took my hand. "I am not really comfortable using your ex-husband's trailer and van," John confided. "You realize that he's *using* you as a free storage lot," he pointed out.

I was startled at first. It took me a few minutes for John's comments to sink in. I began to see what John was getting at. Suddenly acknowledging that John was *right*, I realized that I *had* allowed my ex-husband to store his trailer for the year on our acre-sized-lot. John squeezed my hand affectionately. "You know he did that so he wouldn't have to pay storage fees for a year, as most trailer people have to do."

"I'd never thought about it like that."

"So, you know that he's taking *advantage* of you, don't you?"

It all suddenly became clear to me. *Why the heck do I fall into the same old trap of doing what my ex tells me, as if I'm not a capable woman?* I didn't seem to have punctured that power balloon he'd had over me for years.

Later in the week, Dunchurch had its local fair. We all went. I particularly enjoyed participating in the three-legged and gunny-sack races. The craziest game of all was the boiled-egg-race, where we ran as fast as we could, carrying a boiled egg on a spoon held tight in our teeth. I smile at the memory.

One rainy day, we went into Parry Sound and took the boys to see the first *Star Wars* movie with Harrison Ford, Carrie Fisher, Mark Hamill and Alec Guiness. The boys loved it; they got hooked on the sequels for the next forty years.

Another time that summer, Adam joined us when we went to *Have Some Fun Park*, in Fergus. Unlike its name, it turned out to be anything *but* fun. For that whole blistering week in August, the trailer sat on a flat barren spot without a tree in sight; no shade was to be found anywhere.

I was impressed with Blake's ability to sail the little sailboat that he and his brothers built at their

Dad's when they visited him during the winter months. It is a sport that Blake enjoys to this day, even with his advanced MS, when he sails every summer at the Toronto Disabilities Sailing Club. The other excitement on that trip was when Adam got an asthma attack. We rushed him to Fergus Hospital Emergency Ward! He made a full recovery, thank goodness.

After that summer's camping experiences, John arranged summer holidays at Sauble Beach on Lake Huron for the family. The boys enjoyed those weeks throughout their teenage years.

Summers At Sauble Beach

Summers at Sauble Beach on Lake Huron were some of our happiest vacations. It was John's idea to find a spot there. "I went there as a kid, a preschooler at my Grandmother Clifford's cottages," he told me, a nostalgic look in his eyes as he pulled out his photo album and pointed to a picture of him, a tiny tyke of two, maybe three, digging in the sand. "Mom still owns property east of town," he pointed out. "Sauble will be a great place to take the boys for summer vacations."

John found the *Pine Scene Resort* situated a couple of miles south of the town of Sauble, right on Lake Huron beach, about twenty steps to the water's edge. *Resort* was a misnomer because it consisted of three run-down cottages owned by an ancient couple in their eighties (about the same age as I am currently, and at 86, I don't feel old at all). The cottage we rented most frequently had three bedrooms, a kitchen, and a floor-to-ceiling, glassed-in sunroom that overlooked Lake Huron. It was built from the original pine, which had been cut from the property at the turn of the twentieth century. The walls, which went only halfway up to the wide open space of the rafters, allowed John, at six foot three, to reach up and wrap his fingers over the top of each wall.

The kitchen had a two-burner propane gas stove for cooking, a sink with cold running water, and a refrigerator from the 1950s that coughed and rattled. It competed, each night, with the crashing surf of Lake Huron. The hand-hewn pine cupboards housed the dishes and cutlery we needed for the two weeks.

The old-fashioned electric toaster from the 1930s proved to be a challenge for me. First, I pulled open the two metal flanges, and placed slices of bread on the inside of each flap. The moment the flaps closed, the electric coils immediately turned a bright orange-red to toast the bread. While the bread was toasting, I started setting the table in the sunroom. I suddenly smelled the acrid smell of burnt toast and saw clouds of blue smoke filling the whole cottage.

"What's that awful smell!" Wesley called from his room. "You're burning the cottage down, Mom!" It took many blackened slices of burned toast before I got the hang of using this ancient artifact!

The bathroom was also rudimentary, with only cold water. That was fine for the toilet, and the cold-water sink was fine for washing our hands or taking a sponge-bath. But at the end of the first week, we got into the lake for a *real* scrub-down. I took a bar of ivory soap—it really *did* float—and I went out into the lake for a bath. Lake Huron is the second largest of the Great Lakes.

As I shivered in the frigid water, I called to John. "Next year, let's get a cottage with modern plumbing," wishing like heck I was in my hot bathtub at home.

Flash forward: I am struck by the fact that I had lived on or near three of the Great Lakes: Lake Superior at Thunder Bay; Lake Ontario when we lived in St. Catharines, and, in later years, on Lake Erie at the 'Lodge' in Selkirk. I can cheat by saying I'd spent time on four of the five Great Lakes if I count the summers we spent here on Lake Huron at Sauble! Lake Michigan is the only one to elude me.

On cool August mornings, before I started breakfast, John lit the pot bellied wood stove to take the chill off the cottage. The thick coil of farmer's sausage we bought at the local butcher in town was every bit as good as the peameal bacon *(back-bacon)*. I smile, remembering that Americans call it "*Canadian bacon.*" Once the sausage was cooked, I fried up a mess of scramble eggs. Today, I can still smell the aroma of bacon and sausage, scrambled eggs mingled with burnt toast, and smoke from the wood-burning stove wafting through the air. It is the scent of nostalgia! We took our plates of food to the picnic table in the glassed-in sunroom that overlooked the lake and watched the white-crested waves roll in, and crash, on the deer–coloured sand. It was picture perfect against the azure blue, cloudless sky.

Our ritual after breakfast was to do the dishes, tidy our rooms, sweep the sand out of the cottage floor and head to the beach. After a morning swim, the boys usually walked the two or three miles along the sandy beach to town. The beach at Sauble is the longest fresh-water sand beach in Canada, and the second longest in the world!

Ron remembered what the boys usually did in town: "We went on the giant water slide or just strolled the sidewalk downtown 'picking up' chicks." He started to laugh. "But when Matook, Wesley's Siberian Husky, was with us, it was just great because he attracted girls; he was a real chick-magnet."

Most mornings, John and I took the fibre-webbed, aluminum lawn chairs down twenty paces to the beach, to read. During the afternoons, I continued my professional writing, which had become my obsession at the time. I wrote in cursive, writing long-hand in pencil with scissors and translucent tape at the side of the table to literally cut-and-paste when I changed my mind about something I wanted to say. A secretary at the School Board office, where I worked, would type it up. Occasionally, John was able to persuade me to take a nap with him in the afternoons.

We would all gather at supper time. Whenever we could get it at the harbour, I would cook *splake*. Splake was an experimental type of fish; it was a cross between lake trout and speckled trout and had thick, pink meat that was simply delicious dipped in egg and flour and gently pan-fried it. Unfortunately, it is no longer produced. Other meals were mainly hot dogs and hamburgers.

Many evenings, the boys went back to the quiet resort town; there was no trouble they could get into, so John and I didn't have to worry about them, knowing they were safe with each other.

I loved the evenings when John and I would walk south, down the beach, to get ice cream at the local variety store—double-decker maple walnut for me and French vanilla for John. On the way back, as the waves lapped softly at our feet, a sudden rush of contentment washed over me. "This is perfect," I whispered to John. "We are finally melding into the family I dreamed of; the boys get along with each other and everything is working out perfectly." I remember smiling. "We're going to make it after all." I licked the last of the maple walnut, and started munching on the cone. As we sat on our rickety aluminum lawn chairs, and watched Sauble Beach's famous sunset. I reached over and took John's hand, as purple turned to mauve, magenta, then red, and until the orange sun ball slipped, like an egg-yolk, below the horizon. The sky turned to deep purple, then faded to ink-blue. A few stars blinked at us as we folded up our chairs, walked back to the cottage, rinsed our sandy feet in the water of the blue plastic sauce-pan at the door and went to bed. The rhythm of the waves and the crashing surf lulled us off to sleep. It is a heavenly memory that I will hold dear in my heart, forever.

Visitors sometimes came to Sauble during those two weeks–Christina Grant and Mark and Nancy Kikot. Mark was John's best friend. The summer that sticks in my mind most was the summer that Maureen and Suzie came. Ron and Maureen, and Blake and Suzie, were couples: two brothers with two sisters. On the weekend they were there, Wesley argued vehemently on his brothers' behalf. "Mom, my brothers should be able to sleep with their partners; they've been going out together for a year now." Maureen and Suzie said nothing. A pink surge climbed to their cheeks, burning with embarrassment. "Why are you doing this, Wes," Ron asked, perplexed. "You're the only one that's not going to get laid!"

As the summer came to a close, Wesley rode off on his motorcycle and the rest of us piled into the van.

I took a moment to gaze at the crystal blue lake and the shores of Sauble Beach—knowing that we'd be back again next year.

Hobo: Our Two-Family Dog

Hobo adopted us during our last year at our home on Highway 8. We had to leave him behind, that June of 1979, when we moved.

"Look at that dog pee!" Ron called out to Blake and Wesley, as they walked down the long driveway from the school bus to our house Highway 8, one September day in 1978. "What a funny looking dog; look how he's balancing on his one front leg and two backs to whizz. He's going to fall over if he doesn't watch out." Ron bent down on one knee and called, "Here boy, here boy, let's have a look at you." The dog's long black tail wagged madly. He trotted over with a peculiar waddle, his awkward gait making a lop-sided-soft-kaboom-like sound. His right front leg was positioned directly under his nose, while the shrivelled left limb was held tightly to his broad chest. Coming face-to-face with Ron, the pooch looked up with kind and friendly eyes, and peered through a mass of matted black curls. He seemed to smile, as his red tongue hung down, thick slobber slapped onto the pavement of the driveway. "Looks like an oversized Spaniel," Ron said, patting his unruly coat of hair. "What's wrong with your leg, Boy?" Ron asked, examining the shrunken limb. "It looks deformed to me, and I wonder if you got hit by a car." Ron examined the good leg. "That's why *this* one is so muscular, compensating for your injured one. But look at your smiling face. You're a happy dog in spite of your injury, aren't you?" Ron ruffled his black curly head, as drool dripped from his mouth in a steady stream, like a slow dripping faucet. *He's obviously a farm dog*, Ron thought, *with those mangy black curls matted on his back; he's not groomed enough to be a house dog and there's no collar or dog tag.* "Come on, Boy, let's play fetch."

They ran down the driveway, Ron, Blake and Wesley with their new canine friend. He was no taller than their waists, lumbering along behind them, ker-plunk, ker-plunk. After the boys dropped their schoolbags in the mud-room at the back door, they played fetch, throwing the ball while the dog chased after it. It caught and brought it back to them, every time.

"That dog is pretty darned smart," Blake observed.

Wesley nodded. "Look at how fast he can run on those short three legs of his; he's amazing."

The dog was sitting in our laneway and waiting for the boys to get off the school bus, the next day. They spent the rest of the afternoon playing soft-ball; the dog played too.

"Get the ball," Wesley called to him. In a flash,

the dog took off chasing the ball, grabbing it in his mouth and racing to home plate, just as if he were a player too.

"We have to give him a name," Blake suggested, one afternoon. "We can't keep calling him 'dog.' Got any ideas?"

"I think we should call him *Rover*, Wesley offered, "Because he roves around the fields at night."

"Naw," Ron responded. "We have to call him '*Hobo*' because I don't think he has a home." His brothers agreed. So, Hobo he was.

All fall, Hobo met the boys at the school bus. This pattern repeated—day after day, week after week, for over a month as the dog became a regular visitor, and then faithful friend. "It's as though he can tell time," Ron remarked. "He knows he can count on an afternoon of fun with us, and he's never disappointed."

As the days grew shorter, and the fall air chilled and leaves started falling off the apple trees in the front yard, the boys donned their warm jackets. Every afternoon, they played with Hobo, and every evening when they came in the house for supper, Hobo reluctantly left the property.

One November afternoon, the boys jumped off the school bus, hiked up the collars of their fall jackets against a fierce wind that whipped a mix of rain and sleet across the driveway. It stung their cheeks as they raced to the house, Hobo trotting alongside them. Reaching the front door, the boys opened it, rushed in and slammed it shut with a bang against the cold wind. Hobo sat longingly on the front step as if to ask, *Why can't I come in too?*

Ron complained. "Hobo's so cold outside, Mom—can't we bring him inside? It's too cold for him now that winter is almost here. We can't just let him go off into the fields tonight; he'll freeze to death," he whined as did Wesley and Blake.

"You can put the old green sleeping-bag out into the car-port for him."

Blake immediately dashed into the basement to get it. He dragged it out to the car-port. Wesley unzipped it so the soft plaid flannelette lining was exposed, while Blake moulded it into a basket-like-shape. Hobo sat watching, looking skeptical.

"This will protect you from the cold," Ron told Hobo as he coaxed their curly-headed friend to lie down in his new bed. Hobo looked at the green mound of flannel, sniffed it, walked gingerly around it and finally dropped his three legs as he snuggled into it. Contented, the boys came inside for the evening. The next morning, my three sons rushed outside to check on Hobo. He was not there. There was no sign of him. But there *was* evidence that he'd been there. On the spot where the sleeping bag had been was now a huge mound of green and plaid fluff!

One day in early December, winter jackets, toques and mitts came out of storage. "Can't Hobo come inside the house?" Wesley begged. "Please!"

Relenting, I agreed. "He can come inside, but he has to stay in the basement mudroom."

The boys beamed. "Also, while we are all away for the day, you have to put Hobo outside during the daytime until you come home from school."

The boys nodded and then rushed to the door, "Hobo, Hobo!" they called. Hearing his name, Hobo turned just before he got to the highway and came running back down the lane —flippity-plop, flippity-plop—and down the lane to the back stairs. His tail whipped like a windmill, and thick, sloppy, drool dripped off his grinning black lips.

Hobo became a regular house-guest every night. He left a trail of dark dust on the carpet behind him like *Pig-pen* in Charles Schultz's *Peanut* cartoons.

One morning, we found Hobo lying on the upholstered chair in the family room. John had had enough. "That's it," he said. "Hobo needs a bath and a clipping; we'll get him cleaned up for the holidays." That Saturday morning, as John checked the yellow pages for local dog groomers, Hobo sat at John's feet looking up at him with a curious look across his eyes. John found a dog grooming place called *The Pink Poodle Boutique,* and dialed. "What is your dog's name?"

the groomer asked.

"Hobo," John replied.

"What breed is he?"

"With a name like Hobo what do you think?" John laughed, a grin spreading across his face.

"How big is he?"

"He comes up almost to my knee."

"What would you like done?"

"He needs a wash and cut."

"Can you bring him in next Saturday afternoon at four?"

"Sure; Saturday at four works for us." Hobo suddenly looked up, his ears perking into points. "Hey Hobo, you're going to get a hair-cut, Boy," John said, as he ruffled the mass of matted, dirty, dark curls on the top of Hobo's head.

On the next Saturday at around three in the afternoon, John looked for Hobo. He checked with the boys but they hadn't seen him.

John called, "Hobo, Hobo." But Hobo didn't come.

When Hobo wasn't back by 3:30, John called the *Pink Poodle Boutique* and cancelled the appointment. "The groomer sounded pretty relieved. What's up with that dog?" John asked. "Could he have heard me make the appointment and decided not to come home?" John paused ,... "No, he's not *that* smart ... or is he?"

John found the name of another dog groomer in the area. This time he made sure that Hobo wasn't anywhere near the telephone when he made the arrangements. On the day of the appointment, Hobo was around the whole day! At 3:30 John called him, "Hobo, want to go for a car ride?" opening the passenger side door. Hobo hopped in and they were off to the dog-groomer.

The dog groomer was very gentle with Hobo. While washing him, she was especially tender with his injured leg. She towelled him off, clipped the matted curls and sprinkled him with perfumed powder. Hobo beamed with all the attention.

When John got back home with Hobo, we couldn't believe the change in the dog. His coat was sleek, with a mass of twisty sparkling fluffy curls, and he smelled heavenly!

That evening, Hobo sat on the front step and howled and yowled to signal the world that he was the most beautiful dog in the universe! Now that Hobo was clean and fresh, he was allowed to sleep wherever his heart desired.

During the winter of 1979, John and I purchased a four-bedroom house on Inverness Place in Galt, because living in the country limited the boys' after-school programs. We put our country house up for sale. As June approached, the big question was: *What will we do with Hobo?* "Hobo is a country dog," John reminded us. "He loves the freedom of roaming the fields and going wherever he wants to," John added. "Bringing him into the city would mean he'd be confined to the house or be tied up outside on a leash." John paused, shaking his head. "We just can't do that to him."

Another solution came in a most unusual manner. In early June, the boys had a leaving-the-community pool party and several of the boys' friends came. Hobo was in his glory; he was the centre of attention. As the boys were eating snacks, one of the boys commented, "Hey Wes, isn't that the Knocktor's dog?"

"I don't know," Wes countered. "Hobo is ours; he lives with us."Where do the Knocktor family live?"

"They live down the side-road off Highway 8, down the hill over there," he pointed.

We had to check this out! *What if Hobo does belong to someone else?* On the following Saturday, John and I drove down the side-road until we came to a mailbox with Knocktor's name on it. We got out of the car, went up to the house and knocked.

When Mrs. Knocktor came to the door, we explained the situation with Hobo. She smiled. "Oh," she said laughing, "Rover spends the days with *us*. But every afternoon, he takes off, roams the fields all afternoon and night, and comes back home in the morning."

John started to laugh. "Roams the fields at night!! I don't think so," John corrected her, smiling. "He spends every night with *us*!"

Mrs. Knocktor started laughing. "One thing we *did* wonder about was when he came home at Christmas time shampooed, clipped and looking beautiful," she chuckled. "Frankly, we couldn't figure it out." We all had a good laugh at how smart Hobo was living in two homes at the same time! Our problem was solved.

Until the end of June, Hobo continued his same routine of spending evenings and nights with us and the day at Knocktors. Now that we knew that Hobo had a good home, we felt better that he wouldn't be abandoned when we moved at the end of the month.

Moving day was hectic. The house was a frenzy of activity: men loading furniture, boys gathering bikes and toys, John and I washing breakfast dishes, stacking everything into boxes, and adding to the mountain of cartons at the door. The boys played catch with Hobo in and around the van and cars, and Hobo seemed to thrive on the excitement of it all. Running late, we saw the new owners at the entrance to our driveway. They had trucks, trailers and cars, filled with their belongings, as they lined up along Highway 8 and waited for our moving van to leave so they could move in. The new residents left their vehicles, paced, looked down the driveway, and glanced at their watches. Their yappy poodle barked and barked, adding to the confusion and increasing everyone's anxiety.

My friend Arleen and I did some last minute-cleaning and gathered up the final items like brooms, toys, and clothes We chucked them into the trunk of my car. The movers put the last box into the van and locked the door with a bang. Hobo sat on the front step, alone; he had a forlorn look in his eyes.

John went over to Hobo, bent down, and spoke to him. "Look Hobo, you are going to be fine without us because you have a good home with the Knocktors."

The boys came over to Hobo next; they patted and cuddled him. "Goodbye," they called, as they climbed into my car, ready to go.

Arleen called to me, "I'll do the last check of the house so you and John and the boys can get to the new house on Inverness before the movers."

John gave directions to the van driver and we followed it out the driveway like a convoy. Glancing out the rear-view window I saw Hobo sitting on the front step, as if to say "What about me?"

Arleen did the last walk-through in all the rooms—from top-to-bottom of the three-level home.

Chucking the keys of the house onto the kitchen counter, she closed the door and gave Hobo a pat before climbing into her car and easing down the long lane of Highway 8, home.

When she got to the end of the driveway, the new owner called out to her. "Hey, you forgot your dog!"

Arleen called back out the open window of her car. "He comes with the house!"

THE EIGHTIES:
Building Memories At Inverness Place

Settling in

Life at Inverness Place in Cambridge, where we lived from 1979 to 1989, was filled with adventures and misadventures as the boys completed high school, we solidified careers and worked through the deaths of parents.

The house was a good move and accommodated all of us. It had four bedrooms—Wesley and Ron had their own rooms, and Blake shared a room with Adam, when he came on weekends. The living room, and its large attached dining room, was perfect for entertaining; the kitchen was large enough for a family eating area. John and I loved the study best–it had a fireplace against one wall. John particularly enjoyed it as his reading den on weekends. Within months, compliments of 'Mom and Pop' (John's parents), we had a finished family room in the basement. It was an enormous room; it had a TV and couches. It was a perfect place for four teenage boys and their friends to gather. A bonus was the communal swimming pool, which was free for everyone living in the subdivision. All in all, our Inverness home had been a good choice—especially when I think of today's standards in 2025—we bought it for $79,000 in 1979. It was a steal!

Special Memories of My Teenage Boys

Looking back at that time, I have special memories of each of my boys—the funny things they did, and the ways in which they were unique.

Wesley was a whiz at electronics; I felt confident he could put together a tape-slide presentation for a workshop I was giving. Eager to help, he figured out how to put several slides of Annie–a six-year-old Mennonite girl–along with numerous photographs of her writing pieces that documented her progress over a year. Fortunately, I had a tape-recording of Annie reading her stories in her Amish dialect. Wesley tape-recorded my introduction, put the slides into the projector in progressive order, and dubbed in Annie's voice reading her stories. He located the sound-track from 'The Exorcist' for lead-in music and background. As Annie finished reading her final story, Wesley raised the music volume to a crescendo and then had it fade away. It was an amazing piece of work! I used that tape-slide kit for my presentations throughout my career, giving workshops across Canada and the United States, and later in Southeast Asia. It impressed thousands of teachers around the world—and to think it was created by my talented teenage son, Wesley, in the basement of our home in 1981!

Blake was my stock-broker kid. He learned all about the stock market from a mathematics teacher who taught him in grade seven. They traded stocks by using fake money on various listings on the Toronto Stock Exchange, that were available as a section in the local newspaper. The teacher brought it to class every day. Every student was given $10,000 of fake money, to start. "The stocks we traded were *real* stocks," Blake explained. "It was just that we used *fake* money for the transactions, instead of real Canadian currency." Blake broke into a grin, his grey-blue eyes dancing, "I bought and sold and bought and sold until I'd made over a million dollars—of fake money of course. The teacher was so impressed that he called me the *wonder boy*."

Later, in high school, Blake followed the TSE every day; one day he noticed that, because of the 1981 recession, Rogers' stock was really low. Unannounced to me, Blake called a stock broker and asked him if he could purchase Rogers stocks. When Blake told him that he was only sixteen years old, he told Blake that he was not legally old enough, but he could purchase the stock if an adult co-signed with him. When Blake came to me with his request, I said, "No way—playing the stock market is gambling and you could lose your shirt."

In a conversation with Blake recently, he smiled. "When I look at Rogers stock now, Mom—twenty years later, we could be rolling in dough!"

Ron was my classy teenage son; he oozed style.

For his grade eight graduation Ron wanted to wear a white suit!

"A white suit?" I asked surprised, "Why a *white* suit?"

"I think a white suit would be cool; I want to look like John Travolta in *Saturday Night Fever*."

"Yes, but you won't be able to wear it, afterward," I countered.

The following week, John and I took Ron downtown to a men's shop—actually, it was a dual men's and ladies' shop. "We'd like to see the options you have for a suit for our boy," John told the clerk. The salesman pulled out several selections in grey, navy and tan.

Ron looked them over and grimaced. "Don't you have any *white* suits?"

"None in stock," the clerk announced, apologetically. "But we *do* have white ones you can rent for weddings." Ron's eyes gleamed, and his lips turned up into a smile as we mulled over purchasing a regular one, or renting a white one.

"Ron, you'd look smashing in a navy jacket and grey slacks," I coaxed. "Think about it okay? It would be something you could wear after for some special occasion in the summer or in December for your birthday." Ron's eyes lost their luster and he shuffled his feet, obviously disgruntled. John winked at me. "You go over to the Ladies' side, Gail and leave Ron and me to talk about this."

Sauntering over to the women's section, I spied something royal blue, a skirt, jacket and full-length vest to go with it. *It was such a versatile outfit for work!* Walking back to Ron and John, I saw two suits laying on the counter, a dark blue suit and a white one beside it. Ron was fingering the white jacket, his eyes sparkling, lips spread into a grin.

"Oh Ron, I love the navy one; it will be smashing with a white turtle-neck. You'll be the best dressed guy at graduation," I told him, trying to convince him to take the practical blue one.

John came to Ron's rescue. "Look Gail, a white suit is really important to Ron, even though it may not be practical; and he'll only be renting it for a day," he implored. Suddenly noticing the items slung over my arm, he asked, "What have you got there?" After I explained, a glint shone in his eyes. "I have an idea," John's lips turned into a crafty smile. "You go and try on your outfit, and if you like it, I will get it for you." His eyes twinkled, "On the condition that Ron gets his white suit!"

On the night of graduation, Ron strutted across the stage in his white suit, amid cheers and hoots from his friends. "There goes Mr. Clean! It's Mr. Roark from 'Fantasy Island!' Way to go Ron!" One of his buddies dropped to his knees in front of him calling, "*Look*

Boss, the plane … the plane!" It was just like the character in *Fantasy Island*.

A postscript to "The White Suit Story." One day, I shared a draft of this story with Ron. He responded, "I have some new information to include in the piece, that will make the story even *more* authentic," he said. "When Dad saw me after graduation, he remarked, '*Why the heck did your mother dress you up in that Godawful white suit, gall darnnit?*'

"Because I wanted it," I told him.

~~~

Adam became a natural part of the family—a side kick of Blake's. They did everything together—from selling black-and-white TVs to going to the weekly hockey games to harass the Hornets hockey team. It was our dream to have Adam come to live with us permanently. "Adam is obviously enjoying his time with us," John said. "I hear him laugh when he's with the boys, a sound I've missed for so long." Adam continued to live with us every second weekend and came with us on all our family excursions. Our hope for him to live with us permanently remained a dream for the time being.

'The Boss': Bruce Springsteen Headbands

"Bruce Springsteen's coming to the CNE (Canadian National Exhibition) on the Labour Day weekend!" Andy—Blake's best friend–called out to Blake. He was in the garage, tuning up his motorcycle. Blake's head snapped up at this news. "We could make "The Boss" headbands for him!" Andy's voice rose with excitement. "Toronto *loves* Springsteen, and there'll be more than 100,000 fans there, for sure."

Blake dropped his wrench with a clang. "We could make a fortune." All morning, I heard snippets of their conversation: "love the idea . . . pool our money . . . we'll make a killing . . . what a money-maker . . . rolling in dough."

It was summer, 1985, and our garage became a factory for 'Bruce Springsteen' headbands. The boys borrowed silk-screen equipment from Mr. Weber, their art teacher at Southwood High School. They purchased yards of fabric from the local textile factory and various colours of paint—red, blue and white. They spent hours creating different designs. As the silk-screening process evolved, I was surprised at how intricate and time-consuming it was: it involved cutting-out each design from a hard plastic sheet secured in a wood frame with razor-sharp knives. The design was then placed on top of a fine screen that was, in turn, placed on top of the fabric. Depending on the colour that was desired, the paint was rolled over the plastic; it bled through the screen and onto the fabric. It was amazing!

In the middle of the summer, as the boys printed out 'THE BOSS' headbands, with different arrangements of stars and stripes, Ron joined the assembly-line. The garage floor was a sea of colour. Day after day, week after week, through July and August, the headbands piled up. Blake estimated they had close to a thousand headbands made. As the day of the Bruce Springsteen Concert approached, the boys planned their trip to Toronto. They recruited Wesley to help out. On the day of the opening, August 26, 1985 the boys packed up the headbands into the knapsacks they'd slung onto their backs– they headed out on their motorcycles and drove ninety minutes to the concert in Toronto.

We heard the rest of this story when they returned, later that night. When they arrived at the CNE, they stood outside the stadium to sell the headbands to the people going into the concert. Each of the boys put on a headband, slung a bunch of headbands over their arms and headed off in all different directions to sell them, chanting out, "Want a Boss Headband? Get your Boss Headband here!"

"They were selling like hot-cakes at three bucks-a-piece." Ron told us. "But then I looked over the crowd of people at Blake, and saw a man pull out a portable radio and spoke into it. I knew immediately the guy was a plain-clothed-cop. I waved my arms wildly at Blake, trying to get his attention and to warn him."

Blake butted in. "I was so excited about having sold over twenty headbands already that I didn't see Ron waving at me." Blake took a breath and let out a long disappointed sigh, as if remembering. "This man approached me, wanting to know if I was selling Bruce Springsteen headbands. Thinking he wanted to buy some, I told him the price. When he said he'd take them all, I was over the moon thinking I'd made a killing! ... or so I thought." Blake cocked his head to one side. "But when I put my hand out for payment the guy asked me if I had a permit from City Hall. When I told him I didn't, he gave me a ticket." Blake's face fell and his voice rose angrily, as if reliving the experience earlier at the CNE. He twisted his mouth into a grimace. "At that moment, I knew he was a cop as he confiscated *all* my merchandise and hundreds of dollars profit!" Blake shook his head in disgust.

"Meanwhile," Ron interjected. "I was watching this transaction with Blake from about twenty paces away and decided to distance myself from him so the policeman wouldn't notice *me!*" Ron went on selling headbands at a brisk rate, manoeuvring backwards through a crowd of people. "I suddenly backed into something solid with a bit of give and a slight feeling of warmth. Turning around, I was facing another blasted cop. He seized my entire booty of headbands and ticketed *me* as well. Just then Wesley spotted us and rushed over to us, waving his arms in disgust.

'The cops took all my headbands,' he stormed shaking his head angrily. 'And gave me a ticket to boot!'"

Andy was the luckiest one of all; *his* experience was unique. "My headbands were selling so quickly, people were lining up," Andy said. Then, a wide grin spread across his face. "Two stunning teenage girls approached me and showed interest in the headbands." His eyes lit up. "They had fantastic bods and long blond hair down to their butts!" He started to laugh. "One girl said she loved the headbands, but all she had to pay for it was an extra concert ticket of a friend who couldn't come. She asked me if she could use it for payment for two headbands. "You bet," I told them and handed them two headbands in exchange for the concert ticket. "What a bonus!" Andy said smiling. "As I walked through the gates to the concert, I sold every single one within minutes."

Now, as I write this in 2025, I smile, thinking back to that time in 1985 when the boys worked all summer making the Bruce Springsteen headbands. I have two of them tucked away that survived their great adventure of making and selling *'THE BOSS'* headbands for Springsteen's concert in Toronto at the CNE!

Adam's Lament

As summer ended, John and I thought seriously about bringing Adam to live at Inverness Place permanently. If Adam came to live with *us*, he could still continue to go to his high school in Ancaster—John could drive Adam there on his way to work in Hamilton in the morning, and could pick him up after school on his way home from work. We decided to give it a try.

Unsure of how to go about this, we sought some family counseling and scheduled a session with all four boys.. John and I explained to the two counselors that we were hoping Adam would join our family and live in our house. I recall a general discussion, and then the counselors turned to Adam and probed him for his thoughts and *his* perspective. Adam bolted upright in his chair, tears streaming down his face. "My mother will *never* allow it!" he yelled, charging to the door and slamming it behind him. The rest of us got up and followed, meekly behind.

That was the last time Adam ever came for a weekend in our home! Our dream of having Adam live with us was shattered in an instant.

I have many thoughts about that time. For one thing, we should have talked to *my* boys to hear each of *their* perspectives of Adam joining our family. John might have chatted with Adam about our idea on his way to our home on weekend visits, to listen to how *he* felt about a change in living arrangements. We should, of course, have broached the idea with Adam's mother to get *her* thoughts and *her* perspective. She might have agreed to the possibility. In hindsight, I also realize that we should have done *all* of that before we exposed the boys to the formal counselling session.

The "Shared Custody" concept—where a child spent one week with his mother and the next with his father—was not the norm at that time. Yet, that arrangement certainly could have worked, as far as Adam was concerned.

John's Final Lament

We rarely saw Adam after that—a final lament of John's. On a February night in 2019, the winter before John died, the howling wind flung swirls of snow that obscured our view of Lake Erie. John looked up at me over his "'Granny Smith" glasses that were perched on his nose. He had a book by Leonard Cohen resting on his lap. He murmured something so softly that I could barely hear a word. Pellets of snow snapped at the window pane.

"What's that?" I asked, straining to catch every word.

John's voice lowered to almost a whisper. "I've

helped raise *your* sons at the expense of my Adam." There was an overwhelming sadness in his voice.

My heart lurched at his truth.

Wesley's Misadventures: Car in School Yard

Wesley was an enigma to us ... mostly to *me*. At times he was a wonderful kid; he helped Ron with his Hallowe'en costume, and worked with me to develop the tape slideshow for my work. But on a day-to-day basis, he refused to tidy his room, gather garbage, or take his turn at dishes; it was a constant fight. It was especially confounding as I had, since childhood, *always* done my chores without *ever* being reminded. It was, therefore, impossible for me to understand Wesley's behaviour. To compound my distress, it appeared—at times—that he made a *point* of not following the rules in order to annoy me. Unfortunately, it worked.

Wesley presented us with a list of demands—written down neatly on a piece of paper—his own telephone and phone number; an increase in his allowance to a hundred dollars a month, an extended curfew... the list went on and on. All of this—he stated—"for the pleasure of continuing to live with us." John and I thought the whole thing was preposterous, amusing. We decided not to respond. We also ignored the time he took apart his Mazda and strewed the parts all over the floor of our two car garage, which prevented us from using the garage for over a month. Following John's idea of 'natural consequences,' we turned a blind eye to the mess. Eventually, he cleaned it up.

Everything finally came to a head one frigid night in January. Wesley and I had another fight about chores he hadn't done. I'd had enough. "If you can't follow the rules of the house," I yelled, "then you'd better find another place to live."

Wesley countered, "I am fed-up with this place. I can't stand all your nagging." He stomped upstairs to his bedroom, coming back down moments later with a back-pack over his shoulder. "I'm out of here!" he bellowed, as he grabbed his coat, stuffed his things into his Mazda, and took off. It felt like déjà-vu. I was frantic when he didn't return home during that 20-below-zero Fahrenheit night. . . . Or the next morning!

I received a phone message from the Vice Principal. Wesley was living in his car in the school sportsfield. "Your son is okay," he assured me. "Teenagers are naturally rebellious and he'll come home when he cools off," he chuckled, "Excuse the pun. Wesley can use the school facilities for showering in the meantime." Relieved, I thanked him and asked if there was anything I should do. "For the moment, leave things up to us. We're involving the school counsellor. We agree that a family has to have rules," he shared reassuringly. "Wesley is simply exhibiting typical teenage rebellion. We will be sure he is safe, and we will keep in touch with you."

I was thankful that Wesley was in no immediate danger and pleased that the school was so supportive. But at the same time, I was wretched, and my mind was full of nagging doubts. *What were we doing wrong as parents? Why was Wesley doing this? How could we help him?* My emotions were raw and I had nightmares:I imagined a headline in the local paper— **Teenager Freezes to Death in School Yard.** It was a living nightmare!

During the third week, the Vice-Principal was convinced. "Wesley will come home soon—I'll bet on it." Not a betting person, I wasn't so sure. Wesley lived in his car for more than two months—to me it seemed like a year. When Wesley finally *did* come home, within a week everything returned back to normal—*his* normal. He continued to ignore all household rules—not a thing had changed.

The Missing Pieces to the Puzzle

Now, in my late eighties, I reflect on the many years that I've fretted over how I had dealt with Wesley during his teenage years. I never did connect with him in the way I would have liked. When I look back, there was always something niggling at me—I felt a certain rejection and feeling of disdain of deep-seated anger, toward me. It was unspoken and elusive. I couldn't quite put my finger on it. It felt related, in some way, to his father.

What Their Father Told My Sons About the Marriage Breakup

Two stories that Blake and Ron, when they were adults, shared with me about their father, gave me some illumination.

Blake was fifty-eight when he told me about the summer of 1980, he was sixteen and putting his 500 cc 4-cylinder Honda motorcycle back together after his buddy had wrecked it. "I spent every spare minute of that *whole* summer fixing it up to get it road-worthy again," Blake stated angrily, as if remembering the feelings he had back then. "I was working away with tools and parts all over the garage floor when Dad dropped by." Blake paused for a moment before he went on. "Dad leaned over my shoulder as I worked and said: 'It was your *mother* who broke up the marriage, you know, Blake, because she wrecked my Porsche.' Blake bobbed his chin at me. 'If your *mother* hadn't wrecked the Porsche, you'd be able to be driving it today instead of a motorcycle.'"

Blood blanched from my face and my jaw dropped open. I tried to say something, but nothing came out. I clenched my hands into a fist to steady my trembling fingers as his father's words spun around in my head. *'It was your mother who broke up the marriage because she wrecked my Porsche'. . . .If your mother hadn't wrecked the Porsche, Blake, you'd be driving it today instead of a motorcycle.*

How would those statements have affected my sixteen-year-old son? At sixteen, what would he have thought? How would he have felt toward his mother? What purpose did my ex-husband have in making these statements?

~~~

Ron and I were sitting out on the balcony of the hotel in Huntsville looking out toward the edge of the lake. The half golden moon carved a silver pathway across the water like a lighthouse beacon. I was taking Ron on a golfing vacation to celebrate his pending fiftieth birthday. Ron cracked open his second beer and I sipped a spritzer of white wine and soda. We have a strong bond between us; we reminisced about his fifty years, and we talked and talked about anything and everything. I felt so lucky to have such a delightful son; I was proud of him as a teacher and how he connected with his students—he was always telling stories about them. He is a wonderful storyteller, and I suggested he write down his tales so that he could savor them in his old age. Getting mellow, I mixed one more drink.

Snapping the tab off another beer, Ron stretched

out his legs in front of him. He looked relaxed, as he took a sip. "You know, Mom," he said nonchalantly, as if he was about to tell another story about a student, "Dad blamed *you* for the marriage breakup."

My mouth gaped open, and I almost spilled my drink. *He was blaming me?* That was laughable. It was *he* who left *me*—me, and his three sons—he even asked the Minister *how* to leave us—asking him step-by-step advice. He couldn't skip out on us fast enough. And then *he* blamed *me* for the marriage break-up?

But when I stopped to think about it, Ron knew *nothing* of that. I'd never discussed the breakup with my children. The whole story was in my memoir that I was still writing. It sat on my computer at home.

Ron set down his beer, took out a package of cigarettes from his pants pocket, and lit up. "Dad said that you didn't want to be a stay-at-home mom anymore, that you wanted a career instead."

I gasped. This was so preposterous; I didn't know whether to laugh or cry. *I didn't want to be a stay-at-home mom?* Being home with my sons was the best part of my marriage; it was the part I loved most! Why, I even stated to the marriage counselors that I'd stay in the marriage for the *sake* of the boys; I even fought to have *custody* of them, for heaven's sake. I'd have *preferred* to be a stay-at-home mom, but that became impossible when he left us, leaving me stranded, and forcing me out of the homemaker role. He fought against leaving me anything—no finances, no equity in our property–house, cars, trailer—no alimony, no child support. It is all in the Separation Agreement his lawyer sent me. When left with *nothing*, I *had* to get a job in order to support my children. The whole story was in my unfinished memoir—but Ron knew nothing of that either. He said I left the marriage because I wanted to have a *career?* I chuckled at that. With raising three young children, that was the farthest thing from my mind.

However, as single parent, I *had* to start my BA degree, in order to have a salary above poverty level. The marriage broke up because I wanted a career? *What a joke!*

But Ron had no knowledge of that either. I sat facing him, numb with fury and unable to say a single word in my defence.

But there was more. Ron continued in his calm, relaxed, unperturbed manner. Sucking in a long drag, he blew out a perfect smoke-ring into the cool August night. "Dad said that he would come back to us, but you wouldn't let him."

Thunderstruck, I shook with anger. This was outrageous! In the twenty years after he left us, he never once approached me about this—never sent a letter, or offered a proposal, or sent a notification through his lawyer to negotiate such a possibility. *He would come back, but I wouldn't let him? That* was pure fantasy. I took a deep breath and held it in so I wouldn't shout out or speak my truth and unravel this pack of lies ... But I couldn't risk it. I'd be too emotional, too enraged. What good would result from *that*? And besides, if I *had* set Ron straight, he'd think I was putting his Dad *down*. The words sat silent on my tongue while bile gorged in my chest. It was all I could do to swallow the bitter lump in my throat ... I remained silent and brought my glass to my lips and downed my spritzer in one gulp.

Ron stretched his arms in the air and put his hands behind his neck making himself completely comfortable. "You know, Mom, Dad really *admired* you!" The outer edges of Ron's his mouth lifted, as if somehow applauding his Dad for putting all this messy divorce stuff behind him, and moving on.

My body flinched. I clenched my teeth in disbelief. *What in the world was Ron talking about?* Before I could say a word, Ron added dramatically. Pointing his finger in the air he elaborated. "Dad kept a picture of you on his mantle."

Fury surged through my body. This was too much—it was beyond bizarre. It was downright weird. *He admired me? He'd moved out and left us stranded, left me with nothing to my name and, then he said he admired me? When he looked at my picture, did he admire that I'd survived in spite of how he treated me and his children? Did he pat himself on the back for how successfully he'd screwed me?*

My nostrils flared and I clenched my fists, unable to take any more! Ron was fifty; he was old enough to hear what *really* happened. Bolting upright, I squared my shoulders, my stomach tensed for a fight—to react to this nonsense. I turned to my son, eyes blazing, mouth open ready to blast out the truth . . . "Yeah, right," I began, my voice raw, cracking with rage, struggling to find my voice.

Ron's hands shot up, splaying his hands ready to yell, 'Stop!' "Don't say anything negative, Mom," he said firmly, sensing my change in mood. "After all, he's my *Dad* . . . and besides, I knew that there must be two sides to the story."

It took every scrap of self-discipline I had to clench my mouth shut. But my mind railed. *I am self-silencing once again, squelching my truth* . . . My untold story lay in my heart in grim stoney silence.

What Would My Sons Believe?

It was your mother's fault for the break up

She didn't want to be a stay-at-home mother anymore

She wanted to have a career instead

I wanted to come back to you boys

But your mother wouldn't let me ...

When they heard these words, what would have gone through the minds of Wesley, Blake and Ron? What would they have believed? What would my boys have felt when they heard this tale from their father?

~~~

My Side of the Story

Ten years ago, the boys didn't know that I was writing a memoir. Since that time, I have told them about it, but they have not yet read it. Sometimes, we talk about what we remember of particular times. As I continue to write my memoir, I have faith that each one of my sons will sift through the heap of misinformation that was thrust upon them. A crack will open up to let the light of my love for them shine through. Thank you, Leonard Cohen. In my mind, they will always be my precious little boys. My heart swells with my love for them, now and forever.

"I'll read every word, Mom," Ron promised. Like he said ten years ago on that balcony in Huntsville, "I knew there were two sides to the story."

Season of Good byes

During the next ten years, family members left us. My Dad, John's Mom and then 'Pop', John's Dad.

Auburn Colin Pye: October 28, 1907 – July 27, 1981.

Dad was only 74 years old when he passed on; I have outlived him by 12 years. What I remember most is his joyous laugh, and the warmth of his arms as he wrapped me in a hug. I was honoured to give his eulogy; his life reminded me of a rose. I created a simple handout, with Dad's picture on the cover. I wrote the following: . . . .

To Dad

Dad was not a believer of organized religion, and yet...

He believed strongly in religious values and truly lived them.

Dad's life was like a rose... a hardy Alberta variety... strong stem of character, leaves and thorns of experiences and a delicate blossom of a soul.

Like the rose, Dad's roots began in fertile Newfoundland soil, born in a sod house.

Growing up on a farm in Alberta with a loving brother Ellis and sister Beryl.

He enjoyed the tender leaves of loving children, Merla, Bud, Gail Sharon and Beryl.

His strength of character was like a rose stem...morally strong with value-firm fibre.

He had a varied work, teaching, trucking on the Alaska Highway, farming, owning and managing a general store...trucking in oil-fields in Northern Alberta... owning and operating motels in Slave Lake, Carbon and Bassano.

He suffered through thorns of the great depression, the defeat of political elections, the sorrow of a broken marriage, and the final fight with emphysema.

He sprouted leaves of a new love-filled-marriage with Doris, and adored his rosebud love-child Beryl.

He and Doris were masters in blending the rosebushes of two families into a loving hybrid.

The rosebud was the spirit of Dad's soul ... each petal a gentle reminder of their understanding, acceptance, pride, caring, warmth and empathy for us all.

A most loving attribute of Dad's was that he shared his goodness with all of us, that caused the rose-bud to radiate and bloom.

What we will remember and cherish most, is his infinite love and understanding he had for every single one.

As you walk into the sunset, Dad...

We wish you peace, love and harmony you desired all of us to have.

Margurite Clifford Taylor: –died May, 1986

John's mom died in the spring of 1986. It was such a shock. John walked into the house, his face sallow, eyes cast down. "Mom died," he announced in a halting voice.

"She what?" I exclaimed in surprise. "She was fine when we saw her last week."

"I was at the hospital discussing Pop's discharge. Mom stood up suddenly, saying she didn't feel well. Without warning, she collapsed into my arms. Despite the emergency medical team who rushed to her side, she was gone. She'd had an aneurism in her brain.

"She can't have gone," John's Dad said when he got back to his father's room. "Her coat and umbrella are right here on the bed!"

John's mother was always warm, loving, and kind to me. A memory I cherish is the smell of fresh baked cookies or chocolate cake she had on hand, whenever we visited. I miss her.

John, Stanley Taylor: –September, 1986

John's dad died peacefully at the Cambridge Hospital. However, Pop deserves special acknowledgement of its own.

John's Dad—Pop

Pop, the name we called John's dad, came to live with us after Mom's funeral. He slept in Wesley's room, since he was living in an apartment in Waterloo and going to university at the time. Having Pop in our home full time was an adjustment for Blake and Ron; they had a surrogate grandfather living with us. They were troopers once we explained to Pop that the soft-drinks in the refrigerator were to be shared with everyone!

Pop was a bit of a curmudgeon and had his own way of doing things. It was an adjustment for me, too. It didn't take long, that summer, before he and I got along just fine. One of my favourite images is of him sitting on his red bench on our front veranda, and watching the neighbourhood. He loved that old red bench, the one he made years before from wooden slats from STELCO, a major steel company in Hamilton where he had worked for years.

Summer came. I had workshop commitments in California. During the previous spring, I had made a commitment to present a week-long series of workshops in Fresno and felt obligated to honour my commitment. For the time we would be away, I arranged for a Red Cross Homemaker to come into our home each day to help: she would bathe Pop in the morning, prepare breakfast, and come again in the evening to cook his supper and get him ready for bed. A PSW (Personal Care Worker) came in at noon to prepare Pop's lunch. We installed a Medical-Alert system as an extra safety precaution that Pop could use in the event of an emergency. Blake, who was twenty-three and Ron, who was twenty, agreed to be responsible for Pop during the nights we were away. We stocked up on frozen dinners for the boys. We left emergency phone numbers where we could be reached and planned to call every day to ensure that everyone was okay. John was prepared to fly home in the event of any emergency. Hoping we'd addressed every possible scenario, we flew to Fresno. Thankfully, all was well at home when we called each night.

At the end of the week of workshops we flew home, arriving at O'Hare International airport to connect to a flight on to Toronto. Landing in Chicago in the middle of a torrential rain-storm, we were told all flights were cancelled. I immediately called the boys and explained. Ron, god love him, agreed to be responsible for Pop one more night. It turned out to be an adventure in itself.

RON'S STORY ABOUT POP

"I invited some friends over to play cards in the family room in the basement." Ron started. "The Red Cross Homemaker came to get Pop's supper, and I got Pop ready for bed. I looked in on him after she left and then went back down stairs to play cards. My friends and I were playing a good round of bridge when suddenly we heard a piercing, ear-shattering blast, like a police siren, screaming right inside the house. It scared the living bejesus out of us!"

"'What the hell is *that*?' Al asked, alarmed."

"Oh, my God! Oh my God! It's my Grandpa." I yelled at Al. "It's his heart." I shoved my chair back in a panic, bolted up the two flights of stairs to Pop's room, and opened his door. I rushed in. I was scared that I'd find Pop lying on the floor gasping for air, clutching his chest, or moaning in pain." Ron shook his head, and his head, his lips turned at the corners of his mouth.

"Are you okay?" I asked Pop breathlessly, my heart hammering in my throat. "How is your heart?" I stammered. "Are you alright?"

"Well," Ron continued, "Instead of finding Pop lying on the floor in agony, he was sitting on the side of his bed, in his pyjamas, looking at me with a bewildered frown on his face . . . as though he thought I was an idiot storming into his room like that."

'*It's eleven o'clock,*' Pop said slowly, calmly, nonchalantly pointing to the clock on the night table beside his bed.

"I was so relieved that Pop was all right, I was totally baffled by what he was trying to tell me. "What does eleven o'clock have to do with anything?" I asked, shaking my head confused.

'*Milk and cookies!*' Pop said, deliberately enunciating each word, in a relaxed, unflustered manner, as he took a breath, twisting his mouth as if exasperated that I didn't remember what eleven o'clock signified.

"*It's eleven o'clock and you forgot my milk and cookies!*" Pop said with a hint of disdain in his voice.

"What?" I asked, shocked, surprised, confused and flustered all at the same time at seeing Pop so unperturbed. "Are you kidding me?" I asked, anger rising in my throat. "What the h...." I exclaimed frustration rising. "Is that why you hit the damned button on the 'Medical Alert?'"

'*Yes,*'" Pop said as if it was as obvious as the summer moon shining into the room. '*I pressed the red button to get your attention so you'd get me my milk and cookies.*'

As my heart started to beat slower, I began to understand what had actually happened.

"Okay Pop," I told him, thankful he was okay. "I'll go downstairs and get you your milk and cookies!"

Pop's Red Bench

At his funeral, that fall of 1986, I read a story I wrote, called 'Pop's Red Bench'

POP'S RED BENCH

(To John for sharing
your Dad with me.)

Pop's red bench sits empty now. Fire engine red, it sits framed between the two chocolate brown pillars of the front porch snuggled between the lobster trap on one side and the ebony antique milk can on the other, both spilling over with apple red geraniums.

"The colour's right," I mused. "How could I ever have wanted to paint it chocolate brown to match the house trim?" I wondered.

As I washed off the dust that had blown over from the construction site across the once green corn field, I wiped one crimson slat after another, velvet smooth from the endless sanding and many coats of crimson paint applied lovingly by 'Pop,' at his home in Hamilton.

When Pop first came to live with us, we put an armchair on the front verandah every morning and Pop would shuffle out the front door and onto the porch to sit for an hour or so every afternoon. "I've got a really nice red bench at the old house," he told me. "It would fit right here on your verandah," he said, a mischievous smirk at the corner of his mouth. "It would fit perfectly here on the porch. You and John could sit on it and relax whenever you wanted and watch the neighbours come and go." Pop paused and put a finger to his lips. "You could bring the red bench up from the carport sometime . . . "if you'd like to." Taking Pop's not so subtle hint, John drove over to the old house and picked up the red bench.

Pop wiggled like a puppy when he spotted the patch of red in the back of the station wagon as John drove up the driveway. "You'll see, you'll see. I'll bet it will fit perfectly on the verandah," he chuckled.

"You're right Pop, I laughed as John and I took the bench from the car and set it onto the porch. "It does fit, and think how nice it will look when I paint it chocolate brown to match the trim on the house."

"Benches should be red," Pop said, as he shuffled onto the porch and lowered himself gingerly into his old friend, patting a place on the red bench, an invitation for me to sit with him for awhile. "She's fifty years old, Gail," Pop grinned, shaking his head. "I dismantled these slats from the packing crates that the machinery at the steel mill was packed in. I made bundles of them and tied them together with twine," Pop boasted. "Each night after work I strapped one bundle onto the handle bars of my bicycle and another onto the seat and then pushed the load home. Did the same thing day after day until I had enough to build the bench." Pop smiled. "I designed it for sitting on the front stoop during the long hot summer evenings so I could keep an eye on John and his sister as they played in the street. "I built it high in the back to give support to my aching shoulders but sloped it gently to fit the natural curve at the base of my spine and knees." Pop started to laugh. "I know that your feet are dangling, Gail. Sorry about that but I constructed it higher from the ground than usual to accommodate my long legs!" he said, patting my knee. "The length of the bench was dictated by the length of the pieces of cedar," Pop told me. "It can seat two people comfortably," Pop explained. "But I usually position myself in the middle," he said, "unless I'm in the mood like today to make room for *you!*" He chortled. "When I finished building the bench, I painted it with a red commercial variety I retrieved from the garbage bins thrown there by the painting crews after they had revitalized the machines in the steel mill."

A misty look of nostalgia came over Pop's eyes. "This here bench moved from home to home over the years," he said, proudly. "It sat on every verandah, porch and stoop until it finally retired with me in the carport in Hamilton where I sat in summer, fall and spring as I watched the neighbors shovel their snow, mow their grass and repair their houses."

Pop's forehead furrowed, "Let's get rid of that

old bench," Mom often nagged me. "It's so old and some of the slats are broken. It's such an ugly old thing. People will think we can't afford a decent bench," she'd complained. "Let's throw it out."

Pop smiled wanly remembering. "But I reminded her that it was just the right shape and size for me to ease into without hurting my leg and hip that had been injured in the plant." Pop waved his arms. "And, I told her, it was a perfect fit for the space along the back of the carport between the door and the tool shed." Pop paused, then. "The red bench stayed."

Pop's red bench sits empty now, fire engine red, between the lobster trap on one side and the ebony antique milk can on the other, both spilling over with apple red geraniums. I sat down for a moment and looked up at the blue spruce for the red-headed-sparrow that Pop had discovered. I can't see it today. The white butterflies flit lazily though, the red geraniums their favorite flower, Pop had informed me. My heart twinged remembering.

Pop's red bench sits empty now, fire engine red, between the lobster trap on one side and the ebony antique milk can on the other, both spilling over with apple red geraniums.

"The colour's right," I mused. Benches should be red.

—Gail Heald Taylor 1986

MY CAREER

Primary Consultant

It is hard to believe I was once a nine year old little girl who struggled, until third grade, to unravel the mystery of print. By today's standards, I would have been a candidate for 'Special Education' for sure. Who would have guessed that this same "illiterate" child would later earn three degrees—a Bachelor of Arts, a Master's of Arts and, finally, a Doctorate of Education—and, forty years later, have become a university professor who instructed prospective teachers on how to develop literate classrooms of their own?

But, I am getting ahead of myself.

I was a primary consultant for ten years (1977 to 1987) at the Waterloo County Board of Education; it was both rewarding and challenging work. As one of eight primary consultants, I worked with over a hundred elementary teachers (Kindergarten to Grade Three) and assisted them with implementing language arts (listening, speaking, reading, and writing,), environmental studies and mathematics. It was a daunting role; I felt ill-prepared, despite the numerous courses I'd taken, and my years of teaching. Determined to be the best consultant I could be, I devoured volumes of books on theories of literacy, and studied the Waterloo Board Curriculum, which had been written in the early 1970s. The conferences in Toronto that the Board encouraged us to attend were also significant to my learning; it helped to hear about current research in education. At the time, Donald Graves' (1980) research, which considered communicating through writing, was particularly relevant. It was a departure from the traditional theories upon which the primary curriculum was based. It made me rethink everything I'd once believed.

Birth of 'Natural Language'

Welcoming Graves' shift in philosophies of education, I worked with my primary teachers to put his research into practice in their classrooms. As we observed literacy outcomes grow, I developed handbooks that I called *Natural Language*, through which I outlined step-by-step procedures for teachers to follow. These included—*Natural Language and Dictated Stories*; *Natural Language and Reading*; *Natural Language and Writing* and *Natural Language and Evaluation*. I also created a tape/slide presentation using samples of children's work (Kindergarten/Gr. 1) that demonstrated their progress in reading and writing of children in kindergarten and first-grade. One of these was tape/slides was developed by my son Wesley, in our home. I used these tape/slides at Board Professional Development days; teachers from across the county filled my sessions to learn more about the "Natural Language" processes. They also requested the "Natural Language" handouts from the primary resource facility.

Before long, I was invited to present at conferences in Toronto and attracted educators from across Ontario and beyond. Success with writing the *Natural Language* handbooks spurred me on to write more. At dawn, every weekend, I sat in my home office and drafted hundreds of pages; I sent manuscripts to publishers in the hope that some of the handbooks might be published.

First Publications

My first article, "Scribble in First Grade Writing" (1984) was published in *The Reading Teacher*—the most prestigious international journal on literacy in the world. Until then, no one in Waterloo County had ever received such an honour. In 1985, as a result of my article I was invited to present my work at the International Reading Conference (IRA), which was the largest of its kind in the world—in Atlanta, Georgia. I was the first educator in our county to receive such recognition. Overnight, I'd become known internationally.

For a few years prior, I had been working with Libby Pavey, who was an English Second Language (ESL) teacher in the Board. As part of that work, we documented the writing growth of a Chinese child during her first year in Canada. In 1983, Libby and I presented our work at the Teaching English to Speakers of Other Languages (TESOL) conference, in Toronto. Our presentation was so successful that a gentleman from the Ontario Institute for Studies in Education (OISE) approached us; he was interested in developing a resource book for English Second Language (ESL) teachers. Over the next two summers, I analyzed hundreds of writing samples from young children in Libby's classroom. During one of our family vacations at Sauble Beach, I wrote a first draft at the picnic table.

Trouble Brewing in the Trenches

"Gail, there's a call for you from the literacy consultant in New York City!" our secretary called to me excitedly, interrupting our regular Monday morning meeting with the primary consultants. "Go to your office cubicle to receive the call." My hands trembled with anticipation, and I left the meeting to take the call. "Hello? Yes, I am Gail Heald-Taylor."

A person with a New York accent responded. "I am the Literacy Consultant for New York City and I have copies of two handouts with your name on them, *The 'Natural Language Approach to Reading* and *The Natural Language Approach to Writing*. Did you write these documents?" Her voice sounded breathless with excitement.

"Yes, yes I did." I said, rocking from one foot to the other.

"Oh, thank goodness, I've contacted the correct person," she said eagerly. "I need to tell you that your documents are so good, so practical for teachers. I want to learn more about your work."

Hearing this good news that the top dog in literacy of New York City was interested in my work, I bubbled with excitement, anxious to share my good fortune with my colleagues. As I opened the door to go back to the meeting, heavy silence fell over the room. No one looked up, and all seven heads were bowed, eyes glued to the agendas in front of them. My smile faded, and the thrill of my excitement dissipated like the air from a deflated air mattress. I could hear myself breathing, taking one breath at a time.

"Turn to item # 5," Mary Dobbs, the co-ordinator announced officiously, her finger pointed to her agenda. I stuffed my good news to the back of my mind and I refocused on the meeting. As the meeting carried on, I glanced around the room—no one met my gaze. There was a shift in mood from my consultant friends. It was the sour whiff of resentment, something I'd never experienced before. It made me cringe. At the end of the meeting, my colleagues gathered up their papers, scraped back their chairs and hurried toward the door. "We've got to do something about that *Natural Language* nonsense!"

'Natural Language' Complaints

"It seems that your colleagues are frustrated when their cadre of teachers request your documents on Natural Language." The Assistant to the Director stated, as I sat with my hands clasped in my lap to keep my hands from quivering. "The Primary Department has complained that your "Natural Language" handouts do not follow the county curriculum." *That's because their curriculum is out of date! I'd be happy to discuss my work with them, if they'd only ask.* "And furthermore, requests for your services are pouring in from educators across the Province; they are clambering to visit classrooms where your work is being implemented."

I lifted my eyes. "Would it help if I brought in my Masters thesis to demonstrate the veracity of what I am doing?"

"That would be helpful," he stated. "And do I have your permission to share your Master's work with a professor at the Faculty of Education at the University of Western in London?"

"Of course," I assured him. "I would appreciate *any* review of my work." The next day, I delivered my Masters thesis—all 5 pounds of a 461-page tome—and plunked it down on the Director's desk. When we met a few weeks later, I was greeted with a smile. "The professor at Western is using your 'Natural Language Reading' and 'Natural Language Writing' in her university classes at the faculty. Thrilled with this outcome, I hoped that this was the end of the issue. Of course, it was *not*!

Summoned by the Superintendent of Curriculum

"Mr. McCleary would like to see you, Gail," our secretary informed me as I walked to my office cubical that Friday morning. *Mr. McCleary, the Superintendent of Curriculum, my boss, wants to see me?* Slinging my coat over the back of my chair, I rushed up to the third floor to his office. Mr. McCleary sat, his reddish blond hair slicked backward from his forehead; he had a large, bulbous head. Ripples of flesh hung in waves over a perfect, creaseless shirt collar. A red and navy tie wrapped tightly under the collar; it helped to keep the shirt buttons at the hollow of his neck, from popping. Overall, he had a strangled appearance above his tailored navy suit which, too, was not quite large enough to camouflage his portly body. His blue eyes glared at me. *This was not going to be a friendly meeting!* His lips pulled taut across his mouth in dissatisfaction, he growled, "I'm not hearing very good things about your work, Gail." His voice was officious and caustic.

My skin began to prickle. "I don't understand what you mean, sir," I responded, trying to calm my fluttering nerves.

"Well," he said brusquely, his voice rising, "It seems you are not following the Board language curriculum." He sounded irritated. "And we can't have that, can we?" His voice was filled with sarcasm.

What could I say? Of course, my work didn't follow the Board's curriculum; *it's hot-off-the-press-brand-new following up-to-date-research,* I wanted to tell him. *It's the Board documents that are out of date.*

"I'd like to explain, Mr. McCleary," . . .

Interrupting me, Mr. McCleary raised his index finger and shook it in my face. I saw the wetness under his arm, and smelled the acrid, sour smell of sweat. "If your work doesn't follow the Board curriculum, you have to stop doing it *immediately!*" He bellowed and pounded his fist on his shiny mahogany desk, glowering at me.

Before I could utter another word, he stood up and roared. "I have no more time to talk about this today. I will meet you here at the Education Centre tomorrow morning at ten," he demanded.

"But that's Saturday," I stammered.

"I know," he roared and dismissed me with a wave of his beefy hand.

As I headed home, my mind whirled with conflicting thoughts. My work was being used by the professor at Western University, in London, Ontario. My

Master's thesis had validated Natural Language. *So, what was McCleary talking about?*

A Saturday morning meeting, with my boss, in an empty building.

I couldn't wait to talk to John; he would know what to do!

John set down his coffee mug and took a long drag on his cigarette. "Look Hon, you have accomplished so much in such a short period of time, but there may be something you've overlooked."

"Like what?" I asked, my eyebrows creasing with a sense of concern.

"I wonder how much Mary Dobbs and the other consultants really *know* about all the things you've accomplished."

John had a point. "I guess I've never told them about the article published in "The Reading Teacher" or the ESL book I'm writing for OISE."

"So, you see Hon, the other consultants are only aware that *their* teachers are clamoring for your handouts and that your work is not in the Board curriculum." He sucked in another drag. "Frankly, I think this is all about politics."

"But what about meeting with McCleary tomorrow—a Saturday—isn't *that* abnormal? Don't you think we should call our lawyer to come with me;

a lawyer would sure as heck get McCleary's attention and let him know I'm not a pushover."

John smiled that lazy half grin of his that always calmed me down. "Look, sweetheart, you and I know that McCleary is a buffoon and a bully who thinks he can intimidate everyone— especially women—that's his mode of operation." I nodded. "But he hasn't met *you*, sweetheart," John grinned, patting my knee. "I'll give you some tips on how to handle that jerk, so you don't need a lawyer when you chat with him.

The Saturday Morning Meeting

As I walked up the two flights of stairs to McCleary's office, my footfalls echoed in the empty building. As I neared his open office door, I clenched my fists and fought to remain calm. Pasting a smile on my face, I entered. "Good morning Mr. McCleary," I chirped cheerily, I reached over his desk and dangled my hand for a handshake. Startled, as if I'd caught him off-guard, his hand fumbled as it met mine; he limply shook it. "Before we start, sir," I announced, with more confidence that I felt, "I'd like to know how long this meeting will be; my husband is waiting in the parking lot."

McCleary jerked his head up in surprise at my assertiveness. "Shouldn't take too long," he growled gruffly, in an attempt to take command over the situation.

McCleary coughed and shuffled some papers in front of him. "Now, I want to make something very clear, Gail," he blustered, loudly. "You can't be running around giving workshops all over the county with material that is *not* sanctioned by the curriculum documents. That's all there is to it," he yelled. He pounded his fist on his desk for emphasis.

My body flinched. It was like being interrogated by the police with bright lights in my eyes. My stomach tightened, and my hands began to sweat. "I will not be intimidated," I whispered under my breath, mustering courage to counter this buffoon. "Mr. McCleary," I declared, my voice rising with confidence, "I am sure that you are aware that my work is validated by the current research on literacy. It is written about in my Master's thesis." My voice rose with my conviction. "My article has also been published in a world-renowned reading journal, " I asserted, looking him in the eye. "Furthermore," I added, with aplomb, my voice sounding like the competent author that I was, "I'm working with OISE Press on a future book."

McCleary's eyes widened in surprise—his eyelids fluttered furiously, as if this information was new to him. He reached for a peppermint from his candy dish to settle his nerves. "So," I went on with assurance. "Although my work is absent from the Board curriculum documents, it *is*, nevertheless, up-to-date and reflects current research in literacy."

McCleary's forehead curled, and his lips stretched tight across his face. They quivered with anger. Drawing his fist high above his head, he smashed it on the desk with a whack! "I'm telling you, Gail—so, listen to me clearly." His words snip-snapped with his out-of-control-rage. "You will *not* be allowed to print any more of your Natural Language handouts on the curriculum department budget until this matter is cleared up." His nostrils flared. "Do you understand?" he shouted, his paunchy cheeks puffed out and went a blotchy, bright red.

"Is that all?" I asked, folding my coat over my arm.

"You may go," he yelled, his forehead wet with sweat.

"Thank you, Mr. McCleary." As I left his office, I heard a loud whap as if he had slammed the door behind me. The hollow echo bounced against the walls as I walked the three flights down.

Gail Is the Problem

What to do about Natural Language was the topic of the Monday morning meeting of the primary consultants. I arrived early, got a coffee and headed to the meeting room. I found Mary Dobbs–the coordinator—sitting alone at the head of the table. She was bent over the papers spread out in front of her, reading. She glanced at me; her eyes were stone cold and she grimaced. My heart started to flutter and the palms of my hands began to sweat. At the stroke of 9, the other primary consultants walked in, took their seats and bent their heads over the agenda in front of them.

Mary cleared her throat. "As you know there has been some discussion throughout our Board about our Language Arts curriculum. There was a hard edge to her voice, "Mr. McCleary, our Superintendent of Curriculum, has asked us to develop a policy regarding how the Natural Language material fits with our Language Arts curriculum." She looked around the table. "I invite everyone's input." A stubborn silence filled the room. I heard a shuffling of papers, a shifting of bodies, and a feeling of hesitancy as if the consultants were uncertain of who should begin. "I'll start," announced Ellie across from me, cocking her head defiantly. "This Natural Language material is *definitely* in conflict with the Board's curriculum documents," she stated confidently. I dropped my eyes to my pad of paper, listening intently. *That's not surprising since you wrote the Language Arts document over ten years ago!*

Surprised, I saw many others nod their heads in support of Ellie's comment. I sat mute, but my mind was spinning. *Will we discuss the new research in literacy? Will they acknowledge that the Board curriculum is out of date?*

"What I'm concerned about in Gail's work" responded a colleague to my left, "is that phonics are *not* properly addressed," Her voice had a critical tone. *Oh, my word, she's referring to me in the third person when I'm sitting right beside her!* My mind went numb. *Why doesn't she ask me how I deal with phonics in Natural Language?* In fact, "I've been told that Gail poo-poos the use of phonetics *entirely*," she said caustically, slapping down her pen to punctuate her belief. *It's obvious that she's never read any of my work, or she'd know that phonetics is dealt with effectively in my handouts.*

Perplexed, I looked over at Mary, hoping for some leadership. *When is she going to ask me to explain the research behind my work? Why hasn't she brought my handouts here for everyone to examine, so I could clarify their questions?*

"What I'm concerned about," Janice stated angrily, "Is that Gail has developed a cult-like following."

"Yes," said another colleague. "She buys allegiance by giving out roses to participants in her workshops." She said it with a cynical smirk. "That's bribery, in my books."

Shocked, I couldn't understand why my colleagues were turning on me—we went for lunch together and shared transportation to conferences. I'd entertained them in my home, for goodness' sake.

Ellie addressed Mary Dobbs, directly. "Have

you seen those stories that kindergarten children dictate?" she said, a hint of sarcasm in her voice. "I examined some of them, and it's hard to believe that a five-year-old could tell such elaborate stories." She tapped her pen on the table. "I wonder if Gail *doctors* up those stories for her workshops?" *She's accusing me of fraud!* A lump formed in my throat, and my cheeks burned with anger.

Mary Dobbs nodded to Ellie and asked, "Does anyone else have anything to add?" As Mary glanced around the table waiting, the room fell silent. "Next week we will discuss solutions as to what to do with Natural Language," Mary said crisply, glaring at me. With a scraping of chairs, everyone picked up their papers and shuffled out the door.

I was left alone, My heart sank.

The Solution

The focus of the next primary meeting was to discuss a solution to the issue of Natural Language. After much debate, a resolution was reached. My colleagues drafted a short, two page document. They tucked my Natural Language under the theory of "Language Experience," a well-known term that had been used in the field of literacy for years. In no way did "Language Experience" encompass Donald Graves' new research, upon which my work in Natural

Language was based. The two-page document represented hundreds of pages in my Masters thesis and many hours spent analyzing children's work—all compressed to just a hundred words! "This document will be distributed and mandated to all the primary teachers in the Board," Mary pronounced.

However, that did not satisfy the Primary Department. Mary made a final declaration to me. "We expect that you remove the covers off all the Natural Language documents that are stored in our resource centre."

I straightened my back, pasted a smile on my lips and stared into Mary's eyes in response, I enunciated each word—clearly and distinctly.

"No, Miss. Dobbs. I . . . will. . . not."

Natural Language Gets Bumped Up to the Director

The atmosphere in the Primary Department became so toxic that I applied for a position in the "Gifted" program in the Special Education Department, and was hired., As far as Natural Language was concerned, I continued my work on my own time—weekends and holidays—and gave workshops outside the Waterloo Board boundary. My presentation at the TESL conference (Teaching English to Second Language Learners) drew the attention of Ginn & Company, a major Canadian publishing firm. They hired me, on a part-time basis, to incorporate my Natural

Language philosophy into their new literacy program.

However, problems with Natural Language persisted in the Waterloo Board when educators, from across Ontario, continually requested visits to observe Natural Language in Waterloo classrooms. Now that I was under the umbrella of Special Education, Natural Language created conflict between two main departments—Special Education and the Curriculum Program Department—Mr. McCleary's domain. Consequently, the Natural Language issue was bumped up a notch to the Director of the Board—Mr. Ward. He called high level meetings with the two Superintendents, the Primary Coordinator—Mary Dobbs—and . . . . me. Up against the top political echelon of the county, I felt completely and utterly alone; my only defence was my integrity and my well-researched work.

As I walked up the steps to the conference room, for that first meeting, my body tensed and my sweaty hands clung to the armrail. I was very aware that my future career would depend on the outcome of these meetings. As I approached the open door, I heard muffled voices inside. The moment I entered, the chatter diminished to a whisper, then faded to a deafening silence. My heart pounded furiously, my face fought to remain calm and in control.

"Sit here," Mr. Ward said smiling, pointing to an empty chair. The air crackled with anticipation and every muscle in my body tensed. Glancing around the room, Mary Dobbs sat awkwardly perched on the edge of her chair, her wide girth spilled over the sides. She glared at me disdainfully. Her frown reeked of the odour of accusation. I clasped my hands into a tight ball; I held them in my lap to still the quivering.

"Good morning, Gail." The Coordinator of Special Education whispered, a hint of kindness in his voice.

"Welcome everyone," Mr. Ward began, his lips spreading open in a wide grin. I knew him to be knowledgeable, smart, and politically astute with a warm and pleasant disposition. Mr. Ward turned to Mary Dobbs. "Would you like to begin?" he asked warmly.

Mary nodded and cleared her throat. "I am concerned that the Primary teachers in the county are implementing the Natural Language approach instead of the Primary Language Arts curriculums," she stated, her voice sounding brittle. "Also," she went on. "Natural Language is not consistent with the philosophy of our Board curriculum documents." Mary's eyes narrowed, and anger licked at her words. "Furthermore, my Primary consultants have many concerns about Natural Language. Mary listed all their complaints. "In addition, our Primary consultants are receiving requests from our teachers for documents on how to implement the Natural Language Approach." She took a sip of water. "That's in spite of mandating that teachers employ the concept called Language Experience," she said, with more confidence. "And now, I'm receiving calls and letters from *outside* the county to visit classrooms where Natural Language is being implemented," she said, she shook her head as if that was the final straw. "Natural Language is simply undermining our Waterloo Language Arts curriculum." She smiled, seeming satisfied that she'd made her case.

Mr. Ward smiled and gave a quick nod with his chin "Thank you, Miss Dobbs," Turning to Mr. McCleary, he asked, "Do you have anything to add?"

"Miss Dobbs did a fine job of stating the problem," Mr. McCleary stated, emphatically. "As you can see, Mr. Ward, Natural Language simply conflicts with the Board-sanctioned curriculum—as Mary has so eloquently explained." He tapped his pen on the papers in front of him. "However, I want to point out another major concern we may have overlooked." Everyone cocked their ears, waiting to hear what he had to say. "And that is that Natural Language has caused a *rift* between the two major departments in our Board." His tone was smug. "And that is *not* a healthy situation for our county." His voice rose to a loud pitch. "And that rupture is being perceived in School Boards across the Province of Ontario!" he pronounced, officiously.

"Thank you, Mr. McCleary," Mr. Ward said politely, nodding.

Mr. Ward then turned to me. "Gail," he said calmly, looking directly into my eyes. "Next meeting I would like *you* to share *your* ideas." My eyes lit up and my body tingled with excitement. *Does he really want to hear my thoughts? Is he requesting me to share my work?* Finally, someone has asked me to talk about my research and its application in my Natural Language documents!

Mary's eyebrows shot up in surprise before together in a frown. With a jerk, she gathered her papers, jumped up, and stomped to the door. Mr. McCleary lumbered out behind her.

"Thank you, Mr. Ward, for the opportunity to speak about my work." I held out my arm to shake his hand. Bouncing out of the room, I couldn't wipe off the smile on my lips.

Natural Language Speaks for Itself

I couldn't wait to tell John the good news: "I know what I'll do—"I'll take my overheads and that tape-slide kit that Wesley and I developed. When they see Annie's work it'll impress them for sure. With my Master's research, I'll be able to convince them that Natural Language is well researched and needs to be included in the Board's documents when the primary curriculum is revised."

"Slow down, Hon, don't get ahead of yourself," John cautioned. "This next meeting has far more at stake than convincing them of the validity of Natural Language." Let's look at this as an opportunity to demonstrate your skills in diplomacy and leadership. After all, one day you may want to be a Principal or even a Superintendent," John said. He smiled confidently. "This is the chance to show the Administration what you are made of."

I arrived early on the morning of the meeting; I felt more at ease than the previous one, yet, I was still apprehensive about the approach that I intended to employ.

Mr. Ward started the meeting. "It's good to see all of you this morning. Please help yourself to coffee before we begin."

When everyone was settled, Mr. Ward turned to me. "Gail?" His smile was warm.

Taking a great intake of air, I let it out sparingly bit-by-bit to settle my nerves. "Hello everyone; thank you for this opportunity to chat with you for a few moments," I said. I sounded more confident than I felt. "I want to start by acknowledging that the Primary Language Arts curriculum in Waterloo County is one of the most comprehensive documents of all the School Boards across the province." I took a sip of coffee. "The Primary consultants who developed it did a fine job." I glanced at Mary Dobbs. She scowled at me. "I also want to compliment the Waterloo Board for supporting the Primary consultant team in attending conferences on literacy in Toronto and London, Ontario over the years." I nodded to Mr. McCleary's direction. His lips were spread thin and tight. "Recently, we learned about some very innovative research that challenged many of our former concepts related to the theories of literacy." Mary jerked up her head and pursed her lips to show her disagreement and disdain. "This new research forms the foundation of my Masters work." I nodded toward my thesis. "Out of that work, my article on early writing was published in the world's most prodigious journal, *The Reading Teacher*." I displayed a copy. Mary's eyes glowered at me. "As many of you are aware, that article led to my presentation on Natural Language at the International Reading Conference in Atlanta, Georgia recently." There was an instant collective gasp of surprise at the mention of an international presentation.

Mary's face glowed pink and Mr. McCleary glared, his eyes bulging with anger.

"If anyone has any questions, I would be happy to elaborate."

Silence—stone dead silence. Mary pressed her lips into a thin angry line, and her forehead glistened with sweat, but she said nothing. Mr. McCleary's eyes burned furiously into mine.

There was a shuffling of pages, as Mary and Mr. McCleary sorted through their papers. Mr. Ward moved his eyes around the table, pausing at each person, before asking once again, "Does anyone have any questions for Gail?"

Hearing only the ticking patter of the clock over head and the faint clatter of fingers on keyboards in the outer office, Mr. Ward turned to me. "Thank you, Gail."

Dipping my chin toward Mr. Ward, I concluded, "Thank you everyone for this opportunity to speak with you."

"In conclusion," Mr. Ward said, "I propose that next week we come with ideas for a resolution."

Natural Language: The Final Solution

"John, I know what I'll recommend as a resolution," I said with a half smirk. "I'll demand an apology from Mary Dobbs for the trauma she's caused me. Maybe I'll offer to write a new Primary Language Arts curriculum," I said, laughing, knowing full well that neither of these ideas would be accepted.

Wrestling with this task for a week, John convinced me of a compromise—something I was not completely satisfied with, but which I could live with under these difficult circumstances.

Climbing up those steps to the third floor for the final meeting, I held my solution in my head.

Mary Dobbs and Mr. McCleary sat side by side,

looking calm and self-satisfied. Mr. Ward looked around the room, a pleasant look on his face. "Today we will discuss solutions," he said looking in my direction with his charming smile. "Gail, will you share first?"

"Of course," I said, in an attempt to sound confident while feeling uneasy about my resolution. I sucked in a deep breath of apprehension. Holding up the blue pamphlet, I began: "As outlined in this two-page document, I can support that the Natural Language approach has been placed in the Primary Language Arts Curriculum under the umbrella section called Language Experience." Mary Dobbs head snapped up instantly, her jaw dropping open. "Augh!" she gasped, then called out, "No, No," she shouted. "That will *never* do!" Her eyes burned angrily.

At that moment, Mr. Ward interjected. "Miss Dobbs, help me understand why the blue document doesn't clarify how Natural Language fits with the Primary Language Arts curriculum." Mary became flustered. She was unable to respond. Mr. Ward continued. "That document *is* what your department developed and sent out to all the Primary teachers, isn't it?" He nodded to Mary.

Mary's shoulders hunched, "Well, yes," she sputtered, "But not exactly." Her words were clipped. A deep pink inched up the side of her neck.

Mr. Ward looked intently at Mary, "What is

your proposal then, Miss Dobbs?" There was a slight edge to his voice.

Time seemed suspended as a strange silence filled the room. All eyes turned on Mary, waiting, the question hanging in the air.

Mary shook her head from side to side. Her eyes stared directly into mine with a look of pure rage. Mr. Ward lowered his voice. His words were measured and concise. "Miss Dobbs," he said, as he enunciated each word carefully, succinctly. "Is ... this ... just ... all ... about ... *politics*?" His eyebrows lifted in a question.

Mary's face blanched. She stood up abruptly, gathered her papers, shoved back her chair scraping wood-against-wood and strode out of the room into the hallway. She muttered something to Mr. McCleary as he lumbered after her, trying to catch up.

A Hollow Victory

I sat in an empty room while I was waiting for the Superintendent of Special Education to meet with me. The moment he came into the room, I could tell from his furrowed brow that the news was not good.

He sat down across from me; his eyes were flat. He took in a deep breath and let out a disappointed sound like a tire slowly losing air. He began. "I have been instructed to tell you that you must cease developing and distributing all Natural Language material connected to the Waterloo Board. I jotted down what he said. "It is also demanded that you no longer respond to requests from outside Boards for visits to classrooms where Natural Language has been implemented. *What is the Board doing?* "And, in addition, you are NOT to give workshops to any outside Boards that reflect the Waterloo Board of Education." *They want to disassociate all my work from the Waterloo Board—the Board I've worked in for the past ten years—the Board in which I established my career!* "I will leave you now Gail, to think this over." He left the room. There was a small click as he shut the door behind him.

Numb. I couldn't understand a word of what I'd just heard. My work in Natural Language was validated; my research was sound. It had been accepted by world experts in the field of literacy. The administration knew all that—*why were they doing this to me? What was their purpose?*

At that moment, I felt a heavy boot had come down on my shoulders with a mighty STOMP. They'd stomped on my research; they'd stomped on my career. Stomp!... Stomp!... Stomp!... With a sudden thud, I felt they had stomped on *me*—the very essence of who I was. They were pulverizing me into the ground. Inside, I felt abandoned. Despair wrapped around me, like a shroud.

Coping

"You are depressed, my love," John said, trying to cheer me up.

I sat, silent in my misery.

"Why don't you seek advice?" he asked. "Maybe your Teachers Federation can fight for you," he suggested. "What the Waterloo Board is doing to you, isn't just!"

In a moment of desperation, I called the Provincial Federation. After outlining my situation, the counsellor responded. "It sounds like you have outgrown your Board. My advice to you is to *move on*."

What good was that advice?

I was established in Waterloo County; we owned our home here; our children went to Waterloo County schools. Where was I to move on *to*? I felt worse than before . . . I experienced the combined states of malaise, foreboding, and ambivalence. I was suddenly alienated from all I knew . . . all that had sustained me. My work was what defined me. In a flash, I was became more dejected . . . sad . . . and . . . forlorn.

"You can't go on like this," John said, a few weeks later, an edge to his voice. "You are a fighter, and you have to dig yourself out of this mess. You've got to *do* something productive for *you* to build yourself back up."

His words gave me a glimmer of hope. "This would be a good time to start working on your Doctorate at U of T," (University of Toronto.)

With this beacon of light, I turned the corner toward optimism. I buckled down and finished the courses for my Doctorate at OISE. That summer, I drafted my first book for OISE Press at our family cottage at Sauble Beach.

National Consultant for Ginn

In the summer of 1985, Ginn offered me the job as their National Consultant of Programs. It was quite an honour to be working with a major Canadian textbook company. Taking a leave of absence from the Board, I worked with them from 1985 to 1986. Working from home provided a relaxing routine with the boys. I enjoyed watching them make the Bruce Springsteen headbands, and I remember taking some to the Ginn office staff to sell. Working with a company that valued my background lifted my spirits; I spent time promoting the 'Journeys' program, which sent me across Canada, and I met with teachers in many provinces. On those trips, when I was consulting in a city nearby, I could meet up with family and friends: Aunt Hilda in Vancouver, Mom in Edmonton, and the Townsend's—whom I met one wintery day in Winnipeg.

For decades, the Ginn *Journey's* series supported teachers across Canada. In fact, in 2017, when I was working with a teacher in Hagersville, I came across some of the "Journey's" readers in first-grade classrooms. Picking one up, I smiled to see my name on the inside cover: *Gail Heald-Taylor, Consultant.*

My Near-Miss Plane Crash

It was a trip to remember–my first consulting assignment at the Kirkland Lake Board of Education. Kirkland Lake is hundreds of miles north of Toronto.

From the veranda of our home on Inverness Place, that glorious, warm, sunny fall day, I could see that the leaves on our maple tree had not yet turned orange-brown, and the blood-red petunias that lined the driveway were still untouched by frost. There were two bags beside me, one with my clothes and the other with learning materials for presentations. John and I stood waiting for the limo service to take me to the airport. I was wearing a wool pantsuit and feeling almost too warm in the summer-like autumn sunshine. I threw my long fur vest over my arm in case I needed it for the cooler evenings when I was away.

"Don't you think you should take your coat?" John asked, always worried about me.

"I really don't think I need one," I replied, but to appease him, I went back inside and got the coat that went with the fur vest.

At the Toronto airport, I boarded a twin prop plane along with seven other passengers for the flight North. The passenger galley was only five feet high, and I had to bend my body into a crouch position. My head was inches from the grey carpet on the alley floor, and my nostrils filled with the acrid smell of sweaty runners, spilled coffee, and ancient cigarette fumes. I crawled to my seat and straightened my torso to an upright position. I clicked my seatbelt closed as the engine ground slowly across the tarmac. With a whine and roar, we were airborne for the three and a-half-hour-flight. Margaret Atwood's new book, *The Handmaid's Tale*, kept me engrossed for most of the flight, and I was startled, suddenly, by the ping of ice-pellets against the window pane as waves of white caked the glass like whipped icing. Setting down my book, I saw there was a raging blizzard outside. *My god, I could barely see the wing of the plane!* My body stiffened and my heart lurched as I gripped the arm-rest to steady my nerves.

"It's going to be a rough landing at Kirkland!" the pilot shouted above the roar of the engine. Looking back at us, he yelled again. "But we'll be okay; I've flown in worse conditions." I tried to swallow the lump that was rising in my throat. My heart pounded as gusts of wind piled snow onto the wing. The flight attendant sat white-knuckled, and her face blanched. *This was not reassuring.*

Peeking through a gauze-like veil of snow, I saw buildings below. "We're heading into Kirkland now," the pilot yelled. "Hang on, it's going to be a slippery, bumpy ride." My hands were wet with sweat. The plane rocked and shifted in its descent—the most dangerous part of the flight. With a bang and a jolt, the plane hit the tarmac, bounced, then ricocheted—skittering from side-to-side. Suddenly righting itself, the plane headed toward a mound of snow at the end of the runway. "We're going to crash!" barked the man in the seat behind me.

I could see from the window that the nose of the plane was zigzagging toward the looming snow pile at lightning speed. As I closed my eyes tight, images of the boys and John flashed in my mind. With a jerk, the plane slid—CRUNCH. Full stop.

There was pandemonium—snapping seat-buckles, gabbling voices, zipping duffle bags, and scrabbling feet. The flight attendant snapped to attention, and a flush of pink returned to her cheeks as she pushed open the door of the plane. She let in a blast of frigid air as she lowered the boarding stairs. I pulled on my coat over my fur vest, buttoning it to my chin; it offered meagre protection from the sudden burst of arctic air coming from the wind-whipped tarmac. As I hustled toward the terminal in my high-heeled pumps, I slipped and slid across the runway. Bullets of ice pelted my cheeks, and the howling wind snapped and threshed my hair into rat-tails.

In the terminal, shaking from the near missed tragedy, I wrapped my arms around my body for warmth.

Suddenly, I heard John's voice: *'Don't you think*

you should wear a coat?"... I should have taken a hat and boots too!

Embarrassing Final Day with the Ginn CEO

A final goodbye to Ginn was a bit dramatic. One of the perks of working with them was the beige Chrysler K-Car station-wagon that the company provided. On my last day at the company, I took the CEO out for a farewell lunch in the K-Car I'd purchased. It was *my* treat to take him out to lunch—a classy thing to do, John told me. At the end of our meal, I paid the bill and walked him out to my car in the parking lot of the restaurant. Putting my hand in my purse I reached for my keys as the CEO stood at the passenger side, waiting to get in. Checking every zipped-in pocket inside-and-out of my purse and shoving my hands deep into my jacket pockets, it was of no avail—the keys were nowhere to be found.

Noticing the CEO looking into the car through the passenger window he said, "Your keys are in the ignition." He had a smirk on his face. *Damn, this was definitely NOT a classy ending to my career with Ginn and Company!*

Classroom Teacher / Vice-Principal Roles

My next career move, at Sandown Public School in Kitchener, was as a classroom teacher and half time Vice Principal. For a decade, I'd been the *expert* in my various roles as School Board Consultant, and with Ginn & Company, implementing literacy programs to teachers. In those roles I *showed* teachers how to implement holistic literacy strategies. However, I hadn't actually *taught* children in a classroom of my own. Sure, I'd worked alongside teachers, giving them advice, but that was no substitute for working directly with *real* children in a *real* classroom that was mine. Furthermore, all my teaching experience had been with first and second graders; I had no experience at all with junior students—grades 4 to 6—it was no surprise that I was absolutely overwhelmed as I faced twenty-five, smiling, sixth-graders. I was scared to death.

Two months later, I conducted my first parent-teacher meeting. I had writing samples by my students splashed on the blackboard. Bins of junior novels sat on the shelf along the window ledge of the portable classroom. Professional books—including mine—lined up along the chalkboard ledge. With the screen set up and the overhead projector plugged in, I was ready that Wednesday evening. Was I nervous? You bet.

At 6:45, I reorganized, one more time, the table

at the back of the classroom, fiddled with the orange name-tags, and fluffed the golden chrysanthemums that I'd picked from my garden that morning. They were inside a hollowed-out pumpkin shell, sitting in a glass of water. *Thank goodness I filled the glass with water in the main building of the school.* The portable had no running water.

At 7 o'clock, the door squeaked open, and a woman stepped in, a man following behind. "Welcome," I said, extending my arm to shake their hands. They did not respond. "We're Mr. and Mrs. Watson, David's parents," the woman announced as they picked up the orange cards, wrote down their names, and pinned them to their clothing. They circulated around the room and examined the children's work. Mrs. Watson scrunched her eye-brows together and looked critical; she whispered something to her husband. Other parents arrived, attached name-tags and milled around, chatting, before sitting at the children's desks.

Standing at the front of the room, I cleared my throat. "Good evening," I said smiling. "Welcome to our classroom." My heart was pounding so hard, I wondered if the parents could hear it. "I'd like to begin by sharing a little of my background."

"Oh, we've already heard about *you*," Mrs. Watson interrupted abruptly, a derisive tone in her voice. "You don't teach grammar and spelling," she said scornfully.

My face blanched, my lips went dry. When I tried to speak, my tongue felt as if my mouth was full of peanut butter. A prickly flush of heat rose up my neck to my cheeks; my fingers trembled. *What the heck's wrong with me? I've presented to hundreds of people; how can I get flustered with a comment from that old biddy, for goodness' sake?*

Twenty eyes stared back at me, and not one looked positive. *Boy, how I need a Bloody Mary.* I stretched my lips wide, attempting a smile, and tried to go on. My mouth was parched dry and no words would come. Silence.... Panic. At that moment, I spied the chrysanthemums. Walking past snickering parents to the table at the back of the room, I stopped at the orange blooms, stretched my fingers beneath their stems, scooped them out of the glass jar in the pumpkin, set them down carefully onto the table, sifted the green leaves and spider from the water, wrapped my fingers around the glass, lifted it out of the pumpkin, pried my glued lips apart and ... drank. Back to the front of the room, I turned on the overhead projector—and started.

Putting the Rubber to the Road: Whole Language in Sixth-Grade

Determined to put Natural Language into practice—then called Whole Language strategies—with my sixth-graders, I read and re-read what the experts had written and took the plunge.

The first step was to develop a schedule—a routine for the children and me to follow. On a chart, I labeled "Literature Day" for reading novels and "Writing Day", for writing stories in their notebooks. As the students came into the classroom, they checked the chart; it reminded them of what they were to do. They got to work without any instruction from me. It didn't run smoothly at first, but within a couple of months, they got the hang of it.

On a typical Literature Day, the students had the choice to continue reading their novel from the previous Literature Day, or to select a new one from the hundreds of novels in the bins on the window ledge. As the students read, I moved about the room and helped a student find a book or encourage another to abandon a book they weren't enjoying. Abandoning a book was difficult for Mike. When I noticed him pondering over a page in his book, I stopped and chatted. "I see you haven't gotten very far into *Huckleberry Finn*. What seems to be the problem?"

"Well, my mom says it's a great book, a classic, and she wants me to read it."

"Your mom is correct that, *Huckleberry Finn* is a good book. But if you're not enjoying it, you can choose something else. There are lots of other good novels in the book bins."

"But Mom says I should finish a book once I've started it," he argued.

"A lot of people think that, but in our class you can put the book back into the book bin, if you don't like it, and choose another one you might enjoy better," I suggested. "Maybe save *Huckleberry Finn* for reading at home." Mike beamed. "You have an option, so it's up to you." Mike struggled with "Huck Finn" for a few more days before he returned it to the bin. On his way out for recess, I overheard him ask his buddy, Marve, "What novel are *you* reading?" They continued to chatter about books as they ran outside.

At the end of the Literature Day session, I called the class together for what I called Sharing Time. That's when the class shared titles they particularly enjoyed. Other kids would take their advice and there would be a run on a title. Their classmates had far more influence than I had. In fact, I frequently picked up some of their best loved novels to read, myself. Frankly, I have to admit that it was in *this* class that I too became a reader—a real reader—for the first time!

During Writing Day, the students got out their writing notebooks. They knew that they could write about whatever topic they choose, and on any genre. Some children wrote events from their lives, while others chose to write factual *How To* pieces—how to learn to skate, and how to play soccer. Some students would continue writing the same piece from their last Writing Workshop Day, while others would start something new. It was their choice; the only requirement was that they write something during this time. As the students became busy with their pieces, I walked around the room, glancing at each student, sometimes stopping to whisper a comment, and at other times responding to questions if someone asked me. If I noticed two or three students running into a similar issue, I called them together. "Anyone wanting to talk about new writing topics, come back here for a chat," I whispered.

During Sharing Time at the end of the Writing Day, some students shared their work. When a student read their piece, I encouraged the class to point out *positive* aspects that they appreciated about the piece of writing: for example, Jeffry described the lake at his cottage up north—blue, rippled, and shiny; Jane shared different ways to show anger at her brother when he took her soccer ball without asking—furious, seething, and ticked off. At this point, I would invite the class to consider using interesting descriptions in their own compositions. In that way, they learned from each other as we continually highlighted quality features of each student's work.

Spelling and grammar? How did I deal with developing writing *skills*. Each night, I took home *five* student writing books. I recorded growth on an evaluation sheet I'd developed—you are using contractions well, and you use capital letters in the right places. With spelling, I might celebrate the percentage of words they spelled correctly.

In another column, I pointed out *one* strategy to work on.. I'd point out words that were frequently spelled incorrectly—*said, should, would*. For example, I'd provide the correct spelling, leaving the rest of the misspelled words for an editing session if they wanted to publish the piece.

Five writing books was all I could handle on a single evening; but over a month every child had received a response. In my class there was no need for formal lessons on spelling. What did I do with those commercial spellers? I tossed them out!

By winter break, my grade six students had progressed beyond my wildest expectations. In our "Literature Sharing" sessions, students would point out descriptions that published authors used in *their* novels. For instance, Susan noted, *"his shoulders, lowered, sagged,"* while Jeff liked, *"her voice was soft, low, sounding kind."* Patti was impressed how the author in her book used these interesting phrases, *"his eyes were as black as a shiny piece of wet coal."* I might have mentioned that the phrase was a *'simile,'* knowing that the label wasn't as important as noting the unusual phrase.

As the students discovered strategies that published authors employed, I nudged them to incorporate them into their own writing. In Writer's Workshop sharing sessions, students did just that.

As spring puddles formed around snow banks on the playground, and sprouts of green grass emerged on the soccer field, some of my six-graders edited their pieces by adding new ideas or removing aspects that didn't work well in their compositions—and published their work. At this stage Linda went over her 'skill sheet,' making sure that she'd fixed any grammar and spelling issues before publishing her story. I made any final edits before sending it off to my parent volunteers; they typed up the stories and returned them to my class within a week. We had no laptops in our classroom in 1986. When Lynda got her typed version back from the parents, she bound it together into a cover she'd made from wallpaper samples and put it on display in the *Published Books* bin in our classroom for other students to read during Literature Day.

Marj, the substitute teacher I had once a month, when I was required to attend a principals' meeting, told me she loved my classroom. "I have so little to do," she explained. "The students run the show!" she said excitedly. "I can't believe how the kids check the chart to see what they are doing for the day," she exclaimed. "There's no disciplining required because the kids *love* what they are doing. All I have to do is point out the good stuff in their stories. Piece of cake!!" I, too, was amazed at the children's writing in the last term of the year.

Sean became an amazing writer who revised his realistic fiction story about a fishing trip he had gone on with his Dad. He wrote his story twice–once from *his* perspective, and another draft from his *Dad's* point-of-view. Not bad for an eleven-year-old! And then there was Melissa. On the last day of school, in June 1987, the children were cleaning out their desks, dumping refuge into green garbage bags. I happened to be standing beside Melissa's desk as she reached into it and pulled out sheet after sheet of writing. "Melissa," I asked her, as my eyes grew wide in wonder. "What are all these?"

"Oh, it's just old stuff I've been working on," she laughed, her broad smile exposing the mesh of wire threads wrapped around her teeth. "Just garbage," she said, and cocked her head to one side. The hat that she wore regularly tipped, jauntily, to one side and covered her golden hair.

"Would you give me permission to read them?"

"Sure," she said. "But you can't share them with anyone else!"

"That's a deal." Melissa dragged out several crumpled pieces of writing. It turned out that she had written ten stories in the *third* person about a child who was struggling with her parents splitting up, an astounding body of work! It was undoubtedly a story about Melissa, herself.

Sean and Melissa's work was a testament to how holistic learning could truly happen when students took the lead in their learning. An aside: I Googled Sean and sent him a letter; I never got a reply.

Consultant for HBJ Publishing

The year I taught sixth grade, Harcourt Brace & Jovanovic (HBJ) Publishing from Orlando Florida came knocking at my classroom door. I'd gotten a call from The HBJ literacy consultant, whom I'd met the previous year after giving a presentation in Toronto, called me. In the middle of my teaching year, she invited me to Florida to present my work to their educational team, and the sales personnel of their new reading program "Imagination"—Kindergarten to Grade Eight.

Go to sunny Florida during the Christmas Break? Here we come!

John and I flew to Orlando for a working holiday for me and a relaxing holiday for him. On New Year's Eve, we ate our midnight meal at the window of our hotel room. It overlooked the famous Orlando "Orange Bowl" drop, and we watched the fireworks afterward. They lit up the black, Orlando sky.

The first day that I presented my workshop, their team was so impressed that they offered me a

Consultant position for their program. It was hard to believe my good fortune, that I would be working with such a high profile company in the United States!

One afternoon, I met the President in his enormous opulent office. It had floor-to-ceiling mahogany walls on one side, and sunshine poured through the far wall of glass, casting rays of golden light onto the massive mahogany desk.

"I want to learn more about this new philosophy that's all *the buzz* in the publishing world these days, something I understand *you* know all about, Gail, and are implementing in your classroom up in Canada." He ran his fingers along his wide suspenders. "It is quite amazing, " he said grinning. "We Americans like to think we've discovered *all* that's new in the field of literacy, and here's a Canadian showing us how to do it!" he chuckled at the irony of it.

I learned months later that I'd been speaking to the CEO of the largest educational textbook publishing company in the world! It is just as well that I didn't know it then, or I'd have been way too nervous presenting my work.

HBJ Films My Classroom

That June, 1987, the HBJ film crew descended on my grade six classroom to see my students in action. It was a heady week for all of us. On the first day of filming—oblivious of the cameras shooting pictures of them—my students came into class, checked the chart, Literature Day, and started to work as the film crew shot pictures of them reading their novels, or making notes in their Literature Response Journals. They took shots of Jeremy talking with Judy about other good selections worth reading; Mary-Anne was at the book bin searching for a new novel to read. I circled the room and watched for anyone who needed me. Mike motioned me to come over. "I'm reading *Game On* by Gordon Korman" he told me. "I like it a lot better than *Huckleberry Fin*," he said, with a grin. During circle time at the end of the session, we gathered together and talked about books. Greg waved the book, *Dog Song*, by Gary Paulsen. John asked him what he liked about it, and Greg went on at length. I asked the class if they found any lines in their book that were especially descriptive. Jill always had lines to share. That's when I nudged them to use similar descriptions in their own writing.

The following morning was 'Writing Day.' The kids got out their writing books and took over as they always did. David was conferencing with Adam about his story; Melissa was binding her edited piece she got back from the parent volunteer typist. The best time of all was the end of the session, at circle time, when the film crew shot Sean as he shared his writing about his fishing trip with his dad. His classmates offered praise and asked questions about his piece for clarification. The crew also filmed me as I talked to the class and explained how to use contractions appropriately—a problem many students had in their writing pieces.

On the final day of filming, I caught a fragment of conversation of one of the technicians. "My god, I can't believe what these twelve-year-olds can do." Perking up my ears, I listened as they gathered up their equipment for the day as the other replied. "The writing these kids do is phenomenal!"

Now in 2025, I have had these tapes transferred to DVDs. They sit in a leather basket, at the side of the TV, in the basement of my condo in Port Dover. I will forever look 48 years-old, wearing my favourite royal blue dress, and my smiling face framed by my fashionable Afro-haircut.

On a sad note, all this filming was done in secret, given that my work had been banned in Waterloo County! Imagine, HBJ, the largest textbook company in the world, was filming a classroom teacher in her County. It should have been covered in the local newspaper. Had the board been more progressive, my class would have put Waterloo County on the map!

My First Book

My first book, *Whole Language Strategies for E.S.L Students,* was finally published by OISE Press in 1986. Hot off the press, I signed the necessary papers with Fred, the editor, before going out for lunch. Full of enthusiasm, I imagined a gala lunch at a fancy restaurant on Bloor Street— maybe a reporter or two. We walked along Bloor Street and passed by numerous high-end restaurants without a glance from Fred. My feet were getting tired when we finally stopped and opened the door to . . . 'Swiss Chalet!' There was no publishing team, no celebration and . . . no reporters . . . just Fred and *me*.

While we waited for our order, Fred smiled. "Your book will be a part of a series on ESL (English as Second Language) we've already published," he stated. "It is a very popular series and we anticipate that your book will do very well," he said excitedly as our meals came.

"Great," I said smiling, getting my hopes up. *Wow, I might make some real money— maybe I'll get a new car.*

Fred went on. "I'll explain how the royalties work," he said, as he took a bite of chicken. He pointed to some lines on the document. "There will be *no* royalties for the first 1000 copies," he said as he swallowed some chicken and wiped his mouth with the paper napkin.

My heart plummeted with disappointment. *I won't even get enough to pay for the typing! Not a penny for the hundreds of hours I'd spent gathering data, or the cost of postage to send the manuscripts to Toronto!* "Oh," I gasped as quietly as I could, letting the air out of my lungs slowly, silently.

Fred continued, a positive tone in his voice. "But *you* will receive 5% on sales after that," he added, and smiled and nodded his head. "Like I said, this series is doing *very* well." He scooped up some mashed potatoes.

Finally discovering my voice, I enquired. "What have the sales been like so far?"

"Oh," Fred replied eagerly. "Some of the titles have sold as many as 500 copies!"

A piece of chicken caught in my throat. In other words, *none* of the authors had received a penny so far; they'd gotten *nada*, no royalty at all! My shoulders slumped, and I covered my lips with a napkin to hide my disappointment. There was not a prayer that I'd receive a royal nickel. Taking the last bite of mashed potatoes, I wiped my lips with the now scrunched up flimsy paper napkin. I have no idea if I ordered dessert! But Fred *did* pick up the bill!

In the end, my book defied all odds. The publication, *Whole Language Strategies for ESL Students,* took off. It circulated world-wide for years and was a best seller for OISE Press.

When I was presenting at an ESL conference a few years later, a teacher in the audience came up to me. "Your book was the only resource I took to Africa to teach many years ago, and it proved to be the most useful resource I had." That comment gave me goosebumps, and made all my hard work worthwhile.

My ESL book sold so well that, for over ten years, I *did* receive royalties! I didn't earn enough to purchase a new car, but the royalties *did* pay the costs for the typist!

A Decision About My Future

"You have two choices," John said, over coffee one Saturday morning in February 1987. "To be a Principal or teach at a university." John took a sip of his coffee. "Frankly, now that you have your doctoral work completed, I think you need to work at a university."

"But the advertisements for Principal positions in Waterloo have just come out and I am certainly qualified to apply."

"Yes, I know, but watching you this past year, you're far more interested in your work in literacy; I rarely hear you say a thing about your role as Vice-Principal."

"I guess you're right about that, but nevertheless, I'd be a good Principal too, I think."

John took a sip of coffee. "But look at what you've done with your career so far," John said. "You are a natural for a university position, for goodness' sake. Why the professor at Western is already using your Natural Language work with her student teachers!" He drained the last of his coffee. "And you've already published," John argued. "Look at your ESL book and all the articles you've written," he said, nodding his head. "And those tapes of your kids would be fantastic to use in a Faculty of Education."

"I know, but still," I hesitated for a few moments. . . . "We'd have to move from here and there are the boys to think about." I paused. *What about John's job at USARCO?* I wondered.

"The boys are all away from home anyway, Hon." "Wesley has a D.J. business; Blake is articling for an accounting firm in Toronto, Adam is doing his college placement at Disney in Orlando, Florida and Ron is twenty-one, and working in Cambridge. They'll be fine Hon; you worry too much about them."

"But you can't just leave your good position at USARCO," I emphasized worrying about his work. "We can't jeopardize that!"

"Look, if you're worried about *my* job, Gail, I can get work in the steel industry anywhere in Ontario," he added confidently, taking out a cigarette.

"Are you sure?"

"I am," he said definitely. "And I'm tired of US-ARCO anyway; I need a change," he took a long drag on his cigarette.

So, the decision was made. A week later, I saw an advertisement for a position at the Faculty of Education, University of Windsor. I applied and got the job. We planned to move at the end of the summer of 1987. I was ready for my new adventure as a Professor in the Faculty of Education, at the University of Windsor.

Saying Goodbye to Sauble Beach

The rust-red sun slipped, like a bruise, toward the roiling sapphire-green water of Lake Huron as John and I sat on the old plastic-webbed lawn chairs on the sandy shore of Sauble Beach. We were just steps away from the old rustic 'Pine Scene' cottage; this was the last night of our summer vacation, 1987. Looking out at the white-capped rolling waves, we listened to them crash and slap at my tanned feet, and I turned to John. "It doesn't get any better than this," I said, squeezing his hand. "Sitting here with you is pure heaven, so peaceful. What a perfect summer place this has been for the boys all these years. They are having so much fun with Matook,—Wes' dog—the "chick-magnet," according to Ron. We'll be hearing them coming home soon when the storm hits."

"I love it too," John said wistfully. "Reminds me of when I was a kid at Grandma Clifford's cottages on the edge of town. I can still see her running around cleaning out cottages for the next vacationers; it's how she made a living back in the thirties," he said, a hint of a smile playing across his face. "I loved those days."

"You were so lucky to have lived near this lake, and you've made me love it too. Never had lakes like this in Alberta; the only lake I knew was Sylvan Lake and you could see right around it, from shore to shore, one end to the other. It's not like Lake Huron–which goes beyond the horizon."

"We are so lucky in Ontario to have the five Great Lakes all around us, that's for sure; I think we take them for granted, sometimes."

"The summers here at Huron have gotten into my bones," I said, as the rays of light turned to magenta and mauve. "My God, that is beautiful," I gasped. "Wouldn't it be wonderful if we could buy a house on the water, when we move to Windsor? Wouldn't that be just the ultimate? What do you think?"

"Mmmmm . . . that *is* something to consider."

As the red ball turned from mauve to purple, and then to deep blue, finally inching toward the skyline, it slipped beneath the horizon suddenly and disappeared. My heart lurched; I marvelled at the mystery. *A home on the water; a home on a lake. Moments like this, every night.* The sky was now black, and a cool breeze made me shudder to know that this was the very last sunset we would see at Sauble Beach. Shivering, we folded up the aluminum chairs and headed back to the cottage, hand-in-hand. We rinsed our feet of sand in the blue saucepan outside the door and pulled open the rickety squeaking screen door. We slipped off to bed, dreaming of a home on the water.

The next morning, as we all sat around the sunroom table—John, Wesley, Blake, Adam Ron *and* Wesley's husky, Matook—I was unaware that this would be the last family holiday in which all the boys would be with us: the whole family together for a summer vacation. Sadly, it was the end of an era.

As we packed up our gear for our final trip home, Ron made a great suggestion. "We should leave some memento on the walls, to remind future renters that we were here." Each of the boys found a knot-hole in the pine walls and created an image. Ron's was the most creative; I watched him blacken a large knot-hole and sketch a twisty long tube-like-drawing between two triangles. Ron stood back. A smile flooded his face: "It's a one-eyed-cat!" he exclaimed.

The car was packed, and my heart overflowed with memories as I waved a final goodbye to 'Pine Scene' cottage and Lake Huron. While we drove away, memory after memory came rushing back: images of the boys frolicking in Huron on a sunny warm afternoon; their laughter and the sound of splashing water, the slamming of doors, and the smell of Matook's wet fur. I see an image of John stoking kindling into the pot-bellied stove, smell the aroma of coffee or charred burned toast, or hear the clank of the 1930s metal toaster. As we turned onto the highway for home, I was already missing our walks together. Hand-in-hand, we'd walk down the beach for a double-decker-maple-walnut-ice-cream-cone with its the crunch of walnuts and the release of that lovely maple flavour as I chewed. My heart melted at the memory of that final evening: the image of the sunset on that last night, releasing a myriad of colour as the orange ball slid over Lake Huron– like the final curtain dropping on our last summer at Sauble Beach.

POINTE-AUX-ROCHES

Finding Our Dream Home on the Water

"A home on the water is what we're looking for," John told the real estate agent as we drove down Ouellette Avenue (along the Detroit River), in Windsor, Ontario. Row-upon-row of gunmetal grey skyscrapers, like a concrete wall, towered into the clouds of Detroit, just a stone's throw away. As we passed Dieppe Park, the agent nodded his head. "Windsor is known for its parks and gardens along the riverside–not like that concrete-jungle across the river. A Windsor city by-law limits the height of structures on this side of the river; it ensures that citizens can enjoy the view of the waterfront." As we slowed down at Dieppe Park the agent called, "So, you want a home on the water?"

"Yes," John said. "I grew up on Lake Huron as a kid, and we've just been vacationing at Sauble Beach, so we're dying to find a home on the water." The agent passed us some listings along the river, and our faces fell. "Those are *way* out of our price range," John stated disappointedly. "There's got to be *something* you can show us in our price range, surely."

When we gave him our price range of $175,000, his voice lightened. "How far away from Windsor are you willing to drive?"

"A half hour easily," I replied. After all, I'd driven 45 minutes in Waterloo county.

"That opens up many more possibilities," he said, smacking his hand onto the steering wheel. "I have just the place in mind. I'll call and make an appointment."

We headed east of Tecumseh, passed the village of Emeryville, and zipped down the Main Street of Belle River. We continued across the train tracks and over to the other side of town where the countryside suddenly opened up into flat farmland. "What are those people doing in the fields?" I asked.

"Oh, this is *tomato* country; they're picking for the Heinz factory in Leamington, on the south side of Lake Erie.

Bumping over a set of VIA Rail tracks, the agent announced, "This is about 30 minutes from Windsor," he said, slowing down. "The homes along here are all on Lake St. Clair."

As we passed several seasonal-looking cottages, and an empty lot with a spectacular vista of sapphire green waves rolling to the shore, I craned my neck to the left. *Imagine a home with a view like that!* The agent suddenly slowed to a crawl and turned left into a curved driveway at 2890 St. Clair Rd. A high, red brick entry led to an enormous two story, red brick house. My heart stopped and my breath caught in my throat. *It was absolutely beautiful. And look at that blue lake stretching beyond.* I looked over at John, who was grinning his lop-sided-grin, and squeezed his hand. Scrambling out of the car, I imagined white shutters on the windows and colonial gables around the door. *I'd found the colonial home I've wanted all my life!* John smiled.

"It's a French village," the agent cautioned. "It's called Pointe-Aux-Roches by the locals and most everyone speaks French here." He said this, hesitantly, "I hope that won't be a problem for you." We didn't speak a word of French, but that didn't worry us at all.

"It's listed at $205, 000," but it has almost 3,000 thousand square feet, so that's something to consider. "I'll check with the owners about taking you through."

The house was a dream! Walking into the enormous living room, I couldn't get over the size. My eyes scanned the wall of floor-to-ceiling bookcases of solid, dark-brown walnut that framed the natural stone fireplace. *Gorgeous, absolutely gorgeous!* To our left, John spotted a magnificent, solid walnut bar– it was large enough for six people to gather around comfortably with a bar fridge and wet sink at the end.

Ahead of us was the dining area; it had wall-to-wall windows that overlooked a view of the Lake, sparkling blue on this sunny and warm day. *My antique table and chairs will fit in perfectly; the oak icebox will go into the corner. The black pine subtle bed will look fantastic beneath the windows.* I pictured the family sitting around the table, during the upcoming Thanksgiving weekend, enjoying turkey and mashed potatoes.

The kitchen was to the left of the dining room. Martha Stewart would have died for the same walnut cabinets, designed to sit above a long counter that housed a dishwasher, double-sink and stove–top burner with a grill. Opposite the counter was a centre island; it had a half-sink to one side. At the end, was a giant sub-zero refrigerator and two ovens, one above the other, the top one equipped with a built-in microwave. *This is the family kitchen we need when the kids come to visit with their girlfriends.* Facing across the island was a row of built-in-cabinets of identical walnut, with storage cupboards beneath. Walking through the kitchen, we came to a two-piece bathroom; the cabinets were identical to those in the rest of the house. A doorway to the right led to the laundry room, a washer, dryer, deep freeze and furnace. An extra storage cupboard had been built to one side. John and I cast warm glances at each other. It was a heavenly downstairs.

A three-season sunroom, with floor to ceiling windows, was down two steps from the dining room. I shook my head. I imagined a rainy day. I would be sitting on a lounge chair, an Afghan over my legs, a book in my hand, and looking out at the lake! When we walked outside, we stepped onto a cement patio with lawn chairs here and there. I pictured John sitting on the patio, looking out at the lake, Stetson on his head, a cigarette between his fingers and a mug of cold beer in the other. John squeezed my hand affirmatively.

To get to the upstairs, we walked through the living room and up the stairs. To the left, was a bedroom large enough to park a station wagon. It would make a lovely guest room. On the other side, was a bedroom of equal size that could be my office with the view of the lake. Each bedroom had its own two-piece sink and toilet with shared shower between. There was room for all the kids to come and stay the weekend. It was absolutely perfect!

"Wait till you see the master bedroom," the agent beamed, as we walked across the hallway. My mouth gaped open and I gasped in awe. It seemed the size of a bowling alley; it was half the size of the downstairs. *I pictured John, who'd be sitting in the wing-back French Provincial chair, and me, who'd be lounging on the couch, along the wall.* At the end of the room was a double wide walk-in closet, the likes of which we'd never seen before! The ensuite bathroom had a full bath and tub and shower. The toilet was at one end. Gracing the other wall, were his-and-hers double-sinks that nestled in a long cabinet; there was room for the both of us to bathe and shower at the same time!

"And this door leads to the balcony," the agent announced. He led us across the floor and to an outside door at the north side of the bedroom. We stepped out onto a covered balcony that opened to a full view of the lake. It took my breath away. "Oh John, you can see water for miles with no end-in-sight!"

We reluctantly left the balcony and returned downstairs to the patio where the agent left us alone to chat. "It's absolutely perfect for us," I said. "I love everything about it!"

John paused . . . "Still, it is a lot of money!"

"But we've planned well, John." I said. "We lived on *my* salary while *you* salted your wages into our mortgage, so Inverness was paid off. And we can sell our investment property in Kitchener. With both properties sold, we will surely have enough to purchase this one outright. I paused. "What do you think?" John and I walked slowly, hand–in-hand, toward the agent's car. His gentle squeeze told me his answer. With a little give-and-take we made a deal, and purchased our dream home—at 2890 St. Clair Rd., Pointe-Aux-Roches—all 3,000 sq. feet of it, for $200,000.

My dream came true; we had our home on the water!

Luc Introduces Pointe-Aux-Roches

"Bonjour, bonjour," a stocky man, wearing a ball cap called loudly, as he walked toward us from across the lawns of other properties to the east of us. "Bonjour, bonjour!" he called again. "Je Luc un voisin; bien venue dans Pointe-Aux-Roches!" Wisps of blond hair peaked around the edges of the ball-cap, his round face was weathered-looking, as if he spent most days outside. He wore a blue plaid workshirt and his overalls were well worn and threadbare at the knees. As he stepped onto our property, he called again, "Bonjour; Je Luc un voisin; bien venue dans Pointe-Aux-Roches!" John sat in his Stetson, a T-shirt, and denim shorts, his long legs stretched almost to the end of the cement patio. "Bonjour," John said. He stood up—his arm outstretched and ready to shake hands; he towered over the man.

"Je Luc," he said, his China-blue eyes dancing. A smile filled his entire face.

"I'm John, and this is my wife, Gail."

Instantly shifting to English, Luc apologized, "Pardon me, I assumed you spoke French."

"No, but I'm anxious to learn," John replied, pumping Luc's hand up and down.

"Please sit down, Luc; can I get you a cup of coffee?" I asked, taking John's cup for a refill.

"That would be lovely, Gail." His eyes twinkled merrily, "Black, if you don't mind." His lips turned up in a warm grin.

Passing Luc his coffee, I caught some of his conversation with John. "The lake was originally named Lac Sainte Claire in 1679, by French explorers; it's named after Clare of Assisi, a saint in the Catholic Church. But it's now Anglicized to Lake St. Clair, like most French names in the area." He lifted the mug to his lips. "Everything's Anglicized—like Stoney Point, for instance which should be Pointe-Aux-Roches. Detroit, was originally called De Trois, for Three Straits." Luc's voice rose in frustration. "Soon, no one will ever know that we French settled here about the same time as we settled Montreal; le coureur des-bois travelled here via the Great Lakes and traded furs with the Indians–long before the English arrived." Luc patted his chest. "Some folks, like we Quenneville's, are descendants of those original settlers from the 1600's," he said proudly as he took a long sip of coffee from his mug,

"I had no idea about the history of this place," I said to Luc. "Thank you."

"I've lived here all my life," Luc added. "Was a farmer, grew tomatoes, and invented a drainage system for the farms in Essex County. We learned later that Luc was a millionaire. Retired now, the farmer never left Luc's soul. Swallowing a mouthful of coffee, his lips turned up into a broad questioning grin. "Why the hell did you people move here when you're not French?" he chuckled. "The word around here is that you are a banker from Montreal moving here to retire!"

John smiled. "Don't I wish! No, we came here for Gail's new job at the University of Windsor and I'm going to look for work in the steel industry–I was a Credit Manager for a steel company in Hamilton."

"Well, English speaking folks are sure a rarity in *this* community," Luc laughed, with wonder and confusion in his voice. "But welcome aboard; it's good to have some *English* neighbours to spice things up." His eyes filled with warmth.

"Glad you think so, Luc, and I'm sure we're going to love having *you* as a neighbour too." Smack! A fish leaped abruptly out of the water."Oh, my goodness! A flying fish!" I gasped. "Now *that's* why we wanted to move here, Luc, to be on the water," I observed the ripples the fish had just created. "One day, we'd like to build a deck closer to the shore." I took a sip of my coffee. "I'd also like to extend this patio and build an enclosure on either side to make it more private. Do you know any carpenters in the area?"

There was a long moment of hesitation before Luc spoke. "Good idea to build a deck," he answered, waving his hand toward the water. "But about an enclosure around the patio? I am not so sure about *that!*" He sounded skeptical, and his greying eyebrows pinched together. "No, Gail, that's *not* a good idea," he said bluntly. "It's not the custom here. We are neighbourly on the lake and visit back and forth all the time. A wall would have a *very* unfriendly feel."

A wall was not constructed.

Three Buddies:
A Frenchman, an American, and John

Luc, a French speaking farmer, Stan Mygle, a retired American farmer from Michigan, and John became the greatest of friends. I picture those three buddies sitting on our deck overlooking Lake St. Clair, as I peeked out my office window while taking a break from marking essays. I'd see Luc, his arms waving, head stretched back laughing, Stan sitting quietly puffing away on his giant brown cigar, and John taking a drag on his cigarette—three old buddies shooting the breeze: a French Canadian, an American, and an English-speaking Canadian.

In 2018, when John was failing, I read him an early draft of meeting Luc for the first time at Pointe-Aux-Roches. John interrupted me, a worried look crossing his eyes. "Did you spell *Luc* with a 'c'?"

"I did."

"Thanks, Gail. I'm glad you didn't anglicize the spelling to '*Luke.*' I always believed we should respect Luc's French culture and the Francophone community we'd moved to." A faint smile stretched across John's paper-thin-lips, as if remembering those days in Pointe-Aux-Roches. "Those were very special times," John reminded me. "And Luc and Stan were great friends." John's hazel eyes glowed as he recalled their friendship. "Some afternoons Stan and I sat on the deck and talked about the fish he'd caught that day and . . . the ones that got away," John chuckled. "Luc frequently joined us, and I remember him telling Stan about his French heritage and how he was a descendent from le coureur des-bois, who settled in the community from the 1600s when the French fur-traders came to the area and named De Trois, French for Three Straits—now anglicized to 'Detroit." John broke out laughing.. "That used to annoy the hell out of Stan." John winked mischievously at me. "Of course, *I* had to remind both of them that the area was *first* inhabited by Indigenous people thousands of years before the *French* came and who would have had their *own* name for Detroit."

John continued, smiling. "Remember, too, how Luc thought I was a retired Montreal banker?" John chortled. "He soon found out, when he spoke to me in French, that I couldn't understand much of anything he said!" John looked thoughtful. "Wish I had learned more French when we were there, though—but I was too lazy, and Luc was too proficient in English and that didn't help one bit." A sudden wistful look crossed over John's eyes. "I remember the day Stan died," he said, his eyes growing misty. "I recall that day clearly, even though it happened forty years ago." John ran his hand through his thin white hair and blinked his eyelids up and down quickly, staving off tears. "I was walking across our lawn from our garage when I saw Stan's car was parked at the back door of his cottage with the trunk lid up. I could see the white pails of dirt he brought from his farm in Michigan. I called to him, laughing:'*Hey Stan, bringing soil from the US is illegal, you know.* "Stan just smiled, his cigar hanging out of the corner of his mouth. I waved and called, '*See you later on the deck!*' as I went inside the house." John took a sip of thickened water to moisten his throat. "That was the last time I saw Stan alive." John took a long deep breath before carrying on. "When I went outside an hour later to meet Stan on the deck, he was lying face down on the ground, two pails full of dirt spilled beside him, just steps away from the open trunk of his car. He'd died from a heart-attack right in front of his cottage, the cottage he loved so very much" . . . A long contemplative silence filled the room before John spoke again. "Then a few years later, *Luc* died of cancer and my two good friends were gone."

John's eye lids began to flutter; he stood up, wrapped his long fingers around the handles of his walker, and shuffled down the hallway to our bedroom for his afternoon nap. It was the last year that I had him with me.

Pointe-Aux-Roches: A Family Magnet

At dawn, John and I rushed outside. We took our royal-blue director-chairs to the water's edge so that we could witness the magic of the sunrise. We saw hues of blue, red, and then indigo as the sun rose, inch-by-inch, out of the lake, and until its rays spilled over the water and filled the sky with a glorious golden-yellow. It was a breathtaking moment. The sun hung in the horizon for a few moments before I rushed inside to shower and dress. I grabbed a quick breakfast of toast and peanut butter, and zipped off to the university for the day. Every evening, we went to the water's edge to watch the sunset. As it lowered in the sky, it spilled coloured tones of magenta, mauve and blue over the lake. As the sun crept down the western horizon, the skyscrapers of Detroit turned to grey silhouettes, and then velvety black, as the orange-red ball gradually sunk entirely from view. It was pure magic, every night.

That first fall, our home on Lake St. Clair was a magnet for Ron and Blake and their girlfriends Maureen and Suzie (they were sisters), and Wesley with Kris Steventon. Just as I'd imagined, we had dinners around our antique pine table and then–just as we had at Sauble Beach–we gathered, every evening, to watch the sun set over Lake St. Clair. It sank over the skyline of Detroit and lit the Renaissance Centre in hues of silver and gold. After John and I had gone to bed, we heard the kids' squeals of laughter when someone won a card game.

One weekend Andy—Blake's best friend from high school—came for a visit. "You need a deck," he said. Within minutes, he'd measured and had a design. The next month, Andy brought his crew–including Blake and Ron–and they built the deck one miserable, wet, and muddy weekend. It was massive; it spanned the full width (one hundred feet) of the property. The deck became the place we gathered to enjoy the early morning sunrise and evening sunset vigils.

We spent our first Thanksgiving, Christmas, and Easter with our family. As we slid into our first summer, Pointe-Aux-Roches became party central every weekend. Everyone enjoyed fishing, swimming and lazing on the deck. Those were magical times for us all.

John's Creative Solution for Work

The lake was a cacophony of sound as thousands of white Tundra swans gathered at the shoreline, squawking and hooting, our second spring. John looked down at his coffee, his forehead creased with a wave of worry. "I'm really struggling with what I'm going to *do* with my life now that I'm 55, and still can't find work in the steel industry." A speckle of grey ran through his moustache. "It doesn't help that Luc says the car industry is in a slump. I need to do *something* with my time, *something* to feel useful."

"You help with the dishes, we make the bed together, you tend the bird feeders."

Ignoring me, a pleading look came across John's hazel eyes. "I have something to ask you," a note of seriousness in his voice. He looked so dejected, so forlorn. Taking a deep breath, he held it a long moment before he spoke. I reached over the glass table and put my hand over his.

"I have an idea I'd like to run by you," John said, his voice a hushed whisper.

"Yes?" I waited wondering what was on his mind. He coughed to clear his throat. "How would you feel if *I* took over the workings of the household?"

"What do you mean?" I asked, startled.

"Well, I'm wondering." His voice rose in strength. "What if *I* did the cooking, shopping, cleaning, laundry and lawn-mowing?" He rattled on quickly, like a salesman pitching his spiel. He stopped, then, as if out-of-breath, and took a sip of his coffee.

Taken by surprise, it took me a moment to take it all in and get my wits about me. "You want to take it *all* on . . . *everything*?"

"Yes," He laced his fingers nervously together. "Well?" He looked deeply into my eyes with a distraught look I'd never seen before.

My heart melted. "Well, that is okay with *me*, if that's what you really *want* to do!"

John's eyes brightened as if a weight had been lifted off his shoulders. He put his hand over mine. "The problem is," he said. There was a long hesitant pause. "Do you think we can afford it? Do you think we can live on your salary alone?"

"Hon, we've been living on one salary now for almost two years and we did it as well when we were in Cambridge, so you could pay off our mortgage on Inverness and buy *this* home—so of course we can."

John's eyes lightened, the wrinkles smoothed across his brow.

"Thank you, my love."

The air was suddenly filled with a thunderous roar of flapping wings as the swans took off; the lead swan headed north, directing their way, just as *we* were heading in a new direction with new careers.

I Was Spoiled Rotten

A steaming mug of hot coffee—with just the right amount of sugar and cream—greeted me every morning as I stepped out of the shower. At the table was a bowl of fruit for breakfast. On my way out the door to work, John handed me a packed lunch—a sandwich, cut-up vegetables and fruit—something different every day. In the evening, coming home from work, the house was filled with the aroma of meat and vegetables wafting from the crock-pot. I was spoiled rotten!

That is what life was like for me for the next ten years until I retired. Within a few months, John took over everything—the cooking, cleaning, laundry, grocery shopping, just as he said he would. He was simply amazing!

"I have a whole new appreciation for women in the morning," John explained. "I used to be critical of mothers in their housecoats, with curlers in their hair, who stood at the school bus sending their children off to school." He smiled at the memory. "Now, I know that they'd done a half-a-day's work by eight o'clock in the morning!"

Cooking was the main challenge for John because he'd never done it for himself. Growing up in the thirties, his mothers did the cooking, and then his wife when he got married. After his divorce, he didn't cook for himself either. "I made toast and coffee for breakfast, went out for a big lunch at noon, and picked up a sandwich at the supermarket for supper." John learned fast, discovering crock-pot cooking. "Anyone can learn to cook if you can read." He explained that his favourite dishes came from James Barber. "I watch his show, The Urban Peasant on television as often as I can." John rubbed his palms together. "James Barber never measured a thing . . . it was always a pinch or this or a handful of that, a thimble full of something else." Given John's love of James Barber, I purchased his books as gifts.

The second challenge—cleaning—got resolved, one weekend, when I was getting myself a cup of coffee to take to my upstairs office and mark another box of assignments. Facing the island, I turned to put the cream back into the refrigerator, and my left foot stuck to the floor. Laughing, I called to John, "When was the last time you washed the kitchen floor, Hon?"

"I haven't," he answered back from the laundry room, coming out with a T-towel he'd been folding. "I don't need to," he replied confidently. "I wipe up any spills right away!" We hired a cleaning person immediately.

It didn't take long for gender issues to emerge into John's life. When Luc came to visit and found John in my black chef-apron, he looked at John askance and said, "*Get that damned apron off and come out to play.*" John was secure in his masculinity, so he could ignore Luc's remarks and chauvinistic, out-of-date values.

A grin slid across John's face. "Those sexist values were pretty evident when Luc took me to the Knights of Columbus muskrat dinner at the Catholic Church in town." John chuckled. "The members' wives cooked the muskrats for two days before so the meat was tender enough to eat. At the end of the dinner, all the women came out from the kitchen, red-faced, shiny with perspiration, wiping their hands on their aprons," John said, laughing. "They actually *curtsied*, while the men clapped in appreciation! It was like a scene out of a 1940s movie," he howled.

In 2018, almost thirty years later, I asked John what those days as a house-husband were like for him. A far-away-look swept across his eyes as he took a sip of Ensure, the only drink he could handle then. "Actually, I quite liked the role," he answered. "In many ways, it felt quite liberating." His eyes lit up, remembering. "The best part of the role was seeing the end-result of all I did. When I packed your lunch, I saw the "fruits-of-my-labour" so-to-speak." He smiled, and his brow wrinkled. "It was such a change from industry where clients lied to me every day, telling me they'd put the cheque in the mail—the cheque that never arrived. I found the lack of client morality hard to take." He laced his fingers together. "I was a great Credit Manager, but the job was mind-destroying." John took another sip of Ensure. "So being at home, and looking after you and the house was rewarding, in comparison." His eyes got wistful again. "And I loved that kitchen at Pointe-Aux-Roches," he said with a smile. "While I was working, I could see the lake from three sides, and watch storms come in from Lake Huron over Lake St. Clair." John's eyes softened, remembering."

My conscience eased, I was comforted knowing that our bold experiment was satisfying for both of us.

John's Early Cat Education Centre

There was a sudden, ominous rumble, and men shouting: "Back up a foot more!" A truck engine roared. "That's good!" There was a grinding sound, a sudden whoosh of screeching metal, and a thunderous boom reverberated, breaking the silence of our dreams. John leapt out of bed. "What in the world was *that*?" he exclaimed, rushing to the bathroom window to look out. "They've dumped a load of gravel for the building of the new cottage."

Two mornings later, when I was sitting on the patio and enjoying our second cup of coffee, we revelled in the hush of peace and calm. I heard a sudden tinkling sound. "Do you hear *that*, John?"

"I don't hear a thing," John murmured, as he took a sip of coffee.

I cocked my ear to one side. "There's that sound

again."

"It's probably the wind chimes from next door, Hon."

"I don't think so. Come, let's check it out."

Picking up our cups, we sauntered to the rock pile. There was a jangly, tinny sound. Turning my head, I strained to hear. "It's a mewling sound, John, and it's coming from the rocks; I'm sure of it."

For the next few days, we listened and watched, like two little kids waiting for cookies in the oven to finish baking. Every so often we heard more whining. One morning, a white puff ball of fur—the size of a ping-pong-ball—poked out. "It's a kitten!" I whispered, as it scurried back in at the sound of my voice. Setting out oatmeal gruel at the opening, we saw three more kittens peek out to feed—a grey one, another with spots and a redhead.

"Come see what I've done," John called, waving excitedly as I drove down the lane from the university. He opened the side door of the garage to show a row of cement cinder-blocks, stacked like steps in front of a plastic wading pool. I couldn't believe my eyes. John chuckled. "I found the wading pool on Garbage Day," he laughed, his almond eyes twinkling. "And look what I've done with the old cap of the pickup truck. It makes a perfect place for the kittens to sleep; it'll protect them from the cold in winter." John threw his hands up at all he'd created. "It's the ECE Centre—Early Cat Centre!" I couldn't help laughing at his take on an Early Education Centre at the Board of Education.

Cat lovers too, Ron tells how he and Maureen caught the kittens in the garage. "We were sitting at the side of the rock ruins, sipping cold beers, and watching the kittens scurry in and out of the opening, chasing each other. It was great fun watching them. They'd come and sniff when we wiggled our fingers at them." That's when Maureen nabbed the dark grey striped one because she was calm—John named her Shadow. I caught the red-headed one next—John called her Pekoe, because she reminded him of the fuzz on the leaves of green Pekoe tea before they were picked. Within an hour, the white-spotted one let me pick it up—John named him Spot. Try as I might, I couldn't get the last one out of the rocks. It was *John* who finally lured it out with his hushed and loving voice-he called him Rocky—he was the last to leave the rock pile!

The four kittens in the "ECE Centre" were a frenzy of activity as they chased in and out of the holes of the cinderblocks, scampered up the steps, leaped into the plastic wading pool, and pulled and batted each other's tails. Every chance we got, we went out to the garage to watch our ECE family frolic.

A call to a veterinary clinic, to have the kittens

spayed, was next on the agenda. We found a large box, poked holes in the sides, and then nabbed the kittens, one-by-one. We tucked them in, securely snapped the flaps, and stretched masking tape over top. John put the heaving, wobbling, cardboard box into the van. Amid awful ear-splitting cries, the kittens whined and scratched wildly at the sides of the cardboard; they clamoured to be free. It was bedlam, and the noise was so loud we could hardly hear each other speak.

We were barely out onto Lakeshore Road when Pekoe flew from the back and landed at my feet; an instant later, Shadow slid down my shoulder and onto my lap. Turning my head, I saw Spot ripping around the van like a mad cat–he smashed his head into the car windows in an attempt to break out. And Rocky? His head sticking out of one corner, he was *wearing* the box, his eyes were wild with fear, he bared his teeth in anger as he bounced, shook and heaved the box from one side to the other. He was the veritable "cat in a box!" Cats were everywhere! They raced across the dashboard, clawed at the front seats, and bounced against the windows. They shrieked and cried in their misery as they attempted to flee–it was wild and confused; the van was a mad-house. Arriving at the clinic, we took two cats in at a time. We put them in the duffle bag, and zipped it up for the ten seconds it took to get them from the car to inside the clinic. It was a very subdued crew of kittens on the way back home!

The kittens survived two years in their cat playground in the garage until, one-by-one, they met their destiny. "Pekoe, the smartest of them all, stayed with us the longest, and survived several years. Thinking back, I smile when I remember John's "Early Cat Education Centre"—the cat playground at Pointe-Aux-Roches.

My Career Continues: University Professor

I was filled with excitement, that September of 1987, when I set off to the Faculty of Education at the University of Windsor for my first class. My work was finally valued and respected, and I pushed the dark cloud of Waterloo County behind me. I was free to start my career of teaching, writing and conducting research in the field of literacy, which I loved.

My mind drifts back to my first day of teaching prospective teachers. A group of men sauntered into the classroom; they looked surprised and shocked as they scanned the classroom, noting desks organized into groups of six, instead of the rows-upon-rows of chairs that they were accustomed to seeing. They glanced at the bulletin boards, which were covered with posters that outlined the writing process, along with samples of children's work. Juvenile literature was displayed on tables against one wall. Two comfy couches sat in one corner of the classroom. Restful music drifted from the tape-recorder on one side of my desk, and a vase of flowers from our garden graced the other.

"Come on in." I smiled and waved my hand in greeting as I walked toward them. They looked unsure and clung to the back wall mumbling; I heard snippets of conversation: *Do we have to sit at a desk like in grade school? . . . this is ef-en ridiculous! . . . What's with all the books? . . . I have a science degree . . . I'll bet she knows nothing about quantum physics! . . . A female prof? . . . What the hell can I learn from a woman?*

I smelled disdain.

Other students sauntered in; the women clustered together, like the men, and I noticed a woman wearing a hijab sitting alone. "Welcome to our Language Arts class. I'm Professor Gail Heald-Taylor, and I will be your instructor for teaching literature and writing. In this class, you will be learning from me as well as from each other. That's why I have the classroom organized in groups like this." Skeptical, cynical eyes stared back at me, unconvinced. "Please reorganize yourselves in groups, creating a balance of men, women, and people with diverse backgrounds and race." Chairs scraped, feet shuffled and there were annoyed mumbles, as students reorganized themselves. I reminded myself how important it was for students to learn from people of different genders and cultural backgrounds—it reduced cliques and racial clinging, and, overall, promoted understanding and respect for one another. Working in interactive groups also shifted the learning power from professor to students. I modeled this so that they would consider organizing *their* own classrooms in this way.

Now that students were in groups, I began the class with a question: "Who are your favourite authors? What books are you reading? Think of a book that has influenced your life." There was an awkward silence, as I waited. Then, I asked the questions again. The class sat mutely; they looked at me expectantly. I smiled and took a different tack. "In your group, tell a neighbour about a particular novel you've read recently.... a book you really enjoyed, or one, perhaps, that made you really think." They looked at each other. There were murmurs as I circulated around the groups. A hand waved in the air. I nodded. "Do you *really* want us to talk? Do you actually want to *know* the books we like to read?" He sounded confused, irritated.

"You bet!" I smiled back at him, and asked the question once again. The room suddenly burst into a buzz of chatter as students discussed and listened to each other. When there was a lull, I asked them to designate a spokesperson in their group to share with the whole class what they'd discussed. A woman stood up and shared. "In our group lots of people discussed books they'd read and we also talked about authors we liked." Rubbing her hands together nervously she added, "I have to admit, though, that I haven't read a book of choice since grade school." I heard a murmur of agreement around the room. "But today, I heard about some great books that I intend to get at the library."

Another group reported, "Some of us in our group read novels regularly, but many of us only read textbook material related to specific courses that Professors of English prescribed." I was saddened by his response but not surprised.

Referring to a chart on plastic acetate on the over-head projector, I pointed out characteristics of literature—*Characters, Problems, Point of View, Interesting Language, Solutions*. "In your group choose *one* of these characteristics and listen for that category as I read this chapter from one of my favourite books; *Bridge to Terabithia*, by Katherine Patterson (1978)." When I'd finished reading the chapter, I gave students 10 minutes to discuss and list their ideas, as I walked around the room and listened to their discussions, or answered questions. After 10 minutes, I asked for someone from each group to report and share their ideas with the whole class so that everyone learned from their peers about the many characteristics of literature.

At this point, I gave my mini-lecture: "What I have just modeled today is a lesson that *you* can use on your first day of practice-teaching or, when you eventually have a classroom of your own, when you teach Language Arts yourselves. " I paused and recalled the comments of the science guys earlier. "You don't have to be an English Major to teach Language Arts. Even if your background is Biology, Science, Music, or the Arts, this strategy will work for you with students in grades six through eight. I invite you to try it."

In future classes, I showed my videos of my grade six classroom. I enticed students to write just as I had done, also, with my grade six students. "So, watch what I do and make notes about what you observe, and how you experience it."

Assignments were always expected, and this class was no different. I assigned readings from Nancie Atwell's, *In the Middle* , and asked my students to write a journal about her ideas, how her work compared to how *they* were taught, and how I modelled her ideas in class. I also encouraged them to debate her ideas and mine.

End of class "responders" was a way of gathering feedback that I always introduced to my classes: I asked two volunteers, a woman and a man, to stay after class to provide me feedback. After *this* class, Melissa explained—"This was the first class at university that a professor actually *wanted* us to talk. When you asked us about the books we were reading , we anticipated that it was rhetorical, an introduction to the lecture you were about to give."

"I was surprised too," Bert said. "I expected you to stand at the front of the room and deliver learned information while we copiously recorded what you said, and *our* role was to explore the readings on our own and regurgitate the information on formal tests, essays and exams." He smiled. "I liked this class a whole lot better. I think I actually learned something today."

A few minutes before the end of class I gave them an invitation. "On your way out, I'd like you to examine the novels displayed at the table that are typical selections that interest students in grades four to eight. You are welcome to sign one out."

Recognizing that my instructional approach was revolutionary compared to most university professors, when my students got the hang of it, they enjoyed learning from each other in small groups, and appreciated that I respected and honoured them as learners. I was consciously teaching much more than English Language Arts, I was modeling how to set up a learning community for any subject area, to be adapted for their own classrooms one day.

On reflection, now that we're in 2025, I wonder if my work made a difference to any of the students that passed through my classroom door over those ten years at the Faculty of Education. I wonder if my published work had survived over time and had left a permanent mark on Education, after thirty some years. My name still comes up on a *Google* search. But for me it doesn't matter—because I know in my heart that I taught my best, wrote my best, and did my best. I am satisfied.

Full Professorship: Tenure

Tenure (Full Professorship) was the ultimate goal of my career. The process involved a committee of my academic colleagues who made their decision based on publications, talks, my teaching record, and my professional contributions to the Department. As part of the process, I submitted a 45-page document, in a loose-leaf binder, that outlined my overall academic and professional accomplishments, including my three degrees: BA, Masters, and Ed D. My publications and more are outlined in the **Appendix (p.693)**

I included a letter of support and recommendation by John Savage (internationally respected professor in the field of literacy learning at Boston College, School of Education, in Chestnut Hill, MA). He summarized my work: *"Dr. Gail Heald-Taylor is a respected educational leader who has contributed significantly in the field of literacy instruction. Her research and writing is state-of-the-art and I have used Dr. Heald-Taylor`s work in my own writing. What impresses me most about Gail Heald-Taylor's work is her ability to strike a balance between theory and practice.'*

Evaluation for Tenure is traditionally conducted by one's colleagues. Early in the process, I got a phone call from Dean Awender, who said, "Some of the committee members have asked to *see* the books you co-authored with Harcourt Brace & Jovanovic." He chuckled, "There seems to be a lot of them." The next morning, I loaded up three banker-boxes full of text-books –all with my name as co-author printed boldly inside of each–and plunked them down in Dean Awender's office!

Apparently, that satisfied the committee.

I received Tenure!

Other Accomplishments in my Career:

- The Mace: Another symbolic achievement was being the *first* female professor of the Faculty of Education to carry the Windsor University Mace at the 1997 convocation. It was indeed an honour; I was the first *woman* in the history of the faculty to carry the ceremonial staff! For generations, that designation was the exclusive right of male faculty members!!

- Convocation 1994: Reading son Ron's name at *his* convocation graduation was the proudest moment of my career at the University of Windsor. *Ronald Porter Heald.* As he strode across the stage, I like to believe that he winked at me. It was the highlight of my career. When I glance up at the top of my desk at the picture of the two of us–Ron in his graduating robe, arm around me in my cap and scarlet gown of the University of Toronto– I still get choked-up at the happy memory.

What a fantastic teacher my Ron became; he is so full of enthusiasm and excitement for his students, and his theories of instruction are the same as mine: holistic, student-oriented, and putting learning in children's hands! He makes me proud!

Retirement: Writing and Activism

'Reading Strategies for Beginning Readers;' Heinemann NH (2001) was the most important book I'd written. It is filled with pictures of family reading to my grandchildren, Nathan, Matt and Amy. It was a labour of love.

In 1996, when Conservative, Mike Harris was elected premier of Ontario, I became a political activist. His 'Bill 160' slashed public funding, across the province, for education, health care, and social services. The Bill also froze public service salaries. At the same time, he "cut taxes"—a euphemism for cutting taxes for the very wealthy, while gutting essential programs for the rest of the population.

For teachers, Bill 160 meant increased class sizes and frozen wages. It meant the reduction of programs for special needs students and access to funds for school libraries. In addition, provincial-wide standardized testing was introduced, modelled after the United States. For our family, Bill 160 resulted in Ron losing his first job!

I became an activist overnight. I fought against the cut-backs and the implementation of Charter Schools—for-profit schools as advocated in the United States– and I spoke to thousands of people through CBC television, radio interviews and presentations across Ontario.

In opposition to Bill 160, Unions planned *Days of Action* protest marches in several major cities across the province. John and I marched in Windsor, Kitchener-Waterloo, Hamilton and Toronto (the largest march, with over 100,000 Canadians participating). My protest sign was designed with a picture of six-month-old grandson Nathan that said: **EDUCATE LITTLE NATE.**

Later in the year, I presented at a conference in Bordeaux, France—wearing my vest, which was covered with badges from the various marches—and described how government cutbacks had negatively affected education in Ontario, Canada.

John was absolutely right when he told me that teaching in the Faculty of Education at the University of Windsor was the perfect way to end my professional career.

THE NINETIES & NEW MILLENNIUM

Family Changes: Our Sons Move On

Graduations, marriages and grandchildren were featured at Pointe-Aux-Roches (1987 – 2005).

Adam and Tammy married in Orlando, Florida in 1992 and settled into work at Disney. A few months later, Adam's Mom held a reception for them in Ancaster and graciously invited our whole family to attend. Ron and Maureen married on July 10, 1993, at a beautiful setting at the Ambassador Center. It overlooks the Detroit River, and the skyline of Detroit.

In 1995, Wesley and Shelley married in Toronto– a highlight at the reception was Ron's speech. His toast to the groom had everyone rolling in the aisles with laughter. Later in the evening, Wesley did his imitation of the Blues Brothers, and that thoroughly entertained us all, too.

Blake and Sue moved in together in the early 1990s, when they purchased their home in Mississauga. They experienced great challenges in their relationship when Blake contracted MS during the summer of 1992. I will share more about that tragic episode later.

As for me, I felt both joy and sadness at the

same time–I was happy our sons had found life partners, but I also felt a kind of bereavement and a sense of loss. I felt disconnected from them, now that they had partners of their own. I was no longer the same kind of parent; my sons would rely less on me, diminishing my long role as their mother. I felt at loose-ends and unsure of what my role was. It was a time of readjustment.

On Being a Grandmother

Becoming a grandmother is one of the most rewarding roles I have ever experienced as a woman; it is almost as exciting as birthing my own children. I took delight in all my grandchildren as toddlers, and as active, inquisitive preschoolers; I revelled in their enthusiasm as teenagers, and basked in pride as they moved into adulthood. As a grandmother, I could relax and appreciate each grandchild's stage; I had the luxury of time to be patient, to participate in their fun, and to play games with them and celebrate their development and growth.

Kate Morton's *The House at Riverton* (2006) reminds me of the wonder of being a grandparent.

It's special, grandparents and grandchildren. So much simpler. Is it always so, I wonder? I think perhaps it is. While one's own child takes apart one's heart to use and misuse as they please, a grandchild is different. Gone are the bonds of guilt and responsibility that burden the maternal relationship. The way to love grandchildren is free. (184)

As I reflect on *my* role as grandparent, I realize that I tried to avoid the pitfalls of past parental mistakes. I make amends through my children's children by being a better grandparent than I may have been a parent; I trust that I have left them wisdom along with loads of love and stories . . . lots of stories.

Nathan Alexander Heald: May 10, 1995
My First Grandchild

"It's a boy! it's a boy!" and we're calling him 'Nathan!'" My hand was shaking so hard that I almost dropped the telephone. Tingles of goose-bumps ran up my arms. I couldn't stop smiling. It was such a special day—Nathan's birth and, too, the day I became a grandmother.

Nathan's fingers curled tightly around his Dad's thumb, he was such a tiny baby with tufts of feathery black hair on his head. *Perfect, absolutely perfect!*

Images come flooding into my mind—of Nathan in his car-seat perched on the dining room table, and his mom leaning over to read to him. As that image fades, I see him standing stark still beside a German Shepherd dog, which dwarfed him in size, at the driveway in front of that big old house in Paris. His two-year-old eyes danced, his wee arms waved wildly, and there was an enormous grin on his face. As I drove past them and parked my car, his Dad called, "You can go now. Nathan." He took off and raced to meet me; he jumped into my arms! I blink, and Nathan is in Pointe-Aux-Roches .With radar-like hearing, he hears the VIA train miles away—a sound Grandpa John and I couldn't hear at all. "Train, train," he shouted, as the train ripped by. When the whistle blew at the Pointe-Aux-Roches crossing, Nathan's body wiggled and his tiny hand madly waved. In an instant, Nathan is in his push car with the garden hose, spraying the tree, the cement patio and when I wasn't looking, he turned the hose on *me*!! I wonder if he still has the book that I made for him; it focused on that incident. Nathan loved me reading stories to him; he always named the title and the author. Before long, he knew the titles and authors of all his favourite selections. In his Kindergarten class, he waved to the teacher when she started to read a story to the class. "What's the title of the story and who is the author?" he called out

Nathan's all time favourite memory was the time I took him on a trip to Alberta to visit my family. The trip was my protest against Bill 60 and the introduction of standardized tests. While the grade three children across Ontario were writing the test for the first time, Nathan and I were in a plane flying to Alberta. The first thing he loved was visiting Drumheller at the Royal Tyrrell Museum; it houses the largest display of dinosaur skeletons in the world! Always thinking of his brother, Matt, Nathan purchased a plastic dinosaur to take home to him. While on a dinosaur dig with his Uncle Jim, Nathan found a piece of rock with fern-like imprints on it; it was dated to be thousands of years old. I wonder if he still has it.

Travelling to Waterton Park to see the Rocky Mountains, we stopped at the 6000 year-old, world famous Head-Smashed-in-Buffalo-Jump, – UNESCO Heritage Site. We walked to the top of a steep 300 foot canyon and looked down to where Indigenous people had chased thousands-upon-thousands of buffalo off the precipice, and to their death. Once killed, the meat was preserved into pemmican, the carcasses were harvested for their skins and the hides made into clothing, and the buffalo bones were used for implements. Absolutely nothing was wasted. It was a stark reminder of how many years Indigenous people have been on these lands that we call Canada.

The 'Frank Slide'—a site I'd seen as a child with my grandparents Blakley—was something I wanted Nathan to see. It was dusk when we arrived, and the semi-darkness of the evening cast an eerie light on the blue-grey rock. The rock sat like a giant tombstone; Nathan stood on boulders as big as a car. "The slide happened in April, 1903 when suddenly 82 million tons of rock came tumbling down Turtle Mountain, and buried the east end of the town of Frank. It killed one hundred of the six hundred inhabitants in a matter of seconds." According to local folklore only one little girl survived the ordeal; she was named, Frankie Slide. That gave us a good chuckle.

Nathan became a Calgary Flames fan when we visited my niece Penny; she, who insisted on purchasing him a Calgary Flames T- shirt because the Flames were doing well that year. Nathan maintained his affection for the Flames for many years!

I wanted to visit the Dodd farm in Innisfail with Nathan, because I'd spent the first four years of my life with them. As I drove up the long lane that led to the farm yard, Terry Dodd—Peg's nephew—greeted us. He took us on a ride in his beat-up truck through his farm fields; we saw cattle munching on bales of hay and baby calves suckling their mothers' udders. Later, Terry took Nathan to the barn to see the new baby calves. "Put your hand out to the calf, Nathan," Terry said, laughing. "He'll suck your fingers." Sure enough, Nathan poked his fingers toward the calf, and the calf latched on like a suction cup and made loud smacking sounds! The visit reminded me of how well I'd been loved by the Dodd family when I was a child.

A roller coaster ride at the West Edmonton Mall was a fitting ending to our trip: Nathan took off twisting, turning, racing up to the ceiling and back down, before rolling to a screeching stop. "That was awesome, Grandma; really awesome!"

There are other fun memories Nathan, such as

the day I bought him his first guitar—at Fred Eaglesmith's shop in Port Dover. The guitar became the beginning of Nathan's guitar-playing career.

Now, in 2025, it is hard to believe that Nathan is all grown up – he works in a profession he loves, as an electrician. He is newly engaged to his partner, MacKenzie, and they live together in their condo. He has a bright and promising future ahead.

MATT

HE'S OUT. HE'S OUT

MY BABY BROTHER'S OUT

(Dictated by Nathan, age five.)

I was sleeping and my Dad woke me up. I thought it was morning time, but it was so dark. Dad said it was the middle of the night, and said I had to get up and get dressed because we had to take Momma to the hospital. So, I really hurried. "Burt!" I could hear Momma calling, "It hurts, it hurts."

We drove to the hospital really quick because Momma's tummy was hurting bad. She kept saying, "It hurts. It hurts. It hurts."

When we got to the hospital, we had to go to

number three to the change rooms. Momma got changed and they put her into a high bed that rolled. They put her into a big room with a doctor and nurses. They told me to stand at the door.

I was in the room with Dad and Momma, just a little bit close to Momma's head.

Then they told Momma to push, push, PUSH, PUSH!

And Momma pushed and pushed really hard. And Hard and HARD!"

(Nathan's voice gets louder and louder.)

And then the baby popped out. They held my baby brother by the feet and shook him. Then he started to cry. They measured him and he was 6696. Then we had to wash him and Dad '*holded*' him. And then he started crying and then he went to his mommy. Once he got out, Grandma, he was so small, like the tiniest baby in the whole world. And then he went to his mommy again.

Then Auntie Sue came, but she missed all the fun and all the cool stuff.

Know what Grandma? Mommy's tummy got flat again.

I told the doctor that this was the first time I'd seen a baby get '*borned.*' And the nurse asked me if I wanted to be a baby doctor and come to work with them in the hospital. But I said, "I'll just be an ear doctor."

"And what did you call for, Grandma?" Nathan asked.

"I just wanted to wish your Dad a happy birthday, Nathan and I guess he got the best birthday present ever, a new baby brother for you."

(Recorded by Grandma Heald-Taylor, December 7, 2000)

Matthew William Wesley Heald: December 7, 2000

Matthew bonded to his brother the moment he was born; I chuckle when I remember visiting him for the first time. Matthew was gazing up at his brother and listening to the story "Murmel, Murmel" by Robert Munsch—a perfect story about a baby. Nathan—at the age of five—could read the story word-for-word. It is a sweet image of Matt that I will hold in my mind, forever.

I remember when Matt would crawl around on the upper deck of our home, in Pointe-Aux-Roches. He also rolled around in his scooter on the lower deck outside–paddling his feet to make it go.

One spring break, I took Matt to a maple sugar bush to see how maple syrup was made. Matt was fascinated by the plastic tubes that connected the maple trees and gathered the sap. We watched the sap as it was boiled and reduced into syrup in the sugar shack. Later, Matt poured maple syrup onto his pancakes—his favourite food—in the little restaurant. We learned that Canada produces 71% of the world's supply of maple syrup–most of which was produced in Quebec.

Matt has many special memories of The Lodge. Images come to mind of playing hours of Monopoly, with him as well as miniature ball-hockey on the carpet. Matt also enjoyed playing soccer in the side yard with his brother, and his cousin Amy. He especially loved making chocolate-chip cookies into shapes of dragons, monsters, snakes, and mountains that erupted with chocolate sauce. Speaking of mountains, Matt devoured mountains of Kraft Dinner. Of course, Matt remembers the time I gave 10 cents for every book he read from the easy-read book-bin. I owed *piles* of dough at the end of that experiment. It was worth every dime . . . and a loonie!

Matt has many memories of Port Dover—swimming in Lake Erie, eating foot-long hotdogs at the Arbor, and playing endless games of mini-golf. He enjoyed the July 1st boat parade in the river and the parade of marching bands up main street. In the winter, Matt was fascinated by Santa Claus's arrival at the harbour in a tug boat before leading the Santa Clause Parade. One New Years Day, Matt and the family came to Dover to watch the Polar Bear Dip: a crazy bunch of people jumped into bone-chilling Lake Erie. To warm up, Matt and everyone went to the Marine Museum and had hot chocolate and cookies. Musicians from the area entertained us, with fiddle music while Matt played games with his brother in the children's section. While there, we learned that Port Dover once had the largest fresh-water fishing fleet in the world.

Matt also enjoyed theatre and performances, such as the live performance of Eric Carle's book, *The Very Hungry Caterpillar* at the Lighthouse Festival Theatre. I'd read the book to Matt so often before, and the performance was just like the book!

In 2012, Matt also enjoyed watching the re-enactment of the War of 1812,. It was held in Port Dover to celebrate Canada's victory in the war against the United States, 200 years earlier. Men pretending to be British soldiers shot fake muskets at the Americans. To commemorate the performance, I purchased a replica musket for Matt, much to the chagrin of his parents, who complained that I would never purchase guns for *them* growing up.

Matt wasn't impressed when, that same year, I took him and his brother to Universal Studios in Orlando. He was scared to death on the Harry Potter ride. Afterward, Matt wouldn't go on any rides. Instead, he spent time with me walking around the park, paddling in the large wading pool, or sunning on the sandy beach. Later in the week, he had fun with his American cousins, Kasey and Kody, when they took turns whipping around in my scooter—the one I had for my injured leg—as if he was a race-car driver!

Matt had a lot of interests, and athletics was one of them. He was a goalie for many years; I have memories of him saving goals for many teams. In summer, he played ball hockey, and was a fantastic player. When he graduated from high school, Matt took a fitness course at college; he is now a fitness trainer with a company in Kitchener. As I write in 2025, Matt has a steady girlfriend, Darienne, and is a confident, caring, and sensitive young man.

Amy Carolyn Heald: April 8, 1998
My only Granddaughter

"What would you like me to write in my memoir about you?" I asked Amy. In an instant, she rattled off ideas, one thought tripping over the next. "Baby stories: I want to know about the time I spent with you and Grandpa John in Stoney Point." She paused and took a breath. "And then there was the time you took me to Alberta to all the places *you* grew up. I want to read about them all in your memoir!"

I laughed. "I guess I could write a whole memoir just about *you!*"

"Yep," she countered smugly.

I recall the day I first laid eyes on Amy Carolyn Heald. It was April, 1998. I went to visit her Mom and Dad in Mississauga. She was a chubby, round-faced-baby; she looked as big as a three month old, not a newborn! As she snuggled into my arms, I remember saying to myself, "*A girl, a baby girl! Finally, a baby girl to love!*"

Point-Aux-Roches holds so many memories of Amy as a baby. At seven months old, she stayed with John and me for almost a month when her parents went to Australia. In my mind, I see Amy crawling around in the playpen on the patio overlooking Lake St. Clair. Suddenly, she grasped onto the bars with her chubby little fingers and pulled herself up into a standing position. Wobbly at first, she flopped back down onto her bottom. I clapped my hands in praise. With a huge smile on her face, she did it again. Repeating the climbing and sitting activity she gained greater strength before falling back down. Then, suddenly, all in one motion, she pulled herself up, flipped over the top of the playpen, and landed on the cement patio. In a panic, I scooped her up into my arms, then placed her gently back into the playpen. Scowling at me, she crawled to the bars as if in defiance, pulled herself up and in a flash was over the top again! After repeating this a few more times, she smiled at me as if to say. . . "*Look at me Grandma; see how smart I am?*" When it became a game, I just picked her up and sat her on my knee, so she'd be safe, and I read her stories. The playpen got stored away in the garage. She'd outgrown it!

Amy took her first steps in our living room. As she crawled around on the carpet, she spied the copper kettle. Crawling over to it, she pulled off the lid and peered in. She poked one foot into the opening— a smile spread across her face. With her foot firmly planted, in an instant, she was standing upright. She began thumping across the carpet, using the kettle for balance– step-kerplunk, step-kerplunk, step-kerplunk– as she stumbled across the floor, like a drunken sailor having had one too many drinks! From that moment on there was no more crawling for *Amy!* At seven months, she could walk like a big girl!

Amy cried when I left her room after I'd tucked her in; she was nervous in the unfamiliar crib. In order for her to settle down, I lay down on the carpet beside the crib until she fell asleep. When I woke up in the night with a sore back, I said to myself. "*Something is wrong with this picture—Amy's cozy in her crib and my sixty-year-old-bones are aching.* I made a plan. The next night I had a talk with her. "Amy, now that you are all tucked in and ready for sleep, I am going to *my* bed across the hall. If you need me, you can call me, and I'll come."

Amy nodded her head as if she understood. My head had barely struck my pillow when I heard, "Grandma? Where are you?"

"I'm here, Honey, right across the hall." Getting up, I came to her room, leaned over her crib, and crooned. "See, Amy, I'm right here whenever you need me." She looked at me with a hint of a frown as I shuffled back to my room.

Within moments, I heard, "Grandma? Please come."

"I'm right here in my bed," I called back. There was silence for a few moments before she called out again. I replied, "I'm right here, sweetheart."

"Okay!" she mumbled sleepily. Within moments there was silence. Peeking into her room, her thumb was in her mouth, eyes clamped tight, her breathing a gentle rhythm.

The next morning—before Amy was awake- I went downstairs to the kitchen to help John with breakfast. As I was pouring a bit of milk into the egg mixture for scrambled eggs, the room suddenly filled with a piercing cry, full of anxiety and fear. "Grandma! Where are you?" Dropping the spatula, I tore up the stairs two steps at a time. Amy was wailing tearfully, her voice catching in breathless spasms, **"Grand...ma... Where... Are... you?"** As I ran into her bedroom, she was standing in the crib and rattling its bars. Angry tears streamed down her chubby cheeks as she called: "Grandma! Grandma!" She stretched her arms in the air, and I lifted her up as her wee fingers clung tightly around my neck. By the time we reached the ground floor, Amy's nose was twitching and sniffing the air. The crying stopped. "Eggs," she called out. She wriggled out of my arms, and ran to Grandpa. Always hungry, she gobbled up a plateful of scrambled eggs . . . smiling at us between mouthfuls– she knew she was safe with Grandpa and me right beside her!

Amy loved books. "Book, book, book," she'd call out, sounding like a quacking duck. Turning the pages of the selection, *Crocodile Beat* I asked her, "What's the name of the story, Amy?"

"Crocodile Beat," she responded immediately.

"And who is the author?"

"Gail," she laughed. "It's just like *your* name, Grandma. It's Gail Jorgensen. She opened the cover. "Let's read Grandma, let's read." Her body started bouncing on my lap to the beat, as she chimed in. *"Down by the River in the heat of the day the crocodile sleeps and awaits his prey."* I can still hear the jaunty rhythm in my head; Amy would repeat each line along with me. As we read the final page, and I closed the book, she cried, "Read it again Grandma!" Her blue eyes sparkled, and she grinned.

In 2024, I purchased an old copy of the *Crocodile Beat,* from Amazon. I gave it to her to read to her babies when she had them in the future.

Amy was a story-teller. At three, she told this story based on an incident in the park with her Dad. As she told the story, her Dad copied down the words exactly as she told it.

The Squirrel and the Crow

One day there was a little squirrel that was by the tree eating a cookie. Then the crow came and the crow tried to get the cookie away from the squirrel. And then the squirrel put the cookie in his nest. The crow got it and flied away with it and put it in his nest. Squirrel was very sad. So, crow took the cookie and broke it in two pieces and gave one piece to squirrel and then they all became friends.

By Amy Heald, age 3

Thousands of educators heard Amy's short story when I conducted workshops across Canada, the United States and South East Asia—educators from around the world knew of Amy.

I have many memories of Amy from different places–our house, the Lodge, and various travels. I remember Amy sitting with her cousin Nathan—such as when they walked the shoreline at Pointe-Roches or sat on their little chairs to watch the sunset over the skyscrapers of Detroit. 'The Lodge' is filled with memories of Amy, such as swimming in Lake Erie, playing soccer with her cousins Nathan and Matt, and playing

Monopoly. Of course, there was the reading contest when she earned a pile of Grandma's money. We made trips to Port Dover to the 'Arbour' for foot-long hotdogs, and played mini-golf across the street.

I picture Amy in Montreal at the insect museum, the Quebec Winter Carnival, the Maple Sugar Festival and at soccer games. When Amy was older, she took me to the art gallery to see the Andy Warhol exhibition. Afterward, she introduced me to authentic French poutine.

Amy and I took at trip to Alberta when Amy was 14. This is a precious memory indeed. That particular trip was important to me because I wanted her to meet some of *my* family and show her where *I* grew up so that she would have a better understanding of who I was! We landed in Edmonton; my sister Sharon gave us a home base and she spoiled us rotten with her good cooking! Amy met my brother Bud–her great uncle–and was enthralled by his sense of humour and funny jokes.

A trip to the West Edmonton Mall was a highlight. She saw the Star Wars exhibition—with life-sized characters of Luke Skywalker, Hans Solo, Darth Vader, and Leila. She gathered up brochures for her Dad. A teenager, she loved pawing through many of the 800 stores. We passed by the Ice Palace, which was where Kaetlyn Osmond practised. She won gold at the Worlds in 2017, and bronze at the Olympics in 2018.

"This place is *huge*, Grandma," Amy exclaimed. As we sorted through the brochures, we learned it was one of the largest malls in North America and spanned 48 city blocks. It has the largest indoor wave pool in the world. Our excursion was punctuated with a ride on the gigantic roller-coaster.

Leaving Edmonton, we travelled south toward Red Deer. Nostalgia beckoned, and we made a detour west toward Sylvan Lake. For me, it held memories of family picnics. In an instant, I was ten years old lining up for French fries at a stand on the main street–now a McDonalds! And Sylvan Lake? The giant lake of my childhood had shrunk as I stared at the outer fringes, dotted with trees and homes–a puny body of water compared to the 'Lodge' on Lake Erie. Leaving Sylvan, we passed through Red Deer and memories of my high school, Lindsey Thurber, and my first boyfriend, Peter, flooded my mind. We drove south, to Calgary, where we visited my favourite niece, Penny. On our way back north, I passed the town of Bowden, where I taught elementary school after my one year of teachers' training.

The Dodd farm–the most important visit of the entire trip–was at the town of Innisfail. Passing its famous three-story grain elevators, I spotted the Dodd farm of my childhood. As we drove up the laneway, past the row of tall spruce trees, the white two-story clapboard house came into view. My breath caught in my throat. *I was coming home.* It was dilapidated, and the windows were boarded up. In my mind, I saw it as it was a half century before, vibrant and full of life with Ma and Peg Dodd at the heart of it. "Some of my very first memories are in that old house," I told Amy. "That's where I lived, from a baby until I was four years old, with Peg Dodd and her mother, Ma." My voice suddenly cracked and my eyes stung. "Peg was like a mother to me," I whispered, sighing deeply.

We parked in the middle of the farmyard; I saw a man wearing an old, western-style, slouched hat. He had a tanned, weathered face, and a huge, rusty-coloured, handlebar moustache framing his mouth. Stepping out of the car, I waved.

"Family," he barked as he marched toward me, arms spread wide. He shouted, "Gail, how good to see you!" and embraced me, pressing me into his thick chest.

"This is Amy, my granddaughter." Terry put his hand over hers as if he'd known her all his life. "Terry is Peg's nephew, and the grandson of Ma Dodd," I whispered softly to Amy so she could understand the generational connection.

"You know, Amy," Terry grinned. "I've heard about your Grandma Gail all my life." He smiled broadly. "My grandmother and my Aunt Peg talked about her all the time when I was growing up. Aunt Peg would drag out all the albums and show me pictures of 'little Gail Pye.'" Terry laughed out loud. "But I never met her until just a few years ago!" He shook his head sideways, turning to me. "Little Gail Pye! I feel I've known you forever!"

Getting into his pick-up truck, Terry gunned the motor and we took off. "I'll take you to the new section we just bought down by the Red Deer River," he said excitedly.

"We really can't stay," I argued, knowing I was disappointing him. "We're heading back to Ontario in a couple of days."

"That's too bad," Terry said, whipping the truck around so sharply, we bumped our shoulders against the door. Roaring through the gate to the farmyard, Terry brought the pick-up to a screeching halt. We gave a deep sigh of relief–thankful we were still in one piece! "Will you stay for coffee?"

"Thanks, Terry; but we really don't have time."

I opened my arms for a final hug and he obliged, embracing Amy too. "So glad you stopped by." He winked. "Next time stay a little longer!" Climbing back into our rental car, I turned toward the lane and saw Terry waving at us in the rear-view mirror. That's when it happened!

As I passed the old farmhouse, which peeked out at me through the dark spruce branches, I saw a sudden flash of light and heard a loud roaring in my ears. My heart thudded, and my mind spun in a whirl–

as if I was in some kind of trance. I felt a sudden rush of heat surge throughout my body–a warm and comforting sensation of contentment, solace, and safety. My eyes brimmed with tears; they overflowed, unbidden, down my cheeks. Feelings of being accepted and adored coursed over me. I saw a vision of Peg and Ma Dodd waving a final goodbye, they let me know that I was loved completely and unconditionally, that they'd always be with me.

From a far distance I heard Amy's voice sounding as if she had a mouthful of wool. "Grandma, what's wrong?" I sensed her anxiety and distress, but was so overcome by emotion that I couldn't find words to console her or to let her know that I was all right. I patted her arm and finally whispered, "I'm okay, my love." Taking in a deep gulp of air, I breathed slowly, deeply, out ... and ... in ... out ... and ... in as I tried to figure out why I was feeling this sense of tranquility, peace and serenity.

As my heart beat slowed and my breathing became regular, I heard Amy clearly, "Grandma, Grandma; are you *really* all right? I was so scared, I thought you were having a heart attack and might die!"

"No Amy, I wasn't dying, sweetheart, far from it. I guess that being here on the Dodd farm brought back so many warm childhood memories that I was overwhelmed by the feelings of love that Ma and Peg had for me."

"Thank goodness, you're okay," Amy said grinning, her blue eyes twinkling. "Don't do that again, okay?"

"All right," I said, laughing, as I twisted the key in the ignition and drove cautiously down the rest of the laneway. I reluctantly left the old white house, the home of my heart.

"Buckle your seatbelts," The flight attendant called as the plane revved across the runway. We were heading home to Ontario, and my darling granddaughter, Amy, was sitting beside me. *Does she know me any better?* The wings banked to the east.

RETIREMENT

Who Does the Laundry Now?

"What will my life be like as a wife, now that I'm a retired professor?" I wondered out loud, settling myself on the patio bench beside John. It was June 1999. The butterflies flitted among the pink and white petunias in the gardens, and pristine white gulls flitted high across the azure-blue sky.

John smiled.

"Now that I'm home full time I want to take over some of the household chores. What do you think?"

John was quick to respond. "I hate doing laundry," he stated. "I'd love it if you'd take it over?"

"Of course," I said, and I'll help with the cooking too, if you like."

However, within weeks of retirement Heinemann Publishing, from the United States, contacted me to write a book on early reading. There was a deadline attached to the contract.

White puffy flakes of whipped snow drifted into mounds of white. Fisherman huts dotted the frozen lake under the dull grey sky as I sat at the kitchen table wolfing down breakfast–that John had prepared–before I scurried back up to my office and my computer.

John reached over and placed his hand over mine. "When did you say you would take over the laundry?"

It was a rude awakening, like a brick chucked at my head. Suddenly, I realized that I'd been taking John and his workload for granted. *What irony!* For years, I'd railed against men taking women's roles for granted, and here I was doing the very same thing to my husband. The role reversal ended right then! I started doing my share around the house and carved out a new routine. John continued the shopping and cooking—except on weekends or when we had company–while I took on the cleanup after meals. Finally, I took over the laundry duties. We hired out the cleaning and lawn mowing.

The Beginning Reading Handbook about how literacy was developed with young children—using examples of my grandchildren, Nathan, Amy and Matt, and their pictures gracing many pages—was finally finished in 2001.

Problems in Paradise: Chauvinism Cuts Two Ways

As I took on more responsibility of the household, I thought everything was going well. One evening after supper, I cleared the table and started loading the dishwasher. When I glanced at John, his forehead was wrinkled in worry, as if he'd just received bad news.

What's up?" I asked sympathetically, anxious to hear what was wrong.

John leaned over my shoulder. "You're doing it all wrong!"

"What?" I countered, shocked at his complaint. *What could be wrong about loading a damned dishwasher?*

"You need to put the plates in the correct slots, where they belong, in the bottom. The glasses go in the top rack."

What the hell! I'm helping out and he's criticizing? What's wrong with him? I plunked the rest of the dishes into the remaining spaces and slammed the dishwasher door shut. That is, I *tried* to slam it, but it just retreated slowly, gradually making a final whooshing sound then a final soft click. *Damn it!*

The following week, I was folding laundry on the top of the freezer. There were a stack of teatowels, folded neatly. Grabbing another, I snapped it open and started to fold it when John came in to drop a can into the recycle bin. "Thanks for folding the laundry," he said, examining the stack I'd just folded. "I fold each one over once length-wise and then into folds of three so it fits into the drawer neatly." I felt like a student being scolded by a teacher for not sitting up straight! "And," he went on, "I like my socks folded flat and in half, like this, not smooched into a ball!" He pulled a pair apart to show me. *What does it matter for good-*

ness' sake; why are you being so picky?* I didn't say this out loud; instead, I gave a deep exasperated sigh, and left the pile of folded laundry on top of the freezer for *him* to put away. Grabbing my jacket, I rushed outside, slamming the back door behind me. Stomping to the deck, I sat on the edge and looked out at Lake St. Clair. *Why is he acting like this? Things were going fine all winter. It's not like him to be so critical; he's always so positive and supportive.* I looked out at the water–it was a deep cobalt blue today, with whitecaps hinting a storm. *Maybe he's just tired or having a bad day; perhaps I should just let it go.* A cool blast of wind whipped my face. Cooled off, I shrugged my shoulders and went back to the house. *I'll pick my battles and this is not worth worrying about right now.*

But the criticisms persisted. "*I like the kitchen to be neat, so could you put the dishes away once they're dry?*" "*You waste too much water when you rinse the dishes before putting them into the dishwasher.*" "*I like the sinks to be clean; after you peel the potatoes–would you please put the skins into the garbage can immediately?*" "*You've got to use dish detergent when you wash the pots; you can't just rinse them with water alone because that won't get them clean enough.*"

All I seemed to hear was, "*I wish you'd . . . Why can't you? . . . You've got to . . .*" He'd always been organized and had particular ways of doing things but now he was being ridiculous! I was beginning to feel like a seal in training for a circus act, and it was pissing me off.

This is not what I thought retirement would be; I thought we'd enjoy each others' company, we'd be a team. *I need to talk to him to find out what the heck is going on.*

I approached John right after breakfast one morning, just after he'd clicked off Windsor CBC news. I was silent for a moment, thinking of the right way to start a conversation. Reaching for his hand, I said gently. "What's going on? I can't seem to do anything right!" Taking a sip of tea before going on, I added, "You seem so irritated and angry with me all the time."

John sat quietly for a moment and his brow furrowed in a look of annoyance. "There's nothing wrong, and I'm not angry," he replied, an edge to his voice. "I just like things to be done *right!*" A cold wind of foreboding whistled over me.

The fault-finding stopped for a month before he was at it again. *You lost another sock in the washing machine; You forgot to wipe down the shower with the squeegee!*

On edge all the time, and anticipating criticism and endless nit-picking, took its toll. I needed help. I made an appointment with Joanie, my therapist.

I Sought a Counsellor

Joanie shifted her rotund body into her rattan chair, her feet dangling; she barely reached the carpeted floor. "Good to see you, Gail." Her lips stretched into a broad red-lipstick smile which crossed her entire face. "I just made a potful of ginger tea. Would you like some?"

"Sure." *That's just like Joanie to making me feel comfortable in her tiny, cozy den-like-office in her home.* She was more like a friend than a counsellor to me; she always listened and really *heard* me, frequently understanding *beyond* what I was saying. She had a way of gently nudging me to look beyond *my* point of view. I trusted her! As I wrapped my hands around the warm cup of tea, I knew she'd have answers.

"Now, tell me why you're here."

After giving her a blow-by-blow account of what had been going on since my retirement, I blurted out, "I can't take it anymore. John's constant nit-picking is driving me around the bend."

"Yes, I see how John's behaviour is so annoying to you, Gail."

"That's an understatement!" I added in my pissed-off voice. "I've tried talking to him but nothing changes, so what can I do about it? How can I get him to cut it out?"

"It sounds like it's been quite a difficult adjustment for *John* with you home all the time."

"I'm not sure what you mean?" I was surprised at her comment. "How can this be difficult for *him*? Things should be a lot easier now that I'm helping around the house."

"I understand how you feel." Joanie rubbed her chin. "But now, I'd like you to think about how your being home all the time might be like for *him*."

What's Joanie getting at? "Like, how do you mean?"

"Well, he's been at home for ten years and he's made a fantastic adjustment learning how to cook, do the shopping, laundry and all the necessary jobs around the house."

Warm anger crept up my neck and my forehead wrinkled into a frown, rebuttal clawing in my throat. "Yes, he has; but remember, for the past ten years *I've* been working full time," I snapped back.

Joanie ignored my comment, and it was making me mad. *What's going on here?*

"John has developed his *own* routines, *his* way of doing things."

"Come on, Joanie, folding socks in a ball is not life-threatening for heaven' sake! And not using a squeegee to wipe down the shower is not the end of the bloody world!" I added snarling. "He's being totally unreasonable and I'm sick of it."

Joanie lifted her tea pot and refilled my cup. "I'm curious about something," she said, taking a sip of tea and letting her words hang in the air. "What was it like when *you* were a homemaker full time back in the sixties?" she asked cautiously.

What the heck does that have to do with anything? "Why do you ask?" I was suspicious that I was walking into a trap.

"Did *you* establish routines; have *your* way of doing things?"

"Well . . . yes I did," I admitted sheepishly. *She's turning the tables back onto me and she thinks I haven't noticed.* "Okay, I can see what you're getting at. You want me to see things from *his* point of view." I let my guard down . . . just a little.

Joanie paused and her eyes sparkled. "You see," she grinned, "He has *his* way of loading the dishwasher, and folding his socks," she teased.

My index finger flew to my lips to stifle a grin.

Joanie took a long sip of tea. Her dark eyebrows knitted together, and she drew her lips to the side of her mouth, in deep thought, before she spoke. "On your way home today, I want you to think about something," Joanie said softly, kindly.

I braced myself. *What's she up to now?*

"I want you to do some thinking." She swallowed the last drop of tea. "Is it possible that, over the last ten years, the household has become *John's* territory, *his* domain?" Joanie set her mug on the table and stopped talking, giving me time to mull *this* idea in my mind, before she added, "Do you think he might see *you* as a disruptive force in his space?" She hesitated before adding, "An interloper perhaps?"

My Sudden Realization

As I got into my van, my mind twisted and turned in all directions. "I'm in *John's* domain? *His* territory? *His* space? It's *my* house too, damn it!" I banged my hands on the steering wheel. How can I be an interloper in my own home for goodness' sake! I worked damned hard during those ten years to make a living; it was what we agreed to. It was *his* idea; it was the bargain we made. I thought we'd made it work; it worked for *me*. His incessant nagging makes no sense at all!

Joanie's voice nagged at me, "*What was it like when you were a homemaker in the sixties? Did you have routines?*" Of course I did, but I would have loved it if my first husband had helped me out. I turned up Ouellette, anger rising again. *Why do I have to squeegee the shower, when I wipe it down with a sponge, for heaven' sake. I'm not a slob.* Why do I have to do everything *his* way?

I passed Hotel Dieu hospital to my left, and my body winced. My left hand flew to my breasts; I felt the agonizing pain of a million knife slashes. Breast surgery! My eyes smarting, I sucked in air and let it out slowly. Warm emotions suddenly swept over and around me: the memory of John's arms gently easing me into the van, a blanket wrapped around my quivering body, tender hands lowering me into our bed, fluffed pillows under my head, the soft pressure of John's finger tips pushing the covers onto my body, nudging them gently down the length of my back from the nape of my neck down my spine, loving hands folding me in like a baby. "Sleep well, my love," John whispered.

Turning east onto EC Row, my heart made a gentle turn. *John was there for me after surgery.*

In his ten years as house husband, he'd made quite an adjustment—learning to cook when he'd never cooked in his life. And look at him now! On top of that, he hauled loads of mushroom soil for the gardens. All of a sudden, I recognized the huge adjustment *he* had made over those ten years.

Driving across the bridge through Belle River, I finally understood that John had developed his *own* routines, his *own* ways of doing things. Maybe this role-reversal had given him pride and a sense of accomplishment in running the household so efficiently and effectively all these years. The house had become *his* domain! Maybe I was upsetting his applecart by being home all the time, interfering with *his* way of doing things . . . an *interloper* as Joanie claimed.

Pulling onto Lakeshore Road, and into the driveway at 2890, there was *"Cindy Bear"* greeting me with years of happy memories. I smacked the steering wheel. *I love you, damn it! You are annoying as hell right now. But I love you.*

As I got out of the van, I now had direction and knew what I was going to do. I'd load the dishwasher the way he wanted, fold his socks over flat and the dish towels in thirds! But I drew the line at squeegeeing the shower; sponging would do!

Counselling: Opening Up

"It's good to see you again, Gail," Joanie said with a smile, exuding warmth and care. She offered me green tea, and I wrapped my fingers through the handle. "So how are things going?" she asked.

"Well frankly, I'm angry with you," I said, frowning. "When John and I came to see you a week or so ago, I was disappointed that you asked to see *me* alone again, without John. He's the one that needs some direction, the one who needs counselling!" I stated, annoyed.

Joanie grinned, looking down at her notes.

"Well, you see, Gail, I could see that you and John have difficulty talking about problems that come up in your marriage. But John wasn't ready to open up; he had a way of charming me and getting me off topic.

"That's true about John; he'll avoid disagreement at any cost; his way of dealing with issues is to make wisecracks. Once he has me laughing, then it's game over."

Joanie nodded her head at me. "But *you* seemed willing to explore issues, so I could work with *you*."

My anger evaporated; I began to relax and feel comfortable.

"So tell me about yourself, Gail; I believe that problems you have with John might be related to the way *you* were brought up."

Biting my bottom lip, a shiver inched up my spine.

"So, I'd like you to tell me more about your childhood, where you grew up, about your Mother and Dad, your siblings." Joannie took a sip from her mug. "I'd like to understand more about your childhood," she said, warmly.

A knot began to twist in my stomach, my hands got clammy.

"Okay," I said tentatively, unsure of where to start. Something niggled. *How much does she want to know? How much should I reveal?*

I started by talking about our farm in Alberta, the names of my sisters and brother, and my Dad.

"What was your Mom like?" Joanie asked cautiously, perhaps noticing I hadn't mentioned her.

"I never had much of a relationship with her," I said, dismissively.

Joanie's eye-brows lifted. "Mmmmm," she murmured, making a note.

"Tell me an early memory of your family, any memory at all," Joanie encouraged.

Shifting in my chair, I felt totally lost as to what exactly she wanted.

Sensing my uncertainty, her brow knitted as if thinking of another tact to prompt me to talk. "I'd like you to draw a picture of yourself when you were little," she said thoughtfully, "doing something with your siblings, or with your Mom and Dad." Joannie glanced at the clock on her wall. "We're almost out of time today, so I'd like you to think about this and bring a picture next session."

"You want a painting?"

"Oh no," Joanie said, chuckling. "Use wax crayons, pencil-crayons, coloured markers, anything you like, on any kind of paper."

"I'm not very good at drawing," I told her, old insecurities leaking out.

"Don't worry, you don't have to be," she reassured. "A sketch will do."

"Okay," I'll bring something next week," I agreed, as I got up to leave.

The Portrait: My Identity

It was late. The night before, I had the next meeting with Joanie. John was sound asleep in bed across the hall. *Why did I put this off until the very last minute?* In the darkness, I got out a box of crayons, picked up a piece of discarded computer paper and grabbed a crayon. *Why am I doing this?* I always did as I was told, to avoid getting into trouble with Mom. Finishing the picture, I shoved it into my journal to be ready for my session with Joanie, and headed to bed.

"Here it is," I said, the next day, hesitation in my voice as I handed my drawing to Joanie.

As she examined it closely, her eyebrows pinched together and a long, awkward silence hung in the air.

What's wrong? Doesn't she like my picture?

Deep wrinkles formed on her forehead before she spoke. "Oh, my word," she said, alarm in her voice..

"You've drawn your picture all in *black*!"

"I have?" I answered surprised. "I really wasn't aware."

Once again, Joanie looked intently at my drawing, as if pondering how to respond. Finally, she found her words. "Gail, you have no features on your face; you've drawn no eyes or mouth, not even a nose!" a note of incredulity in her voice. "And you are sitting up in a tree alone all by yourself!"

So? That's what I liked to do as a kid! Why is she making such a fuss about the picture?

Beginning to feel defensive, I reached for my drawing. Joanie was right; it was all black and I had no face. Blinking in surprise, I sat there, mute, wondering what she would make of this. *What the heck does it mean?*

Joanie studied the picture once again. Folding her hands together in a prayer-like clasp she looked at me with the kindest eyes. She cleared her throat, and lowered her voice to a whisper. "No one has reflected who you really are."

"I'm not sure what you are talking about." This sounded *gobbledy-gook* to me. And yet, I felt a wave of empathy and compassion from her.

Joanie went on to explain. "When a baby is born," Joanie began, looking deeply into my eyes, "she develops her identity from the messages she receives from her parents, usually from their mother, especially in your case–born in 1938–when mothers were the primary caregivers for their babies."

I was totally engrossed in what Joanie was telling me.

"A mother tells her infant she is beautiful."

I knew that feeling. I had marvelled at my own boys when they were born.

Joanie continued. "As a mother strokes her babe, she tells her she's going to be a great writer some day, a nurse, a teacher . . . that she looks like a friend or movie star, even. It's the messages that an infant receives," Joanie stressed, "that gives a child her basic identity and worth as a human being."

All that cooing and cuddling my boys gave them *their* identity, *their* value as human beings?

Joanie went on. "She gains *her* sense of identity from the messages *she* receives from her mother."

As I stared at my portrait, the implications of Joanie's words suddenly came tumbling into my mind. They filled me with unanswered questions. *What did it mean that I drew no facial features? Could I have internalized the fact that my mother gave me no value or worth?*

A cold chill crept up my spine.

"I'd like to know more about you and your mother." Joanie stroked my arm empathetically. "Let's talk about *her* the next time we meet."

My Birth Story

"I've done a lot of soul-searching about our last session," I told Joanie, as I took the mug of green tea. "I found your interpretation of my self-portrait—as to why I drew my face with no features—troubling." I chewed on my left thumbnail, nervously. "It's an odd thing about that faceless-me," I said, hesitantly. "I find it difficult to look into the mirror at my reflection. Oh, I look at myself when I'm putting on make-up; but other than that, I avoid mirrors," I rattled on. It's like I don't acknowledge the image of *me,* the person I *am* inside." I stopped talking. I'd said too much. This was sounding crazy even to my own ears.

Joanie nodded affirmatively, urging me on.

Feeling encouraged, I said thoughtfully, "I wonder if it has anything to do with that picture I drew... "that no-one had reflected who I was." I paused then. "Maybe I'm afraid if I look into the mirror a blank slate will be reflected back."

"You could be on to something," Joanie agreed.

Then, she turned to her notes. "I think we agreed at the last session to talk some more about your mother. What do you think?

Do I have enough courage to tell mom's response to me when I was born? Can I trust how Joanie will respond to that tale? Will she dismiss it as a way to seek attention? And yet, Joanie seemed genuinely interested in my welfare. With her I'm feeling accepted, validated and safe. An overwhelming feeling of trust wrapped around my shoulders like a warm blanket. With a sudden surge of confidence, I opened up. "I think I'm ready to tell you the story of my birth," My heart thumped anxiously.

"Good for you," Joanie said kindly. "I can tell by the frown on your face that this will be difficult for you." Joanie leaned forward, anxious to hear every word.

Breathing in deeply and exhaling slowly, I began. "When I was a little girl of six, my mother told me this story about her reaction to *my* birth." I blinked, and I was suddenly in the kitchen of our farmhouse in Innisfail, Alberta, seventy-five years earlier. My six-year-old hand swatted at a housefly that was buzzing around my Baby sister Sharon's head, which lay on my mother's lap as she changed her diaper. I stood admiring Baby Sharon's little round fat body, her rosy pink cheeks. As Mom secured a safety pin into the cloth diaper, she purred softly, admiringly. *"What a beautiful baby you are, Sharon, with your clear porcelain China skin, blue eyes. What a darling baby,"* Mom crooned. *"You're going to be such a beauty when you grow up."*

"Glancing at me, Mom's face twisted into a grimace, her eyes cold as ice, and her voice coming through the mist of time. *"Oh Gail,"* she exclaimed, sardonically, *"You were so ugly when you were born, I couldn't stand the sight of you. You looked just like old Mrs. Brett, the ugly old crone that lived down the road from our farm when I was growing up."* Mom lifted up Baby Sharon and patted her back for a burp. *"I was so ashamed of how ugly you were, Gail, that I had to cover your face with a blanket so no one could see you."*

Joanie's mouth gaped open, shock written across her face. "Oh, my word," she gasped. "This is unbelievable." A long, uncomfortable, silence filled the room. Joanie's eyes blazed with anger. "I am furious at your mother," she said enraged. "It is incomprehensible to blame *you* for *her* inability to look at you. How cruel to blame *you*–an innocent baby–for being the cause of *her* failure to accept you, to appreciate you. And it was vicious of your mother to remind you so frequently of how ugly she thought you were. What a damaging thing to do to a baby . . . to a child . . . to *you!*"

My body shuddered and my fingers trembled taking this all in. *Joanie is mad at my mother? Cruel? Damaging? Innocent baby?*

"This is not about *you*, Gail, nor your sister Sharon," Joanie stated emphatically, before continuing. "This is about your *mother*." Her eyes locked into mine and I could see the black flecks in her irises. "It was your *mother* who couldn't look at you; it was *she* who was unable to accept you when you were an innocent baby."

It was about *Mom* and *her* inadequacies; it's not about me at all. I was struck by this twist of perspective. *I am not responsible for Mom covering me up! Is this why I drew such a gruesome picture of myself with no face, no identity? Is it because Mom couldn't accept me, couldn't look at me–wishing me invisible, a blank, a nothing? Was she blaming me and my appearance as justification of her rejection of me, giving her permission to dismiss me and to refuse the love I deserved?*

Turning to Joanie, I reflected on all this. "I always felt that it was *my* fault that Mom couldn't love me, that I was un-lovable. I always thought that if I did as she wished, never offended her, never crossed her, and always tried to please her, that I would *earn* her love. "At age fifty-seven, I speculate now whether getting all those degrees, even my Doctorate, I was subconsciously trying to make her proud of me, to please her, to make me acceptable in her eyes so that, eventually, she might love me!"

Joanie nodded.

A pensive look came across Joanie's eyes. "I'd like to know more about your relationship with your mother. "We will explore that next time."

Earliest Memory of My Mother
Cigarette Story

"What are your earliest memories of your mother?" Joanie asked. "Perhaps they can give us insights as to what was going on with her during that time back in the 1940s."

Foreboding washed over me. "I was afraid of her; she was mean, she beat me," I said, my eyes stinging.

Joanie placed her hand over mine. "I can see that this is very difficult for you," she said empathetically.

Comforted by Joanie's response, the tension in my shoulders softened, my thumping heart slowed, and my emotions settled. Even after more than fifty years, the event is clear in my mind: I recall every detail, every word spoken, and every emotion I felt as a barely three year old toddler.

"Mom gave a white note wrapped around green paper (dollar bill), and told me to get her a package of cigarettes at the drugstore on the corner. I knew the way because I'd been there many times before. I squeezed the papers into my hand, and walked past Mr. Rogers Park on my way up the block. I remember the clerk reaching way down, taking my crumpled mess of papers, and handing me a blue package with a picture of a sailor on the cover. On the way home, I bit into the package and released the lovely aroma with every bite. As I handed my mother the package of cigarettes, her eyes went wild, her lips twisted in a grimace and she screamed, "'You've punctured every single cigarette; you've ruined them all." She wrenched me up by the arm, ripped a thin branch from a nearby shrub, and whipped the switch across my tiny legs and bum again and again. The lash cut into my bare legs, thighs and bum. Pain pierced my armpit, and my feet dangled off the ground as the switch struck across my wee legs. Throwing the damaged cigarettes on the ground, Mom screamed at me. "Now get back to the drugstore and get another package of cigarettes!" Blubbering, I stumbled back up the street and all the way to the drugstore, once again."

Blinking back tears, I whispered to Joanie, "I was only three years old."

Joanie gasped; she clapped her hand over her mouth, her eyes wide in horror. "I am so very sorry," she murmured. "And you were a helpless toddler; what a painful memory!"

Joanie dipped her head to the side, deep in thought. "You know, Gail, by today's standards your mother's behaviour would be considered *abusive!*"

Abusive? The word rang in my ears and it took a moment to think about what I'd just heard. *Abusive?* It was certainly bad parenting, neglectful even . . .

but abusive? Sending a three year old to a store unaccompanied and whipping her for ruining cigarettes! Yes, that is abusive behaviour all right. When I think back, Mom treated our family dog with more humanity than me!

Joanie nodded sadly. "I am so sorry that your early years were so unhappy," Joanie said, dejectedly. "It is a miracle you survived, being unwanted and so abused by your mother."

"I guess so," I agreed. "Thank God for Peg," I added as an aside.

"Peg?" Joanie asked, surprised. "Who is Peg?"

"Oh, it's Peg Dodd's family. I lived with them as a preschooler.

"What?" Joanie responded, eyes wide with surprise. "A family you lived with other than your own?"

"Yes," I said smiling, "I have very special memories of my time with the Dodds."

Joanie's eyes lit up. "I want to know more about Peg Dodd when we meet next.

The Dodds

"I've never seen so many baby pictures of a single child!" Joanie said, as she thumbed through the album Peg Dodd had put together of a dewy-faced baby of two months, a toddler in a sleigh, a little girl in cowboy boots and a western hat, and a little girl sitting on the hood of a car and her tiny hand saluting, an airman standing beside her. She returned the album to me. "Who *was* Peg and what was her relationship with your family?"

"From what Ma Dodd told me, decades later before she died, she and Mom were friends. Her daughter, Peg, baby sat my six-year-old sister, Merla, and my brother Bud, who was eighteen months older than me, while Mom and Dad worked at the Bulk Oil Business in Innisfail. Peg was excited to see the new baby when my mother came home from the hospital. When Peg saw me in the bassinet with a coverlet over my face, she pulled it off and fell in love with me instantly. I remember Ma smiling as she explained how Peg brought me home with her every chance she got, until I was living with them full time from the age of two until I was four years old.

"There was no hiding my head under a blanket with *Peg!*" I exclaimed to Joanie. From these pictures, you can see that Peg thought I was the most beautiful baby in the world. She showed me off to her girlfriends and male friends alike with a smile on her lips and love in her eyes.

When I was older, I recall feeding calves with Peg's father, Ernst, and patting pigs with her brother Bruce. I also have happy memories of gathering eggs with Ma and making a scarecrow to ward off crows in the cornfield. I sighed wistfully. "I felt loved by that whole family!" I said stroking the album lovingly.

"Judging from how Peg looked at you and showed you off, one might suspect that you were *her* child."

Joanie's words struck a chord as I recalled Peg's gentle touch, the way she stroked my hair, the kind way she spoke to me and the way she doted and adored me. An overwhelming sense of belonging came over me. "You know Joanie, deep inside I feel that Peg was like a mother to me." I tented my fingers deep in thought. "It was *Peg* who was the mother I never had. I folded my fingers into my lap . . . "Perhaps that's why she wanted to adopt me."

Joanie gasped. "Adopt you?" she cried out. "I certainly want to know more about that."

The Adoption Story

The adoption story was something Mom had told me about many years before. But I hadn't given it much thought at the time. Now, in my the meetings with Joanie, my interest was piqued.

Mom was in her late seventies, and I spoke with her weekly. I dialed her number: "Hello Mom." We bantered about weather in Ontario to that in Alberta before I brought up the Dodd's. "I'm thinking about writing my memoir and wondered if you could tell me more about the Dodds and our move to Dawson Creek." Mom's voice lit up. "*We were moving up north near the Yukon border, in 1942, when your dad got the job of hauling goods up the Alaska Highway during World War Two,*" she said, excited at the memory. "*Ada Dodd, (Ma) and Peg approached me about adopting you.*" Mom's voice was matter-of-fact, unperturbed at such a serious request. "*Ada and Peg were worried about your moving so far away from them, that they'd miss you.*" Mom's voice suddenly rose in angry defensiveness. "*I told them, in no uncertain terms, that I wouldn't consider adopting any of my children out!*" She sounded angry at the *Dodds* for asking. It was as if Mom had suddenly realized the implications of what Peg and Ma were suggesting and how it might affect *her*. "*NO WAY*" she repeated, caustically, "will I adopt any of my children out!" But it was *me* the Dodds wanted to adopt, not my siblings. It felt like she was protesting too much–as if playing to an audience. I wondered if the notion of adoption tugged her. Maybe she felt guilt that I'd spent so much time with them and not with my biological family. Her refusal felt more like an obligation to refuse in order to avoid outside criticism.

I also speculated as to why Peg and Ma felt I would be better off with *them* than Mom. *What did they know? What were they worried about? Had they seen the welts on my thighs?*

Thinking back, I felt Mom was ticked off with *me* for asking her about the adoption in the first place, as if I was accusing her of something, of being caught out.

Of course, what I really wanted to hear was that she couldn't *possibly* adopt me to the Dodd's, because she valued, cared about me . . . or even loved me a little.

When I told all this to Joanie, she shook her head sadly and tapped her pen against her note-book. "I am perplexed about your mother in so many ways," she said sadly. "What caused her to think you were an ugly baby? Why did she cover you up? How could she beat a helpless three year old? Why did she allow you to live with the Dodd's for such an extended period of time? And what was it about your mother that Peg and her mother feared about leaving you with her? Why did they think you'd be better off with them?"

Joanie seemed deep in thought. "There's something," she said, shaking her head. "There is something that caused your mother to reject you, to allow you to be raised by another family when you were so little." She tapped her pen on her notebook. "The whole thing is a mystery to me." It was to me as well, I thought, as I left the session for the day.

The New Year's Baby

"A letter from the government, " I said to John, as we sat in our sunroom having lunch. I'll bet it's my application for my CPP (Canada Pension Plan)," I said, ripping the envelope open to read the form. "It says I have to go to the office in Windsor to apply."

Inside the CPP office, I pulled a number from the dispenser–43—found a seat, dug out my novel and read. "Forty Three," came over a loudspeaker. I shoved my book into my satchel, got my CPP forms out, and walked to agent number 10. "Martha" was on her name tag. "Good morning. How are you today?" she greeted me.

"I'm good, Martha," I told her, passing my papers to her.

"So, you're applying for your CPP," she said smiling. "You don't look a day over fifty; certainly not old enough to be collecting CPP!"

"Thanks," I replied, smiling at the compliment.

Martha ran her finger down the form checking all the boxes. Suddenly, her finger stopped. She looked up. *Had I filled out something incorrectly?*

Martha smiled. "So, you're a New Year's baby, I see," she said with a giggle.

"No," I corrected her, pointing to my birth date on the form. "I was born in October, on October 1, 1938."

"I'm just teasing," Martha smirked, her blue eyes flashing. "What I meant was, you were probably *conceived* on New Year's Eve," she chuckled.

I felt my face blanche, and my heart thudded in my chest. Scenes of the past year with Joanie flashed before me like the rewinding of a B-rate movie. *You were conceived on New Year's Eve.* I suddenly felt numb all over, and there was a piercing ringing in my ears. *I've got to get out of here.*

"Is there something wrong?" Martha asked, her eyes wide with worry. "Are you all right?"

Drawing in a deep breath, I exhaled slowly. "I'm okay," I mumbled, as the knot in my stomach loosened. "Is the application filled out correctly?"

"Yes, everything's in order," Martha said, shifting to a formal professional tone. "You should be getting your first payment in two months."

"Thanks," I murmured, turning toward the stairs. Everything suddenly became blurry. Grasping tightly to the handrail, I descended the stairs and stepped cautiously to prevent falling. I stumbled out the door into the sunshine. I took quick short breaths, in and out. I found my car and crawled into it. Martha's words flashed through my mind . . . *"So, you were a New Year's baby; you were conceived on New Year's Eve!"* Was this a clue to the mystery–the mystery of my mother? My mind raced with a jumble of thoughts . . . I started the engine, and turned up Oullette, toward home. *I was conceived on New Year's Eve.* I heard Joanie's voice. *"Your mother covered you up because you were ugly . . . Was your mother reminded of something when she looked at you? . . . of something she was ashamed of?"* I turned onto E.C. Row. What was it about my birth? Memories rippled through me. *It was the war years . . . Penhold airbase . . . airmen in Peg's photos . . . lots of service-men . . .* The light turned green and I tried to focus on the road. "I wonder if your mother had some kind of indiscretion." My eyes blinked. *Indiscretion? Shame? Is that why Mom shipped me off to Peg and the Dodd's? The Dodd's wanted to adopt me.* It was all very strange. My car bumped over the Belle River bridge. *Did Mom have an indiscretion? Was I a secret of some sort? Would seeing me remind her of it?* My mind kept spinning . . . . *I was born in 1938* . . . Veering left onto Lakeshore Rd., I turned into our driveway. Home at last, I couldn't wait to talk to John.

Digging for My Alberta Roots

"You were a New Year's baby?" Joanie blurted out when I told her about the visit to the CPP office. "Your life is such a mystery: I'd like you to do some digging into your past. Take a trip to Alberta to chat with your family–your siblings and your mother since she is still alive–to uncover this mystery."

"Mom will be 87 in December, so I don't have much time!" I said.

Home from my session with Joanie, I sat with John at our dining room table, watching the snowflakes settle on the window sill as I mulled over what Joanie proposed.

"You're awfully quiet," John said, touching my arm. "Do you want to tell me how your session went with Joanie?"

"She was pretty supportive, as usual. Since I wasn't getting anywhere with Mom on telephone calls, she suggested I explore my family history with my siblings to see if *they* have memories of my background in our family." I paused and looked at the heavy sky. Grey clouds threatened a blizzard. "She suggested I go on a 'family odyssey.'"

"So, what do you think of the idea, love?" John twined his fingers through mine.

Glancing out at the storm, I shuddered. "It could just stir the pot, open old wounds."

"But, can you turn back now after coming so far with Joanie?" John looked deep into my eyes. "You know that you *are* different from the rest of your family," he said gently. "You're smarter, have more drive, kinder, more beautiful..." he said, his hazel eyes shining mischievously, "and I'll bet none of them can make baked Alaska!"

I laughed out loud. "How the heck can I be serious, you rascal, when you make jokes."

"Okay, okay!" he grinned. "A trip to Alberta might fill in some of the missing pieces of the puzzle about you and your mother," he offered, his eyebrows lifting. "Your mother's birthday is coming up in a few weeks; that might be the time to go and do your investigating, since the family will be on hand to celebrate her special day."

Landing in Edmonton, Sharon met me at the airport. "You've sure got Mom in a tizzy," she lashed out, giving me a dirty look. "She's worried sick about you coming."

"How so?" *I had no idea I was the topic of their conversations.*

"She's afraid you'll bring up all that crap about the Dodd's and how you spent so many years with them."

"But it's a fact," I mumbled under my breath, not willing to open up the mess with her.

"It sure as hell upsets her!" Sharon spat out angrily, pulling out a cigarette. "Calling me every hour." She shrugged her shoulders at me. "She's *my* mother too, and at 88 I don't want *you* giving her a heart attack, for God's sake." She hacked and puffed on her smoke. "And don't bring up that garbage of how *you* were raised differently from the rest of us; she treated us kids all the same!" *She's bought Mom's line—hook-line and sinker.*

Sharon's voice raised in volume. "I can't believe you are so damned insecure," she shouted. "You're a doctor for God's sake! Smarten up!"

"Hey Mom, it's Gail here. I'm at Sharon's and I'm coming to Red Deer for your birthday party on the weekend." It was an eternity before I heard her response. Taking a deep breath, I added gently, "I'd like to come down today so that I can give you your birthday gift privately and spend a bit of time with you before the party tomorrow."

"Is Sharon coming with you?"

Sharon waved her hands indicating no. "She has to work," I said wondering if that was actually true.

Mom coughed and sighed. "Humm, well, maybe not today; I'm not feeling well." There was a long pregnant pause. "Maybe come tomorrow for my birthday lunch at The Steak House"

As I stepped into my rental car, Sharon handed me a card to give Mom. "You're not coming to Mom's birthday party?" She shook her head no, without an explanation.

I fared better with my sister Merla on the day before Mom's birthday party, when we chatted in a restaurant in Red Deer. She took out a cigarette, and lit up as we ordered. "Do you have any memories of Mom and Dad when you were little and living in our house in Innisfail?" I asked, hoping she could fill me in with some details about the family from back then.

"Not much," Merla said, taking a long drag. "I was only 7, Gail; hell, that was 6 0 years ago; in fact, I don't remember you at all." *That's because I'd been with the Dodds.*

"What was Mom like, growing up back then?" I asked, changing the topic back to Mom.

"She was mean," Merla said. I can't remember a kind word she ever said to me. *She was mean all right; I remembered the sting of lashes on my thighs.*

"We had a lot of sitters, though, when Dad was away, sometimes overnight," she said, blowing a cloud of smoke in the air. Peg Dodd was one of them." Merla stubbed out her cigarette when the server brought our hot beef sandwiches—the special. Merla cocked her head to the side, recalling something. "I do remember that Mom and Dad fought a lot; they were drinkers too, based on the number of beer bottles that littered the floor some mornings." Merla took a bite of the roast beef, chewed and swallowed. "I loved watching Mom get all dolled up in fancy dresses to go to dances." Merla smiled at the memory, taking a scoop of mixed vegetables. "When Mom left the house, I heard the sitters make comments . . . *"she was a party girl"* . . . *"he messed around . . . but she was no angel"*. . . . Merla took a final scoop of mashed potatoes. "I didn't understand what the baby sitters meant back then, as I do now." She took out a cigarette. "I remember seeing lots of service men on the streets in town; after all, it was during the war years."

My head was spinning . . . *Dad was a philanderer . . . Mom a party girl . . . Penhold air-base . . . airmen in Peg's photos . . .* Pieces of the puzzle—one bit of information after another—began to fall into place.

Mom's Birthday Party

Arriving at The Steak House early, I was escorted to the table reserved for Merla Burchell. Sitting down, I set the book and card on the table beside me, and placed Sharon's card on top. As the family arrived, I got caught up on all their news.

"Here they come," someone called out as Merla and Jim came in with a small diminutive woman on

Jim's arm. *Oh, my word, it is Mom.* She seemed so much smaller than on my last visit. Her wispy panda-white curls framed her wizened face of spiderweb creases. Her powder–blue eyes sparked. Everyone waved, calling out birthday wishes.

"Hello, hello," Mom announced. I motioned her to sit beside me. I passed her Sharon's card, and she spent a moment reading it. Then, a smile flashed across her entire face. "Good for Sharon," Mom exclaimed, waving the card so everyone could see. "Sharon couldn't come but she sent me this lovely card." Sitting down, she turned to me. Mom tapped my parcel and muttered, "Another Munro book, I suppose?" She lifted her eyebrows in disdain. "Don't like Munro anymore," she snarled. "Sharon loans me romantic novels that are a lot more interesting." she snipped.

Her comment cut deep. I took a deep breath and whispered, "I'd like to have a visit before I go back to Ontario."

"Well, I don't know," Mom replied hesitantly. "Maybe come over after my nap at around 7." *After 7? That means I have to stay another night in the motel!*

Just then, cake came in with a myriad of lit candles. We sang Happy Birthday. The slices were devoured, and everyone got ready to leave. When I nodded to the server, the bill came to me. My card . . . and gift . . . remained unopened on the table.

The Toe Incident:
A Nice Little Visit

Ringing Mom's doorbell, I was filled with hope for a good visit. I pushed the buzzer once again and waited. It seemed forever before I heard the lock unsnap and the door open. "Come in," she bellowed gruffly, in her gravelly voice. "Shut the door, you're letting the cold air in," she complained. "And take off your boots, so you don't wreck the carpet," she roared, as she tromped up the hallway. She seemed nervous, agitated.

Removing my boots, I set them neatly together like two stiff soldiers on duty. A bone-chilling cold struck my stockinged feet as they hit the icy, sodden carpet. Whipping off my socks, I hung them over my boots to dry before rushing up the hallway to the warm carpet in Mom's living room. Mom sat at a chair at her dining room table, rows of playing cards in front of her as if she'd been playing solitaire. I set her gift and birthday card on the table. "Put your coat on the settee," she barked, "And sit down on the couch over here." She pointed to the floral chesterfield in colours of orange, yellow and brown. I followed her orders like a trained seal, just as I had as a child. *This is not a good omen.*

Mom stared at me, her brow furrowing. I felt an attack coming. "You've got bare feet," she snapped critically.

I flinched.

"Yes," I retorted, defensively. "The entry way is soaking wet so I took off my socks to dry them."

"It's not *that* wet," Mom argued. "It was fine when I came home earlier." *She always has to have the last word... has to be right... even when she's not.* "Bare feet ruins carpet pile," Mom asserted. *What the hell is she talking about? Is she making that up just to criticize me?*

Bending her head over to one side, Mom looked quizzically at my feet, as if surprised at something. *What's she up to now?* I asked myself, feeling something sinister coming. Instinctively, I tucked one leg under my hip hiding my foot.

"Look at your second toe," Mom cried out caustically, her eyes piercing into a squint.

My body cringed as my eyes darted down to my toes. I curled them under in an attempt to retreat, preparing for a strike.

"That's so odd," Mom growled, her lips pressed tight together like a purse snapped shut.

"Your *second* toe is longer than your *big* toe," she blurted out in a puzzled tone.

The air prickled with disapproval as I yearned for my offending toes to disappear. *What the hell is she talking about? I haven't been here five minutes and all she's done is attack me from the moment I came through the door.*

Mom bent over. She drew her eyes together, fascinated with my toes. "Mmmm. I don't think anyone else in *our* family has a second toe like *that*," she insisted, frowning. "I'm sure of it."

My face blanched, my forehead rutted in a furrow of anxiety. *What the hell is she trying to say?*

Taking a breath, she leaned out toward me to get a better look. "No," she smirked. "No one in *our* family has second toes like *that!*" she repeated, her mouth turning up in a half-taunting grin.

Attempting to get my toes covered, I searched for a throw-blanket, anything to cover-up my disgraced toes. Finding none, I arched my foot, bent my knees back and tucked my offending toes under the skirt of the couch and out of sight! Shame burned my cheeks. I gasped for air. I'd been assaulted and had no bruise; I had been struck without a hand laid on me.

Mom pulled back, and sat up straight again; her lips settled into a thin, brittle line as if satisfied that she'd hit her mark. Turning to her playing cards, she gave me a dismissive look. "Well, we've had a nice little visit, haven't we?"

Stumbling outside into the squeaky Alberta snow, I retched, emptying my stomach. What the hell was this thing about my toes?

Mom Is Dying: Will I Go?

"Mom broke her hip; she's in bad shape, Gail," Sharon cried on the telephone. "At 92, she won't allow surgery; she's given up." Fear gripped her every word. "Will you come?"

My mind went blank as if all the air had been sucked out of the room. "I'll get back to you." As I placed the receiver on the hook, memories of Mom's 88th birthday charged through me. *I rented a motel room just blocks from her house, instead of staying with her; she discarded me like a worn-out slipper. She left my gift unopened and my card unread.* The memory cut like a knife. *And then that thing about my toes.* Anger surged through me. *Why the hell should I go? She's treated me like shit forever. Hell, no, she can rot in hell, for all I care. I'm not going.*

In a foul mood, I went down stairs to talk to John. "What are you going to do?" he asked.

"Why the heck should I go after all she's done to me?"

"You're right, Love; she's caused you nothing but heartache all your life. Why ask for more abuse?"

"I'll tell Sharon that I'm not coming."

All night thoughts haunted me, interrupting my

sleep. *Can I withstand another putdown, another caustic comment? Hell no!* I twisted and turned, wrenching the sheets. *But if I don't go, can I live with myself? But then again, she's done nothing but abuse me. Do I want more of that? But what daughter doesn't go to her mother's bedside when she's dying? I want to do the right thing, be a decent daughter.* I fell into a fitful sleep.

The Slice

Sleep would not come. Images haunted me. Burning rage crawled up my spine and ignited my emotions; I was flipped back in time—in Mom's condo packing up her belongings for her move to the Assisted Living facility in Coronation. A razor sharp memory cuts deep in my soul as I remember the bouquet of Gerber daisies and freesias that sat in the middle of the dining room table. I'd bought them at the beginning of the week to brighten the room during our week of packing up Mom's things. I arranged the lovely mix of colour in the blue Delft vase–a gift I'd given Mom from Holland, years ago.

All week Mom sat in her blue recliner chair. It swallowed up her diminished, ninety-one year old body. She clung to it like Velcro; it was the last of her possessions she'd take. All week, from her blue throne, she barked orders in her usual bullying way. I did as I was told; I filled boxes with dishes, bedding, and knick-knacks. The flowers remained on the table every day and brought us a bit of cheer when we took breaks. At week's end, I surveyed the flowers. *The bouquet is pretty fresh!* Only a few stems needed trimming. *I'll throw them out in the morning, before we leave.*

Just then Mom called out in a loud, caustic voice. "Throw those damned flowers out; they're stale and wilted."

"They're still okay," I replied. "I'll get rid of them in the morning."

"No, you won't," Mom argued, her voice rising, her fists clenched. "Throw them out right now, damn it."

I'd had enough of her bullying. I remained seated right where I was.

A fierce look crossed Mom's eyes as she slowly, cautiously inched her way out of her throne. She lowered her feet until they touched the floor. She leaned forward, stood up, turned around and toddled to the table.

She's going to throw the flowers out. *That's okay with me.* I smirked at how ridiculous she was behaving. Leaving the flowers in the vase, she shuffled toward the kitchen. *She's going to pitch them in the garbage,* I surmised.

I was wrong.

Mom came back to the table with . . . a cutting

board and . . . a knife.

What the hell is she going to do now? I wondered to myself. Perplexed, I watched as she lifted the flowers out of the vase and laid them across the cutting board. Her blue eyes glared, menacingly at me and her lips creased in a brittle grimace, she took the knife . . . held it out in from her . . . pointing it directly at me! . . . With a flourish, she swung the blade in the air then lowered it, drawing it across the stem of a Gerber, leaves falling away . . . ... *Slice* . . . yellow petals fell to the floor. My mouth dropped open, horror struck to the marrow of my bones. *What the hell is she doing?* Glancing over at me as if checking my reaction, Mom lifted the knife into the air once more and brought it down with a *thud* through a white daisy . . . *Slice* . . . the leaves fell away . . . *Slice* ... the sunny white petals spilled onto the floor.   My heart went cold as one-by-one each flower was sliced into several pieces, and stems and petals fell. The crimson Gerber was the last to go . . . *Slice* . . . the stems. . . *Slice* . . . the leaves . . . *Slice* . . . the crimson petals fell to the floor like droplets of blood.

My execution.

"*John, John!*" I screamed, waking up with a start, my pillow wet with tears.

John held me close as my body convulsed in sobs. "What's wrong?" he asked, gently. I couldn't speak, my breath caught in loud gulps. "How could she hate me that much," I sobbed.

John stroked my back, as I told him my dream. "Oh sweetheart, how terrible," he said calmly. "You know this is not about you, my love. It's about your mother; it's something about *her*."

"I know," I blubbered, swiping at my tears. I blew my nose. "Nothing has really changed," I murmured. I shook my head and collected my thoughts. "I still have to go, if only to prove to myself that I can rise above my pain and anger–to be a better person. Who knows, perhaps on her death-bed Mom will acknowledge my existence!

I packed my bag.

The Blind Assassin

It was June, 2001, and I was in an airplane, flying off to see my dying mother. From my window seat, Lake Ontario was a royal blue, and dotted with toy-like white sailboats. The wing banked, turning west to an entirely unpredictable terrain. *What will greet me in that landscape?* I adjusted my seatbelt and rummaged in my satchel for *The Blind Assassin,* Atwood's novel that won the Man Booker Prize last year. As I gaze at the title, the irony of *The Blind Assassin* strikes me. In *my* case my mother was the *assassin* and I was *blind*– at least that's how it felt. I was blindsided—never knowing when or how she would strike. Flipping to my bookmark, I settled back into the story, which focused on women in the 1930's. *Iris,* the main character in the story, was stuck in an arranged, loveless marriage—like many women of the time. What options were open to her should she leave her husband? With no qualifications, no career, and no ability to earn a living, she'd be thrown out of her home, have no claim to their property, and no right to alimony.

And Mom? Based on scraps of memory of stories told to me—Mom was unhappy in her marriage too. Like Iris, she was stuck with no career and no means to support herself. But unlike Iris, Mom had children to raise. If *she* left the marriage, her options were limited: she could clean houses, move in with her parents, or put her children up for adoption. Her choices were bleak. Iris' on the other hand, seemed blind to the fact that *she* could become pregnant.

Secrets! —Iris had an affair–I was fascinated with how Atwood kept the family secret so well hidden in the story. How were extramarital affairs dealt with in the 1930s? If it were the *wife* committing adultery, she'd be an instant outcast, a scarlet-woman, a pariah, or a worthless slut who brought shame not only to herself but also to her husband and the family as a whole. And what of *men* who had affairs at that time? Well, *that* was a different story entirely. They were given a free pass and let off the hook.

Mom's secret? "You were a New Year's baby," the CCP agent chuckled. I imagined New Year's Eve in 1937... Mom and Dad had a fight... Dad went away on deliveries for a few days... Mom got dolled up and went out –she was a party girl... *Was I conceived that night? Was that my mother's secret? She got pregnant with me! Oh my God, could that be it? I was an unwanted pregnancy born on October 1, 1938!*

But who fathered me? Was he a serviceman in the war? Or was he Dad? She would never be entirely certain whose baby I was—she simply didn't know. As I think about it now, a chill runs up my spine and my body quivers.

The strange outburst about my toes! What did they signify? *"None of my other children have second toes longer than their big ones."* At the time, I thought Mom intended the comment as another insult. But *now*, I wonder if it was a clue. Was my father's second toe longer than his big toe? The answer would never be known; he died decades earlier. I don't think Mom knew, either. It remains, forever, a mystery.

Not knowing who fathered me could explain Mom's resentment of me—why she couldn't look at me... why she covered me up. So many questions sat on my tongue. Was *I* the reality, the *truth* she couldn't face? Was *I* her shame, the boil waiting to be lanced? Is that why she felt relieved when Peg Dodd whisked me off to their farm?

For decades Mom's secret was safe . . . until I started asking questions. I was in my 50s, and Mom was in her 80s—about family history of the Dodd's and why they wanted to adopt me.

Now that my mother was dying, there was no chance to reveal her secret. I had to figure it out on my own. And yet, I was somehow implicated; the two of us knotted at the heart like twists in a linen rope. *Now Mom was dying, damn it and I'd never know!*

"Buckle your seat belts, ready to land," Packing up Atwood's novel, I braced myself as an image of Mom suddenly appeared how smooth will *that* landing be? The engine cuts, the tarmac rises to meet me.

Bump. . . bump. . . bump.

"Welcome to Edmonton."

RECONCILING

My Final Journey with My Mother
My Sister's Reception

Welcome to Coronation, the town sign beckons, where Mom was dying in hospital, and I was feeling apprehensive, with a sense of foreboding. *What will I find at this final destination?* I parked at the Pioneer Hotel and met Sharon. "I'm so glad you're here," she exclaimed, her arms wide, inviting a hug.

I was surprised at her positive reception given how she'd railed against me on my last visit; I felt uneasy, on guard. "How is Mom? Have I gotten here in time?"

"She's hanging in, but the nurses say it could be any day now." Dropping my luggage in my room, I got into her car and we drove to the hospital. "Mom is in a lot of pain with her broken hip," Sharon said. "So they have her doped-up pretty much; but she's awake sometimes and is able to visit with us. They told us someone should be with her when she passes, so we've been taking turns in her room. Merla is with her right now."

"I'll take my turn too," I offered, as Sharon guided me to Mom's room.

"I'll check with Merla," Sharon responded. *Check with Merla? It was Sharon who called me to come when Mom was dying.* I think this in my head; no sense in rocking the boat. As if Sharon read my mind, she added, "Merla's kind of taking charge since she has Power of Attorney and has been looking after Mom the past year," she explained. "I think she feels she's carried the ball so far, and her reward is taking control."

"But I can help," I volunteered, once more recalling how I sat with Dad when he was dying, in 1981. "I have my book and I can read if Mom is sleeping."

"I'll check with Merla," Sharon said, getting up and going into Mom's room. I heard murmuring, as they discussed the issue. *Some things never change; I'm always odd-man-out in this family--forever on the outside looking in!* Feeling powerless and at their mercy, I waited anxiously for their verdict.

"Mom isn't up to it now, Gail," Merla said brusquely in a take-charge-voice before going back in snapping the door shut like a trap door to keep the skunks at bay. Annoyed at her abruptness, I sat. *What's up with her?* Then, my mind rewound to the phone call I got from her daughter Penny, two years ago; she explained that Merla had a gambling addiction. After an enormous struggle, I insisted the POA be shared between Merla and a friend of Mom's. *Is that why she is so prickly, still pissed off with me?*

Sharon turned to me. "I'm so glad you came; you give me such comfort and strength to face Mom's death." *To comfort her?* There was no point saying anything, knowing how volatile she could be.

At that moment Merla came out. "I've got to have a smoke, Sharon; it's your turn now," she stated like a sergeant giving orders.

"You know that I can take a turn," I reminded Merla, beginning to feel anxious, wondering if I'd ever get to see Mom.

"I'll let you know later," she quipped, as she barrelled down the hall to an outside exit. I felt uneasy. *Was I being closed out all together?*

For the rest of the afternoon, my sisters took turns while I sat outside the door–an emotional wall of concrete separated me from Mom as she took her final breaths.

"I've just *got* to see Mom before she passes," I blurted out to Sharon feeling exacerbated. "Couldn't *you* just slip me in when Merla is out for a smoke?"

"I don't know, Gail," Sharon hesitated. "You know how Mom *is* about *you*." She coughed nervously. "I don't want Mom to turn on *me*!"

For the next two days, Merla and Sharon manned Mom's room. They took turns, day and night, while I stayed at the hotel at night and returned in the morning to try to see Mom.

One morning Merla came with news, her eyes glistening. "Warren and Laura are coming to visit

Mom," she exclaimed excitedly. "They'll be here sometime this afternoon." Warren and Laura had been friends of Mom's for over 40 years. When they arrived that afternoon, Merla opened the door of Mom's room and led them in, with Sharon following like a puppy. The door slammed shut like a slap in my face. From outside, I heard high-pitched voices, though I could not make out a single word said. There were roars of laughter. I was sure I heard Mom's voice in the mix. Scanning page after page in my novel, I was unable to retain a hint of understanding. *What is wrong with this picture?* I screamed in my head as a flush of anger inched up my neck and my eyes misted. They are all chatting and laughing and having a great time, as I sit alone banished like a leper. *I've got to get out of here.*

At that moment, the door burst open and Sharon rushed out, a huge smile on her face. "Mom has rallied with Warren and Laura here, reminiscing about old times. It's wonderful to see Mom so alive and happy," she exclaimed excitedly. "They've been on the road for hours and haven't eaten." She rustled in her purse, and tossed me her car keys. "Would you get a pizza for us?" She pointed down the hall. "The nurse at reception will know a good pizza place in town."

Mom Won't See Me

"I've been here for three days now, and it's time I saw my mother!" I told Merla firmly, staring directly into her eyes.

Merla shifted her feet from one-foot-to-the-other, her mouth twisting into a thin line, letting me know that *she* was in charge.

"Well, that's a problem," she said in a smug tone.

"Mom *doesn't* want to see *you*."

It was as if all the air had been sucked out of the room. Gasping for breath, my stomach turned into cold hard steel. *How could you do this to me? How could you be so fucking cruel?* Grabbing my satchel and purse I raced down the hall, out the door, years of hurt pouring down my cheeks. *So, this is your final act, Mom!*

Leaving the hospital, I walked, my mind in a whirl. *What the hell, Mom. I'm your daughter too, damn it.* Down a sunny street, I walked. What right did the sun have to shine when my heart was breaking? *For years you'd closed me out, ignored me like a shadow, trying to wipe me out, erase me from your life . . .* Dark clouds gathered, the wind picked up as I walked some more. *You'd rather take your secret to the grave than acknowledge that I existed, the secret you've been hiding for six decades.* Tears rained down my cheeks, as I walked faster to beat the storm, my heart wrenched in a vice of sadness, and pain—the kind Richard Wagamese knew so well.

> *Life can strip you raw;*
> *Some holes are never filled;*
> *Some gaps not chinked,*
> *Some chill winds relentless in their pitch and yowl.*
> (Medicine Walk; 2014 pg. 207)

Shall I Stay or Shall I Go?

Do what your heart tells you, love," John counselled. "If you follow your heart, you'll know what to do."

Mom was clinging tight to her secret, right to the bitter end. I was left with a festering open wound; it was a throbbing ache. I will never know her secret? Should I pack up and go home to John?

Something was stopping me. *What is it?* I asked myself as I crawled out of bed and rushed to the shower. As the water splashed over me, I wished it would wash away the pain of these past days. I should check out and leave right now... What is stopping me? As I picked the hair dryer, I turned on the heat, full blast. *Why don't I look after myself? Why do I stay to be crapped on yet again?* I put on makeup to cover the dark circles under my eyes. The word *'integrity'* popped into my mind. *What daughter doesn't come to the bedside of her dying mother?* But, what do I think will change if I stay? Maybe Mom will wrap me in her arms and tell me she loves me--that's not going to happen; she doesn't even want to see me, for God' sake. Why have I hung on to hope long after hope has expired?

I pictured myself getting the pizza for Mom's company. *Why hadn't I told them to go to hell!* But, that little voice in the dark recesses of my mind yelled out. *I must do the right thing; I'm not going to let my sisters point their fingers at me:* "Gail just up and left, giving us no support, leaving Mom on her death bed and wouldn't even see her to say her last good bye." I stepped into my white slacks and slipped on my navy striped top. Squeezing my eyes shut, I jutted out my chin. *I'm not going to give them the satisfaction!*

My Final Good Bye

Sharon had her suitcase at her feet. "I'm going back to Edmonton today," she said, as she took the last bite of scrambled eggs. "I've been here for a week and need clean clothes." She took a sip of coffee. "Mom seems to have perked up with Warren and Laura's visit." She paused and got out a cigarette. "By the way, where did *you* go yesterday? I saved you a piece of pizza." I glared at her in stony silence. "So, I'll stay overnight in Edmonton and come back in the morning." *A breakthrough; this could be my chance to see Mom!*

Parking myself in the hallway outside Mom's room, I read Atwood until Merla came out in the late afternoon, looking exhausted. "You can go back to the hotel, Gail. I'm going home tonight, and I've made arrangements for the nurses to look after Mom while I'm gone."

"Okay" I said as I packed up my things as if ready to leave. "I'll just go to the washroom before I head to the hotel."

"I'll be back tomorrow morning," Merla called out. She hurried down the hall and turned the corner, out of sight. Waiting a few moments to be sure she'd gone, I took a deep breath of relief. *I'm coming Mom!*

The smell hit me first—odour of old urine mixed with cleaning fluid stung my nostrils. Mom lay sleeping, the oxygen tubes attached to her nose, a tall metal intravenous rack stood to the side, the tube held firm with a piece of medical tape. She seemed swallowed up in the hospital bed, like a baby in a cradle, tiny, wizened up, a shadow of her old self, her face a mass of wrinkles like crumpled tissue paper, blue veins running like tributaries through a mass of crepe-like-flesh, and her eyes closed tight.

I sat at her bedside as close as I could in order not to disturb the catheter bag hanging below the bed. I held her frail and limp hand, resting it in the palm of mine. It was warm to the touch—and was the first time I'd ever held my mother's hand. It was a strange feeling to find it so soft, so gentle, so utterly foreign from the sharp sting of the flesh-on-flesh smacks I felt as a child. Pushing that thought to the side, I caressed each finger, around each ragged cuticle one at a time. My imagination ran wild. *What a time we could have had together, had you not been so full of fear and guilt.* "What fun we might have had!" I whispered tenderly to her silent ears, her blind eyes. *And all I have now is your hand and dreams of what might have been.*

I ran my fingers gently up to her protruding blue veins. In deep sleep, she slumbered on, her heart beating in time with the whosh, whosh of her breath as she sucked the oxygen from the plastic tube. *Will you drift off now, never knowing that I came, never looking into my eyes, never hearing my voice, never feeling my touch?* My heart wrenched at the thought as I swallowed the lump that rose in my throat. *Have I come too late?* "I'm here, Mom; it's Gail," I said in a hushed murmur. "I'm right beside you." Her body flinched; she moaned. *Did she hear me? Does she know I'm here?*

What will Mom do if she wakes up? Will she scowl and order me to leave, to get me out of her sight like she'd done all my life? How will I ever stand it if she does? My stomach lurched. *Oh, my God—maybe I shouldn't have come after all.*

The glowing orange light of sunset streamed through the window. I sat frozen holding my mother's hand. The room darkened. The nurse came in to roll

Mom over. "Won't be too much longer now," she said, kindly, after she took Mom's blood pressure and pulse.

My eyes stung. I'd come too late, too late to give me comfort. The touch of her hand was all I had left. I sat and waited and listened to the whosh, whoosh of the oxygen, the only sound in the room.

It became dark and the rays of moonlight caught on the metal intravenous rack casting a shimmer of light and twinkling like silver across Mom's face. Suddenly she stirred and her eyelids fluttered as she struggled to open them. They were misty and watery now, only a hint of the old China blue. Her forehead pinched as she squinted to focus. *Oh my God she's awake!*

"Who are you?" she asked, her voice just a murmur, rough as sandpaper. "Is it you Merla? Sharon?"

My heart plunged; my hands trembled. *Will I tell her it's me?* Taking in a great gulp of air to gain courage before I spoke, I lowered my voice to a soft hush. "No, it's *me, Gail*."

Mom's eyes opened wide in recognition and surprise. *She knows it's me. I'm sure of it!* I sucked my breath waiting nervously. Her thin lips trembled. She coughed lightly to clear her throat as if wanting to speak. Her lips pursed open slightly. Her voice was a tiny peep I could barely hear. It was a tone I'd never heard before, softer, gentler, with a hint of warmth.

Did I feel a tiny pat of her fingers on my palm?

"Oh, Gail, you *came!*"

Her thin sparse lashes fluttered then and her lids slowly closed over her eyes.

Those were the last four words my mother spoke before she died.

YOU CAME

The baby she couldn't look at

The child she couldn't accept

The woman who wouldn't go away

No matter how she tried

Came to her deathbed

"You came"

Her mother murmured

Forgiving herself

THE LODGE

Move to Port Dover

As we drove down Brant Hill, crossing the lift bridge to Port Dover, we met a spectacular view of Lake Erie and the Lighthouse (built in 1842). We were so impressed with Port Dover that we purchased a condo as a weekend holiday home, to be closer to our family and grandkids. During the first year, we took the grandkids to watch Santa arrive in town by tugboat, and then went to the Christmas parade afterward. On New Year's Day, we watched the brave diving into Lake Erie for the Polar Bear Dip. Canada Day festivities included a boat parade, followed by a giant parade. On July 13th, 2008, we were bowled over when 100,000 bikers roared into our town of 7,000. There was always something going on in Dover. We loved Dover so much, that we sold our home in Pointe-Aux-Roches and moved there permanently. John brought Qigong to Dover, and volunteered his services for years. With Qigong, John came into his own.

The Lodge

While I loved the harbour and lighthouse of Port Dover, I longed for a cottage right on the water, like we had in Pointe-Aux-Roches. I started looking.

On a beautiful January day in 2006, the sun was

high in the cobalt blue sky, Lake Erie a steely blue, and the icy shoreline slushy. I found it. A gigantic cottage, with 165 feet of frontage (the size of a city block) and the look of an estate—had a For Sale sign thrust into a snow bank. It was a real find!

The day we drove out to The Lodge, as it would soon become known—was wind-whipped. We met Lynda Purves, the agent, who led us through snow banks to the front door. We stepped into the two immense rooms, partially divided by a long wall. I was struck by the two-story height of the ceilings. John's eyes lit up in surprise; he stretched his arms above his 6 foot 3 height, with lots of room to spare. Out of the two large picture windows, I imagined future spring gardens with rows of lemon daffodils blowing in the wind. "What a wonderful living room," I remarked, thinking the corner to the left could be a perfect reading corner. We followed Lynda down a cavernous hallway that was covered with loose asbestos tiles. The floors can be covered with hard-wood, I rationalized, picturing our antique pine jam-cupboard on the right-hand wall. To the left, was a tiny two-piece bathroom with a filthy toilet and an ancient pedestal sink. It was grimy with dust and the caustic, sour smell of urine. In my mind, I saw a large vanity, toilet and shower. *It will be absolutely beautiful!*

Across the hall, there was a bedroom large enough for a queen bed and dresser. Peacock blue curtains sagged and cobwebs dripped from each corner. I pictured new window treatments and a fresh coat of paint.

As we entered the kitchen, my mouth hung open as I stared at its enormous size, as big as a restaurant with ten tables and chairs. It had room to spare! My mind went into overdrive–I mentally placed our black antique subtle bench under the plate-glass window, the pine dining table and chairs in the centre, and the 1930's ice box in the corner. *What a marvellous room for the family!* Along one wall were cupboards with brown, louvered doors. Painted white, they would give the place a cottage feel look, especially when the blue drapes and peeling wallpaper were removed.

The kitchen island was a disaster—brown pressboard, an ancient stainless steel sink that was grey with ground-in-dirt, a leaky faucet had left permanent water stains. But, I rationalized, with crisp white cupboards, an island with a new sink and counter top, it had great potential.

We looked at the lower wing next: it had a magnificent pool table, right in the middle of the room. *Wait till the boys see this; they'll love it.* When the panelling was painted, it would be a fantastic games room. Two tiny bedrooms, large enough for a single bed and dresser, would be perfect for the grandkids. The hallway led to the master bedroom; it was a room large enough for a king-sized bed, side tables, end cupboards, a dresser and a lounge chair to boot! A four-piece ensuite bathroom with a giant jetted bath tub, separate shower, toilet and sink was next to it. I knew it could be a lovely ensuite, despite the room's hanging cobwebs and filthy fixtures. The price was right—$189,000—and I loved it. John looked at me and shook his head, knowing I was crazy about new projects. "If you like it, then go for it!" he said smiling. We took possession in February 2006!

It took a year to complete the renovations. The final touch was the nautical design on the peak above the picture window, on the outside. It was pure genius. "It was the Haney Place of *Green Acres* from the 1970 sitcom," a friend said, chuckling after the renovations were completed.

The following year, to pull the disjointed architecture together, we built a veranda around the cottage. The roof, supported by white pillars, gave the place an aura of class. In early October, I designed raised flower beds around the circumference of the property. At an open house, we invited family, friends and contractors to join us in celebrating our achievement. As a final gesture, the family brainstormed a name. We came up with "The Lodge". It became the centre piece for family gatherings and for entertaining—and a playground for our grandkids—Nathan, Matt and Amy.

The Lodge was also a place that enabled John to perfect his Qigong. He continued teaching Qigong in Dover, as well as with neighbours on the lake, every

Thursday morning at 11 o'clock. There was green tea afterwards, a Thursday tradition.

An image suddenly comes to mind of John, in the side yard—his long arms extended far out in front of him, his back bent in a perfect arch in a gentle move as he draws his arms back, his body straightening vertically before it bends and stretches again like a well-oiled machine in slow motion. His body is a silhouette against the backdrop of the waving, cobalt water of Lake Erie. He came into his own.

In later years, as we aged, The Lodge became a peaceful place for John and me. We spent hours looking out at the lake and the changing hues of colour over the seasons; we smiled at the goslings waddling down Lakeshore Road behind their mama, we marvelled at the heron gliding gracefully into Maple Bay, the flitting of monarchs in the flowering shrubs preparing for their flight south, and the lifting of the migrating geese and the golden glow of sunsets as the sun took its last breath over the crimson maples of Maple Bay.

We were blessed with family, friends and life at our beloved Lodge we loved so much. It was our final home together before John passed, in August 2019.

CAREGIVER ROLE

Chicken Pox and Blood Clots

June 20, 2013 will forever be etched in my mind; it was the day John contracted chicken pox and son Blake suffered blood clots on both lungs!

Just moments before, John and I were sitting in the Emergency Ward in Hagersville hospital. We suspected that John had sunstroke or a very bad cold. After the physician took John's blood pressure and checked his lungs and heart, he looked into his throat. His eyes opened wide in surprise. "Oh, my word! You have chicken pox! How old are you?" the doctor asked, noting John's thinning white hair.

"I just turned 80," John replied in his croaky voice.

"This certainly *is* an anomaly," the doctor joked, "for an 80 year old to come down with full-blown chicken pox." He laughed out loud. "Go home and drink lots of fluids; that's about the only recommendation I can give you, and come back if you observe any signs of fever."

John was slumped in the passenger seat, with moist beads of perspiration shining on his forehead, and his eyes sunken and dull, when my flip phone hummed. Pulling onto the shoulder, I reached into my purse, and I pulled it out. A message flashed. "*Blake is in intensive care with blood clots on both lungs. Doctor needs permission to operate!"*

"Look Hon, Blake is the priority here," John croaked in a gravelly voice. "I'll be just fine with all the juices and soups we've got," he assured me. After asking a neighbour to check on John while I was gone, I packed my bag.

That was the beginning of my summer of hell running between two hospitals—Hamilton and Mississauga–for weeks on end.

Blake: In ICU

The smell hit me smack in the face; the mix of antiseptic and urine caught in my nostrils. A maze of tubes snaked in all directions from Blake's body: an IV bag of solution hung on a rack, a catheter bag dangled under the bed, and a clear plastic line gurgled under his nose as it pumped oxygen into his lungs.

As Gina jumped up and opened her arms, I said, "Thank God, you were there with him when it happened. If it wasn't for you, he'd have died,"

As we sat quietly at the foot of Blake's bed, all we heard was the whoosh of the oxygen machine. Whoosh in-and-out; whoosh in-and-out. A nurse came in to take Blake's blood pressure; the machine made a wu wu sound. Blake winced in pain and opened his eyes.

"It's Mom," I whispered. "How are you doing? *Such a stupid thing to ask!*

He nodded. "Aaa ri I ess." *Why was he sounding like that? Maybe it was the drugs he was on.* Then he added, "Ad ur errr" sounding like, *"Glad you are here."* –a ghost of a smile on his face.

Gina and I sat watching as my darling boy struggled to survive. Worry clawed at my heart.

Blake Battles MS

Whoosh in, whoosh out, whoosh in, whoosh. The sound made my mind wander. It seemed only yesterday that I heard the *Thump, Thump, Thump* coming up the stairs in our home at Pointe-Aux-Roches. It was the July 1st weekend of 1991– Canada Day, thirty years ago. Thump, Thump, Thump! *What was that sound?* We found out the next morning.

Blake staggered into the kitchen grumbling. "My legs felt like they were stuck in cement blocks, and I had to hang on to the wall for dear life so I wouldn't fall over, as I pounded up each step," he said, as he stumbled across the floor, planting his feet wide apart as if on the deck of a boat trying to balance. "Now I've got a splitting headache, " he complained, rubbing his hand across his forehead. He suddenly called out: "My eyes, my eyes!; I can't focus!" His eyelids fluttered and he squinted, straining to see. The hairs on the back of my neck stood up and goose bumps prickled my arms. *There was something wrong, really wrong!*

Wondering what to do, I peppered Blake with

questions. "Would you like a cold compress on your head? Do you want to lie down? What would that make you feel more comfortable?" Blake took my arm as I helped him to the sofa, lowered him down, and tucked a pillow under his head. "I'm going to talk to Dr. Yee, our neighbour, just a minute away. He's a GP and maybe he can tell us what's going on and what we should do."

After Dr. Yee examined Blake, he nodded to me and we stepped out to the patio. "I believe this could be something serious," Dr. John said somberly. "I suggest he go back to Mississauga, right away, to see his *own* doctor." He paused, before adding thoughtfully, "It sounds like it may be a neurological issue." *Oh my God! It's worse than I thought.* My heart sank to the bottom of my stomach.

Suzie packed up their gear to get ready to head back to Mississauga.

"Would you like me to come, son?" I desperately wanted to be with him.

"Don't worry Mom, I'll be okay with Sue."

Reluctantly, I pulled back. *After all he was a 27-year-old man; I have to respect that.*

As Suzie and Blake rolled out of the driveway, I waved my hand until they slipped out of sight, completely. John wrapped his long arms about me, and I nuzzled my head into his chest and wept.

Blake's MS Diagnosis in 1991

"Blake wants you to come." Suzie's voice was strained, urgent. "He's in the Credit Valley Hospital going through a battery of tests. I'm waiting on the 6th floor."

"I'm on my way."

After the gruelling three-hour drive on the 401, I pulled into the hospital and found Suzie sitting on a bench in front of the elevator. She smiled wanly, dark circles under her amber eyes. "Thank goodness you're here." We wrapped our arms tightly about each other in a deep hug.

"Where's Blake? How is he doing?" I whispered in her ear. At that moment, Blake glided through the glass door in a wheelchair, an orderly parking him at the elevator in front of us. "I'm here, son," I called. He moved his head toward the sound, his eyes blinking trying to focus. *My goodness, I don't think he can see us!* His face was ashen, his cheeks hollow, his forehead a wave of furrows.

"Thanks Mom," he murmured, nodding his head.

The door of the elevator opened and the attendant whisked the wheelchair onto the platform facing us. Blake looked out, his eyelids bulging wide; they were the size of loonies, and filled with terror. The elevator door drifted shut, and he sank from view.

We waited in Blake's room until the neurologist came. He was a tall man wearing a white jacket, and he exuded confidence. "I'm your son's neurologist," he said, directing his gaze to me. "A sample of the cerebrospinal fluid revealed damage to the central nervous system," he stated officiously, without an ounce of emotion. My throat tightened and my mouth went dry as I copied down this information in my notebook. "We also tested for brain aneurisms, ALS, Epilepsy, Parkinson's, Polio and Lupus and the results were negative." *Well, that was good, wasn't it?* I was grasping for hope. He paused . . . examining his notes. "We found damage to your son's optic nerves, in both eyes." My hands trembled so much my scribbles were illegible.

"So . . .", the word hung in the air for a long, anxious, uncomfortable moment. The doctor coughed to clear his throat. "So, we suspect that your son has . . . Multiple Sclerosis. *Oh my God! This can't be happening. Tell me it isn't so!* Suzie gasped, and twisted her hands anxiously in her lap.

"How do you know for sure?"

"In your son's case, tests revealed two significant results." My pen was ready. "Damage to the nervous system and damage to the optic nerves. But, in your son's case the optic nerves in *both* eyes are affected," he stated emphatically. "The *only* disease that damages *both* optic nerves is MS," he said, as if to *punctuate* the accuracy of his diagnosis. My stomach knotted. *Oh my God, will he be paralyzed and be in a wheelchair for the rest of his life?*

Wiping my eyes with the back of my hand, I mumbled, "What about his vision? He can't see. Will he be permanently blind?"

"Regarding your son's blindness, I predict it will be temporary, but we don't know for sure because every MS diagnosis is "case-specific", meaning that every person may experience symptoms only attributable to *them*.

Blake Battling Blood Clots

Coming out of my daydream, in 2013, I stared at Blake battling for his life. I asked myself, "What now?" How can this be happening to him on top of his MS? *He could die!* My hands trembled, and my stomach wrenched at the thought. Time stood still as I sat, waiting, watching and worrying about Blake's future. Nurses came to take his blood pressure and change the IV bag. When they left, the room was quiet except for the whoosh of the oxygen tank. Whoosh in, whoosh out, whoosh in, whoosh out. Suddenly, the door opened. A woman entered; she wore a white jacket over a blue-striped dress, and carried a stethoscope around her neck. She checked on Blake and wrote something onto her clipboard before turning to me. She extended her hand. "I'm Dr. Lee, your son's cardiologist," she said, her eyes smiling. "Your son is lucky to be alive." *My heart soared!* "The blood clots were caught in time." She paused before going on. My heart twinged. *Is there something else?* "But I am afraid a small blood clot travelled from his lungs, up through a tiny hole in his heart, to his brain." Her eyes clouded ruefully . . . "He's had a stroke."

Oh, no! I gasped. "Is that why he was speaking so strangely? Will it affect his MS? What is the treatment?" My questions dripped with anxiety and fear.

"It's too soon to say," Dr Lee answered. "Only time will tell." *What else could possibly happen to my son?*

Once Blake was breathing on his own, Dr Lee removed the oxygen. "The worst is over," she assured us. "We're moving him to the cardiac recovery wing. *He's made it! My God, my boy's made it!*

With Blake in recovery, I spent more time with John. At the same time, I was anxious to know how Blake was dealing with the aftermath of his stroke. *How could I see Blake and leave John?* I had to make a choice. Knowing that John was safe in hospital for a day, I decided to go to visit Blake. Pulling onto 403 heading to Mississauga, I felt torn to pieces with guilt. *How the hell can I be in two places at once?*

Blake Re-learns to Speak

Blake's eyes lit up when I walked into his room. "It gd se u," he muttered, his eyes smiling.

"Good to see you too, son." He waved a piece of paper in the air. "What's that in your hand?" I asked him.

"dis is fr spsh trpy," he said, sounding as if his mouth was full of cotton balls. But if I listened carefully, I understood what he was telling me—*This is speech therapy*. He points to the letter 't' as he makes a 't t t t' sound like a toy Tommy gun, before pointing to the letter 'p'. Full of determination he continued going down the list of letters attempting a sound for each.

Suddenly his cell phone buzzed and he responded. "lo?" he paused, listening. "K, shrl," he answered. It was Cheryl, his secretary. *My word, he's running his company from his hospital bed! There's no stopping my boy!* As I listened, I was struck by inspiration. "Think about *texting* your messages to Cheryl," I suggested. "That way your communication will be more authentic." This was a strategy I'd written about professionally in my ESL book. Blake hesitated at first, but then tried it. "Hi Chrl." He was surprised she responded. They texted away for a few minutes, as Cheryl deciphered and responded to Blake's texts.

Since Cheryl's texts in reply were correctly spelled, Blake's speech and spelling improved dramatically. Today, in 2025, his speech is perfect.

Advocating for Blake

Although Blake's language was gradually improving, the operation and stroke set him back physically. One day, I watched two attendants–one on each side–hoisting him up into a chair. so they could make his bed. He had lost the strength he'd once had in his legs and now was unable to stand up or take a few steps alone. *It was so damned hard to witness such a quick decline.* At the same time, I was glad he could get the physiotherapy he needed. Before he went back to his condo, he'd have to gain back some of the strength he'd lost.

One morning at home, my flip phone thrummed. Flipping it open, I read a message from Blake, "Hd nrs dsrge . . . cm..." It took a second to decipher. *Head nurse discharge . . . come. Oh my God! They're going to discharge him!* I threw on some clothes, slapped a washcloth over my face, brushed my teeth, and ran a brush through my hair. Grabbing my purse and tote, I tore to Credit Valley before Dr. Lee made her rounds. I got there just in time. I dropped my bag and had just sat down when Dr. Lee came in. "Good morning," she said a big smile spread across her face. "Blake, I have good news!" Her eyes gleamed with delight. "You've made fantastic progress; your haemoglobin and blood count are great, and your lungs are clear," she chimed excitedly. "So, you're good-to-go; we can discharge you today, and you can go home!"

"Noooo," Blake managed to call out. "Ned fzo tharpe." His forehead wrinkled into a frown, his face blushing pink with anxiety.

Interjecting, I said as calmly as I could, "Dr. Lee, I am thankful that you saved my son's life." I took a breath before I added, "But he is certainly *not* ready to be discharged. As you can hear, Blake requires more speech therapy and physiotherapy for his body so that he can manage on his own when he gets back to his condo."

"He can get physiotherapy as an out-patient," Dr. Lee suggested, dismissing me.

"But you don't understand," I responded, trying to explain, without success. "Blake has MS and the operation and stroke has set him back so much that he can't even get out of bed by himself," I countered, my voice rising with anxiety. "It takes two nurses to lift him out of bed. He lives alone. He can't get out of bed by himself—how in the world would he be able to get to 'Out-Patient' services for physiotherapy?"

"Oh," Dr. Lee remarked, her lips pursing in thought. "I didn't realize that," she said, as she filled out a requisition for speech and physiotherapy at the ReHab (rehabilitation) Center in the hospital. She lifted up her pen and spoke directly to me. "You are a good advocate for your son, and I recommend that you inform staff in *all* other departments of the hospital to make them aware of your son's overall condition, so they can *realistically* assess his needs."

On that day Dr. Lee learned that Blake was much more than a healed heart!

Blake's Hospital Adventure

"You've got your electric scooter, Blake," I said smiling. "I hear you took it for a spin the other day." Blake's eyebrow raised, a quizzical look in his eyes.

"Ow u no?" He smiled impishly.

"Wesley called and told me all about it." I chuckled remembering the story he told me. ...

"The day after I got Blake his scooter from his condo, I came to visit him. I came to his room and he wasn't there. So, I checked with the nurse at the desk. She told me Blake had been riding around the Cardiac Wing in his scooter. But when I looked up and down the halls, I couldn't find him anywhere. When I reported that to the Head Nurse, all hell broke loose. They initiated a Code Blue alert. **"Patient missing! Patient missing! In a red wheelchair; his name is Blake Heald."**

When Wes told me the story, I couldn't stop giggling, as I imagined how Blake must have looked from the perspectives of visitors and patients as he ripped down hallways in his flaming red scooter, his blue hospital gown flapping out behind him. I pictured the quizzical looks on faces as he whipped into the elevator, pushing buttons to the rehab centre to visit buddies he knew from his previous stay in hospital. I visualized the shock of patrons and staff at Tim Horton's when they saw this half-naked guy in his scooter ordering a double-double . . . and not paying for it. What did people think of this semi-clad guy, sipping coffee beside the fountain in the garden, as they entered Tim's?

Blake looked at me and grinned. "I cm bk wn I hr nm cld." He shook his head puzzled. "I dn'no th fss wz bt." He paused then, his eyebrows raised. "u gt go tms to pa fr mi cfe!"

When I went down to Tim's and offered to pay, the cashier laughed. "It's on us; your son made our day!"

Final Reflection

Today, in 2025, I think back over the three decades since Blake was diagnosed with MS, and I am saddened by the myriads of losses he's endured. Now his body has let him down completely. Even his right hand—the one he successfully texted with just months ago—has failed him. In spite of it all, he is in his office every single day. He's planning to purchase a houseboat this summer and travel the waterways of Ontario. *Why not*? Last summer, he rented one, hired his PSW to address his personal needs, and commandeered his brothers, Wesley and Ron, to go with him down the Port Severn locks one weekend. At sixty-one, he plays a mean game of Bridge with all the old ladies in his condo every Tuesday night. He loves debating politics with me on our nightly phone calls, though we both agree that Donald Trump is an ass. Blake still maintains his sense of humour. After a recent pub night with his brothers, the waitress ran out with one of his shoes. Blake looked down at his shoeless foot, his lips curling up into his lop-sided-grin.— "You know, they're only cosmetic!"

As the end draws near for my amazing son, I have one wish—that I will pass first.

Home to John:
Could It Get Any Worse?

"Blake survived," I told John excitedly, when I called him. "He's going into rehab so I'm on my way home!" I was so excited that I hadn't noticed that his voice was raspy and weak.

As I pulled into the driveway and leapt out of the car, my heart was bursting with happiness at being home, a huge smile on my face. There was John coming around the corner of the Lodge to greet me. He shuffled, in slow motion as if knee-deep in water. Panic bubbled in my throat. *Why was he walking like that? What had happened to him?* He began to sway ready to topple over! Racing over, I reached him just in time, holding his arm to steady him, seeing him up close. His face was gaunt, his eyes hollow, and his sweatshirt hung limp on his six-foot-frame. My chest tightened in fear. Holding him like a fragile doll in my arms, we shuffled inch-by-inch at a snail's pace one-step-at-a-time until we were inside and he was settled into his blue wingback chair. Questions gushed out of me like a geyser. "Did you drink the fluids? Didn't Alison check on you? Why didn't you tell me when I called?" Anger churned through me.

"Alison called." John's voice was ragged; it was coming out in short spurts. "But, I told them I was okay." He grabbed at his throat in agony. "Because I thought I *was*."

I suddenly felt guilty and sympathetic at the same time. "What have you been eating?"

"Ice cream to soothe my raw throat."

"Oh, my goodness," I stammered. "That wasn't enough sustenance; you're probably dehydrated; I've got to get you to the hospital!"

"No," John croaked. "You just got home from looking after Blake, and you need a break. We'll go to the hospital tomorrow—if we have to." *Oh, my darling, you are always thinking of me!*

John went to St. Joe's Hospital in Hamilton to recover. Travelling from the Lodge each day, I sat with my sweetheart, stroking his forehead and holding his hand. His throat filled with pox, he could eat nothing solid; he could only sip on water, juice and broths. He slept most of the time as I sat, day after day, fretting, feeling helpless, with dread creeping up my body. *Will he survive this? Will I lose him?*

Days crawled into weeks, with no improvement. As I made the trek from home to St. Joe's—a daily ritual—I got weary. One morning, I was so exhausted, I could hardly get out of bed. I'd left John sleeping peacefully the night before, so I took a break for the day. Sitting on the deck to eat my breakfast, I finally relaxed. The early morning dew glistened on the flowering shrubs as I sat sipping my tea; it was peaceful, serene. The shrill of my landline shattered my solitude. Anger licked through me. I needed this moment to last. I'd come to the end of my tether. Closing my eyes, as the last of my tea slid down my throat, I reluctantly lifted the receiver and pressed *talk*.

"Gail?" Anne, John's favourite nurse answered, her voice sounding anxious.

"Yes?" I replied, a feeling of foreboding washing over me.

"John fell."

"Oh no!" Panic leapt in my throat.

"He struck his head and may have a concussion," she said, desperation in her voice.

"I'll be there as soon as I can." My stomach tightened, tense.

"Good," Anne replied, her voice softened with relief. "He's asking for you."

When I got to the hospital, John was in a wheelchair with an IV contraption on wheels trailing behind him. He looked pale and drawn, with deep shadows under eyes that had become sunken. He smiled wanly. *Oh my word, he's going to die!* Memories suddenly swam into my mind –our first date . . . those eyes, like gazing into deep pools of coffee. . . Our first kiss . . . in his jeans and Stetson, tourists asking directions thinking he was a Calgarian . . . .

I want him back!

"Oh Gail," John croaked hesitantly, so softly I had to strain to hear. "I'm so glad you are here," he whispered. He coughed before adding, "I thought this was the end." His velvet eyes faded then, like melting chocolate as he fell into a deep sleep.

John eventually recovered from pneumonia and came home. He was a frail skeleton of his once healthy self, he had lost over 30 pounds from his six-foot-three, 175 pound-frame, and was now just 145 pounds. At home I nursed him back from the abyss of almost losing him.

A Monitor or Not

Gaunt, frail and weak, John and I sat on the deck that fall. We held hands; the cone flowers were fading, humming birds were sucking the last of the nectar from hydrangeas, and Canada geese squawked south —all the signs of hunkering down, and closing up for winter. John was up every morning, napped in the afternoon, and watched 'Judge Judy' in the evening. Though weak, his humour was back.

"You've stolen my covers," I complained, one October morning.

His amber eyes sparkled. "Good thing you've got *me* to keep you warm," he quipped with a grin. Nevertheless, John required personal support workers (PSWs) for his personal care. He was unsteady on his feet, and I worried he'd fall and break a hip. A health monitor would give me peace of mind. When I brought up the subject, John balked. "Why are you against it?" I asked. *It's was a no-brainer to me!* John's forehead twisted in waves; he was silent for a long moment before he spoke. "It's just that I've lost so much." His eyes were pools of pain. "I'm unable to bathe myself, need help dressing, can't eat cheese, potato chips and Kielbasa, foods I used to love so much, or drink beer and wine any more. Driving is out of the question." His voice was filled with disappointment. "And now you want to tether me like a dog on a leash," he barked.

I felt a momentary pang of guilt. "I can see how a monitor would be another loss, but it would mean the world to me to know you were safe when I was out getting groceries."

John let out air in his lungs in a deep sigh. "I know you are suggesting a monitor because you love me," he muttered, tears in his voice. "A monitor would give you comfort. But for *me* it would spell a loss of power and control." His voice cracked like a whip. "As caregiver, you'd have all the power and control over every decision . . . for me it means a complete loss of who I am."

After years of pondering, I wonder if, subconsciously, I believed the monitor meant John would be with me longer.

How Do I Cope?

"Look after yourself, Gail," my friends told me, empathetically. "You've been looking after

John and Blake for months now." There was worry in their eyes. "You have to look after yourself or you'll burn out, and then what good are you for John or Blake?" Terry quoted statistics, "Caregivers frequently die before the patient!" he stated with authority. "You'd better heed that data."

After all their comments, I realized that I didn't have a clue of what it meant to look after myself–I had no point of reference—my own care had never been a priority I could afford myself. How could I look after myself when John's and Blake needed me more? *How does one do that?* "What are practical, doable ways?" I asked myself.

Looking back, after months of the regimens at both hospitals, exhaustion had set in. I woke up several times in the night stressed about John's pneumonia . . . his weight loss . . . The next night I was plagued with anxiety for Blake, about whether the rehab was doing enough for him. *How will he manage when gets back to his condo? What kind of care will he need?* One evening, driving home after seeing John, I got so confused that I took the wrong road. At times, I found myself hyperventilating and trying to focus my thoughts; I felt completely out of control. One morning, I woke up in a cold sweat, having no idea what to do, or where to go– immobilized, confused, in a daze with no energy to shower or get dressed.

In a panic, I called Marylin, our geriatric counsellor. *Why hadn't I called her sooner?* She listened intently as I told her what was happening with me.

When I stopped talking, she began. "For starters, you need to stop travelling to both hospitals and running yourself ragged." Her tone was more direct than I was used to. "Going at *that* pace you'll burn out!" she warned. "You need to take time for *yourself*." Her voice softened with empathy. "John and Blake are safe where they are, and in hospitals with professionals looking after their needs," she reminded me. "You need to start looking after *you*."

"How do I do *that*?" I asked, frustration in my voice.

Marylin began asking me questions rather than telling me what to do. "When was the last time you sat on your deck and meditated as you looked at your gardens, or watched butterflies, before heading out to a hospital? Have you considered going to a museum? When did you have coffee with a friend? Are you exercising, or reading anything enjoyable?"

"No, no, no, and more no's," I countered, tears smarting. "It's my *job* to look after them; I don't have the right while they lay suffering." I stuttered with excuses.

"Well, you *do* have the *right*," Marylin, insisted warmly. "*You* are valuable too. And *you* are the only person who can make a change in this terrible situation; no-one can do it *for* you." she admonished, kindness and understanding in her voice.

Tension eased from my stomach as I took her advice. Within days, I started an exercise regimen, and took time for a pedicure—the whole time feeling guilty for looking after myself! On an inspiration, I called my friends from Dover to come to the Lodge for afternoon drinks. Their friendship gave me strength, and filled my soul. Over the weeks, I was gradually replenished, and able to give my best to both John and Blake.

I realize, now, that writing my memoir, also became a form of self care—once Blake was settled in his condo attended by PSWs. Up at 4 am, I checked on John to be sure he was breathing and sleeping soundly, before I settled into my swivel chair at the computer to work on my memoir. My mind fresh, thoughts flowed; my dream-world of words insulated me from the reality I was facing down the road. Those four hours were *my* time and I coveted every moment. John and my writing were my world . . . until the end came.

Forgiveness Meditation

On a July day in 2018—the year before John passed—we were sitting on the deck of the Lodge, our final home. John was bundled up in a fleece-lined-hoodie. Even the light breeze off the lake cut through his thin emaciated body. Quiet, the only sounds were the waves lapping the shore, that John no longer heard.

I sat in my rocking chair reading *Marrow*, by Elizabeth Lesser about the power of forgiveness. It struck deeply. Moving over to the wicker couch, I turned to John. "Is there anything I have ever done that has upset or hurt you in any way?" I asked gently, folding our hands together as we did our hearts.

"Yes," he snapped abruptly, without giving it a second thought.

Stunned, speechless, I swept my mind for what it might be. "What did I do?" I stammered, stuttering my words.

"You sold my painting of the Conquistador at the yard sale at Port Dover," a hint of annoyance in his voice.

That was thirty years ago! Has he been harbouring that hurt all this time? I felt a pang of guilt. "I didn't realize the picture meant that much to you," I muttered, feeling embarrassed.

"It was the first painting that I hung in my apartment after my divorce." His eyes ached.

A twinge of remorse gnawed at my heart. "I'm so sorry," I said ruefully.

"It was kind of thoughtless of you," John muttered in a brooding undertone.

Recalling the incident, I had to admit that John was right; I *hadn't* considered his feelings about the painting; it didn't fit our décor... *my* décor... *my* colour-scheme. When I stopped to think about it, I never even asked him if he wanted to keep it. I reached for his hand. "I see now that I ignored your feelings–will you forgive me?"

"I forgave you a long time ago," John chuckled with a wink and a lop-sided-smirk. He squeezed my hand. Pensive for a moment, he looked thoughtfully at me." Is there anything *I* have done to hurt *your* feelings?"

"I can't think of a single thing" I blurted out laughing. "I aired all my grievances in counseling, years ago." I patted his hand, savouring the moment of understanding and appreciation of each other's perspective—a kind of reconciliation.

A tormented look suddenly came across John's almond-brown eyes as if something deep was bothering him. "There is *one* thing I regret," he lamented, tears in his voice. "I have such a terrible time remembering your birthday." He pulled his lips to the side of his mouth. "In my head, I know it's October first," he said, giving his head a shake. "But September is usually such a warm month, and I don't think about the cool days coming. Then, September 30th has passed, and I flip over the calendar page, and there it is, October first, and I'd missed your birthday . . . again!" His eyes were pools of pain.

"John, in all our years together you've only forgotten it once or twice, and I knew you didn't do it on purpose," I said, patting his hand attempting to assuage his guilt.

My mind at peace after airing and resolving our grievances, I snuggled into his shoulder; the bond between us entwined us together so powerfully. With John I could truly be myself, accepted as I was . . . feeling loved as I'd never been before- more honest and trusting. *Will we have another summer together?*

No matter–this moment was complete.

As I reflect on that exchange now–after John has passed–I marvel at how our relationship became ever deeper from the moment we said our vows on April 21st in 1979–almost forty years earlier—and we continued to discover new things about ourselves, until the very end.

Birthday Traumas Put to Bed

A goldfinch pecked at the seeds on the antique chair sitting in the corner of the garden that summer before my birthday. A lonesome loon–an elegant duck in a black and white tux—wailed as it called to its mate across the lake–a mournful sound that John couldn't hear.

"You'll be 80 in October," John remarked, his voice strained to sound light. "We should do something *special*." his voice was tender and warm. "Birthdays are so stressful for you, Hon; you were never properly *birthed*."

"What do you mean?" I queried, confused by his comment.

"Your mother never properly celebrated you when you came into this world—you were never valued, not really wanted."

I was touched by the depth of John's understanding: he understood how waves of sadness swept over me when my birthday rolled around each year; it struck me to the very marrow of my bones. John was silent for a moment, words thick on his tongue.

"I'm plagued with worry about how you will manage your birthdays, when I'm gone."

"Don't talk like that," I cried, tears clogging my throat. "You'll be with me a long while yet." But in my mind, fear gripped my heart. I'd depended on John to get me through my birthdays over the years. *How will I ever manage when I'm on my own?* John's eyes brightened.

"Let's celebrate your 80th this summer when the gardens are at their best?" John suggested, squeezing my hand. *Is he wanting my party four months sooner, afraid he won't be around in October?* Sliding the thought aside, I suggested, "How about a garden party in August when the hydrangeas are at their best. It can be my *fake* birthday party," I called out gaily, trying to sound positive. "We'll bill it as our *thank-you* to our friends and neighbours for all the help they've offered over the past year. No one will guess that it's my 80th birthday celebration too."

The house crackled with activity on the day of the party. My dear friend Tracey arrived with boxes of wine, fruit and vegetable trays, birthday cake and sunflowers. Taking John's hand, we shuffled to his blue wing-back chair, my heart swelling with gratitude at the sacrifice he'd made over the years validating my value and worth and quelling the dark clouds of birthdays past.

As the room filled up, I waved my arms. "Welcome everyone. I want to thank all of you for your kindness over the past year; your generosity was overwhelming." People nodded their heads.

Son Ron spoke up. "This is also a pre-celebration for Mom's 80th birthday." There was a collective gasp. Tracey came out with the birthday cake and led everyone in singing "Happy Birthday," before taking the cake to the kitchen, for later.

Alison, my teaching colleague of twenty years, spoke up next. "When I married my first husband, Verner, our wedding was a spontaneous affair." She paused. "I wasn't pregnant," she added hastily, amid much laughter. "Gail and John were our only guests. John walked me down the aisle, and Gail stood up as my bridesmaid." Alison looked out over the crowd. "Now, I'd like *you* to tell me something you appreciated about Gail." Comments flowed . . . "Gail is the heart of our Maple Bay . . . a great neighbour; . . . hates barley soup! . . ."

Ron took out a slip of paper from his jean pocket and surveyed the crowd . . . such a handsome man at 52: his body was sleek and trim; his eyes sparkled with mischief. "An important thing about Mom is her acceptance of all people. Growing up, there was a boy on our street who was mentally challenged. *You never know what he might do to your children,* the neighbours warned. "But Mom invited him to all of our birthday parties, to make him feel like he belonged."

Friend Penny waved her hand. "I've known Gail for over 20 years, and she has always been like a mother to me, always there cheering me on."

John, Alison's husband, smiled to the crowd.

"You might not know that Gail was the first woman—in a hundred years--to carry the Mace at the graduation ceremony of the Faculty of Education, at the University of Windsor."

At that juncture Alison and Ron got into a friendly spat. "I want to go last," Ron said.

"No," argued Alison, "I need to go last."

"But I'm her *son*," Ron insisted, "*I* should go last."

"Sorry," Alison said, taking control. "It's important that *I* go last because I have a special ending.

Gail

When I think of you now,

I see your lovely home,

Your peaceful lake (mostly!) and your beautiful garden,

I see your garden in particular,

As a reflection of your life

You <u>planted</u> yourself in Waterloo

When I first met you.

Your desire to further educate yourself and others

Took you to many countries, universities and schools

You <u>spread the seeds</u> of how children learn,

With your lectures, the books you wrote and published

By heading up a department at the University of Windsor…

You still do so at your local school in Hagersville.

(Do they even know the treasure they have, I wonder?)

Your published works will explain to those who wish to follow

How children acquire language, writing and reading skills

These were the days you <u>bloomed</u>

And yes, there were times

Like all of us have,

When you <u>wilted</u> and <u>fell</u>.

Those days were dark and difficult for you

However, as challenging as these days were

Like dots on a map

They have taken you on your life's journey and

Made you the woman you are today

You <u>transplanted</u> yourself

Set down your <u>roots</u> at the lake

Here you began to grow again

You have regained your courage

You have compassion

You have made many connections

You have a wonderful generosity of spirit

You have <u>weeded</u> out the unnecessary

With John at your side

You have created and nurtured an environment

Of love and peace

You are in <u>full bloom</u> again

You have found your "self."

'There are no roots more intimate

Than those between the mind and body

That has decided to be whole.' (rupi kaur)

So what else will you do?

There is still that wild rose in you!!

You go into your 8th decade

Stronger, wiser and timeless

And in the words of Reba McIntyre,

'To succeed in life:

We need three things:

A wishbone

A backbone and

A funny bone.'

You have all three!!!

Alison
August 19, 2018

Reflecting now, in 2025, and John gone, I sit alone on the deck. My eyes sweep across the gardens and a warm glow comes over me. Closing my eyes, I reach back to memories of birthdays past, leaving a deep emotional hole that waits to be filled. For years, I expected John to chink the cracks, to make me whole. He did his job well for over forty years.

It is no longer *his* job to rescue me on October first . . . to chase away the phantoms of my mother who was unable to nurture her third child. Because of John's love, I must finally take on that responsibility *myself* to nurture my own soul and celebrate my arrival on this earth. Full of love for myself, I will spend the rest of my time living and loving others, until the end.

Final Months: The Palliative Kit

Over the dark days of November, when the snow kissed the ground, and the garden showed nothing but wilted dead leaves, the wind whipped through the maples along Lakeshore Road. Their naked limbs were like arms of skeletons, and reached up into the low-hanging sky. Winter was coming. John was tucked in bed for his morning nap before the careworkers came—I ignored the fact he'd been sleeping almost 20 hours a day. Dust danced in the shaft of sunlight that streamed through the kitchen window as I washed our breakfast dishes, the only sounds were the tinkle of the porcelain bowls against glass tumblers. Quiet and lost in thought, I folded the hand towel and hung it on the rack inside the door under the kitchen sink.

The telephone screamed, jarring the silence.

"Do you have the *kit*?" I recognized the voice of the palliative care supervisor.

"What kit? I'm not sure what you mean."

"*The End-of-Life-Kit!*" she snapped, as if I should know what it was. "You need it now that John's assessment is downgraded on the palliative scale—he's close to death."

Fear stung my heart. "No," I quipped. "He's not dying; he was reading Leonard Cohen's book yesterday; he's doing just fine!"

Denial.

The Last Christmas

Winter came with a vengeance. Wind-whipped snow pelted windows so crusted with frost that I could barely see the drifts outside. They swirled, reaching almost to the rooftop. John sat, morose in the corner in his blue wing-back chair, his granny glasses perched on his nose. He was reading Leonard Cohen's latest book of poems. He looked up, a forlorn look in his eyes. "I don't think I can manage another winter here in the Lodge." I tucked his warm log cabin quilt in around his emaciated body.

He looked so miserable, so disconsolate, I wanted to do something special to cheer him up. With Christmas coming, I recalled the tale he told me about the doll he'd gotten under the tree when he was in kindergarten.

One morning—or was it afternoon–while John slept–I sat at my computer and started the story, "Jackie's Doll." John was called 'Jackie' until age ten.

That Christmas morning–our last Christmas together–John unwrapped the tissue from his present. His eyes grew large and his mouth stretched into a broad smile, "*Jackie's Doll,*" he said, his voice low as he stroked the cover with loving eyes. "This brings back wonderful memories." His voice was filled with nostalgia. His shoulders relaxed as if remembering that time, over 80 years before. "Would you read it to me?"

"Of course!" I said, thrilled at his reaction. He handed me the book, and I started. His eyes lit up when I came to the part about his Dinky cars. "I had a lot of them and I kept them organized in a special box." When I read the part, "*he scraped the hoarfrost with his chubby little fingers,*" John stopped me. "I never had chubby fingers; my fingers have always been long and skinny, even as a child." He hesitated a moment and rubbed his chin. "But I guess, for a children's story, it sounds better to have the little boy have *chubby* ones!" I smiled and continued reading as John nodded his head at the parts he liked. However, every so often he'd interrupted me waggling his long index finger to set me straight on certain details. At the end of the story, John nodded. "You certainly got the ending right; that kindergarten teacher was really kind." John rubbed his finger on his white-bearded chin. "I really loved that doll."

JACKIE'S DOLL

Jackie sat on the cold linoleum floor playing with his metal cars as they flew under the ironing board and crashed into the radio.

"Stop that racket," his mother scolded, "I'm trying to listen to 'Lux Radio Theatre.' You know it's my favourite radio program. You'll have to put your cars away if you can't do as you're told," his mother said angrily. "Why can't you play quietly like your sister Gloria does in her bedroom?"

Jackie tried to play quietly, but the cars seemed to have a mind of their own. "Besides," he thought, *I don't have a bedroom of my own like Gloria; my bedroom is under the stairs and isn't big enough to play with my cars*. Rrmm, rrmm crash, rrmm, rrumm crash, rrumm rrumm... crash.

"All right that's it," railed his mother, "I can't hear any of my program with those noisy cars; you'll have to put them away."

Jackie gathered his cars one by one and lined them up neatly along the windowsill and admired the designs the frozen dew had made on the windowpane. He couldn't see through, so he scraped the hoarfrost with his chubby little fingers until he'd made a hole big enough to look out into the yard at the drifts whipped by the howling wind. He thought of his Dad up north in the lumber camp and wondered if it was as icy cold as this when he cut the trees and hauled them out of the bush with the team of horses. In his last letter, he included a note just for him that his Mom read to him. Oh, how he wished he could read those letters himself. Maybe he'd learn to read next year in Grade One. Even so, he remembered every word his Dad wrote about how he had to get up early before the sun came up, how warmly he had to dress before going out to the bush, and how he appreciated the wool hat and mitts mom had sent him. He told how he loved the two giant workhorses, Rex and Barron, he worked with. His dad had even drawn little pictures of the horses pulling the trees along the snow. But the best part of his letter was when he described how he and his friend Pete could saw trees faster than any of the other loggers. He always ended his note by telling him to be a good boy for his mother. Jackie thought of his Dad's long arms and how warm and cuddly he felt when he lifted him off his feet and pressed him into his chest. Jackie missed his Dad and wondered why he had to work so far away from home.

"Will Dad be coming home for Christmas Mom?" he asked. "He didn't last year, remember?"

"We'll see," was all she whispered, tears in her voice.

Last spring and fall his dad had been laid off when the ground up north was too soft and soggy for the horses to go into the bush. That's when Dad had to go on "relief." Mom and Dad were really upset about it, but Dad had explained, "No work, no pay; no pay, no food. "Damned Depression!" he heard him exclaim under his breath.

But Jackie was happy that his Dad was "on relief" because he had time to carve a wooden train for him, and made building blocks and string toys. Jackie would sit for hours and watch in wonder as his dad carved magic from a block of wood.

As Jackie made designs in the frosty windowpane, he remembered when Dad took his hand in his and walked him to his first day of kindergarten. Jackie liked playing with the other boys in the class and especially enjoyed the building block centre even though the blocks were not as big as the ones his dad had made at home.

And he recalled that day after school when he and Dad went for a walk in the park to see the fall leaves–red, gold and bronze. Many had begun to fall to the ground, so Jackie gathered the brightest ones to take home so Mom could iron them between wax paper. Before they left for home, they sat on a park bench and Dad gently put his burly arm around Jackie's shoulders and whispered, "You know I'll have to go back up north soon, Jackie, now that the muskeg is hardening with frost. I'll be leaving sometime next week."

Jackie's heart sank with disappointment, but

he knew from the way Pop was whispering that he was reluctant to leave as well. So, Jackie wanted to cheer him up. "That's all right, Dad," he managed to say, "You'll still write me letters, won't you?"

"You bet," was his response.

It wasn't long before the fall winds blew all the leaves to the ground and the first snow fell as Jackie trudged to school in his high galoshes. True to his word, Dad wrote letters every week but it just wasn't the same as having his Dad with him every day.

On one particularly cold day, just before Christmas, Mom's friend, Hazel, came over for tea. "Go into the living room to play," his mother told him, "I want to talk to Aunt Hazel." So, Jackie reluctantly took his wooden train into the living room and made it chug around the furniture, choo choo, whooooo, under the Christmas tree and back to the living room door.

He heard his mom making crying noises. "I don't know what we're going to do," she sobbed. "Stanley sends his cheques regularly, but with rent and groceries, we can hardly make ends meet." Jackie stopped his engine and listened. "I managed to get a doll on sale for Gloria, not the one she wanted, mind you. You know all the girls want the "Eaton's" doll. But I just can't afford that. Heaven's, I don't even have enough money for a present for Jackie. And to top it all, Stanley wrote to say he wouldn't be home for Christmas!"

A lump came up in Jackie's throat and he could hardly breathe. *Dad's not coming home for Christmas again this year!* He struggled to keep the tears from rising in his eyes and crawled to his bed under the stairs so he could think by himself. He missed his Dad so much and knew that there wouldn't be any of Dad's hand-made toys under the Christmas tree on Christmas morning. This was not a Christmas he was looking forward to.

On the Saturday before Christmas, Jackie decided to walk to the outdoor skating rink down the street. The big kids played hockey while Jackie and his friends slid around the ice with a piece of wood playing their version of hockey. Playing with his friends made him forget that his Dad would not be home for Christmas. They played for several hours, going into the ice shack periodically to warm their hands and feet on the pot-bellied stove stoked with firewood. The smell of sweaty socks and steamy woollen mittens filled the air. Jackie couldn't seem to get warm so he headed for home.

On his way, Jackie met his mom's friend Hazel, who stopped to wish him a Merry Christmas. She had a giant bob under her arm. When Jackie arrived home, he put his boots in the shed, hung his mitts on the hook and stepped into the kitchen. The heat burst upon him with the smell of cookies and hot chocolate, a welcome from the frigid cold outside. He tiptoed across the freshly washed floor to the heat register where he stood gingerly allowing the heat to rise over his frozen toes and up his pant legs.

"You must be frozen half to death, Jackie. Look at your cheeks, they're beet red. You should have come in ages ago! Come here and let me rub your feet to get some feeling back in them. I'll get you some hot chocolate and shortbread in a few minutes."

Jackie felt a whole lot better after both his feet and tummy were warmed up and didn't feel nearly as sad as he had before.

On Christmas Eve Jackie and Gloria got ready for bed and were allowed to open one present . . . it was their new pajamas, which they wore as they prepared snacks for Santa. They sat on the sofa watching the lights on the Christmas tree blink off and on, making the long strips of silver icicles sparkle in different colours. After hot chocolate and cookies, they went off to bed to wait for Santa. 'Maybe Santa could bring Dad home for Christmas. After all, Santa *was* magic!

Gloria woke up first and pulled at Jackie's arm to get up. They rushed to the tree.

"Look," cried Gloria, "Santa brought me an Eaton's doll, just what I wanted. It's so beautiful!"

Jackie looked and saw another package with his name on it, a pretty pink box, large enough for a dump truck. When he ripped off the paper and lifted the lid there was the most beautiful doll he had ever seen. It wasn't as big as Gloria's but it had soft arms and a head that moved and eyes that clicked open and shut. It was even wrapped in a fuzzy blue blanket. He carefully eased it out of the box and held it close to him and he thought of how his Dad rocked him on his knee. Even though his Dad couldn't be with them for Christmas, just holding the doll made him feel close to him.

Just then the phone rang. It was Dad. As his mom talked Jackie bounced from one foot the other waiting for his turn to talk. Finally, it came. "Hi Dad," he said, "Santa gave me a beautiful doll. When are you coming home?"

"Not till spring son, but I've made lots of building blocks for you and I'll bring them home for you then, OK? Can I talk to your mom now?"

Fortunately, Jackie was out of earshot when his mom described how Jackie had gotten the doll. "You see," she whispered, "Hazel gave me the Eaton's doll for Gloria because she knew how hard-up we were. So, then I gave Jackie the doll I'd gotten for Gloria. He seems so pleased with it."

For the rest of the holiday Jackie played with his doll. He fed her, dressed her and rocked her in his arms. He could hardly wait to take it to school for 'Show and Tell.'

On the first day after the holidays, he carefully

bundled up his doll–partly to keep her warm and partly to keep her hidden–so no one could see his surprise.

"What did you get for Christmas, Jackie?" his friends asked

"I'm not telling–you'll see at 'Show and Tell time.'"

After the children took off their coats, boots and hats, they gathered around the circle for sharing time. One by one the children brought their objects and set them in front of them. Eddie shared first, showing the class how his bulldozer could move across the floor and raise the blade up and down. Shirley brought a stuffed bear and demonstrated how its arms moved around and around. When it was Jackie's turn, his eyes sparkled as he unfolded the blanket from around his doll.

"Look," he grinned, "her eyes click back and forth, her hair is curly and look at her arms, they're soft as velvet. Want to feel them?"

"Oh," the class murmured; some of the boys pointed and giggled. "Jackie got a girl's present." Jackie's heart sank, and he wrapped the doll up so no one could see her.

Fortunately, Miss Oak, the kindergarten teacher, rescued the situation. "What a beautiful doll, Jackie," she exclaimed. "And I love how you cuddle and nurse it just like a real father would do with a newborn baby. I'll bet your father held you like that when you were little." Jackie beamed and thought his father probably had done that. "Would you like to put your doll in the home centre so the other boys and girls can play at being good parents?"

"No," Jackie said, "She's too special. I'd like to take her home." So, Jackie wrapped up his doll into a bundle and placed it gently beside his galoshes in the cloak-room. He could hardly wait to get home so he could play with his doll.

This was a Christmas Jackie would always remember.

****

Our Last Valentine's Day

The wind raged; it whipped snow into waist-deep drifts across the road and into the yard on that day in February 2019, just months before John died. He was wobbly on his feet, and had less energy than last month; he needed a walker to prevent a fall. The bookmark in Cohen's memoir hadn't moved in weeks. But he was still with me . . . giving me hope.

"I have no Valentine for you, Hon" John said with a saddened heart. "And the roads are too bad for you to go to town to get one for me.

"Not to worry, love, I have one for *both* of us in my file of cards," I responded, hoping that would cheer him up.

"That's not the same," he lamented, his words dripping with tears. "I want a card from *me* alone."

A memory tugged at my heart, as I recalled the first Valentine card John gave me –a red construction paper heart with lace doily paper trim. It was so sweet. "Would you like to make one this year?" A ghost of a smile curled his lips. "I have construction paper and glue. What do you think?"

John's eyes glowed warm. "Okay," he replied, his face lighting up. "But I'm not sure I can cut out the heart."

Is he too weak to handle scissors? "What if I cut it out so you can fill in the words you want to say." *I'd better keep this simple!* "Three words would be great."

"I love that," he said, relief dripping off his tongue as I handed him a cut out heart of cherry-red paper. "Thanks Hon," he said and tucked it into the back of Cohen's book. "I'll work on it later."

The day before Valentine's Day, I sneaked a peek at the red heart in his book. Not a word was on it. A chill of guilt ran through me. *Maybe the task was too difficult.* I went to my card file and located my Valentine card. *It will have to do.*

Just as I snapped the book shut, John tottered out of the bedroom shuffling his walker toward my desk, lowering himself onto my armless-swivel-chair. I rushed over, alarmed. "That chair is too unsteady for you; it could tip over," I said, fear licking through me. Placing my hands at his arm, I guided him gently onto the seat of his walker, clamping the lock in place. "What is it you want, and I'll get it for you?"

He pointed to the top shelf. "That dictionary up there." I handed it down to him and went to the kitchen to prepare his breakfast. Pages rustled as he flipped through the dictionary stopping at times peering at lines of print. "This isn't a very good dictionary," he called to me. "It doesn't give a detailed description of the word I want." His brow waved into a furrow of frustration as he slapped the volume shut. In one swift movement his bottom lifted from the walker, his arm swung up and the dictionary flew out of his hand. He swayed, his body quivered, eyes racked with fear. I tore in from the kitchen and caught his arm, just in time. He hesitated for a moment as I got him turned around. He clung to the walker, handles tottering toward his wingback chair. As he moved away, I noticed the bent-over-stoop of his shoulders and how gaunt his body had become; he was a shell of his former self. My heart lurched at his sudden loss of stamina and balance. Pushing down the brake handle, John lowered himself cautiously, gingerly, into the wing-back-chair, clutching to the firm arm-rests.

"What the heck were you doing with the dictionary, anyway?" I said, trying to be cheerful and hiding my distress.

Waves of worry wove across his eyes. "I was looking up a word I wanted to put on your Valentine's card, and I couldn't find the definition in the dictionary," he moaned, lacing his fingers together. "I've been struggling the last two days about how I was going to create this card for you." There was such torment in his voice. "And I couldn't find the words I needed." His eyes cast downward. "And now I don't have the strength to even write them down."

A tender ache bruised my heart. "No problem; I can do that for you," I said, as he passed the Valentine heart to me.

"Print the word . . . *beautiful* . . . " I smiled as I wrote it down in my best primary hand-writing as I speculated what the next two words would be? . . . *loving . . . kind . . . fantastic?*

John looked up, a sense of purpose written across his face. "Now write *political*."

Political? I was startled, dismayed. *At least he hasn't lost his sense of humour!*

"That's the word I was having so much difficulty with, and the dictionary was no help at all." John looked at me, his eyes soft and kind. "I admire how you see things from a *global* perspective . . . the relationships between ideas—universally . . . in such a caring, and empathetic way. You care about the world." A look of satisfaction spread across his face. "So, on my Valentine—beside the word 'political'– write 'sees relationships; is a global thinker.'"

John chuckled then. "But now I've gone over the three-word-limit!"

Spring Brings Grief and—Acceptance

March was biting cold. Rain, mixed with snow, slashed down the window panes with a vengeance. The promise of spring was in the distance. Signs of John's decline became more evident—walking was slower and more unsteady; his hearing was getting worse, and his body so stooped, his head curled toward his slippers. An English Major, a writer of poetry, he no longer wrote and Cohen's book lay silent on the table.

That's when John stopped winding our antique oak clock, something he'd done every evening since the day we purchased it, 30 years earlier. The last time he put the key into the slot and twisted it till taut, the final turn before placing the key behind the clock face, its terminal resting place was April 20, 2019. When the hands wound down the next day, the long hand sat reposed at the Roman numeral V, the short hand sat half way to the V1—at 25 minutes past 5. This is where the hands remained forever. . . on that 21st day of April, our anniversary of 40 years.

In the days that followed, twin threads ran through me, grief for the future without him, and happiness when he survived another day. Happiness and grief—the waiting game was excruciating. Kubler-Ross described this experience as "Preparative Grieving"; I called it hell! The future without him was so painful that I'd rather die myself than have him leave me. I felt responsible for keeping John alive; it was my job to address his every need. I couldn't take time away from him in case he needed me... for fear he...

Daylight lengthened, maple buds swelled ready to pop, forsythia splashed clouds of yellow and tulips were ready to explode crimson—and I finally came to grips with reality; there was not a single thing that I could possibly do to prevent John from dying.

It was a moment of *acceptance*.

TIME STANDS STILL

Time stands still
on the hands of the ancient oak clock
encasing the black Roman numerals
the clock he faithfully wound
every Sunday evening
marking time for meals and meds
for over thirty years
till his shrivelled fingers
could no longer heave the hefty spring
the worn and darkened turn-key
the clock gave out its terminal sigh
the frail needle-thin slivers
of steel coming to a full stop
locked forever at half past five
as the low slanting rays of sun
cast shadows over the forsythia
on that Sunday evening
the spring before
my beloved made his final trek
into the unknown

Gail Heald-Taylor
October 2024

Frail Days: Final Conversations

It was the middle of the afternoon, July 2019, just weeks before John died. "It's a gorgeous day," I whispered softly to John. "Would you like to go out onto the deck for awhile?" There was a ripple of movement as he rolled over onto his back, his hazel eyes opening, bleary and watery, as he tried to focus. I wanted to believe the faint stretching of his lips was a grin. John dragged his legs over the edge of the bed and slowly wrenched himself up into a sitting position. He stretched his right foot as he reached for his black leather slipper and attempted to wiggle his foot into it. I reached down, pushed his foot completely in, and lifted the back of the slipper up over his heel, doing the same with the left. He gripped the walker handles firmly and hoisted his body up gradually, shakily, until he was standing.

Donning his red hoodie and blue-plaid quilted jacket and matching navy cap with the University of Windsor logo, he was ready to go. He grasped the handles of the walker, and took slow, plodding steps out the door to the deck. He parked the walker and he stepped tentatively, sliding onto the soft cushion of the wicker chair. Looking out at the lake, the sun made ripples on the water. "They are fairies, dancing," John said, a bit of drool oozing from the corners of his mouth. *Always so fastidious, this drooling must be so embarrassing to him.* But not to me. I'd wipe his drool forever, if only he could stay with me one more year... or two.

"You created this garden," John said, squeezing my hand. It is a show piece." His bony fingers stroked my hand. "It gives me comfort knowing you will continue living here." His eyes glistened as he cleared his throat. . . .after I'm gone."

I blinked quickly to stave off tears.

John's voice turned soft and low. "You work so hard at looking after me, and I'm so useless now." he whispered dejectedly. "What good am I to you?"

"Oh, my goodness," I replied, swallowing the lump rising in my throat. "You've given me the *world*! You help me solve life's problems, helped raise my boys. You loved me, valued me. You've given me everything I've ever wanted and needed." I stroked his hand gently. "How will I ever manage without you?"

That was the last conversation we had.

RENEWAL

Reaching back in memory,

I review my life more clearly now

how your unconditional love

is pivotal in my rebirth

With you I am

adored not abandoned

accepted not rejected

worthy not worthless

valued not criticized

affirmed not spurned

encouraged not belittled

hopeful not hopeless

empowered not powerless

truly loved unconditionally

Reality Strikes: Who Tells John?

The horizon woke slowly, spilling yellow light that welcomed that summer morning of July 30, 2019. The gardens were lush with colour: the pink verbena, shasta daisies—a wash of white—and the sweet scent of lavender permeated the early morning dew. These gardens always beckoned John; this was the place he loved to sit to watch for butterflies, orioles and the sassy cardinal. *Maybe we will sit out later.* A damp chill ran up my spine. Taking the last sip of tea, I went inside to prepare John's smoothie for his breakfast. I whipped in an extra raw egg and ignored the fact that over the past week he'd only drunk one Ensure for the whole day. Checking on John, I asked if he'd like come out for breakfast.

"Sure," he mumbled as I got the walker ready for him to swing out of bed.

"I can't move," he said," his voice filled with surprise and fear.

"Can you roll onto your side like you usually do?"

"I just can't seem to do it," he stammered, sounding frustrated as he pushed his arms to no avail. He didn't have the strength to roll his body in *any* direction!

Jennifer, John's personal care worker bounced in, then. "How's John doing today," she chirped.

"Not well," I said, explaining to her that he refused to eat, was sleeping most of the time, and his weight was down to 120 pounds. "And now he hasn't the strength to get out of bed."

She called palliative care.

Within an hour, Susan, the palliative care nurse, came. She smiled warmly, her eyes full of empathy as we tiptoed softly past our bedroom so we wouldn't disturb John. We settled in the sitting area. "So, tell me what's going on?" Susan asked, taking out a notepad from her satchel, peppering me with questions—about John's intake of food, sleeping, his weight, his strength. When Susan finished her notes, she laced her fingers together and put her index finger up to her lips. "It sounds as though John's body may be shutting down," she murmured softly, with alarm in her eyes. She reached for my hand and stared deep into my eyes. I knew that look. Silence hung in the room; I waited for the words that clung silently on her lips—the words I feared the most—the words I knew were true.

Susan eased out of our driveway. *Who will tell John?* Her car glided west onto Lakeshore Road. *Will I have to tell him?* I tracked Susan's car as it rolled around the curve of Maple Bay fading out of sight. *How do I tell John?*

Coming away from the window, I noticed Leonard Cohen's book on the drop-leaf table. John's Granny-glasses were perched on top and an envelope stuck out, marking the last page John had read—the poem Leonard Cohen had written . . . Opening the book, I read the poem aloud to the silent room.

You Got Me Singing

You got me singing,

Even tho' the news is bad;

You got me singing;

The only song I ever had;

You got me singing;

Ever since the river died

You got me thinking

Of the places we could hide

You got me singing

Even though the world is gone

You got me thinking

I'd like to carry on

You got me singing

Even though it all looks grim

You got me singing

The Hallelujah hymn

You got me singing

Like a prisoner in a jail

You got me singing

Like my pardon in the mail

You got me wishing

Our little love would last

Like those people of the past

(Leonard Cohen,

The Flame Poems and Selections from Notebooks).

A shadow of loneliness folded over my heart as I shuffled down the hall to tell John.

The Final Goodbye
August 2, 2019

In the palliative care room, I unloaded our things. The moment John saw the wool-lined-log-cabin quilt, his eyes glistened with surprise. "You brought my blanket," he exclaimed joyously, as I lay it on his shivering frail body and right up to his chin. I pressed it tightly along his spine, just as I had at home, and settled in a chair beside him, reaching for his hand. Days pass, visitors come.

John's long fingers stroke the red and blue quilt. He lifts a corner, motioning me to crawl in. His eyes wash over me like a kiss, saying his goodbye.

Vigil

In the palliative care bed

they lie asleep

like children, changelings curled

and cupped for warmth.

They look at home, at peace,

accepting

that the time is near

and ready now

for what's to come.

Him dying

slow

with each short breath.

Her trying

hard

to ease his death.

Her arm

draped over him

a part

of his frail frame.

Their bodies landscaped

by a favourite log-cabin quilt;

its yellow, red and orange angles

starred with knotted deep green wool

like bone-meal nourished blades of grass.

I take a chair

and wait for them

to wake.

Mark Kikot
August 6, 2019

Ron Is Coming

The air was thick and heavy. Only a few fluffy cotton-ball clouds floated in a sky as blue as Venetian glass. *It was not right for the sun to be shining. John is gone! The sky should be overcast in gloom to mark his passing.*

I suddenly needed Ron's support. He'd been on the road for hours; he was coming from the teacher's camp at Eagle Lake, north of Huntsville. I watched and waited, sitting on my deck-couch, the wicker chair, beside me, now empty. Ron was coming, and I could hardly wait. I spotted a dark vehicle turning onto Lakeshore, winding around the copse of trees at Maple Bay. It was shiny and sparkling in the sunlight; it slowed down, as it eased up the driveway to the Lodge. My heart leapt into my throat. Ron was here. My 52-year old son was a handsome man! Trim body, hair cut short–just so– his golden goatee flecked with strands of silver, his eyes sparkled and his lips stretched into a broad infectious grin. "How are you doing Mom?" My eyes bubbled over, every time I heard that phrase. I nodded, my feelings raw. Ron sat in John's chair. My heart pinched. He took a drag on his cigarette. "We talked a lot about John, last night around the campfire, and the kids were all pretty upset," he said, blowing out a puff of smoke. "John was their *real* grandpa as far as they were concerned, Dad and their Grandpa Sivier gone."

A pensive, far-away look drifted over Ron's eyes. "You know Mom, John was a *good* man. He modeled what a *good* man should be." Ron said, a serious look in his eyes. "I appreciated that he never pretended to take over the role of our Dad or be a disciplinarian, like a lot of Stepdads do." I wondered if Ron had picked up John's dry, off-beat sense of humour, and perhaps John's distinctive fashion style as well.

"When did you last eat," Ron asked me. I shook my head. "You relax; I'm making us something." In the kitchen, he opened drawers, got frying pans out, scoured the refrigerator, and found backbacon and a carton of eggs. It was like he'd been working in my kitchen forever! As the bacon sizzled in the pan, I realized that this was a new experience– to be pampered, waited on by my adult son. It felt so comforting. Within minutes, Ron handed me a steamy plate of scrambled eggs, laced with the pungent smell of garlic (even at the age of ten; his favourite red sweater reeked of it), framed with slices of bacon.

Back outside, Ron shifted in his chair, a serious look coming over his eyes. "What are your plans for John?"

Building my courage to answer, I took a deep long breath. "John wanted something informal, here at The Lodge in this garden," I managed to stutter. "John's last wish was to spend one more summer here in this garden and . . . he made it!" Ron reached over and patted my hand, just as a Monarch butterfly landed on a coneflower. "I'd like to have a celebration of his life, something informal with people telling stories about things they remember about him."

Within a few moments, we decided to have the event on the Sunday of Labour Day weekend; we discussed who would speak. "Mark will have to speak, of course; he was John's best friend. And I'd like Alison too; she knew John really well and she will make things light with her funny Scottish sense of humour." Ron agreed, smiling.

"I want to speak as well," I said, my throat catching. "And I'd like *you* to be the Master-of-Ceremonies, Ron."

"I'd be happy to do that, Mom. You make the plan and give it to me, and I'll make the whole thing run smoothly."

"I know you will Ron; I can count on you." I reached over and patted his tanned hand. "I have a month to make the plans."

Will I Stay or Will I Go?

We sat on the deck, a beer in Ron's hand, as the sun cast shadows and the sky lit up in colour., "Now that you are alone, are you going to stay here at The Lodge?"

"Actually, John and I discussed purchasing a condo for *me* to move into after he passed—in Dover or Paris."

Ron took a swig of his beer. "There's no need for you to move to a condo to see more of *me*. We meet at the Rez restaurant about every two weeks or so; it's only a half hour drive for you and I'd like to continue that as long as we can. And furthermore, if you get to the point that you can't drive, then I will drive the *extra* half hour *here* to the Lodge to visit you."

Suddenly, Ron stood up and walked out to the edge of the deck. "This is a beautiful spot, Mom. Just look at the royal blue of the lake tonight." As if on cue, a mother goose swam by, her several goslings whisking the water like miniature propellers, struggling to keep up. "Do you always have so many geese?"

"Yes; the geese are here all year round, and we have cormorants too, and if you watch closely, you may see the herons glide toward the reeds in the corner over there; he comes most evenings."

"And your gardens, Mom! This place is a showpiece right out of *Better Homes and Gardens*!" Ron walked back to the sitting area and sat on the chair opposite me. "I can't imagine you on a dinky deck in a condo in Paris, when you have *this*!"

Ron's eyes suddenly sparkled with glee, and his lips turned up into an impish grin. In an instant, he became a different person as if–a blind had drawn down over his face, his voice changed into that of an old woman (as if it were me):

"Hey Judy," he scoffed. "I like this little bathtub-sized-patch of deck here on my Paris condo! Come on over, it's certainly big enough for two of us to sit comfortably." Ron's eyes twinkled with laughter. "You know Judy, I used to have an enormous deck that went around three sides of 'The Lodge'; that's what we called our cottage. It was covered too, so that we could sit out if it rained, or snowed, even. It had three different spots I could sit, depending on the weather."

I smiled at my son being *me* in the future.

"And Judy," Ron went on. "I love this pot of petunias I got at Sobeys last week– just the right size to fit in this soup bowl, perfect for the condo deck. But at The Lodge, Judy, I had giant containers the size of wash-tubs that overflowed with petunias! They were positioned everywhere around the property. And we had flowering shrubs—I had something blooming from early spring to late fall."

I laughed out loud and drained the last of my drink. "Hey Mom, do you want a refill?"

"Sure," I snapped back at him at him, laughing, "and put some rum in it this time!"

Ron came back with my drink and another beer for himself and stood looking out at the side yard, to the double lot on the other side of the row of flowering shrubs. "*And Judy,*" he pointed out. "*see that patch of green between us and the next row of condos that the guy mows in two sweeps? At The Lodge we had a huge property, as big as a baseball diamond from the nearest neighbour!*"

I felt a sharp stab of loss at how I'd miss my lake friends if I moved. "Okay, okay. Enough, Ron!".

"But I haven't started on the lake and or the birds yet," Ron teased. "Seriously Mom, I want you to *really* think about this." He smiled at me. "Do you want to be the lady who *sits* on her puny deck in a condo in Paris, the lady who *used* to live at the lake?" Ron reached over for my hand and looked deep into my eyes. "Or do you want to be the lady who *lives* at this wonderful place?" That scene came back to haunt me two years later.

John's Celebration of Life

Dawn breaks on Lake Erie, red and orange, like an oil painting on the still water. A mantel of cheesecloth mist hangs low on the deck; it is an August morning, the day of John's celebration of life. I picture him in the chair opposite me, drinking coffee, just as we always did each morning. He'd reach over and pat my hand. *How many mornings had we done that-- Hundred's? Thousands?* I took them for granted, believing those days would last forever. Now that he is gone, only memories remain.

Grey-rimmed clouds gather to the west, above Maple Bay, hinting of rain. Why can't the sun shine like yesterday, or be hot and humid, as predicted for tomorrow? *John deserves a bright joyous day for his celebration.* I shake my head angrily at the Gods.

It is time.

I recall only bits and pieces of the afternoon—Ron was relaxed and comfortable as Master of Ceremony. Looking out at waves of people gathered on the lawn, he introduces Adam, John's son, then acknowledges the rest of the family. He invites everyone gathered to share anecdotes of John.

Art, hands shaking nervously, picked up the microphone. "One day, I came over to see John and noticed that he was sitting facing the lake instead of the garden as he usually did. "Hey John, you're not sitting at your usual place, what's going on?" John sat quietly for a moment before responding. He rubbed his chin and gave me that sideways half-grin. *"Today I feel adventurous!"*

Granddaughter Amy steps up, "This is the letter I wrote to Grandpa last year, when he fell and we thought he was going to die."

"Dear Grandpa,"

"I wanted to write this letter so that you would know how much you mean to me. You are the only grandfather I have ever known; you spent endless days with me when I was young. Some of my earliest memories are of planting flowers at the house at Stoney Point. You read to me; you went on walks with me, and gave me the greatest gift you could give, your time. I will always cherish the time we had together. I could always count on you for a laugh and a joke with a perfect straight face. I am so 'gratelle' that you took the time to know me and share your stories with me. I love you so much, and I hope that you know you have a very special place in my heart."

Absolute silence.

At that moment, a silver van drove slowly along Lakeshore Road and past The Lodge. A passenger leaned out the window and waved his hand. "Congratulations!" he yelled, thinking it was a wedding! *Over in the corner, John chuckles!*

Mark, John's best friend, delivered the poem he'd written...

"How does friendship start? When does it end?"
In Memory of John Taylor
(May 11, 1933 – August 2, 2019)

How does a friendship start? When does it end?

We try, as best we can, to meet the need

That's shared, but cannot fully comprehend

The way it moves like Apostle's creed.

The words we choose become the bread we break,

Then sip the silence like communion wine,

And pray, or hope, that we give and take

Will make our souls a little more divine.

But since we can't be sure, we talk it out,

Or work a poem for the perfect word,

Until, beyond a shadow of a doubt,

The line is solid, true, forever heard.

Though life is gone, our memories don't die;

They gather love and make death a lie.

Mark's sonnet has perfect form, cleverly chosen words, skillfully arranged. *John would have loved it!*

Microphone in hand, Alison shared an anecdote.: "John had many words-of-wisdom for me. Coming over one time with a problem about a family, I went on and on about what the *other* person should do to fix it. Finally, I stopped and sat quietly for a moment. John looked at me intently and rubbed his chin, as if composing something insightful before he spoke. *"Alison,"* he said softly, *"It seems to me that you have a need to solve other people's problems."* His lips turned up at the corners of his mouth. *"You know, you are not perfect yourself,"* he said, gently. *"Sometimes you have to listen and attend to your own issues."* John clasped his hands together in a prayer-like fashion. *"After all you have cracks too."* He took a deep breath, *"As Cohen would say, 'there is a crack, a crack in everything; that's how the light gets in.'"*

I am reminded of the poem Alison had given John on his birthday, May 11, just two months ago.

John

Of nimble body

Quiet soul

Inquisitive mind

You have taught me many things:

To stretch before eating

To eat when I am hungry

To observe without speaking

To let the birds come to me

To listen and just be

To sit where the wind doesn't blow

To always face the sun,

To avoid seeing the shadows

To problem solve rather than create

To smile through my eyes into my soul

John of the lake

I wish you a bountiful year!

My Farewell

It is now *my* turn to speak. I stand, my legs wobbly, wondering if I will make it to the microphone before they buckle. Ron smiled lovingly as he handed me the microphone. Over at the right corner of the garden, I imagined John nodding silently.

I began.

"I am wearing this peasant blouse today in remembrance of my dear John. Images of elephants are woven into the Egyptian cotton. According to Hindu and Buddhist philosophy elephants are a symbol of sensitivity, wisdom, stability, intelligence, grace and reliability. Slow to anger, elephants are calm, patient and peaceful . . . All these characteristics embody my beloved John. . . . . John was a writer of poetry," I said, looking out at the crowd. "I found this poem a few days ago, in a folder in his desk. It was as if John was contemplating his final journey—his eulogy.

The Garden

Shadows ebbing

Sunbeams anticipating

Heaven anointed

Earth affirmed

Ourselves created

Eden germinating

Creatures realized

"And it was good."

Sun smiling

Wind laughing

Children playing hide and seek

In the garden

Providence cruciated

The garden gnome meditates

Sun foreshadowing

Wind crying

Son

Praying garden

Light of the world crucified

And in the place where he was crucified

There was a garden

And in the garden a new sepulchre.

The Last Dance

Penny stood. "I'd like to read a story about John and Gail's very special relationship. It is called, 'Our Last Dance.' It's a story Gail wrote."

OUR LAST DANCE

We sit watching TV one evening as John surfs channels . . . CTV, Global, CBS. . . Clicking on PBS, I hear Pat Boon croon, 'April Love'. "Stay there." I wave to get John's attention, until he yanks off his earphones wondering what I want. "I'd like to hear 'The Best of the Fifties'; is that okay with you?" I bellow, so he could hear.

"Sure thing," he responds, snapping onto PBS just as 'The Four Lads' belted out, *Standing on the corner, watching all the girls go by.* "John chuckles, "You can't get away with *that* song today," he exclaims, "with the Women's Movement.'"

"Right," I answer. "But let's not get politically correct tonight. Let's just enjoy the music." I couldn't help swinging my shoulders to the rhythm of the songs. "Let's dance, love." John struggles up and raises his left hand, folding mine in his, just like he did forty years before. Holding him close, I close my eyes nestling my head on his chest, his collar bone poking into my cheek, my fingers sliding down the protruding ribs of his declining body. *Only 120 pounds now, a fraction of his original weight when I first met him. . . a six-foot-three-gentle-giant.* Images of past times flood my mind—the first moment I saw him at McMaster in his navy pinstriped suit, the one I loved so much; our first date to see the 'Ink-Spots' in that nightclub in Hamilton. Back then, he stood his full six feet three inch straight-as-an-arrow elegant body–the handsomest man in all of Hamilton. My mind meanders on . . . .

Old Love

At dusk a young couple, hand-in-hand, is walking up Lakeshore Road, the red sun hanging in the air just above the charcoal treeline of Maple Bay. The sky is streaked with orange and red, and then fades to pink and purple as if a child's water colour paints have spilled dripping a kaleidoscope of colours blending into one another. In the fields west of the road, the windmills loom silently; they lazily turn their gigantic mystical limbs inch-by-inch in a clockwise direction, like the monstrous hands of Big Ben. It is quiet now, the crimson and white Canadian maple leaf flags wilt on their masts in the warm spring evening, and the mosquitoes are not yet whining for blood. Lake Erie, slate grey tonight, is smooth as ice, with barely a ripple; the evening is hushed, except for the rustling of new yellow-green leaves on the hundred year old maples along Lakeshore Road, and the muffled coo of a mourn-

ful dove. A trumpet blare from geese breaks the silence, as they rise up with a splash of flapping wings and chattering and head across the lake to scrabble for discarded soybeans left from the harvest last fall.

The young man in jogging shorts, a T-shirt, and a Blue Jays ball cap on his head looks up at the sign on the cross-beamed post, **'Maple Bay Lodge.'** "Just look at those gardens!" he says, nodding to his partner. She turns her head, her long waist-length-blond hair falling off her forehead and into her baby blanket blue eyes. "I want to have gardens like that some day, if we can ever buy our own house," she sighs, wistfully, squeezing her partner's hand.

"The hues of mauve and pink of the shrubs are more beautiful in the twilight against those pear-shaped magnificent blooms hanging from that tall bush," she points out with her finger. "They are absolutely gorgeous."

He turns to her. "They're hydrangeas, I think; my Oma has them in her garden in Hamilton." He spots the giant flower tubs. "And those pink petunias!" he adds. "They are magnificent."

"The people who live here are really old," she explains to him. "My Gran says the woman celebrated her 80th birthday, last year, at a big garden party on the lawn out front."

The ripples on the lake, of rosy-magenta-blue, fade to ebony as the sun slips under the trees, the only light now a silver path floating across the water from the third-quarter moon. Standing in front of the sprawling cottage, a pathway of stepping stones lead to the four white pillars jutting out from the deck.

"I hear music," the young girl announces, turning her head to the side as if straining to hear. "It sounds old-fashioned." She stops walking, cocking her head to listen. "I've heard that music before at Gran's cottage when I was little. "It's from the 60's . . .or 50's maybe . . . really old stuff." She starts to laugh as if the lyrics are funny and so out of fashion now.

"Look, at the window," he mumbles softly, almost a whisper. "Their lights are on and I see the old couple," he says, tipping the peak of his cap up to have a better look. "Can you see them?" he whispers to her, putting an arm around her waist.

The girl turns and looks, a smile dancing across her face as she witnesses a tall, slight man, his shoulders stooped way over, the wispy hair on his head as white as afternoon gulls, his chin cupping the head of the old woman, her hair streaked with grey, the top of her head nestling perfectly under his chin, and her arms wrapped around his thin waist. "Look at that scarlet top she's wearing, with cut-outs in the shoulders; I have one just like it in green. It's all the rage this summer," she comments, sounding surprised. "The old lady's a pretty spiffy dresser for an ancient broad of 80 years old!"

Stopping beside the mailbox, the shape of a bread-

loaf and black as the eyes of a crow, they listen to the rhythm of the crooning wafting out into the night air, tunes they've never heard before. "Look," *the young man calls out.* "They're dancing for Christ' sake." *He starts to laugh.*

Shh," she cautions, "They might hear you."

"Or maybe they are just holding each other up so they don't fall down," he chuckles jokingly, his voice softer so he won't disclose their presence.

"Oh, my goodness, he looks like he is ready to topple over any second!" she murmurs sucking in air holding her breath anticipating he'll fall.

"That's possible, I suppose; he seems pretty wobbly to me."

Peering more closely inside the cottage, the young girl sees how closely the two old people are entwined with their eyes closed and contented smiles on their faces. She pauses, taking in a deep breath, her heart pounding and sending shivers up her spine as she speaks: "You know, Hon" *she mutters, stroking his arm.* "I think they are dancing . . . dancing a dance of love.*

****

John falters. "I'm dizzy," he mumbles, his legs going all rubbery.

"Don't worry," I whisper. "I'll hold you close, so you won't fall." I strengthen my grip around his waist.

"Just sway to the music, my love," I assure him, pulling him close. We cling to each other as images float through my mind—the concerts we went to, the trips we enjoyed, the parties we held in this very room. John's left arm drops to his side. I take his frail right arm, his veins are taut to the touch.

"I'm ready for bed now," he mumbles, his eyelids flickering.

We totter down the hall as a new song comes on. . . *'Wise men say, only fools rush in . . .'* "It's Elvis," I call out. "They're playing *our* song." *'Shall I stay? . . . Would it be a sin'*

"I can't hear it," John shrugs, his shoulders sagging. *'Like the river flows surely to the sea . . .* "I know, I know," I counter excitedly, "I'll hear it for both of us." . . . *'darling so it goes . . . some things are meant to be.'. . .* Goose bumps ripple along my arms and up both legs as we shuffle toward our bedroom to the last lines of our song.

'Take my hand; take my whole life too. . . For I can't. . . help. . . falling. . . in. . . love. . . with. . . you.'

****

I stand and read my poem to John.

I See You

On sad days I look out at the lake

I see you in the waves

I hear your voice whisper in the wind

When a butterfly flits by,

I feel your fingers grace my hand and

Heart.

August 2019

Dark clouds suddenly swirl overhead; the sky darkens and the wind scatters papers. An angry clap of thunder rolls, churning the waves as they crash to the shore. Rain pounds down as if the gods can hold off no longer.

John had spoken; he's had enough!

The Gift of John's Hats

The chill in the late August evening forces the family inside. Pictures of John greet us everywhere. In every shot, John is wearing a hat, his signature look—he wore a hat for all occasions, and every mood. An inspiration suddenly strikes me. *Why not give a hat to everyone.* I quickly gathered John's hats from the pegs off the wooden racks in the hallway, his stack of caps from the closet shelf. There are dozens of them—fedoras made of felt, sheared rabbit, straw and canvas, and cotton caps in a variety of colours. I set them around the room—on chairs, across the coffee tables, and on every surface.

Adam and his boys looked at me quizzically, as if wondering what was going on. I smiled and held my arms out wide surveying the hats. "Your grandpa loved to wear hats; he had so many that I'd like you to choose one in remembrance of him."

They gasped. "You mean we can each have one?" they asked, astonished at the gesture.

"Absolutely—and please take one of his canes too," I added, pulling out the antique cream can full of them. There was a flurry of excitement as they checked them out and finally chose one to wear.

Suddenly, I spied John's 'Charlie-1-Horse-hat' hanging on top of John's black Australian oilskin longrider coat, his black, tooled, walking-boots underneath. It was one of John's classic outfits. In an instant, I saw Adam in the outfit, the image of his Dad twenty years earlier—the same tall stature as John. I set them down in front of Adam. "I wonder if you'd like any of these pieces, Adam?"

Adam's eyes glistened. "Are you giving them to me?"

"And the hat too, if you like it. It's a genuine 'Charlie-1-Horse-hat' your Dad got in Nashville." Adam picked it up, caressed the felt and stroked the feathers tucked into the one side of the band. He slid his arm in the oilskin coat, and then the other, grabbed the front left flap and pulled it over to the centre, then stretched the right one over and pressed the metal dome fasteners together with a metal-on-metal clap. It was a perfect fit! With the 'Charlie-1-Horse-hat' Adam looked just like his Dad.

Hugs and more hugs, they ambled to the door wearing one of John's hats and swinging a cane as they waved goodbye, taking a little of John with them.

My Heald grandkids also had fun choosing one of John's hats and canes. Nathan liked the winter fleece with ear flaps. Matt chose a brown fedora; I have a great picture of Matt proudly wearing it and holding a cane at his side. Amy found a white straw hat with a wide brim. Ron looked great in a number of fedora's; I cannot recall which one he finally chose.

Gifts of John's Passing

As August slid into September, 2019, the gardens were still lush, buzzing with hornets; Monarchs gathered nectar for their sojourn south; humming birds whirred by as I sat on the deck sipping my tea . . . alone with my memories. Pictures of John still graced the Lodge. Like talismans, they brought meaning and comfort, as if John was somehow still with me. They were treasures, *gifts*, and they renewed my spirit to carry on and to face the future alone. A sudden feeling of enthusiasm, optimism, unexplainable joy—a whirlwind of gratitude—came over me, as I found new meaning in John's death. I call them "gifts of John's passing."

With a new bounce in my step, I hopped into my car and drove three hours to Grand Bend, to Oak's Inn, to reconnect with Nancy, John's cousin. Their laughter and their stories of childhood endeared them to me; they helped bring me even closer to John. Visiting Nancy was a gift, and eased the pain of John's death, just a month before.

Going down to Lake Huron beach on that cold, windwhipped day, I sat on the same bench we'd sat on when he was recovering from chicken pox. I recalled harbouring so much guilt about putting myself first, when John was still so weak. *Had I done enough for him, listened enough, cared enough?* As the waves crashed to the shore, I was struck by a memory from six years earlier. John and I had sat on this exact same bench, our hands folded into each other, watching the gentle surf roll in to lap at our feet. What he said stuck with me. *"You know, Hon, had it been up to me, I would have preferred to be at home in bed at the Lodge. But now that we've been here these past few days, I feel that they have been good for me too."* He caressed my cheek. *"When you do something you need for you, it usually turns out to be something good for me as well."*

Angry autumn waves crashed across the wharf as I came back to the present. John's words relieved my guilt and were another gift of John's passing.

As my birthday loomed—my first birthday without John—I faltered; I was wary. *Would I need John to see me through it?* As I woke up, in a lather of sweat on Oct. 1st, I was on John's side of the bed, the space he'd held for over forty years. The *other* remained unruffled, the side that used to be *mine*. *If I go back to my side, will he come back and look after me on my birthday?* I yanked the covers up overhead and sorted my thoughts. John was the only person who really understood why birthdays were so important to me; he knew how I always wondered about my true beginning. Under my cocoon of covers, memories merged of past birthdays: how John filled in the chinks and crevices with a mortar of love over forty years; the silver heart he gave me on my first birthday with him; a single red rose; birthday lunches at David's, our favourite restaurant; and my seventieth birthday at Cottonwood Mansion. My heart wrenched as I thought about my 80th party, just months ago, when he was so fragile, so ill. *"I worry about how you will manage your birthday when I am gone."*

Basking in the warmth of memories, my soul lightened with John's love, and gave me the resilience to overcome my past, and the courage to face my birthday alone. With a joy I'd never experienced before, I dressed and made a reservation for lunch at Davids. Sitting alone at our favourite table, I waved to the server. "Could I have my orange juice in a champagne glass?" As I toasted myself, I thought of John—it was the ultimate gift of John's passing.

As I write my memoir, I think of those early mornings at 3 a.m. when I was alone with my thoughts and creating stories about my life—while John lay sleeping. When he awoke, I shifted gears and cared for him. This memoir—the last chapters devoted to John—is the final gift of his passing.

Upon reflection, I hold steadfast in my belief that it is the many gifts of John's passing that gave me the courage to embrace my new life alone. Recalling them gives me the depth of his love even more intensely. They diminish the rawness of grief and lessen the pain of John's *actual* death, as I face my life without him.

THE TWENTY TWENTIES

Depression and COVID-19

In November 2019, the days grew shorter, clouds hung heavily in the sky, and the lake was as cold and black as death. My world shrunk into my red wingback recliner, and I would spend hours staring off into space. The birthdays of my son Ron, and grandson Matt, were a blank in my mind; Christmas was a blur. Did I watch *A Wonderful Life* on Netflix?? I can't recall. Time ticked by in slow motion, hours rippled into days; days melted into weeks, and my life turned into grey, like the shades of colour in black and white movies.

I puttered aimlessly around the house with no purpose and no idea of what to do. Last year, John was with me, my whole world revolved around him. Now, with absolutely nothing to occupy my time, I felt like an immigrant in a new land navigating the frigid Canadian winter, as if for the first time. My spirit withered, my mind spiralled down, the promise of spring seemed to be years away.

That a new year would brighten my days was a hollow wish. News flashed of some disease in China— Covid 19; there was a case or two reported in the United States, countries in Europe, and the first case in Canada was diagnosed in Toronto, on January 21st. Alarm bells rang in my head. *What is this?* By the end of February, the count in Canada had climbed to 10. On the morning of March 13, Sophie Trudeau, the prime minister's wife, contracted the virus, increasing the Canadian case count to 155, by evening to 198, the next day, 253 cases . . . . . on March 15—321. *The cases had more than doubled in three days!* Each morning, I sat with notebook and pen in hand, waiting anxiously for the new Canadian count—345 . . . 441 . . . 598 . . . 833. . . .

Ron called. "The US border is closed, so we've cancelled our trip to Florida and are heading to Blue Mountain in Collingwood for a week; we just wanted you to know where we were." The next day another call. "Mom, we were in the hot tub at the resort when suddenly they announced the resort was closed!"

COVID-19 had hit my world!

As numbers climbed, so did my anxiety. I was obsessed with counting: by March 25th my notebook page was full of statistics, and there was barely room on the last line to jot down the latest count—2,982! *Oh my god, what is happening?*

Shopping malls suddenly closed, as did restaurants, gym-clubs and schools. Ontario had clapped shut tighter than a drum. Only essential service establishments were open—pharmacies and grocery stores, and liquor stores too. *Booze would numb the mind with nothing to do!* The virus spread easily via droplets in coughs and sneezes; there was a run on disinfectants–

toilet paper—for some unknown reason!!

Feelings of doom closed in on me. Being safe became my obsession; I washed my hands constantly, disinfected surfaces, and purchased tons of fabric masks!

When advised to stay home and avoid contact with other people, I kept a distance of six feet from others. When neighbour Cathy walked onto my property, I cringed and kept a cars length away, too panicky to invite her onto the deck. I'd become paranoid. Ron visited, but wouldn't come inside for fear of contaminating me. I felt incarcerated; I reduced my interactions to telephone calls with friends Marty, Jill and Tracey. But when I shared how I was feeling they quickly changed the subject as if depression was contagious.... April 12—23,318.

When I attempted to read my novel, the words were meaningless and disconnected. The work on my memoir turned inward; I chastised my mothering, wondered if I'd loved John enough, if I could have kept him with me longer. My negative internal chatter was oppressive, and I tortured myself with questions that had no answers.

I had difficulty getting out of bed, wore sweatpants all day, and had no desire to shower or wear makeup. With no energy to cook a meal, I snacked on ham sandwiches and cheese and crackers.

A liquid drowsiness poured over me, and filled the empty hours with naps. *I lived for my naps!* "Don't call me from 12 to 2," I told Tracey. "That's when I nap." But to be honest, I napped again at four in the afternoon and again over the news hour at 6 and fell asleep at 8:30 right after I'd talked to Ron and son Blake. . . May 17—75, 800 cases!

My world shrunk, it dribbled out of me and into a deep, dark hole. As I peered into my mirror one morning, I flinched. *Who is this woman?* Staring back was a face:a roadmap of lines criss-crossing sallow cheeks, double bags under sunken, hollow eyes, and hair stringy, lank and lifeless. I felt invisible, my very life was being erased, like notes on a blackboard—rubbed out.

It didn't help that I saw my neighbours managing so well: Donna and Jim painted every room in their house; Katie power-washed her deck and hauled gravel from the beach to ward off weeds around her cottage. She told me all the clothes she'd ordered online and continued to cook up a storm on her BBQ, while I could barely make a trip to the grocery store on my own.

Worried I was becoming unhinged, I called my therapist. "Depressed? No kidding," he said. "You are still mourning John and now this pandemic? I'd be surprised if you *weren't* depressed."

Dissatisfied with his response, I called Marylin

our geriatric counsellor and friend. "Oh, for goodness' sake, Gail. Get up off your duff and plug into 'YouTube' and find something useful to do." *How the hell could I do that with a flip-phone?*

In desperation I turned to Patti, my social worker, writing-coach and friend. "*Everyone* is feeling the stress of COVID. You are doing okay; you write every day and always have something to share during our weekly conferences," she reminded me. "And you nap? No kidding! If I were up at 3:30 every morning I'd be napping every chance I got too! You're doing just fine!" Always putting a positive spin on everything, Patti gave me a glimmer of hope. Perhaps writing could ease the uncertain times when everything else in my life seemed turned upside down and inside out. *If only John were here!*

Invitation to Change Came Knocking

A surprise visit from Evelyn, a dear friend from Port Dover, came on a steamy day in August. She was from the condo complex where we used to live before John and I moved permanently to the Lodge. She stepped out of her car and walked gingerly across the stepping stones to the deck. Wearing a colourful mask across her mouth and nose (the mask attached with rubber bands), she looked like a masked bandit from comic book days of childhood. As she stepped onto the deck, she swung her arms into a circle, fingertips barely touching. "Virtual hug, Gail, virtual hug," she repeated, as she settled into the rocking chair that faced the lake. Anger licked through me. *Wearing this bloody mask was unnatural, and I hated it!* Why couldn't we give each other a *real* hug like we would have last year, before COVID-19 struck? Back then, I'd have rushed to her, arms opened wide wrapping them around her chest, feeling the heat of her body next to mine, the pat of her fingertips on my back. *What had the world come to since Covid?* Will we have to live like this for rest of our lives, keeping our distance from the people we love?

Waving back a virtual hug, I shuffled over to the far corner of the wicker settee so we could keep our safe distance of six feet and drop our masks. A positive, cheery soul, Ev had a friendly smile and merry eyes framed by a full head of dark, chestnut, wavy hair; her hair had only a few strands of white threading through. She was so 'with it,'; she'd mastered all her cell phone apps while me, six years younger, had just purchased a cell phone and could barely tap out a text! I loved telling my friends that Ev was my 87-year-old-friend going on 50!

"What a lovely spot you have, Gail. Your gardens are absolutely gorgeous; they'll soon be turning in a month or two, as fall comes." The gulls swooped and dipped into the silver water for fish. *Oh, how John loved a day like this when the sky was a deep blue, the lake calm as glass, sun sparkling on the water like dancing fairies, as he used to call them.*

"It's so good to see you Ev, I've missed you. Would you like a soft drink?"

"Why, thank you."

"That's a lovely top you're wearing," I said, admiring how Ev looked. "I love the navy, red and white stripes; those colours really suit you and look terrific with your white slacks."

"Thank you, Gail. I got them online."

Suddenly embarrassed by the condition of my well-worn-white shorts, I instinctively crossed my legs so she couldn't see them. I'd been wearing these same shorts since before John got chicken pox six years ago, and alternating them with my three-year-old Capri's. I had only a couple of short sleeved tops, decent enough to wear with them. *My word, I looked frumpy beside Ev.* Her shoes looked brand new, too. I quickly tucked my feet under the settee so she couldn't see the scuff marks on the four year old sandals. I'd been too apprehensive with COVID to go to a mall to shop for spring clothes, which I so badly needed. I hadn't a clue how to go online like Evelyn had. I was looking drab and dowdy! *Does Ev notice my scruffy look, my out-dated clothes?* Nervously I fingered my dank unkempt hair. A puzzled look came over Ev's face, the crease of a frown above her nose. I imagined her thinking. *What's happened to Gail, the Gail known for her smart outfits, choosing just the right scarf to enhance a dress or jacket? This is not the Gail I know; where did that old Gail go?*

Ev's eyes shifted past the gardens to the expansive lawn stretching to the next property. "This is such a beautiful spot, Gail; it's so lovely in the summer." Her eyes grew distant, as if she had something on her mind: "How will you ever manage all this property this winter with COVID-19 ramping up?" She looked at me with worried eyes.

Winter? I dabbed the sweat off my forehead. It was a sweltering hot day. *Winter?* I lived my life moment to moment, unable to predict the next hour; I couldn't visualize tomorrow. *Winter?* Next week was far in the future, next month a year away. *Winter?* Forcing my eyes forward, across the stepping stones to Ev's car, was a hundred miles away; inching my gaze— past Lakeshore Road to the water—was a continent from where I was sitting. I suddenly felt like an insignificant speck on the horizon.

The deck had become my essential safety point, the outer reaches of my universe. Deep, incomprehensible, trepidation prevented me from taking one single step off. *With nothing solid beyond, where would I land?* Feeling like a trapped bird, I was unable to *will* my feet to take a single step from the deck!

Ev paused and took a sip of her drink. Her eyebrows met in a frown. "We're all really concerned about you, Gail, and how you will manage all this property by yourself. You are such a social person and you'll be so isolated from neighbours because of this darned COVID thing." Eve's eyes grew wide with a hint of a scowl. "You know that someday soon you'll have to move from here, don't you?" She said it as if it were a statement, rather than a question. "You'll need a smaller place as you get older and are less able to manage all this property."

My mind slowed to a standstill. I was unable to compute what my ears were hearing and what it meant. *I won't I be able to manage on my own as I get older?!* I asked myself. *Winter is coming?* A hush hung as I tried to understand.

Ev's eyes widened and she tipped her head to her shoulder as if an idea had suddenly occurred to her. A flurry of words suddenly spilled from her mouth. "Lorie is selling her condo beside *me*; she is selling it privately for a good price; it depends on her health, what her doctor says about the state of her cancer, and if she's improved enough to move to Kingston with her partner. She'll know by September 24th."

I couldn't make sense of this wash of information until the next day. I was making a cheese sandwich for lunch when Ev's words drifted in and out of my consciousness. *Lorie's selling her condo... it's right beside mine.* I got out a plate and glass from the cupboard. *I knew that condo complex... I had lots of friends there.*

As I sat on the deck that afternoon, I pondered. *Lorie's been sick... she's moving... she'll know on Sep-*

tember 24th. I tucked the knowledge into the back of my mind.

It was a turning point for me.

Making the Decision

With a screech of tires, a black pickup pulled to a sudden stop in front of the Lodge, its crimson caution lights blinking to warn oncoming traffic. Startled, I dropped my book in my lap as a tall man loped across the lawn; he clutched something in his hand. "Hello," he called, his blue eyes twinkling as he wrestled with his black COVID mask, slipping the left strap over his ear to reveal his face. "I wonder if you are interested in selling your property," he asked smiling, setting his card on the deck.

Surprised by the sudden interruption, I stuttered, incoherent, "Nooo, not right now."

He rushed back to his truck, hopped in and roared down Lakeshore Road. He stopped at various properties along the way. Although I didn't know it then, it was the beginning of the property bonanza caused by the Covid scare.

Sell? Sell the Lodge? Not a chance!

Ordinarily, I'd have tossed the card into the garbage, but for some reason, I tucked it into the back of my book and then stored it, more carefully, into my business-card file by the telephone. Over the following days, thoughts jostled and joggled in my mind as I remembered Evelyn's visit and noted the red of the real estate card peeking out at me every time I made a telephone call. *Had this place become too big to manage?* I suddenly began to see the Lodge through jaundiced eyes. The deck needed preserving and a few rotting boards needed replacing. The steel around the pillars was corroding and the trim could do with a fresh coat of paint. *Maintenance was looked after in a condo!*

But then, I thought of John and the promise I'd made. '*I'm so glad that you're staying in the Lodge after I'm gone!*' he'd said. But he was not here and the Lodge was simply not the same without him. It was so darned lonely living here by myself! "*Lorie is selling her condo; it's right beside mine!*" I knew I'd need to move from the Lodge sometime in the next ten years, but the idea terrified me. *But, if I don't move now, then when, and where?* These questions coiled and crisscrossed through my mind. *I'd feel comfortable at Ev's condo complex; I'd have friends there and they might help me get over this emotional slump.*

When I checked with family, Ron said it was up to me. "I'll support whatever you decide. Granddaughter Amy was adamant. "Oh Grandma, I'm so happy you're thinking of a condo; you'd be safe, close to people, grocery stores, hospitals, and a taxi if you can't drive. I'd be so relieved if you were in a condo!"

There was Blake to consider! The Lodge was perfect for him: all on one floor, it was the only family place he could come to in his electric wheelchair. Coming to the Lodge was something he'd done almost every Sunday since he got his accessible van six years ago. He *loved* the lake. *How could I take this away from him, one of the few pleasures he had as MS ravished his body? How could I be so selfish? Why couldn't I stay here a couple more years for his sake? That's what a good mother should do shouldn't she?*

As I wrestled with my conscience over my duty to my son and *my* needs in my old age, I twisted and flailed at night. My brain shouted questions. *What to do? What on the earth to do?*

When Scott, my handyman, came to cover the air-conditioners and winterize the Lodge, I shared my thoughts. "Oh, Gail, a condo would be good for you."

"How do you mean?" I asked, surprised at his quick response yet valuing his opinion. "Right now, you are physically able to manage here, but for how long?" His eyes grew warm. "And frankly, I've been worried about your emotional well-being since COVID-19. You are completely isolated here, both socially and emotionally, so you'd be much better in a condo in Dover."

It was something to consider. I could make the move while I was still physically able, while I had all my faculties, while my health was good, and while I could still drive.

"But what about Blake? There's no way he'd be able to get into the condo with his electric wheelchair; there are too many steps!"

"A wheelchair ramp could be built, no problem!"

Lorie got a clean bill of health; I made an offer on her condo. The decision made, I put the Lodge up for sale.

Sale of the Lodge: Its History

The wild, howling wind swirled and almost whipped the sign out of the real estate agent's hands as he wrestled with it on the front lawn. With a final whack, it stuck in the ground and wavered on its flimsy metal legs. It was October, 2021; our beautiful Lodge had gone up for sale.

"What's the history of this place?" the agent asked, a clipboard clutched in his hand as he wandered through the Lodge measuring rooms, the wing and the basement for the listing. "The layout is so different from most cottages."

"You've got that right," I said smiling. "2890 Lakeshore Road has quite a history; I've gathered some of it, over the years, from the neighbours."

"Tell me about it," the agent suggested. "Owners often like to know the history of the place they purchase."

I took a deep breath and started.

"Up until the 1950's, most of the land, for miles around, was owned by the Edgar Wardell family. "The Lodge" was nothing but a field. Then, the Wardell's started selling lakefront lots on the east and west side of Wardell Lane for $500.00 a lot. But on this lot where The Lodge is, Edgar Wardell hauled a chicken coop down to the corner of Wardell Lane and Lakeshore for his wife to sell her eggs and home-made pies. She was known as Grandma Wardell. The original chicken coop still exists near the old Wardell homestead up Wardell Laneway. Eventually, Edgar Wardell built a proper building for his wife; she not only sold her eggs and pies, but also newspapers, chips, pop and candy. She ran that little store right into the 1970s. I showed the agent a picture of Grandma Wardell, a stout woman with merry eyes and a friendly face; she wore a floral housedress that she probably made herself, as women did in those days.

But *this* place was originally built by a guy called Boris Dimov. He bought it off the Wardell family, with investment money from doctors and lawyers in Europe, to construct a resort on Lake Erie for them to come to holiday in Canada. That was why he constructed the huge great-room with high 7 foot ceilings and picture windows that overlook Lake Erie. It was a grand entrance, like that of a hotel. The area at the back, where the kitchen is now, was to be a kind of banquet hall or something of the sort for entertaining dignitaries and guests. But when the European investors came to inspect the place and it didn't meet their standards, the money dried up and Boris sold it in the mid 1980s to some people called the Haggerty's. They made it into a restaurant and ice cream parlour. But they eventually closed down the operation in the early 1990s and lived in it until 2001 or 2002."

"When did *you* buy it?" the agent asked.

"John and I purchased it in the winter of 2006 and it became officially "The Lodge." We had it completely renovated with a wraparound veranda and gardens all around. Now, in 2021, I'm moving on and taking with me treasured memories of our 'Lodge.'"

"That's a wonderful history of your place, and I suggest you do a write-up for the prospective purchasers."

I did that.

I smile now in 2025 thinking that *we* would be a part of The Lodge's history. I imagine what people might say about the Lodge when I am gone. . . . .

The Final Goodbye

I woke up with a start, morning sunlight streaming through my bedroom window. This would be the last time that I would sleep in this room. I showered and put on the clothes I'd laid out the night before, folded my nightclothes, and stuffed them into my overnight suitcase along with the wet towels and wash cloth. Stripping the bed of blankets and quilt, I shoved them into my large suitcase and rolled everything out the back door and into my van. The freshness of the morning breeze caught in my throat; the red of the sun was blinking over the horizon. Lake Erie crashed against the rocks on the shore. *What have I done? Why have I sold my beautiful Lodge? It was what John and I created together these past fifteen years; my heart and soul are here with John. What in the world have I done!*

The moving truck rolled up to the front door, men stretched dropcloths across the floors, and started loading the boxes stacked floor to ceiling of the sunroom.

It was done!

I stood in the middle of the room as men scurried past me, and I forced my mind to shift. I imagined the condo living room, the floral wing-back chairs on either side of the dry-sink with the pine window frame filling the wall above it. The spindle settee would fit perfectly along the opposite wall. In the corner of the bedroom, I imagined John's blue wing-back chair where he'd greet me every morning. With the condo basement finished, it was surprising how much of the furniture I was taking with me. Ron and Maureen had chosen some pieces I couldn't take, and I'd sold others to neighbours or to the new owners.

Friends burst in suddenly. Katie's eyes glowing with tears. "I'll miss you," she whispered. Art squeezed my hand goodbye. Cathy opened her arms and wrapped me in a hug, and Al shook my hand.

As the bed frame—the final item—was loaded into the moving van, the men rolled up the dropsheets, I set the keys on the counter, and I shut the door. Waving to my friends, I backed out of the driveway and followed the moving van up Lakeshore Road. Looking back into the rear-view mirror, memories flooded my mind. The Lodge had been everything I imagined it could be, and more. It was a playground for the grandkids whenever they visited on weekends, and holidays, playing mini-hockey or soccer games in the extra lot. My nostrils filled with the scent of peanut butter and chocolate chip cookies we'd baked. The Lodge had become our family gathering place for special holidays. It accommodated Blake's electric wheelchair so he and Gina could come to visit almost every weekend. It was where Adam and the twins came from Florida, and family from Alberta. But mainly, the Lodge had been a peaceful haven for John and me, his final resting place.

As I rounded Maple Bay and swung north onto Fisherville Road, I swiped my eyes with the back of my hand. Everything had fallen into place. At 82, I got the condo I wanted close to old friends and did it on my own terms while I was still able. In some ways, it felt as if it was all meant to be. Stopping at Rainham Road, I took a deep breath.

I swung west toward Dover and the next chapter of my life.

EPILOGUE: TREASURES TO KEEP

What treasures would I cherish as I made my last move—to an old folks home off in the future. What would I take with me? What would be the reminders of my life? Huddled on a shelf in my condo family room are the treasures I will take with me—there is a lopsided dish that I nestle into my cupped hand; a warm feeling swells up in my heart. It was the precious glazed candy dish that Ron made—50 years ago in elementary school. He'd moulded it from clay into the shape of a bowl, and dabbed on black and royal-blue spots—my favourite colours. The teacher told him that the hues would blend and fuse into each other when it was fired in the kiln. However, for some strange reason, they didn't, so Ron ended up with a blue and black spotted candy dish. It is precious just as it is. He gave it to me for Mother's Day. I will treasure it as long as I have life in these old bones.

The paper maché piggy-bank winks back at me. Blake made it in art class, in Grade Three, as well as the yellow lion puppet with the glued-on eyes and orange hair around its face.

Wesley made the multi-coloured wooden sculpture, in wood-working class in Grade Eight, as well as the bas-relief copper sailboat and green decoupage gingerale bottle overlaid with the Canadian flag, which was made to commemorate Canada Day. Squeezed in the shelf are samples of hand-stitched weaving that my sons created, years ago.

I envisioned each boy at work, bent over at their school desks, their little hands immersed in clay, moulding a bowl. Their tiny fingers cut out dimes of felt for eyes and glued on golden pupils to make the lion puppet more life-like. I see another pair of fingers immersed in gloopy wallpaper paste and newspaper as one son covers a balloon to take on the shape of a pig, adding ears and a tail and painted-on eyes and nose, a slit cut in the back for coins. I marvel at the patience of the young weavers as they designed and wove their works of art; I admired the ingenuity of my artist son, Wesley, as he cut and glued his wooden sculpture and pressed out the shape of the sailboat from a flat copper sheet.

Staring up at the row of treasures, my breath catches in my throat. These works of art are precious to me. They've survived five decades; they've been packed up and moved to seven homes; they've graced many shelves in a myriad of rooms in various houses we'd lived in over the years. These items suddenly take on enormous meaning. . . . They are symbols of fifty years of love.

ACKNOWLEDGEMENTS

My memoir is a labour of love that I put together over the past fifteen years or more. It couldn't have been written without the help of Patti M. Hall, my writing coach; she taught me how to write with more depth and literary quality as I revised my memoir multiple times. I am also grateful to my publisher, Robyn York who read every page, offered valuable feedback on my work and gave me the confidence to acknowledge that I could call myself a 'writer' beyond that of a non-fiction author of books for educators. As my publisher, she also guided me through the self-publishing process from hiring a professional editor, creating a cover and taking the manuscript to press. I particularly appreciated Editor Chris Turnbull, who tightened some pieces, made changes of tenses and suggestions of photographs to add.

I owe an enormous dept to the Dodd family—especially Peg and Ma Dodd, who loved me as an infant as if I were their own--and Peg's nephew, Terry who reaffirmed a few years ago, my adult place in the 'Dodd' family.

I am especially grateful to my husband John, who loved me unconditionally, with whom we built a loving life together as we blended our family. He gave me the courage to deal with the trauma of my birthdays on my own.

I acknowledge too the friends who read pieces of my memoir—Penny McBride, Joyce Hamilton, Penny Hope, Jean Mottashed and Beverley Robertson--and encouraged me on.

To Alison Wasielewski I am grateful for believing in me as a consultant in primary education and valuing my ability to adapt current research for classroom practice. I appreciate as well, Michael Awender, Dean of the Faculty of Education at the University of Windsor, who valued my work as an administrator and researcher in education.

To my four sons—Wesley, Blake, Ron and Adam—who kept me honest as their mom and gave me insights into life. A special thanks to son Ron, who promised to read every page of the master document—all 900 pages of it. I am grateful to Ron as well, for giving me fresh understanding of my birth mother's final words.

I am especially thankful for my grandchildren, Nathan, Amy, Matt, Kasey and Kody, for giving me such joy and laughter to my life.

I dedicate this memoir to my granddaughter, Amy, the keeper of the family history.

APPENDIX

Academic Accomplishments—three degrees; BA, Masters, Ed D

Published Books:

- 5 published books;
- 40 books co-authored
- 10 published chapters in other authors' work

Published Articles:

- 26 published articles in reputable Journals

Text Book Publications Co-Authored:

- HBJ, Orlando, Florida *'Imagination' K to 8 Program* (largest text book company in the world in 1985)
- Ginn & Company Canada 'Journey's' program (1980's)

Professional Presentations:

- 346 professional presentations in the United States, Canada, Bordeaux, France, Japan, South Korea, Singapore, Taiwan and Indonesia.

Professional Positions:

- Professor at the Faculty of Education, University of Windsor- --19 87 to 1994.
- First Dean of U of Windsor Chatham campus 1991 to 1994.

Professional Commentary on Professional Work:
Overall Work in Literacy Education:

- The Reading Teacher (the most widely acclaimed literacy journal in the world.

- *"Regarding the 5 articles by Dr. Heald-Taylor published in "'The Reading Teacher,'" of all the manuscripts submitted to our journal, the acceptance rate for feature-length manuscripts has ranged from 8% to 11% during the past 8 years. By that criteria alone, one might conclude that Dr. Heald-Taylor`s scholarly contribution of five articles, is exemplary."*

- Response by. John Savage– the internationally respected professor in the field of literacy learning at Boston College, School of Education, in Chestnut Hill, MA: *"Dr. Gail Heald-Taylor is a respected educational leader who has contributed significantly in the field of literacy instruction. Her research and writing is state-of-the-art and I have used Dr. Heald-Taylor`s work in my own writing. What impresses me most about Gail Heald-Taylor's work is her ability to strike a balance between theory and practice.'*

- *Whole Language Strategies for ESL Students*, OISE Press (1986).
Response by Dr. Lloyd-Brown, Administrator for DeKalb County Schools, Georgia: "The Whole Language Strategies for ESL Students (1986), is a hand book for teaching literacy strategies to students for whom English is not their first language. The book is a well-organized

handbook including Dictate Stories, Literature Strategies, Process Writing, Themes and Evaluation. The strategies are appropriate for new ESL students across the spectrum, in primary, upper primary and secondary grades. It is a valuable resource for our burgeoning immigration population that grew in ten years from 135 to 3,600 international students. Therefore, it is exciting to review this hand book."

- *Administrator's Guide to Whole Language*: Richard C. Owens (1989).
  Review by Dr. Dave Johnson, secretary of the California Reading Association (1990). "*The Administrator's Guide is a must for all educators who are interested in learning how to implement Whole Language in their school or in a whole school district.* "*The Administrator's Guide should be on the best seller of the 10 most read by educators; a 'must read' for implementing Whole Language in a whole school district.*"

Professional Presentation Responses:

- Teachers of English of Other Languages (TESOL)

- Conference, New Jersey (1991): "*I could have listened to Gail all day . . . Gail Heald-Taylor is a wonderful presenter, she is vibrant . . . Her warmth and humility shine through. She presents a truly humanitarian and valued philosophy of education.*'

FAMILY PHOTOGRAPHS

Peg took these pictures of Merla, Bud and me at our home in Innisfail I would have been 4 months old.

Merla, Bud & Gail

BUD, GAIL AND SHARON, 1953, PENHOLD, AB

Gail on Rosie, our pony 1947

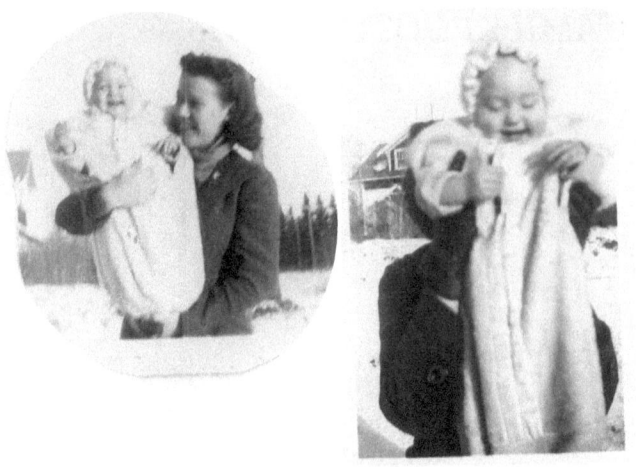

PEG DODD AND BABY GAIL

Ma Dodd and Gail

GAIL ON THE
DODD FARM

Gail, Bud, Sharon and Dad
Taken 1953 at Penhold, Alb.

HIGH SCHOOL

PRAZAK, SHIRLEY R., Tawatinaw
PREUS, VIOLET N., Edmonton
PYE, GAIL B., Penhold
QUILLIAM, CONNIE H., Edmonton

Teacher From Red Deer Off To Germany

Miss Gail Pye, former teacher at Riverglen School, will leave Red Deer tomorrow (Saturday) for Soest, Germany, where she has accepted a position on the teaching staff of a Canadian Army school for children of service personnel.

Miss Pye, who taught at Bowden before coming to Red Deer, is one of 28 Canadian teachers being added to the Soest army school. Employed by the Department of National Defence, the group will sail from Montreal Tuesday on the Empress of England, docking at Liverpool.

Well known in Red Deer during her stay here, Miss Pye expects to tour France and Germany before the school term begins. She will be away two years.

OFF TO TEACH IN EUROPE

A LETTER HOME FROM SOEST, GERMANY, 1959

1959 is almost gone, and that time of year is here again when I wish to send you my sincerest Christmas and New Year Greetings. This will be my first Christmas away from all of you and as I walk down through the town of Soest, and see the Christmas decorations across the streets, and as I look in every shop window, I become a little nostalgic for dear old Canada.

Many of you asked me before I left home to be sure to write and tell you of my experiences travelling to Europe, and my first impressions of the few countries I have visited. I know I have neglected all of you, but hope this letter will help you to form a picture of "Gail in Europe".

My train trip east was quiet but very pleasant. In Calgary, we joined two girls from Vancouver, and as we progressed Eastward, many teachers boarded, so that, in Montreal, there were about fifteen of us. We had all had come from the West together on the same train, and, since we were all embarking together on the adventure of school-teaching in Europe, we had formed our own special Western Canadian group, even before we walked up the gangplank of the "Empress of England".

During the first day on board ship, we explored the ship's promenade, entertaining rooms, lounges, barber shops, souvenir shops, and even the swimming pool. Each day's programme followed a similar routine. I didn't rise until twelve noon. My drowsiness was caused by the change of altitude, no doubt! Our room stewards would bring us breakfast in bed if we so desired. We ate lunch and in the afternoon, played desk tennis, read, played "horse racing" (a game designed for boat travel), wrote letters or listened to an afternoon concert by the ship's orchestra. Our evening meal was a strictly formal occasion. Although the meals were not the highlight of our cruise, they were certainly interesting. It was the first time I had tasted frog's legs, caviar, crepes suzettes, and escargots (snails). Following dinner we danced or had sing-songs until 2 a.m. each morning.

The trip was fun, but we were all glad when we saw the lights of Ireland. We docked at Greenock Scotland, where one of our friends disembarked. Maureen was a Scottish girl who had taught in Canada, and then was hired by DND to teach abroad. She planned to visit her family before coming to Germany to teach.

We left the ship at Liverpool England, and took the boat train to London. One of my first impressions of England was the fantastic number of chimney-pots on each house (one for every fire-place in the building). London is a very beautiful city, with enough attractions to interest one for weeks. Our brief visit allowed us to see only the highlights- Westminster Abbey, St. Paul's, the Tower of London, and the Changing of the Guard, at Buckingham Palace. One evening three of us went to see the Royal Ballet.

Our trip to Harwich from London, by train, across the channel by ferry, and by train again from the Hook of Holland across the Netherlands and Northern Germany to Soest, was long and exhausting. After three days in Soest, I felt rested, and had made plans for further travel, during the two weeks before school.

Before I left home I met Ernie, a German fellow who has been in Canada for four years. He wrote to his friends and family in Hamburg, telling them to expect a visit from me. So my plan was to visit Hamburg.

In Hamburg, Ernie's friends were to meet me at the conductor's booth on the platform, but, due to my failure to read Ernies instructions properly I found myself at the information booth instead of the conductor's booth. Repeating like a parrot to all and sundry the phrase Ernie had taught me, "Ich kann nicht Deutsch sprechen; sprechen sie Englisch, bitte?" I finally got the answer "Yes" from a very pleasant German gentleman. He ushered me back to the platform had my name called over the public address system, telephoned each of Ernie's friends, put me into a taxi, and told the driver, the address to which I was to go. Ernie's friends, Rolf and Wolfram arrived half an hour later.

I stayed with Wolfram and Ursula for one week and the other week with Jurgen and Gisi, all of them friends of Ernie. They were just wonderful to me. They all spoke English in varying degrees and made me feel most welcome throughout my full two week stay.

Hamburg is a fascinating city. In the centre of the city are two lakes called Alsters, which are dotted with white sailboats during the weekends. In "Planten un Blomen", is an outdoor roller skating rink, a miniature golf-course, an outdoor and indoor orchestra, an open-air resturaunt, and lily covered streams, banked with almost every variety of flower. It is the largest park I think I have ever seen.

I visited some of Hamburg's museums and cathedrals. How much more interesting to see original works of art, than to study them from books!

You would have laughed had you seen me at the market-place. Of course, I had never been to a market before, and I'm afraid it was quite obvious to all. I'm sure everyone wondered who this person was who was staring in at every stand, but who didn't buy anything. Everything from fresh fruits and vegetables, to American records, were sold at the little booths, which resembled the booths at a Fair. A man was even skinning eels, which the North German people consider quite a delicacy.

Jurgen is a teacher, and I visited him at a camp where he was spending two weeks with his pupils. This is standard procedure in Germany. A teacher spends two weeks getting acquainted with his pupils before the new term begins, which is in the middle of August. The German school day is from 8a.m. until noon, including Saturdays, but the students have much more homework than Canadian students of a similar grade, and are expected to spend most of each afternoon on complete lesson preparation and homework. A teacher has the choice of specializing in a particular grade, or progressing with his pupils from Grade One through to Grade Nine. There are three types of German school- the Volksschule, Mittel Schule and the Hoch Schule. Every child begins in the Folk school which he attends for four to six years. After that period the slower pupils attend the Middle School where they learn trades, and the better pupils attend the High School. Only pupils who graduate from this school may attend one of the many Universities in Germany.

I was shown through a Middle School in Hamburg. It was a very modern school and the Zoology students could study in a tropical room where live turtles, lizards, snakes, alligators, monkeys, ant-eaters, horned-toads and tropical birds live in their natural habitat.

When I left Hamburg for Soest, I realized how much it had meant to have English speaking German friends to show me around their wonderful city.

On our first long weekend in Soest, three of us, all teachers, went to Belgium. In Brussells we saw the famous statue of the "Manniken Pis", about which there is a very ancient story. According to legend the men of Brussells were defending their city for an infant Monarch. The Monarch's men were losing the battle, when they noticed the tiny Prince, answering the call of Nature. They interpreted the act as contempt for their cowardice, took new Courage and won the battle. The statue, illustrating the exact posture of the young boy, and serving a dual purpose as a fountain, was erected in Brussells 600 years ago, to commemorate this historic event. The disillusioning fact about the statue is that it is less than life-size; however, he deserves special recognition as "Brussells oldest Inhabitant."

On our way to Bruges, we stopped at Breendonk, to see the German concentration camp there, which is now a National War Memorial. All of the cells and chambers were just as they were during the war. It was most depressing to see the tiny solitary confinement cells, with pleas for peace scratched into the stone. In many cells were tape recorded testimonies of the men who were imprisoned there. The torture chamber, gallows and firing squad posts are all as they were during the war. It's no wonder the Belgians are as bitter as they are towards the Germans.

We arrived in Bruges to find the people celebrating the Liberation of 1944. Since Bruges was liberated by Canadians we were made most welcome. After a thrilling gymnastic display, by a group of Flemish High School boys, a native of Bruges showed us his city. He spoke eight different languages.

On our way home we drove through Flanders, and stopped at the many cemeteries. There are several very impressive War Memorials to the Canadians who died in both World Wars. In Ypres, we saw the huge War Memorial Menin Gate, where the names of Commonwealth soldiers who died in the First World War and whose graves are unknown, are inscribed.

Another weekend, four of us went to St. Goar to see the "Rhine in Flames." I have never seen such a brilliant display of illuminations. The old castles on either side of the river glowed with many coloured lights. In front of every major building, was a red flame, produced by chemical bonfires, which were lighted in succession to illustrate the burning of the town from one end to the other, by the French invaders, in the seventeenth century. Then for twenty minutes the sky was filled with dazzling light, as the fantastic coloured fireworks were set off over the ancient town. After the fireworks hundreds of Germans and tourists gathered together in the Gasthauses (Taverns) to spend the remainder of the evening, singing, drinking and dancing. As we drove away from St. Goar in the morning, I was surprised to see by daylight how tiny and narrow the famous Rhine river really appeared. It looked hardly wider than my own Red Deer River, but the amount of river traffic, barges, tugs, steamers, scows and freighters make one realize that it is the river of Europe which carries more traffic than any other.

Thanksgiving weekend was a long weekend, so five of us drove to Amsterdam to spend the holiday there. The highlight of our tour was the visit to a small Dutch village on the island of Marken, about five miles from Amsterdam. The farming folk go to Amsterdam, by boat in summer, and on skates in winter, to sell their produce in the Amsterdam markets. The people have adhered to all their centuries old traditions. We were very impressed by their costumes. The women wear long colourful skirts, lace caps covering their long hair while the men are dressed in navy coloured billowing trousers, and tight fitting vests, with large white buttons. All children are dressed like their mothers until they are six years old. Then the boys have their hair cut and are dressed in trousers. Of course, all the people wear wooden shoes. Since we were travelling on a tour, we suspected that the people were living in this manner, only to attract tourists, but a clerk in our hotel assured us that there were several other villages in Holland where the people live in a similar manner. In spite of the materialistic world about them, these people have preferred to live the simple but happy life they have always known.

Amsterdam is an exciting city to drive in, especially for the driver, because one has to be continually on the alert to dodge all of the literally thousands of bicycles which crowd the streets, especially during rush hours. Everyone travels by bicycle. There are more bicycles in Amsterdam than in any other city in Europe, and they have the right-of-way over all other traffic, by Dutch law.

Holstein, may be a province in Germany, but it will be surprising if the province contains more Holstein cows than there are in Holland. One sees the familiar black and white animals grazing in every field that is not being used for growing tulips. The other familiar sights of Holland, of course, are the dikes and windmills, and they are just exactly as one would have imagined them to be. Nowhere have I seen neater or better kept farms.

And now, back to Soest. I am really enjoying my twenty-three Grade One children, and at times it is even quite relaxing to get back into the classroom after a hectic weekend of travel. I am teaching in a very new and modern school with twenty eight other very friendly teachers and a wonderful principal.

After my first month here I moved into the town of Soest with a very warm and friendly German family, so that I could learn more about the German people, their customs and their language. Through this family I have made several other German friends, and have learned much more of the German language. I have been well rewarded for giving up the relative comfort of life in the Officer's Mess, in order to gain more of the cultural benefits of life with the German people.

I hope that this letter has given you a fairly good picture of my life here in Germany. Everything is new and wonderful to me. I know that if the remaining time in Europe is as enriching for me as the first four months have been, I will consider the experience a valuable one.

Wishing you a very Merry Christmas and success and happiness in 1960.
I will be looking forward to hearing from you in the New Year.

Travels in Europe, 1959-1960

*Gail and Wes,
Proposal and
marriage, 1960*

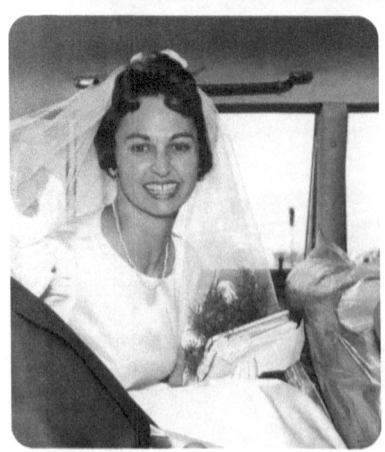

A Paris Original

GAIL + BOYS

JULY 1967

MOTHERHOOD

Gail Heard
Ronnie, Blake, Wes.
"Lucky" Anne the beagle
Easter Sunday. This is taken
April 14, 1968 in our own backyard.
Galt, Ontario
We have had the beagle for
two months now and the
boys love her. She was a stray
who came to stay, so we had
her "spayed" and bought a
license.

Circa 1970 - 1971
L to R
Gail
Wesley Randy Ron Morgan Jim Sharon Robin Blake Kenny

Wesley, Adam, John
Ron, Gail, Blake

Gail & John
Wedding Day,
April 21, 1979

John Taylor

Qigong on Lake Erie

Alberta Grain Elevators

Springsteen Headbands

Gail & John

Career

The Lodge
(Before & After)

Grand children

Family

ABOUT THE AUTHOR

Gail Heald-Taylor

Gail didn't learn to read until she was 10 years old and yet obtained a BA, Master's and a Doctorate of Education. Her teaching career began as a classroom teacher. At 19, she taught children of the armed services in Germany. Returning to Ontario, she taught elementary grades, was a Consultant in Primary Education, and then professor at Windsor Faculty of Education. After publishing several books, she was hired as a consultant with a Canadian (Ginn) and American (HBJ) textbook companies to develop language programs. In that capacity, Gail gave workshops across Canada and the United States to audiences of up to a thousand educators. In retirement she provided professional development in American International schools in Singapore, Japan, South East Asia, Philippine's, Korea and Taipei. She won the Norfolk Literacy Award in 2021. This memoir culminates over ten years of writing, editing and revising and is her first full length non-academic publication.

REVIEWS & COMMENTS

When I read Gail's memoir I knew I was in the midst of a great writer and feminist, a cross between Atwood and Steinem. She's travelled the world speaking to educators about literacy while raising her boys.
—Penny McBride

Gail has such a way of describing her characters and situations that draws the reader into the story. Her story of her husband John's decline moved me ...She did such a superb job of writing about his last months that I actually felt I was sitting in the Adirondack chair beside him, watching the scene play out...It was poignant powerful, emotional, authentic...what fine literature should do.
—Jean Mottashed, *Lynnwood Arts Center Writing Group*

As a professor I used Gail's instructional strategies to help my university class of student teachers to process the '9-11 attack in New York. Gail was an amazing educator ...in large part from her profound understanding of human beings.

—Rheta Rubenstein, *Professor of Teacher Training, University of Michigan*

www.ingramcontent.com/pod-product-compliance
Lightning Source LLC
Chambersburg PA
CBHW030849170426
43193CB00009BA/544